WAR and peace

POSSIBLE FUTURES from analog
Edited by Stanley Schmidt

ANTHOLOGY #6

WAR and peace

POSSIBLE FUTURES from **analog**
Edited by Stanley Schmidt

The Dial Press
Davis Publications, Inc.
380 Lexington Avenue, New York, N.Y. 10017

FIRST PRINTING

Copyright © 1983 by Davis Publications, Inc.
All rights reserved.
Library of Congress Catalog Card Number: 80-69078
Printed in the U. S. A.

COPYRIGHT NOTICES AND ACKNOWLEDGMENTS

Grateful acknowledgment is hereby made for permission to reprint the following:

E for Effort by T. L. Sherred; copyright 1947 by Street & Smith Publications, Inc., renewed 1974 by the Condé Nast Publications, Inc.; reprinted by permission of the author.

The Weapon Shop by A. E. van Vogt; copyright 1942 by Street & Smith Publications, Inc., renewed 1969 by The Condé Nast Publications, Inc.; reprinted by permission of the author.

The Wabbler by Murray Leinster; copyright 1942 by Street & Smith Publications, Inc., renewed 1969 by The Condé Nast Publications, Inc.; reprinted by permission of the author's Estate and the agents for the Estate, Scott Meredith Literary Agency, Inc., 845 Third Avenue, New York, New York 10022.

Conquest by Default by Vernor Vinge; copyright © 1968 by Vernor Vinge; reprinted by permission of the author.

Warrior by Gordon R. Dickson; copyright © 1965 by The Condé Nast Publications, Inc.; reprinted by permission of the author.

Hawk Among the Sparrows by Dean McLaughlin; copyright © 1968 by Dean McLaughlin; reprinted by permission of the author.

The Mercenary by Jerry Pournelle; copyright © 1972 by The Condé Nast Publications, Inc.; reprinted by permission of the author.

No Shoulder To Cry On by Hank Davis; copyright © 1968 by The Condé Nast Publications, Inc.; reprinted by permission of the author.

The Bully and the Crazy Boy by Marc Stiegler; © 1980 by Davis Publications, Inc.; reprinted by permission of the author.

Thunder and Roses by Theodore Sturgeon; copyright 1947 by Street & Smith Publications, Inc.; renewed 1974 by The Condé Nast Publications, Inc.; reprinted by permission of Kirby McCauley, Ltd.

Late Night Final by Eric Frank Russell; copyright 1948 by Street & Smith Publications, Inc., renewed 1975 by The Condé Nast Publications, Inc.; reprinted by permission of Scott Meredith Literary Agency, Inc.

Cover art: Joe Burleson

CONTENTS

INTRODUCTION
Stanley Schmidt — 6

E FOR EFFORT
T.L. Sherred — 8

THE WEAPON SHOP
A.E. van Vogt — 49

THE WABBLER
Murray Leinster — 82

CONQUEST BY DEFAULT
Vernor Vinge — 90

WARRIOR
Gordon R. Dickson — 115

HAWK AMONG THE SPARROWS
Dean McLaughlin — 133

THE MERCENARY
Jerry Pournelle — 173

NO SHOULDER TO CRY ON
Hank Davis — 220

THE BULLY AND THE CRAZY BOY
Marc Stiegler — 227

THUNDER AND ROSES
Theodore Sturgeon — 241

LATE NIGHT FINAL
Eric Frank Russell — 260

INTRODUCTION
Stanley Schmidt

In 1944—in the thick of World War II and a little before Hiroshima and Nagasaki—*Analog*'s earlier self, *Astounding Science Fiction*, published a story called "Deadline," by Cleve Cartmill. A key element of the story was a description of an atomic bomb—which in reality was still top secret—sufficiently accurate to bring FBI agents to the *Astounding* office to find out where the security leak was. Editor John W. Campbell told them there was no leak: anyone who had been following even nonclassified developments in atomic physics could see the possibility, and in fact *Astounding* had been publishing stories and articles about that and related matters for quite some time. When the agents suggested that it should stop, Campbell pointed out that the sudden dropping of a very hot topic would arouse far more suspicion than continuing a line of speculation and discussion already well established.

The atomic bomb and its direct and indirect descendants have been an important area of science fictional speculation ever since—and reality hasn't been far behind. We (or our governments, which may not be quite the same thing) now have nuclear fusion bombs which make the fission devices of World War II look like damp firecrackers, to say nothing of self-guiding long-range missiles, high-powered lasers, and the imminent possibility of orbiting weaponry which can pose an ever-present threat to huge areas of Earth. Science fiction writers have foreseen all these things and many others, and have been busy exploring the possible ramifications of the problems—and possible solutions—because they haven't been kidding about any of them. The rest of the world has been gradually realizing that the weapons we already have, and their descendants to come, constitute a danger of such unprecedented magnitude and character that we *must* try to learn how to neutralize it.

There have been many anthologies of war stories, both in science fiction and in literature at large. This is hardly surprising. War has always been a fertile ground for stories, because it throws people into conflicts of such intensity that it brings out their best and worst qualities as do few situations in everyday life.

But this is *not* just an anthology of war stories. It is no mere collection of battle adventures for those who see such things as light entertainment and would rather not think beyond the physical action on the battlefield. There is plenty of action and entertainment here, but these writers have looked beyond the front line to explore various aspects of the *causes* of war—and possible *alternatives* to it, which we sorely need. These are, as the title says, stories about both war and peace; and I know of few, if any, other books which have approached the subject in quite this way. You can read the stories in any order you like, of course, but I recommend the order in which they appear, and have written the introductions accordingly.

I don't think you will "like" all these stories. I do hope you will enjoy reading them all, but I don't think you can comfortably agree with all the ideas they present. I know I can't; the range they cover is too broad, and if you happen to agree with everything in one, you'll find another that clashes. That is as it should be. If a few of these stories make you uneasy enough to take a fresh look at some ideas you have always taken for granted, the experience may nudge you a little closer to some solution that you and your fellow sentient beings urgently need.

My first hope for *anything* I edit or write is that you will enjoy reading it and feel, when you finish, that your time was well spent. In this case I hope that you will also find these stories thought-provoking, and that you will come away from the book not only entertained, but perhaps a little wiser.

We need all the help we can get. ■

Other Books in the
Analog Anthology Series
Edited by Stanley Schmidt:

**FIFTY YEARS OF THE BEST
SCIENCE FICTION FROM ANALOG
ANALOG: READERS' CHOICE
ANALOG'S CHILDREN OF THE FUTURE
ANALOG'S LIGHTER SIDE
ANALOG: WRITERS' CHOICE**

Joel Davis, President & Publisher; **Leonard F. Pinto,** Vice President & General Manager; **Carole Dolph Gross,** Vice President, Marketing & Editorial; **Leonard H. Habas,** Vice President, Circulation; **Fred Edinger,** Vice President, Finance.

Stanley Schmidt, Editor; **Elizabeth Mitchell,** Managing Editor; **Ralph Rubino,** Corporate Art Director; **Gerard Hawkins,** Associate Art Director; **Terri Czeczko,** Art Editor; **Carl Bartee,** Director of Manufacturing; **Carole Dixon,** Production Manager; **Iris Temple,** Director, Subsidiary Rights; **Barbara Bazyn,** Manager, Contracts & Permissions; **Michael Dillon,** Circulation Director, Retail Marketing; **Robert Patterson,** Circulation Manager; **Paul Pearson,** Newsstand Operations Manager; **Rose Wayner,** Classified Advertising Director; **William F. Battista,** Advertising Director (NEW YORK: 212-557-9100; CHICAGO: 312-346-0712; LOS ANGELES: 213-795-3114)

E FOR EFFORT
T. L. Sherred

Human history has been a turbulent succession of wars and interludes of more or less shaky peace, and what we know of both has been heavily filtered, not only through historians, but through barriers deliberately built into original sources. The wheelings and dealings of politics, diplomacy, and finance, which often lead to armed conflict, are commonly conducted in secret, with a great deal of effort expended on creating semi-fictitious accounts of those dealings to shape public opinion. But suppose the reality could be got out in the open—that what really went on behind closed doors in history both ancient and very recent could be laid bare for all to see. Could not that unprecedented understanding of historical reality be used to nip the causes of war in the bud?

THE CAPTAIN WAS MET AT THE AIRPORT by a staff car. Long and fast it sped. In a narrow, silent room the general sat, ramrod-backed, tense. The major waited at the foot of the gleaming steps shining frostily in the night air. Tires screamed to a stop and together the captain and the major raced up the steps. No words of greeting were spoken. The general stood quickly, hand outstretched. The captain ripped open a dispatch case and handed over a thick bundle of papers. The general flipped them over eagerly and spat a sentence at the major. The major disappeared and his harsh voice rang curtly down the outside hall. The man with glasses came in and the general handed him the papers. With jerky fingers the man with glasses sorted them out. With a wave from the general the captain left, a proud smile on his weary young face. The general tapped his fingertips on the black glossy surface of the table. The man with glasses pushed aside crinkled maps, and began to read aloud.

Dear Joe:
    I started this just to kill time, because I got tired of just looking out the window. But when I got almost to the end I began to catch the trend of what's going on. You're the only one I know that can come through for me, and when you finish this you'll know why you must.
    I don't know who will get this to you. Whoever it is won't want you to identify a face later. Remember that, and please, Joe—*hurry!*
        Ed.

It all started because I'm lazy. By the time I'd shaken off the sandman and checked out of the hotel every seat in the bus was full. I stuck my bag in a dime locker and went out to kill the hour I had until the next bus left. You know the bus terminal: right across from the Book-Cadillac and the Statler, on Washington Boulevard near Michigan Avenue. Michigan Avenue. Like Main in Los Angeles, or maybe Sixty-third in its present state of decay in Chicago, where I was going. Cheap movies, pawnshops and bars by the dozens, a penny arcade or two, restaurants that feature hamburg steak, bread and butter and coffee for forty cents. Before the War, a quarter.

I like pawnshops. I like cameras, I like tools, I like to look in windows crammed with everything from electric razors to sets of socket wrenches to upper plates. So, with an hour to spare, I walked out Michigan to Sixth and back on the other side of the street. There are a lot of Chinese and Mexicans around that part of town, the Chinese running the restaurants and the Mexicans eating Southern Home Cooking. Between Fourth and Fifth I stopped to stare at what passed for a movie. Store windows painted black, amateurish signs extolling in Spanish "Detroit premiere . . . cast of thousands . . . this week only . . . ten cents—" The few 8 × 10 glossy stills pasted on the windows were poor blowups, spotty and wrinkled; pictures of mailed cavalry and what looked like a good-sized battle. All for ten cents. Right down my alley.

Maybe it's lucky that history was my major in school. Luck it must have been, certainly not cleverness, that made me pay a dime for a seat in an undertaker's rickety folding chair imbedded solidly—although the only other customers were a half-dozen Sons of the Order of Tortilla—in a cast of second-hand garlic. I sat near the door. A couple of hundred-watt bulbs dangling naked from the ceiling gave enough light for me to look around. In front of me, in the rear of the store, was the screen, what looked like a white-painted sheet of beaverboard, and when over my shoulder I saw the battered sixteen-millimeter projector I began to think that even a dime was no bargain. Still, I had forty minutes to wait.

Everyone was smoking. I lit a cigarette and the discouraged Mexican who had taken my dime locked the door and turned off the lights, after giving me a long, questioning look. I'd paid my dime, so I looked right back. In a minute the old projector started clattering. No film credits, no producer's name, no director, just a tentative flicker before a closeup of a bewhiskered mug labeled Cortez. Then a painted and feathered Indian with the title of Guatemotzin, successor to Montezuma; an aerial shot of a beautiful job of model-building tagged Ciudad de Méjico, 1521. Shots of old muzzle-loaded artillery banging away, great walls spurting stone splinters under direct fire, skinny Indians dying violently with the customary gyrations, smoke and haze and blood. The photography sat me right up straight. It had none of the scratches and erratic cuts that characterize an old print, none of the fuzziness, none of the usual mugging at the camera by the handsome hero. There wasn't any handsome hero. Did you ever see one of these French pictures, or a Russian, and comment on the reality and depth brought out by working on a small budget that can't afford famed actors? This, what there was of it, was as good, or better.

It wasn't until the picture ended with a pan shot of a dreary desolation that I began to add two and two. You can't, for pennies, really have a cast of thousands, or sets big enough to fill Central Park. A mock-up, even, of a thirty-foot wall costs enough to irritate the auditors, and there had been a lot of wall. That didn't fit with the bad editing and lack of sound track, not unless the picture had been made in the old silent days. And I knew it hadn't by the color tones you get with pan film. It looked like a well-rehearsed and badly-planned newsreel.

The Mexicans were easing out and I followed them to where the discouraged one was rewinding the reel. I asked him where he got the print.

"I haven't heard of any epics from the press agents lately, and it looks like a fairly recent print."

He agreed that it was recent, and added that he'd made it himself. I was polite to that, and he saw that I didn't believe him and straightened up from the projector.

"You don't believe that, do you?" I said that I certainly did, and I had to catch a bus. "Would you mind telling me why, exactly why?" I said that the bus—"I mean it. I'd appreciate it if you'd tell me just what's wrong with it."

"There's nothing wrong with it," I told him. He waited for me to go on. "Well, for one thing, pictures like that aren't made for the sixteen-millimeter trade. You've got a reduction from a thirty-five-millimeter master," and I gave him a few of the other reasons that separate home movies from Hollywood. When I finished he smoked quietly for a minute.

"I see." He took the reel off the projector spindle and closed the case. "I have beer in the back." I agreed beer sounded good, but the bus—well, just one. From in back of the beaverboard screen he brought paper cups and a Jumbo bottle. With a whimsical "Business suspended" he closed the open door and opened the bottle with an opener screwed on the wall. The store had likely been a grocery or restaurant. There were plenty of chairs. Two we shoved around and relaxed companionably. The beer was warm.

"You know something about this line," tentatively.

I took it as a question and laughed. "Not too much. Here's mud," and we drank. "Used to drive a truck for the Film Exchange." He was amused at that.

"Stranger in town?"

"Yes and no. Mostly yes. Sinus trouble chased me out and relatives bring me back. Not any more, though; my father's funeral was last week." He said that was too bad, and I said it wasn't. "He had sinus, too." That was a joke, and he refilled the cups. We talked awhile about Detroit climate.

Finally he said, rather speculatively, "Didn't I see you around here last night? Just about eight." He got up and went after more beer.

I called after him. "No more beer for me." He brought a bottle anyway, and I looked at my watch. "Well, just one."

"Was it you?"

"Was it me what?" I held out my paper cup.

"Weren't you around here—"

I wiped foam off my mustache. "Last night? No, but I wish I had, I'd have caught my bus. No, I was in the Motor Bar last night at eight. And I was still there at midnight."

He chewed his lip thoughtfully. "The Motor Bar. Just down the street?" And I nodded. "The Motor Bar. Hm-m-m." I looked at him. "Would you like . . . sure, you would." Before I could figure out what he was talking about he went to the back and from behind the beaverboard screen rolled out a big radio-phonograph and another Jumbo bottle. I held the bottle against the light. Still half full. I looked at my watch. He rolled the radio against the wall and lifted the lid to get at the dials.

"Reach behind you, will you? The switch on the wall." I could reach the switch without getting up, and I did. The lights went out. I hadn't expected that, and I groped at arm's length. Then the lights came on again, and I turned back, relieved. But the lights weren't on; I was looking at the street!

Now, all this happened while I was dripping beer and trying to keep my balance on a tottering chair—the street moved, I didn't and it was day and it was night and I was in front of the Book-Cadillac and I was going into the Motor Bar and I was

E for Effort

watching myself order a beer and I knew I was wide awake and not dreaming. In a panic I scrabbled off the floor, shedding chairs and beer like an umbrella while I ripped my nails feeling frantically for that light switch. By the time I found it—and all the while I was watching myself pound the bar for the barkeep—I was really in fine fettle, just about ready to collapse. Out of thin air right into a nightmare. At last I found the switch.

The Mexican was looking at me with the queerest expression I've ever seen, like he'd baited a mousetrap and caught a frog. Me? I suppose I looked like I'd seen the devil himself. Maybe I had. The beer was all over the floor and I barely made it to the nearest chair.

"What," I managed to get out, "what was that?"

The lid of the radio went down. "I felt like that too, the first time. I'd forgotten."

My fingers were too shaky to get out a cigarette, and I ripped off the top of the package. "I said, what was that?"

He sat down. "That was you, in the Motor Bar, at eight last night." I must have looked blank as he handed me another paper cup. Automatically I held it out to be refilled.

"Look here—" I started.

"I suppose it is a shock. I'd forgotten what I felt like the first time I . . . I don't care much any more. Tomorrow I'm going out to Phillips Radio." That made no sense to me, and I said so. He went on.

"I'm licked. I'm flat broke. I don't give a care any more. I'll settle for cash and live off the royalties." The story came out, slowly at first, then faster until he was pacing the floor. I guess he was tired of having no one to talk to.

His name was Miguel Jose Zapata Laviada. I told him mine; Lefko. Ed Lefko. He was the son of sugar beet workers who had emigrated from Mexico somewhere in the Twenties. They were sensible enough not to quibble when their oldest son left the back-breaking Michigan fields to seize the chance provided by a NYA scholarship. When the scholarship ran out, he'd worked in garages, driven trucks, clerked in stores, and sold brushes door-to-door to exist and learn. The Army cut short his education with the First Draft to make him a radar technician, the Army had given him an honorable discharge and an idea so nebulous as to be almost merely a hunch. Jobs were plentiful then, and it wasn't too hard to end up with enough money to rent a trailer and fill it with Army surplus radio and radar equipment. One year ago he'd finished what he'd started, finished underfed, underweight, and overexcited. But successful, because he had it.

"It" he installed in a radio cabinet, both for ease in handling and for camouflage. For reasons that will become apparent, he didn't dare apply for a patent. I looked "it" over pretty carefully. Where the phonograph turntable and radio controls had been were vernier dials galore. One big one was numbered 1 to 24, a couple were numbered 1 to 60, and there were a dozen or so numbered 1 to 25, plus two or three with no numbers at all. Closest of all it resembled one of these fancy radio or motor testers found in a super super-service station. That was all, except that there was a sheet of heavy plywood hiding whatever was installed in place of the radio chassis and speaker. A perfectly innocent cache for—

Daydreams are swell. I suppose we've all had our share of mental wealth or fame or travel or fantasy. But to sit in a chair and drink warm beer and realize that the dream of ages isn't a dream any more, to feel like a god, to know that just by turning a few dials you can see and watch anything, anybody, anywhere, that has ever happened—it still bothers me once in a while.

I know this much, that it's high frequency stuff. And there's a lot of mercury and copper and wiring of metals cheap and easy to find, but what goes where, or how, least of all, why, is out of my line. Light has mass and energy, and that mass always loses part of itself and can be translated back to electricity, or something. Mike Laviada himself says that what he stumbled on and developed was nothing new, that long before the war it had been observed many times by men like Compton and Michelson and Pfeiffer, who discarded it as a useless laboratory effect. And, of course, that was before atomic research took precedence over everything.

When the first shock wore off—and Mike had to give me another demonstration—I must have made quite a sight. Mike tells me I couldn't sit down. I'd pop up and gallop up and down the floor of that ancient store kicking chairs out of my way or stumbling over them, all the time gobbling out words and disconnected sentences faster than my tongue could trip. Finally it filtered through that he was laughing at me. I didn't see where it was any laughing matter, and I prodded him. He began to get angry.

"I know what I have," he snapped. "I'm not the biggest fool in the world, as you seem to think. Here, watch this," and he went back to the radio. "Turn out the light." I did, and there I was watching myself at the Motor Bar again, a lot happier this time. "Watch this."

The bar backed away. Out in the street, two blocks down to the City Hall. Up the steps to the Council Room. No one there. Then Council was in session, then they were gone again. Not a picture, not a projection of a lantern slide, but a slice of life about twelve feet square. If we were close, the field of view was narrow. If we were further away, the background was just as much in focus as the foreground. The images, if you want to call them images, were just as real, just as lifelike as looking in the doorway of a room. Real they were, three-dimensional, stopped by only the back wall or the distance in the background. Mike was talking as he spun the dials, but I was too engrossed to pay much attention.

I yelped and grabbed and closed my eyes as you would if you were looking straight down with nothing between you and the ground except a lot of smoke and a few clouds. I winked my eyes open almost at the ends of what must have been a long racing vertical dive, and there I was, looking at the street again.

E for Effort

"Go any place up to the Heaviside Layer, go down as deep as any hole, anywhere, any time." A blur, and the street changed into a glade of sparse pines. "Buried treasure. Sure. Find it, with what?" The trees disappeared and I reached back for the light switch as he dropped the lid of the radio and sat down.

"How are you going to make any money when you haven't got it to start?" No answer to that from me. "I ran an ad in the paper offering to recover lost articles; my first customer was the Law wanting to see my private detective's license. I've seen every big speculator in the country sit in his office buying and selling and making plans; what do you think would happen if I tried to peddle advance market information? I've watched the stock market get shoved up and down while I had barely the money to buy the paper that told me about it. I watched a bunch of Peruvian Indians bury the second ransom of Atuahalpa; I haven't the fare to get to Peru, or the money to buy the tools to dig." He got up and brought two more bottles. He went on. By that time I was getting a few ideas.

"I've watched scribes indite the books that burnt at Alexandria; who would buy, or who would believe me, if I copied one? What would happen if I went over to the Library and told them to rewrite their histories? How many would fight to tie a rope around my neck if they knew I'd watched them steal and murder and take a bath? What sort of a padded cell would I get if I showed up with a photograph of Washington, or Caesar? Or Christ?"

I agreed that it was all probably true, but—

"Why do you think I'm here now? You saw the picture I showed for a dime. A dime's worth, and that's all, because I didn't have the money to buy film or to make the picture as I knew I should." His tongue began to get tangled. He was excited. "I'm doing this because I haven't the money to get the things I need to get the money I'll need—" He was so disgusted he booted a chair halfway across the room. It was easy to see that if I had been around a little later, Phillips Radio would have profited. Maybe I'd have been better off, too.

Now, although always I've been told that I'd never be worth a hoot, no one has ever accused me of being slow for a dollar. Especially an easy one. I saw money in front of me, easy money, the easiest and the quickest in the world. I saw, for a minute, so far in the future with me on top of the heap, that my head reeled and it was hard to breathe.

"Mike," I said, "let's finish that beer and go where we can get some more, and maybe something to eat. We've got a lot of talking to do." So we did.

Beer is a mighty fine lubricant; I have always been a pretty smooth talker, and by the time we left the gin mill I had a pretty good idea of just what Mike had on his mind. By the time we'd shacked up for the night behind that beaverboard screen in the store, we were full-fledged partners. I don't recall our even shaking hands on the deal, but that partnership still holds good. Mike is ace high with me, and I guess it's the other way around, too. That was six years ago; it only took me a year or so to discard some of the corners I used to cut.

Seven days after that, on a Tuesday, I was riding a bus to Grosse Pointe with a full briefcase. Two days after that I was riding back from Grosse Pointe in a shiny taxi, with an empty briefcase and a pocketful of folding money. It was easy.

"Mr. Jones—or Smith—or Brown—I'm with Aristocrat Studios, Personal and Candid Portraits. We thought you might like this picture of you and . . . no, this is just a test proof. The negative is in our files. . . . Now, if you're really interested, I'll be back the day after tomorrow with our files. . . . I'm sure you will, Mr. Jones. Thank you, Mr. Jones. . . ."

Dirty? Sure. Blackmail is always dirty. But if I had a wife and family and a good reputation, I'd stick to the roast beef and forget the Roquefort. Very smelly Roquefort, at that. Mike liked it less than I did. It took some talking, and I had to drag out the old one about the ends justifying the means, and they could well afford it, anyway. Besides, if there was a squawk, they'd get the negatives free. Some of them were pretty bad.

So we had the cash; not too much, but enough to start. Before we took the next step there was plenty to decide. There are a lot who earn a living by convincing millions that Sticko soap is better. We had a harder problem than that: we had, first, to make a salable and profitable product, and second, we had to convince many, many millions that our "Product" was absolutely honest and absolutely accurate. We all know that if you repeat something long enough and loud enough many—or most—will accept it as gospel truth. That called for publicity on an international scale. For the skeptics who know better than to accept advertising, no matter how blatant, we had to use another technique. And since we were going to get certainly only one chance, we had to be right the first time. Without Mike's machine the job would have been impossible; without it the job would have been unnecessary.

A lot of sweat ran under the bridge before we found what we thought—and we still do!—the only workable scheme. We picked the only possible way to enter every mind in the world without a fight; the field of entertainment. Absolute secrecy was imperative, and it was only when we reached the last decimal point that we made a move. We started like this.

First we looked for a suitable building, or Mike did, while I flew east, to Rochester, for a month. The building he rented was an old bank. We had the windows sealed, a flossy office installed in the front—the bullet-proof glass was my idea—air conditioning, a portable bar, electrical wiring of whatever type Mike's little heart desired, and a blond secretary who thought she was working for M-E Experimental Laboratories. When I got back from Rochester I took over the job of keeping happy the stone masons and electricians, while Mike fooled around in our suite in the Book where he could look out the window at his old store. The last I heard, they were selling snake oil there. When the Studio, as we came to call it, was finished, Mike moved in and the blonde settled down to a routine of reading love stories and saying no to all the salesmen that wandered by. I left for Hollywood.

I spent a week digging through the files of Central Casting before I was satisfied, but it took a month of snooping and some under-the-table cash to lease a camera that would handle Trucolor film. That took the biggest load from my mind. When I got back to Detroit the big view camera had arrived from Rochester, with a truckload of glass color plates. Ready to go.

We made quite a ceremony of it. We closed the venetian blinds and I popped the cork on one of the bottles of champagne I'd bought. The blond secretary was impressed; all she'd been doing for her salary was to accept delivery of packages and crates and boxes. We had no wine glasses, but we made no fuss about that. Too nervous and excited to drink any more than one bottle, we gave the rest to the blonde and told her to take the rest of the afternoon off. After she left—and I think she was disappointed at breaking up what could have been a good party—we locked up after her, went into the studio itself, locked up again and went to work.

I've mentioned that the windows were sealed. All the inside wall had been painted dull black, and with the high ceiling that went with that old bank lobby, it was impressive. But not gloomy. Midway in the studio was planted the big Trucolor camera, loaded and ready. Not much could we see of Mike's machine, but I knew it was off to the side, set to throw on the back wall. Not *on* the wall, understand, because the images produced are projected into the air, like the meeting of the rays of two searchlights. Mike lifted the lid and I could see him silhouetted against the tiny lights that lit the dials.

"Well?" he said expectantly.

I felt pretty good just then, right down to my billfold.

"It's all yours, Mike," and a switch ticked over. There he was. There was a youngster, dead twenty-five hundred years, real enough, almost, to touch. Alexander. Alexander of Macedon.

Let's take that first picture in detail. I don't think I can ever forget what happened in the next year or so. First we followed Alexander through his life, from beginning to end. We skipped, of course, the little things he did, jumping ahead days and weeks and years at a time. Then we'd miss him, or find that he'd moved in space. That would mean we'd have to jump back and forth, like the artillery firing bracket or ranging shots, until we found him again. Helped only occasionally by his published lives, we were astounded to realize how much distortion has crept into his life. I often wonder why legends arise about the famous. Certainly their lives are as startling or appalling as fiction. And unfortunately we had to hold closely to the accepted histories. If we hadn't, every professor would have gone into his corner for a hearty sneer. We couldn't take that chance. Not at first.

After we knew approximately what had happened and where, we used our notes to go back to what had seemed a particularly photogenic section and work on that awhile. Eventually we had a fair idea of what we were actually going to film. Then we sat down and wrote an actual script to follow, making allowance for whatever shots we'd have to double in later. Mike used his machine as the projector, and I operated the Trucolor camera at a fixed focus, like taking moving pictures of a movie. As fast as we finished a reel it would go to Rochester for processing, instead of one of the Hollywood outfits that might have done it cheaper. Rochester is so used to horrible amateur stuff that I doubt if anyone ever looks at anything. When the reel was returned we'd run it ourselves to check our choice of scenes and color sense and so on.

For example, we had to show the traditional quarrels with his father, Philip. Most of that we figured on doing with doubles, later. Olympias, his mother, and the fangless snakes she affected, didn't need any doubling, as we used an angle and amount of distance that didn't call for actual conversation. The scene where Alexander rode the bucking horse no one else could ride came out of some biographer's head, but we thought it was so famous we couldn't leave it out. We dubbed the closeups later, and the actual horseman was a young Scythian that hung around the royal stables for his keep. Roxanne was real enough, like the rest of the Persians' wives that Alexander took over. Luckily most of them had enough poundage to look luscious. Philip and Parmenio and the rest of the characters were heavily bearded, which made easy the necessary doubling and dubbing-in the necessary speech. (If you ever saw them shave in those days, you'd know why whiskers were popular.)

The most trouble we had with the interior shots. Smoky wicks in a bowl of lard, no matter how plentiful, are too dim even for fast film. Mike got around that by running the Trucolor camera at a single frame a second, with his machine paced accordingly. That accounts for the startling clarity and depth of focus we got from a lens well stopped down. We had all the time in the world to choose the best possible scenes and camera angles; the best actors in the world, expensive camera booms, or repeated retakes under the most exacting director can't compete with us. We had a lifetime from which to choose.

Eventually we had on film about eighty per cent of what you saw in the finished picture. Roughly we spliced the reels together and sat there entranced at what we had actually done. Even more exciting, even more spectacular than we'd dared to hope, the lack of continuity and sound didn't stop us from realizing that we'd done a beautiful job. We'd done all we could, and the worst was yet to come. So we sent for more champagne and told the blonde we had cause for celebration. She giggled.

"What are you doing in there, anyway?" she asked. "Every salesman who comes to the door wants to know what you're making."

I opened the first bottle. "Just tell them you don't know."

"That's just what I've been telling them They think I'm awfully dumb." We all laughed at the salesmen.

Mike was thoughtful. "If we're going to do this sort of thing very often, we ought to have some of these fancy hollow-stemmed glasses."

The blonde was pleased with that. "And we could keep them in my bottom drawer." Her nose wrinkled prettily. "These bubbles— You know, this is the only time I've ever had champagne, except at a wedding, and then it was only one glass."

"Pour her another," Mike suggested. "Mine's empty, too." I did. "What did you do with those bottles you took home last time?"

A blush and a giggle. "My father wanted to open them, but I told him you said to save it for a special occasion."

By that time I had my feet on her desk. "This is the special occasion, then," I invited. "Have another, Miss . . . what's your first name, anyway? I hate being formal after working hours."

She was shocked. "And you and Mr. Laviada sign my checks every week! It's Ruth."

"Ruth. Ruth." I rolled it around the piercing bubbles, and it sounded all right.

She nodded. "And your name is Edward, and Mr. Laviada's is Migwell. Isn't it?" And she smiled at him.

"MiGELL," he smiled back. "An old Spanish custom. Usually shortened to Mike."

"If you'll hand me another bottle," I offered, "shorten Edward to Ed." She handed it over

By the time we got to the fourth bottle we were as thick as bugs in a rug. It seems that she was twenty-four, free, white, and single, and loved champagne.

"But," she burbled fretfully, "I wish I knew what you were doing in there all hours of the day and night. I know you're here at night sometimes because I've seen your car out in front."

Mike thought that over. "Well," he said a little unsteadily, "we take pictures." He blinked one eye. "Might even take pictures of you if we were approached properly."

I took over. "We take pictures of models."

"Oh, no."

"Yes. Models of things and people and what not. Little ones. We make it look like it's real." I think she was a trifle disappointed.

"Well, now I know, and that makes me feel better. I sign all those bills from Rochester and I don't know what I'm signing for. Except that they must be film or something."

"That's just what it is; film and things like that."

"Well, it bothered me— No, there's two more behind the fan."

Only two more. She had a capacity. I asked her how she would like a vacation. She hadn't thought about a vacation just yet.

I told her she'd better start thinking about it. "We're leaving day after tomorrow for Los Angeles, Hollywood."

"The day after tomorrow? Why—"

I reassured her. "You'll get paid just the same. But there's no telling how long we'll be gone, and there doesn't seem to be much use in your sitting around here with nothing to do."

From Mike: "Let's have that bottle," and I handed it to him. I went on.

"You'll get your checks just the same. If you want, we'll pay you in advance so—"

I was getting full of champagne, and so were we all. Mike was humming softly to himself, happy as a taco. The blonde, Ruth, was having a little trouble with my left eye. I knew just how she felt, because I was having a little trouble watching where she overlapped the swivel chair. Blue eyes, sooo tall, fuzzy hair. Hm-m-m. All work and no play— She handed me the last bottle.

Demurely she hid a tiny hiccup. "I'm going to save all the corks— No I won't either. My father would want to know what I'm thinking of, drinking with my bosses."

I said it wasn't a good idea to annoy your father. Mike said why fool with bad ideas, when he had a good one. We were interested. Nothing like a good idea to liven things up.

Mike was expansive as the very devil. "Going to Los Angeles."

We nodded solemnly.

"Going to Los Angeles to work."

Another nod.

"Going to work in Los Angeles. What will we do for pretty blonde girl to write letters?"

Awful. No pretty blonde to write letters and drink champagne. Sad case.

"Gotta hire somebody to write letters anyway. Might not be blonde. No blondes in Hollywood. No good ones, anyway. So—"

I saw the wonderful idea, and finished for him. "So we take pretty blonde to Los Angeles to write letters!"

What an idea that was! One bottle sooner and its brilliancy would have been dimmed. Ruth bubbled like a fresh bottle and Mike and I sat there, smirking like mad.

"But I can't! I couldn't leave day after tomorrow just like that—!"

Mike was magnificent. "Who said day after tomorrow? Changed our minds. Leave right now."

She was appalled. "Right now! Just like that?"

"Right now. Just like that." I was firm.

"But—"

"No buts. Right now. Just like that."

"Nothing to wear—"

"Buy clothes any place. Best ones in Los Angeles.'

E for Effort 19

"But my hair—"

Mike suggested a haircut in Hollywood, maybe?

I pounded the table. It felt solid. "Call the airport. Three tickets."

She called the airport. She intimidated easy.

The airport said we could leave for Chicago any time on the hour, and change there for Los Angeles. Mike wanted to know why she was wasting time on the telephone when we could be on our way. Holding up the wheels of progress, emery dust in the gears. One minute to get her hat.

"Call Pappy from the airport."

Her objections were easily brushed away with a few word-pictures of how much fun there was to be had in Hollywood. We left a sign on the door, "Gone to Lunch—Back in December," and made the airport in time for the four o'clock plane, with no time left to call Pappy. I told the parking attendant to hold the car until he heard from me and we made it up the steps and into the plane just in time. The steps were taken away, the motors snorted, and we were off, with Ruth holding fast her hat in an imaginary breeze.

There was a two-hour layover in Chicago. They don't serve liquor at the airport, but an obliging cab driver found us a convenient bar down the road, where Ruth made her call to her father. Cautiously we stayed away from the telephone booth, but from what Ruth told us, he must have read her the riot act. The bartender didn't have champagne, but gave us the special treatment reserved for those that order it. The cab driver saw that we made the liner two hours later.

In Los Angeles, we registered at the Commodore, cold sober and ashamed of ourselves. The next day Ruth went shopping for clothes for herself, and for us. We gave her the sizes and enough money to soothe her hangover. Mike and I did some telephoning. After breakfast we sat around until the desk clerk announced a Mr. Lee Johnson to see us.

Lee Johnson was the brisk professional type, the high-bracket salesman. Tall, rather homely, a clipped way of talking. We introduced ourselves as embryo producers. His eyes brightened when we said that. His meat.

"Not exactly the way you think," I told him. "We have already eighty per cent or better of the final print."

He wanted to know where he came in.

"We have several thousand feet of Trucolor film. Don't bother asking where or when we got it. This footage is silent. We'll need sound and, in places, speech dubbed in."

He nodded. "Easy enough. What condition is the master?"

"Perfect condition. It's in the hotel vault right now. There are gaps in the story to fill. We'll need quite a few male and female characters. And all of these will have to do their doubling for cash, and not for screen credit."

Johnson raised his eyebrows. "And why? Out here screen credit is bread and butter."

"Several reasons. This footage was made—never mind where—with the understanding that film credit would favor no one."

"If you're lucky enough to catch your talent between pictures you might get away with it. But if your footage is worth working with, my boys will want screen credit. And I think they're entitled to it."

I said that was reasonable enough. The technical crews were essential, and I was prepared to pay well. Particularly to keep their mouths closed until the print was ready for final release. Maybe even after that.

"Before we go any further," Johnson rose and reached for his hat, "let's take a look at that print. I don't know if we can—"

I knew what he was thinking. Amateurs. Home movies. Feelthy peekchures, mebbe?

We got the reels out of the hotel safe and drove to his laboratory, out Sunset. The top was down on his convertible and Mike hoped audibly that Ruth would have sense enough to get sport shirts that didn't itch.

"Wife?" Johnson asked carelessly.

"Secretary," Mike answered just as casually. "We flew in last night and she's out getting us some light clothes." Johnson's estimation of us rose visibly.

A porter came out of the laboratory to carry the suitcase containing the film reels. It was a long, low building, with the offices at the front and the actual laboratories tapering off at the rear. Johnson took us in the side door and called for someone whose name we didn't catch. The anonymous one was a projectionist who took the reels and disappeared into the back of the projection room. We sat for a minute in the soft easychairs until the projectionist buzzed ready. Johnson glanced at us and we nodded. He clicked a switch on the arm of his chair and the overhead lights went out. The picture started.

It ran a hundred and ten minutes as it stood. We both watched Johnson like a cat at a rathole. When the tag end showed white on the screen he signaled with the chairside buzzer for lights. They came on. He faced us.

"Where did you get that print?"

Mike grinned at him. "Can we do business?"

"Do business?" He was vehement. "You bet your life we can do business. We'll do the greatest business you ever saw!"

The projection man came down. "Hey, that's all right. Where'd you get it?"

Mike looked at me. I said, "This isn't to go any further."

Johnson looked at his man, who shrugged. "None of my business."

I dangled the hook. "That wasn't made here. Never mind where."

Johnson rose and struck, hook, line and sinker. "Europe! Hm-m-m. Germany. No France. Russia, maybe, Einstein, or Eisenstein, or whatever his name is?"

E for Effort

I shook my head. "That doesn't matter. The leads are all dead, or out of commission, but their heirs . . . well, you get what I mean."

Johnson saw what I meant. "Absolutely right. No point taking any chances. Where's the rest—?"

"Who knows? We were lucky to salvage that much. Can do?"

"Can do." He thought for a minute. "Get Bernstein in here. Better get Kessler and Marrs, too." The projectionist left. In a few minutes Kessler, a heavy-set man, and Marrs, a young, nervous chain-smoker, came in with Bernstein, the sound man. We were introduced all around and Johnson asked if we minded sitting through another showing.

"Nope. We like it better than you do."

Not quite. Kessler and Marrs and Bernstein, the minute the film was over, bombarded us with startled questions. We gave them the same answers we'd given Johnson. But we were pleased with the reception, and said so.

Kessler grunted. "I'd like to know who was behind that camera. Best I've seen, by Cripes, since 'Ben Hur.' Better than 'Ben Hur.' The boy's good."

I grunted right back at him. "That's the only thing I can tell you. The photography was done by the boys you're talking to right now. Thanks for the kind word."

All four of them stared.

Mike said, "That's right."

"Hey, hey!" from Marrs. They all looked at us with new respect. It felt good.

Johnson broke into the silence when it became awkward. "What's next on the score card?"

We got down to cases. Mike, as usual, was content to sit there with his eyes half closed, taking it all in, letting me do all the talking.

"We want sound dubbed in all the way through."

"Pleasure," said Bernstein.

"At least a dozen, maybe more, of speaking actors with a close resemblance to the leads you've seen."

Johnson was confident. "Easy. Central Casting has everybody's picture since the Year One."

"I know. We've already checked that. No trouble there. They'll have to take the cash and let the credit go, for reasons I've already explained to Mr. Johnson."

A moan from Marrs. "I bet I get that job."

Johnson was snappish. "You do. What else?" to me.

I didn't know. "Except that we have no plans for distribution as yet. That will have to be worked out."

"Like falling off a log." Johnson was happy about that. "One look at the rushes and United Artists would spit in Shakespeare's eye."

Marrs came in. "What about the other shots? Got a writer lined up?"

"We've got what will pass for the shooting script, or would have in a week or so. Want to go over it with us?"

He'd like that.

"How much time have we got?" interposed Kessler. "This is going to be a job. When do we want it?" Already it was "we."

"Yesterday is when we want it," snapped Johnson, and he rose. "Any ideas about music? No? We'll try for Werner Janssen and his boys. Bernstein, you're responsible for that print from now on. Kessler, get your crew in and have a look at it. Marrs, you'll go with Mr. Lefko and Mr. Laviada through the files at Central Casting at their convenience. Keep in touch with them at the Commodore. Now, if you'll step into my office, we'll discuss the financial arrangements—"

As easy as all that.

Oh, I don't say that it was easy work or anything like that, because in the next few months we were playing Busy Bee. What with running down the only one registered at Central Casting who looked like Alexander himself, he turned out to be a young Armenian who had given up hope of ever being called from the extra lists and had gone home to Santee—casting and rehearsing the rest of the actors and swearing at the costumers and the boys who built the sets, we were kept hopping. Even Ruth, who had reconciled her father with soothing letters, for once earned her salary. We took turns shooting dictation at her until we had a script that satisfied Mike and myself and young Marrs, who turned out to be clever as a fox on dialogue.

What I really meant is that it was easy, and immensely gratifying, to crack the shell of the tough boys who had seen epics and turkeys come and go. They were really impressed by what we had done. Kessler was disappointed when we refused to be bothered with photographing the rest of the film. We just batted our eyes and said that we were too busy, that we were perfectly confident that he would do as well as we could. He outdid himself, and us. I don't know what we would have done if he had asked us for any concrete advice. I suppose, when I think it all over, that the boys we met and worked with were so tired of working with the usual mine-run Grade Bs, that they were glad to meet someone that knew the difference between glycerin tears and reality and didn't care if it cost two dollars extra. They had us placed as a couple of city slickers with plenty on the ball. I hope.

Finally it was all over with. We all sat in the projection room; Mike and I, Marrs and Johnson, Kessler and Bernstein, and all the lesser technicians that had split up the really enormous amount of work that had been done watched the finished product. It was terrific. Everyone had done his work well. When Alexander came on the screen, he *was* Alexander the Great. (The Armenian kid got a good bonus for that.) All that blazing color, all that wealth and magnificence and glamor seemed to flare right out of the screen and sear across your mind. Even Mike and I, who had seen the original, were on the edge of our seats.

The sheer realism and magnitude of the battle scenes, I think, really made the picture. Gore, of course, is glorious when it's all make-believe and the dead get up to go to lunch. But when Bill Mauldin sees a picture and sells a breathless article on the similarity of infantrymen of all ages—well, Mauldin knows what war is like. So did the infantrymen throughout the world who wrote letters comparing Alexander's Arbela to Anzio and the Argonne. The weary peasant, not stolid at all, truding and trudging into mile after mile of those dust-laden plains and ending as a stinking, naked, ripped corpse peeping under a mound of flies isn't any different when he carries a sarissa instead of a rifle. That we'd tried to make obvious, and we succeeded.

When the lights came up in the projection room we knew we had a winner. Individually we shook hands all around, proud as a bunch of penguins, and with chests out as far. The rest of the men filed out and we retired to Johnson's office. He poured a drink all around and got down to business.

"How about releases?"

I asked him what he thought.

"Write your own ticket," he shrugged. "I don't know whether or not you know it, but the word has already gone around that you've got something."

I told him we'd had calls at the hotel from various sources, and named them.

"See what I mean? I know those babies. Kiss them out if you want to keep your shirt. And while I'm at it, you owe us quite a bit. I suppose you've got it."

"We've got it."

"I was afraid you would. If you didn't, I'd be the one that would have your shirt." He grinned, but we all knew he meant it. "All right, that's settled. Let's talk about release.

"There are two or three outfits around town that will want a crack at it. My boys will have the word spread around in no time; there's no point in trying to keep them quiet any longer. I know—they'll have sense enough not to talk about the things you want off the record. I'll see to that. But you're top dog right now. You got loose cash, you've got the biggest potential gross I've ever seen, and you don't have to take the first offer. That's important, in this game."

"How would you like to handle it yourself?"

"I'd like to try. The outfit I'm thinking of needs a feature right now, and they don't know I know it. They'll pay and pay. What's in it for me?"

"That," I said, "we can talk about later. And I think I know just what you're thinking. We'll take the usual terms and we don't care if you hold up whoever you deal with. What we don't know won't hurt us." That's what he was thinking, all right. That's a cutthroat game out there.

"Good. Kessler, get your setup ready for duplication."

"Always ready."

"Marrs, start the ball rolling on publicity . . . what do you want to do about that?" to us.

Mike and I had talked about that before. "As far as we're concerned," I said slowly, "do as you think best. Personal publicity, O.K. We won't look for it, but we won't dodge it. As far as that goes, we're the local yokels making good. Soft pedal any questions about where the picture was made, without being too obvious. You're going to have trouble when you talk about the nonexistent actors, but you ought to be able to figure out something."

Marrs groaned and Johnson grinned. "He'll figure out something."

"As far as technical credit goes, we'll be glad to see you get all you can, because you've done a swell job." Kessler took that as a personal compliment, and it was. "You might as well know now, before we go any further, that some of the work came right from Detroit." They all sat up at that.

"Mike and I have a new process of model and trick work." Kessler opened his mouth to say something but thought better of it. "We're not going to say what was done, or how much was done in the laboratory, but you'll admit that it defies detection."

About that they were fervent. "I'll say it defies detection. In the game this long and process work gets by me . . . where—"

"I'm not going to tell you that. What we've got isn't patented and won't be, as long as we can hold it up." There wasn't any griping there. These men knew process work when they saw it. If they didn't see it, it was good. They could understand why we'd want to keep a process that good a secret.

"We can practically guarantee there'll be more work for you to do later on." Their interest was plain. "We're not going to predict when, or make any definite arrangement, but we still have a trick or two in the deck. We like the way we've been getting along, and we want to stay that way. Now, if you'll excuse us, we have a date with a blonde."

Johnson was right about the bidding for the release. We—or rather Johnson—made a very profitable deal with United Amusement and the affiliated theaters. Johnson, the bandit, got his percentage from us and likely did better with United. Kessler and Johnson's boys took huge ads in the trade journals to boast about their connections with the Academy Award Winner. Not only the Academy, but every award that ever went to any picture. Even the Europeans went overboard. They're the ones that make a fetish of realism. They knew the real thing when they saw it, and so did everyone else.

Our success went to Ruth's head. In no time she wanted a secretary. At that, she needed one to fend off the screwballs that popped out of the woodwork. So we let her hire a girl to help out. She picked a good typist, about fifty. Ruth is a smart girl, in a lot of ways. Her father showed signs of wanting to see the Pacific, so we raised her salary on condition he'd stay away. The three of us were having too much fun.

The picture opened at the same time in both New York and Hollywood. We went to the premiere in great style with Ruth between us, swollen like a trio of bullfrogs. It's a great feeling to sit on the floor, early in the morning, and read reviews that make you feel like floating. It's a better feeling to have a mintful of money. Johnson and his men were right along with us. I don't think he could have been too flush in the beginning, and we all got a kick out of riding the crest.

It was a good-sized wave, too. We had all the personal publicity we wanted, and more. Somehow the word was out that we had a new gadget for process photography, and every big studio in town was after what they thought would be a mighty economical thing to have around. The studios that didn't have a spectacle scheduled looked at the receipts of "Alexander" and promptly scheduled a spectacle. We drew some very good offers, Johnson said, but we made a series of long faces and broke the news that we were leaving for Detroit the next day, and to hold the fort awhile. I don't think he thought we actually meant it, but we did. We left the next day.

Back in Detroit we went right to work, helped by the knowledge that we were on the right track. Ruth was kept busy turning away the countless would-be visitors. We admitted no reporters, no salesmen, no one. We had no time. We were using the view camera. Plate after plate we sent to Rochester for developing. A print of each was returned to us and the plate was held in Rochester for our disposal. We sent to New York for a representative of one of the biggest publishers in the country. We made a deal.

Your main library has a set of the books we published, if you're interested. Huge heavy volumes, hundreds of them, each page a razor-sharp blowup from an 8×10 negative. A set of those books went to every major library and university in the world. Mike and I got a real kick out of solving some of the problems that have had savants guessing for years. In the Roman volume, for example, we solved the trireme problem with a series of pictures, not only the interior of a trireme, but a line-of-battle quinquereme. (Naturally, the professors and amateur yachtsmen weren't convinced at all.) We had a series of aerial shots of the City of Rome taken a hundred years apart, over a millennium. Aerial views of Ravenna and Londinium, Palmyra and Pompeii, of Eboracum and Byzantium. Oh, we had the time of our lives! We had a volume for Greece and for Rome, for Persia and for Crete, for Egypt and for the Eastern Empire. We had pictures of the Parthenon and the Pharos, pictures of Hannibal and Caractacus and Vercingetorix, pictures of the Walls of Babylon and the building of the pyramids and the palace of Sargon, pages from the Lost Books of Livy and the plays of Euripides. Things like that.

Terrifically expensive, a second printing sold at cost to a surprising number of private individuals. If the cost had been less, historical interest would have become even more the fad of the moment.

When the flurry had almost died down, some Italian digging in the hitherto-unexcavated section of ash-buried Pompeii dug right into a tiny buried temple right where our aerial shot had showed it to be. His budget was expanded and he found more ash-covered ruins that agreed with our aerial layout, ruins that hadn't seen the light of day for almost two thousand years. Everyone promptly wailed that we were the luckiest guessers in captivity; the head of some California cult suspected aloud that we were the reincarnations of two gladiators named Joe.

To get some peace and quiet Mike and I moved into our studio, lock, stock, and underwear. The old bank vault had never been removed, at our request, and it served well to store our equipment when we weren't around. All the mail Ruth couldn't handle we disposed of, unread; the old bank building began to look like a well-patronized soup kitchen. We hired burly private detectives to handle the more obnoxious visitors and subscribed to a telegraphic protective service. We had another job to do, another full-length feature.

We still stuck to the old historical theme. This time we tried to do what Gibbon did in *The Decline and Fall of the Roman Empire*. And, I think, we were rather successful, at that. In four hours you can't completely cover two thousand years, but you can, as we did, show the cracking up of a great civilization, and how painful the process can be. The criticism we drew for almost ignoring Christ and Christianity was unjust, we think, and unfair. Very few knew then, or know now, that we had included, as a kind of trial balloon, some footage of Christ Himself, and His times. This footage we had to cut. The Board of Review, as you know, is both Catholic and Protestant. They—the Board—went right up in arms. We didn't protest very hard when they claimed our "treatment" was irreverent, indecent, and biased and inaccurate "by any Christian standard." "Why," they wailed, "it doesn't even look like Him," and they were right; it didn't. Not any picture *they* ever saw. Right then and there we decided that it didn't pay to tamper with anyone's religious beliefs. That's why you've never seen anything emanating from us that conflicted even remotely with the accepted historical, sociological, or religious features of Someone Who Knew Better. That Roman picture, by the way,—but not accidentally—deviated so little from the textbooks you conned in school that only a few enthusiastic specialists called our attention to what they insisted were errors. We were still in no position to do any mass rewriting of history, because we were unable to reveal just where we got our information.

Johnson, when he saw the Roman epic, mentally clicked high his heels. His men went right to work, and we handled the job as we had the first. One day Kessler got me in a corner, dead earnest.

"Ed," he said, "I'm going to find out where you got that footage if it's the last thing I ever do."

I told him that some day he would.

"And I don't mean someday, either; I mean right now. That bushwa about Europe might go once, but not twice. I know better, and so does everyone else. Now, what about it?"

I told him I'd have to consult Mike and I did. We were up against it. We called a conference.

E for Effort 27

"Kessler tells me he has troubles. I guess you all know what they are." They all knew.

Johnson spoke up. "He's right, too. We know better. Where did you get it?"

I turned to Mike. "Want to do the talking?"

A shake of his head. "You're doing all right."

"All right." Kessler hunched a little forward and Marrs lit another cigarette. "We weren't lying and we weren't exaggerating when we said the actual photography was ours. Every frame of film was taken right here in this country, within the last few months. Just how—I won't mention why or where—we can't tell you just now." Kessler snorted in disgust. "Let me finish.

"We all know that we're cashing in, hand over fist. And we're going to cash in some more. We have, on our personal schedule, five more pictures. Three of that five we want you to handle as you did the others. The last two of the five will show you both the reason for all the childish secrecy, as Kessler calls it, and another motive that we have so far kept hidden. The last two pictures will show you both our motives and our methods; one is as important as the other. Now—is that enough? Can we go ahead on that basis?"

It wasn't enough for Kessler. "That doesn't mean a thing to me. What are we, a bunch of hacks?"

Johnson was thinking about his bank balance. "Five more. Two years, maybe four."

Marrs was skeptical. "Who do you think you're going to kid that long? Where's your studio? Where's your talent? Where do you shoot your exteriors? Where do you get your costumes and your extras? In one single shot you've got forty thousand extras, if you've got one! Maybe you can shut *me* up, but who's going to answer the questions that Metro and Fox and Paramount and RKO have been asking? Those boys aren't fools, they know their business. How do you expect me to handle any publicity when I don't know what the score is, myself?"

Johnson told him to pipe down for a while and let him think. Mike and I didn't like this one bit. But what could we do—tell the truth and end up in a strait-jacket?

"Can we do it this way?" he finally asked. "Marrs: these boys have an in with the Soviet Government. They work in some place in Siberia, maybe. Nobody gets within miles of there. No one ever knows what the Russians are doing—"

"Nope!" Marrs was definite. "Any hint that these came from Russia and we'd all be a bunch of Reds. Cut the gross in half."

Johnson began to pick up speed. "All right, not from Russia. From one of these little republics fringed around Siberia or Armenia or one of those places. They're not Russian-made films at all. In fact, they've been made by some of these Germans and Austrians the Russians took over and moved after the War. The war fever had died down enough for people to realize that the Germans knew their stuff occasionally. The old sympathy racket for these refugees struggling with faulty equipment, lousy climate, making super-spectacles and smuggling them out under the nose of the Gestapo or whatever they call it— That's it!"

Doubtfully, from Marrs: "And the Russians tell the world we're nuts, that they haven't got any loose Germans?"

That, Johnson overrode. "Who reads the back pages? Who pays any attention to what the Russians say? Who cares? They might even think we're telling the truth and start looking around their own backyard for something that isn't there! All right with you?" to Mike and myself.

I looked at Mike and he looked at me.

"O.K. with us."

"O.K. with the rest of you? Kessler? Bernstein?"

They weren't too agreeable, and certainly not happy, but they agreed to play games until we gave the word.

We were warm in our thanks. "You won't regret it."

Kessler doubted that very much, but Johnson eased them all out, back to work. Another hurdle leaped, or sidestepped.

"Rome" was released on schedule and drew the same friendly reviews. "Friendly" is the wrong word for reviews that stretched ticket line-ups blocks long. Marrs did a good job on the publicity. Even that chain of newspapers that afterward turned on us so viciously fell for Marrs' word wizardry and ran full-page editorials urging the reader to see "Rome."

With our third picture, "Flame Over France," we corrected a few misconceptions about the French Revolution, and began stepping on a few tender toes. Luckily, however, and not altogether by design, there happened to be in power in Paris a liberal government. They backed us to the hilt with the confirmation we needed. At our request they released a lot of documents that had hitherto conveniently been lost in the cavernous recesses of the Bibliotheque Nationale. I've forgotten the name of whoever happened to be the perennial pretender to the French throne. At, I'm sure, the subtle prodding of one of Marrs's ubiquitous publicity men, the pretender sued us for our whole net, alleging the defamation of the good name of the Bourbons. A lawyer Johnson dug up for us sucked the poor chump into a courtroom and cut him to bits. Not even six cents' damages did he get. Samuels, the lawyer, and Marrs drew a good-sized bonus, and the pretender moved to Honduras.

Somewhere around this point, I believe, did the tone of the press begin to change. Up until then we'd been regarded as crosses between Shakespeare and Barnum. Since long-obscure facts had been dredged into the light, a few well-known pessimists began to wonder *sotto voce* if we weren't just a pair of blasted pests. "Should leave well enough alone." Only our huge advertising budget kept them from saying more.

I'm going to stop right here and say something about our personal life while all this was going on. Mike I've kept in the background pretty well, mostly because he wants it that way. He lets me do all the talking and stick my neck out while he sits in the most comfortable chair in sight. I yell and I argue and he just sits there; hardly ever a word coming out of that dark-brown pan, certainly never an indication showing that behind those polite eyebrows there's a brain—and a sense of humor and wit—faster and as deadly as a bear trap. Oh, I know we've played around, sometimes with a loud bang, but we've been, ordinarily, too busy and too preoccupied with what we were doing to waste any time. Ruth, while she was with us, was a good dancing and drinking partner. She was young, she was almost what you'd call beautiful, and she seemed to like being with us. For a while I had a few ideas about her that might have developed into something serious. We both—I should say, all three of us—found out in time that we looked at a lot of things too differently. So we weren't too disappointed when she signed with Metro. Her contract meant what she thought was all the fame and money and happiness in the world, plus the personal attention she was doubtless entitled to have. They put her in Class Bs and serials and she, financially, is better off than she ever expected to be. Emotionally, I don't know. We heard from her some time ago, and I think she's about due for another divorce. Maybe it's just as well.

But let's get away from Ruth, I'm ahead of myself, anyway. All this time Mike and I had been working together, our approach to the final payoff had been divergent. Mike was hopped on the idea of making a better world, and doing that by making war impossible. "War," he's often said, "war of any kind is what has made man spend most of his history in merely staying alive. Now, with the atom to use, he has within himself the seed of self-extermination. So help me, Ed, I'm going to do my share of stopping that, or I don't see any point in living. I mean it!"

He did mean it. He told me that in almost the same words the first day we met. Then I tagged that idea as a pipe dream picked up on an empty stomach. I saw his machine only as a path to luxurious and personal Nirvana, and I thought he'd soon be going my way. I was wrong.

You can't live, or work, with a likable person without admiring some of the qualities that make that person likable. Another thing; it's a lot easier to worry about the woes of the world when you haven't any yourself. It's a lot easier to have a conscience when you can afford it. When I donned the rose-colored glasses half my battle was won; when I realized how grand a world this *could* be, the battle was over. That was about the time of "Flame Over France," I think. The actual time isn't important. What *is* important is that, from that time on, we became the tightest team possible. Since then the only thing we've differed on would be the time to knock off for a sandwich. Most of our leisure time, what we had of it, has been spent in locking up for the night, rolling out the portable bar, opening just enough beer to feel good, and relaxing. Maybe, after one or two, we might diddle the dials of the machine, and go rambling.

Together we've been everywhere and seen anything. It might be a good night to check up on François Villon, the faker, or maybe we might chase around with Harounel-Rashid. (If there was ever a man born a few hundred years too soon, it was that careless caliph.) Or if we were in a bad or discouraged mood we might follow the Thirty Years' War for a while, or if we were real raffish we might inspect the dressing rooms at Radio City. For Mike the crackup of Atlantis has always had an odd fascination, probably because he's afraid that man will do it again, now that he's rediscovered nuclear energy. And if I doze off he's quite apt to go back to the very Beginning, back to the start of the world as we know it now. (It wouldn't do any good to tell you what went before that.)

When I stop to think, it's probably just as well that neither of us married. We, of course, have hopes for the future, but at present we're both tired of the whole human race; tired of greedy faces and hands. With a world that puts a premium on wealth and power and strength, it's no wonder what decency there is stems from fear of what's here now, or fear of what's hereafter. We've seen so much of the hidden actions of the world—call it snooping, if you like—that we've learned to disregard the surface indications of kindness and good. Only once did Mike and I ever look into the private life of someone we knew and liked and respected. Once was enough. From that day on we made it a point to take people as they seemed. Let's get away from that.

The next two pictures we released in rapid succession; the first, "Freedom for Americans," the American Revolution, and "The Brothers and the Guns," the American Civil War. Bang! Every third politician, a lot of so-called "educators," and all the professional patriots started after our scalps. Every single chapter of the DAR, the Sons of Union Veterans, and the Daughters of the Confederacy pounded their collective heads against the wall. The South went frantic; every state in the Deep South and one state on the border flatly banned both pictures, the second because it was truthful, and the first because censorship is a contagious disease. They stayed banned until the professional politicians got wise. The bans were revoked, and the choke-collar and string-tie brigade pointed to both pictures as horrible examples of what some people actually believed and thought, and felt pleased that someone had given them an opportunity to roll out the barrel and beat the drums that sound sectional and racial hatred.

New England was tempted to stand on its dignity, but couldn't stand the strain. North of New York both pictures were banned. In New York State the rural representatives voted en bloc, and the ban was clamped on statewide. Special trains ran to Delaware, where the corporations were too busy to pass another law. Libel suits flew like spaghetti, and although the extras blared the filing of each new suit, very few knew that we lost not one. Although we had to appeal almost every suit to higher courts, and in some cases request a change of venue which was seldom granted, the documentary proof furnished by the record cleared us once we got to a judge, or series of judges, with no fences to mend.

It was a mighty rasp we drew over wounded ancestral pride. We had shown that not all the mighty had haloes of purest gold, that not all the Redcoats were strutting bullies—nor angels, and the British Empire, except South Africa, refused entry to both pictures and made violent passes at the State Department. The spectacle of Southern and New England congressmen approving the efforts of a foreign ambassador to suppress free speech drew hilarious hosannas from certain quarters. H. L. Mencken gloated in the clover, doing loud nip-ups, and the newspapers hung on the triple-horned dilemma of anti-foreign, pro-patriotic, and quasi-logical criticism. In Detroit the Ku Klux Klan fired an anemic cross on our doorstep, and the Friendly Sons of St. Patrick, the NAACP, and the WCTU passed flattering resolutions. We forwarded the most vicious and obscene letters—together with a few names and addresses that hadn't been originally signed—to our lawyers and the Post Office Department. There were no convictions south of Illinois.

Johnson and his boys made hay. Johnson had pyramided his bets into an international distributing organization, and pushed Marrs into hiring every top press agent either side of the Rockies. What a job they did! In no time at all there were two definite schools of thought that overflowed into the public letter boxes. One school held that we had no business raking up old mud to throw, that such things were better left forgotten and forgiven, that nothing wrong had ever happened, and if it had, we were liars anyway. The other school reasoned more to our liking. Softly and slowly at first, then with a triumphant shout, this fact began to emerge: such things had actually happened, and could happen again, were possibly happening even now; had happened because twisted truth had too long left its imprint on international, sectional, and racial feelings. It pleased us when many began to agree, with us, that it is important to forget the past, but that it is even more important to understand and evaluate it with a generous and unjaundiced eye. That was what we were trying to bring out.

The banning that occurred in the various states hurt the gross receipts only a little, and we were vindicated in Johnson's mind. He had dolefully predicted loss of half the national gross because "you can't tell the truth in a movie and get away with it. Not if the house holds over three hundred." Not even on the stage? "Who goes to anything but a movie?"

So far things had gone just about as we'd planned. We'd earned and received more publicity, favorable and otherwise, than anyone living. Most of it stemmed from the fact that our doing had been newsworthy. Some, naturally, had been the ninety-day-wonder material that fills a thirsty newspaper. We had been very careful to make our enemies in the strata that can afford to fight back. Remember the old saw about knowing a man by the enemies he makes? Well, publicity was our ax. Here's how we put an edge on it.

I called Johnson in Hollywood. He was glad to hear from us. "Long time no see. What's the pitch, Ed?"

"I want some lip readers. And I want them yesterday, like you tell your boys."

"Lip readers? Are you nuts? What do you want with lip readers?"

"Never mind why. I want lip readers. Can you get them?"

"How should I know? What do you want them for?"

"I said, can you get them?"

He was doubtful. "I think you've been working too hard."

"Look—"

"Now, I didn't say I couldn't. Cool off. When do you want them? And how many?"

"Better write this down. Ready? I want lip readers for these languages: English, French, German, Russian, Chinese, Japanese, Greek, Belgian, Dutch and Spanish."

"Ed Lefko, have you gone crazy?"

I guess it didn't sound very sensible, at that. "Maybe I have. But those languages are essential. If you run across any who can work in any other language, hang on to them. I might need them, too." I could see him sitting in front of his telephone, wagging his head like mad. Crazy. The heat must have got Lefko, good old Ed. "Did you hear what I said?"

"Yes, I heard you. If this is a rib—"

"No rib. Dead serious."

He began to get mad. "Where you think I'm going to get lip readers, out of my hat?"

"That's your worry. I'd suggest you start with the local School for the Deaf." He was silent. "Now, get this into your head; this isn't a rib, this is the real thing. I don't care what you do, or where you go, or what you spend—I want those lip readers in Hollywood when we get there or I want to know they're on the way."

"When are you going to get here?"

I said I wasn't sure. "Probably a day or two. We've got a few loose ends to clean up."

He swore a blue streak at the iniquities of fate. "You'd better have a good story when you do—" I hung up.

Mike met me at the studio. "Talk to Johnson?" I told him, and he laughed. "Does sound crazy, I suppose. But he'll get them, if they exist and like money. He's the Original Resourceful Man."

I tossed my hat in a corner. "I'm glad this is about over. Your end caught up?"

"Set and ready to go. The films and the notes are on the way, the real estate company is ready to take over the lease, and the girls are paid up to date, with a little extra."

I opened a bottle of beer for myself. Mike had one. "How about the office files? How about the bar, here?"

"The files go to the bank to be stored. The bar? Hadn't thought about it."

The beer was cold. "Have it crated and send it to Johnson."

We grinned, together. "Johnson it is. He'll need it."

I nodded at the machine. "What about that?"

"That goes with us on the plane as air express." He looked closely at me. "What's the matter with you—jitters?"

"Nope. Willies. Same thing."

"Me, too. Your clothes and mine left this morning."

"Not even a clean shirt left?"

"Not even a clean shirt. Just like—"

I finished it. "—the first trip with Ruth. A little different, maybe."

Mike said slowly, "A lot different." I opened another beer. "Anything you want around here, anything else to be done?" I said no. "O.K. Let's get this over with. We'll put what we need in the car. We'll stop at the Courville Bar before we hit the airport."

I didn't get it. "There's still beer left—"

"But no champagne."

I got it. "O.K. I'm dumb, at times. Let's go."

We loaded the machine into the car, and the bar, left the studio keys at the corner grocery for the real estate company, and headed for the airport by way of the Courville Bar. Ruth was in California, but Joe had champagne. We got to the airport late.

Marrs met us in Los Angeles. "What's up? You've got Johnson running around in circles."

"Did he tell you why?"

"Sounds crazy to me. Couple of reporters inside. Got anything for them?"

"Not right now. Let's get going."

In Johnson's private office we got a chilly reception. "This better be good. Where do you expect to find someone to lipread in Chinese? Or Russian, for that matter?"

We all sat down. "What have you got so far?"

"Besides a headache?" He handed me a short list.

I scanned it. "How long before you can get them here?"

An explosion. "How long before I can get them here? Am I your errand boy?"

"For all practical purposes you are. Quit the fooling. How about it?" Marrs snickered at the look on Johnson's face.

"What are you smirking at, you moron?" Marrs gave in and laughed outright, and I did, too. "Go ahead and laugh. This isn't funny. When I called the State School for the Deaf they hung up. Thought I was some practical joker. We'll skip that.

"There's three women and a man on that list. They cover English, French, Spanish, and German. Two of them are working in the East, and I'm waiting for answers to telegrams I sent them. One lives in Pomona and one works for the Arizona School for the Deaf. That's the best I could do."

We thought that over. "Get on the phone. Talk to every state in the union if you have to, or overseas."

Johnson kicked the desk. "And what are you going to do with them, if I'm that lucky?"

"You'll find out. Get them on planes and fly them here, and we'll talk turkey when they get here. I want a projection room, not yours, and a good bonded court reporter."

He asked the world to appreciate what a life he led.

"Get in touch with us at the Commodore." To Marrs: "Keep the reporters away for a while. We'll have something for them later." Then we left.

Johnson never did find anyone who could lipread Greek. None, at least, that could speak English. The expert on Russian he dug out of Ambridge, in Pennsylvania, the Flemish and Holland Dutch expert came from Leyden, in the Netherlands, and at the last minute he stumbled upon a Korean who worked in Seattle as an inspector for the Chinese Government. Five women and two men. We signed them to an ironclad contract drawn by Samuels, who now handled all our legal work. I made a little speech before they signed.

"These contracts, as far as we've been able to make sure, are going to control your personal and business life for the next year, and there's a clause that says we can extend that period for another year if we so desire. Let's get this straight. You are to live in a place of your own, which we will provide. You will be supplied with all necessities by our buyers. Any attempt at unauthorized communication will result in abrogation of the contract. Is that clear?

"Good. Your work will not be difficult, but it will be tremendously important. You will, very likely, be finished in three months, but you will be ready to go any place at any time at our discretion, naturally at our expense. Mr. Sorenson, as you are taking this down, you realize that this goes for you, too." He nodded.

"Your references, your abilities, and your past work have been thoroughly checked, and you will continue under constant observation. You will be required to verify and notarize every page, perhaps every line, of your transcripts, which Mr. Sorenson here will supply. Any questions?"

No questions. Each was getting a fabulous salary, and each wanted to appear eager to earn it. They all signed.

Resourceful Johnson bought for us a small rooming house, and we paid an exorbitant price to a detective agency to do the cooking and cleaning and chauffeuring required. We requested that the lipreaders refrain from discussing their work among themselves, especially in front of the house employees, and they followed instructions very well.

One day, about a month later, we called a conference in the projection room of Johnson's laboratory. We had a single reel of film.

"What's that for?"

"That's the reason for all the cloak-and-dagger secrecy. Never mind calling your projection man. This I'm going to run through myself. See what you think of it."

They were all disgusted. "I'm getting tired of all this kid stuff," said Kessler.

As I started for the projection booth I heard Mike say, "You're no more tired of it than I am."

From the booth I could see what was showing on the downstairs screen, but nothing else. I ran through the reel, rewound, and went back down.

I said, "One more thing before we go any further: read this. It's a certified and notarized transcript of what has been read from the lips of the characters you just saw. They weren't, incidentally, 'characters,' in that sense of the word." I handed the crackling sheets around, a copy for each. "Those 'characters' are real people. You've just seen a newsreel. This transcript will tell you what they were talking about. Read it. In the trunk of the car Mike and I have something to show you. We'll be back by the time you've read it."

Mike helped me carry in the machine from the car. We came in the door in time to see Kessler throw the transcript as far as he could. He bounced to his feet as the sheets fluttered down.

He was furious. "What's going on here?" We paid no attention to him, nor to the excited demands of the others until the machine had been plugged into the nearest outlet.

Mike looked at me. "Any ideas?"

I shook my head and told Johnson to shut up for a minute. Mike lifted the lid and hesitated momentarily before he touched the dials. I pushed Johnson into his chair and turned off the lights myself. The room went black. Johnson, looking over my shoulder, gasped. I heard Bernstein swear softly, amazed.

I turned to see what Mike had shown them.

It was impressive, all right. He had started just over the roof of the laboratory and continued straight up in the air. Up, up, up, until the city of Los Angeles was a tiny dot on a great ball. On the horizon were the Rockies. Johnson grabbed my arm. He hurt.

"What's that? What's that? Stop it!" He was yelling. Mike turned off the machine.

You can guess what happened next. No one believed their eyes, nor Mike's patient explanation. He had to twice turn on the machine again, once going far back into Kessler's past. Then the reaction set in.

Marrs smoked one cigarette after another, Bernstein turned a gold pencil over and over in his nervous fingers, Johnson paced like a caged tiger, and burly Kessler stared at the machine, saying nothing at all. Johnson was muttering as he paced. Then he stopped and shook his fist under Mike's nose.

"Man! Do you know what you've got there? Why waste time playing around here? Can't you see you've got the world by the tail on a downhill pull? If I'd ever known this—"

Mike appealed to me. "Ed, talk to this wildman."

I did. I can't remember exactly what I said, and it isn't important. But I did tell him how we'd started, how we'd plotted our course, and what we were going to do. I ended by telling him the idea behind the reel of film I'd run off a minute before.

He recoiled as though I were a snake. "You can't get away with that! You'd be hung—if you weren't lynched first!"

"Don't you think we know that? Don't you think we're willing to take that chance?"

He tore his thinning hair. Marrs broke in. "Let me talk to him." He came over and faced us squarely.

"Is this on the level? You going to make a picture like that and stick your neck out? You're going to turn that . . . that thing over to the people of the world?"

I nodded. "Just that."

"And toss over everything you've got?" He was dead serious, and so was I. He turned to the others. "He means it!"

Bernstein said, "Can't be done!"

Words flew. I tried to convince them that we had followed the only possible path. "What kind of a world do you want to live in? Or don't you want to live?"

Johnson grunted. "How long do you think we'd live if we ever made a picture like that? You're crazy! I'm not. I'm not going to put my head in a noose."

"Why do you think we've been so insistent about credit and responsibility for direction and production? You'll be doing only what we hired you for. Not that we want to twist your arm, but you've made a fortune, all of you, working for us. Now, when the going gets heavy, you want to back out!"

Marrs gave in. "Maybe you're right, maybe you're wrong. Maybe you're crazy, maybe I am. I always used to say I'd try anything once. Bernie, you?"

Bernstein was quietly cynical. "You saw what happened in the last war. This might help. I don't know if it will. I don't know—but I'd hate to think I didn't try. Count me in!"

Kessler?

He swiveled his head. "Kid stuff! Who wants to live forever? Who wants to let a chance go by?"

Johnson threw up his hands. "Let's hope we get a cell together. Let's all go crazy." And that was that.

We went to work in a blazing drive of mutual hope and understanding. In four months the lipreaders were through. There's no point in detailing here their reactions to the dynamite they daily dictated to Sorenson. For their own good we kept them in the dark about our final purpose, and when they were through we sent them across the border into Mexico, to a small ranch Johnson had leased. We were going to need them later.

While the print duplicators worked overtime Marrs worked harder. The press and the radio shouted the announcement that, in every city of the world we could reach, there would be held the simultaneous premieres of our latest picture. It would be the last we needed to make. Many wondered aloud at our choice of the word "needed."

We whetted curiosity by refusing any advance information about the plot, and Johnson so well infused the men with their own now-fervent enthusiasm that not much could be pried out of them but conjecture. The day we picked for release was Sunday. Monday, the storm broke.

I wonder how many prints of that picture are left today. I wonder how many escaped burning or confiscation. Two World Wars we covered, covered from the unflattering angles that, up until then, had been represented by only a few books hidden in the dark corners of libraries. We showed and *named* the war-makers, the cynical ones who signed and laughed and lied, the blatant patriots who used the flare of headlines and the ugliness of atrocity to hide behind their flag while life turned to death for millions. Our own and foreign traitors were there, the hidden ones with Janus faces. Our lipreaders had done their work well; no guesses these, no deduced conjectures from the broken records of a blasted past, but the exact words that exposed treachery disguised as patriotism.

In foreign lands the performances lasted barely the day. Usually, in retaliation for the imposed censorship, the theaters were wrecked by the raging crowds. (Marrs, incidentally, had spent hundreds of thousands bribing officials to allow the picture to be shown without previous censorship. Many censors, when that came out, were shot without trial.) In the Balkans, revolutions broke out, and various embassies were stormed by mobs. Where the film was banned or destroyed written versions spontaneously appeared on the streets or in coffeehouses. Bootlegged editions were smuggled past customs guards, who looked the other way. One royal family fled to Switzerland.

Here in America it was a racing two weeks before the Federal Government, prodded into action by the raging of press and radio, in an unprecedented move closed all performances "to promote the common welfare, insure domestic tranquillity, and preserve foreign relations." Murmurs—and one riot—rumbled in the Midwest and spread until it was realized by the powers that be that something had to be done, and done quickly, if every government in the world were not to collapse of its own weight.

We were in Mexico, at the ranch Johnson had rented for the lipreaders. While Johnson paced the floor, jerkily fraying a cigar, we listened to a special broadcast of the attorney general himself:

" . . . furthermore, this message was today forwarded to the Government of the United States of Mexico. I read: 'The Government of the United States of America requests the immediate arrest and extradition of the following:

" 'Edward Joseph Lefkowicz, known as Lefko.' " First on the list. Even a fish wouldn't get into trouble if he kept his mouth shut.

" 'Miguel Jose Zapata Laviada.' " Mike crossed one leg over the other.

" 'Edward Lee Johnson.' " He threw his cigar on the floor and sank into a chair.

" 'Robert Chester Marrs.' " He lit another cigarette. His face twitched.

" 'Benjamin Lionel Bernstein.' " He smiled a twisted smile and closed his eyes.

" 'Carl Wilhelm Kessler.' " A snarl.

"These men are wanted by the Government of the United States of America, to stand trial on charges ranging from criminal syndicalism, incitement to riot, suspicion of treason—"

I clicked off the radio. "Well?" to no one in particular.

Bernstein opened his eyes. "The rurales are probably on their way. Might as well go back and face the music—" We crossed the border at Juarez. The FBI was waiting.

Every press and radio chain in the world must have had coverage at that trial, every radio system, even the new and imperfect television chain. We were allowed to see no one but our lawyer. Samuels flew from the West Coast and spent a week trying to get past our guards. He told us not to talk to reporters, if we ever saw them.

"You haven't seen the newspapers? Just as well— How did you ever get yourselves into this mess, anyway? You ought to know better."

I told him.

He was stunned. "Are you all crazy?"

He was hard to convince. Only the united effort and concerted stories of all of us made him believe that there was such a machine in existence. (He talked to us separately, because we were kept isolated.) When he got back to me he was unable to think coherently.

"What kind of defense do you call that?"

I shook my head. "No. That is, we know that we're guilty of practically everything under the sun if you look at it one way. If you look at it another—"

He rose. "Man, you don't need a lawyer, you need a doctor. I'll see you later. I've got to get this figured out in my mind before I can do a thing."

"Sit down. What do you think of this?" and I outlined what I had in mind.

"I think . . . I don't know what I think. I don't know. I'll talk to you later. Right now I want some fresh air," and he left.

As most trials do, this one began with the usual blackening of the defendant's character, or lack of it. (The men we'd blackmailed at the beginning had long since had their money returned, and they had sense enough to keep quiet. That might have been because they'd received a few hints that there might still be a negative or two lying around. Compounding a felony? Sure.) With the greatest of interest we sat in that great columned hall and listened to a sad tale.

We had, with malice aforethought, libeled beyond repair great and unselfish men who had made a career of devotion to the public weal, imperiled needlessly relations traditionally friendly by falsely reporting mythical events, mocked the courageous sacrifices of those who had *dulce et gloria mori*, and completely upset everyone's peace of mind. Every new accusation, every verbal lance drew solemn agreement from the dignitary-packed hall. Against someone's better judgment, the trial had been transferred from the regular courtroom to the Hall of Justice. Packed with influence, brass, and pompous legates from all over the world, only the congressmen from the biggest states, or with the biggest votes, were able to crowd the newly installed seats. So you can see it was a hostile audience that faced Samuels when the defense had its say. We had spent the previous night together in the guarded suite to which we had been transferred for the duration of the trial, perfecting, as far as we could, our planned defense. Samuels has the arrogant sense of humor that usually goes with supreme self-confidence, and I'm sure he enjoyed standing there among all those bemedaled and bejowled bigwigs, knowing the bombshell he was going to hurl. He made a good grenadier. Like this:

"We believe there is only one defense possible, we believe there is only one defense necessary. We have gladly waived, without prejudice, our inalienable right of trial by jury. We shall speak plainly and bluntly, to the point.

"You have seen the picture in question. You have remarked, possibly, upon what has been called the startling resemblance of the actors in that picture to the characters named and portrayed. You have remarked, possibly, upon the apparent verisimilitude to reality. That I will mention again. The first witness will, I believe, establish the trend of our rebuttal of the allegations of the prosecution." He called the first witness.

"Your name, please?"

"Mercedes Maria Gomez."

"A little louder, please."

"Mercedes Maria Gomez."

"Your occupation?"

"Until last March I was a teacher at the Arizona School for the Deaf. Then I asked for and obtained a leave of absence. At present I am under personal contract to Mr. Lefko."

"If you see Mr. Lefko in this courtroom, Miss . . Mrs.—"

"Miss."

"Thank you. If Mr. Lefko is in this court will you point him out? Thank you. Will you tell us the extent of your duties at the Arizona School?"

"I taught children born totally deaf to speak. And to read lips."

"You read lips yourself, Miss Gomez?"

"I have been totally deaf since I was fifteen."

"In English only?"

"English and Spanish. We have . . . had many children of Mexican descent."

Samuels asked for a designated Spanish-speaking interpreter. An officer in the back immediately volunteered. He was identified by his ambassador, who was present.

"Will you take this book to the rear of the courtroom, sir?" To the Court: "If the prosecution wishes to examine that book, they will find that it is a Spanish edition of the Bible." The prosecution didn't wish to examine it.

"Will the officer open the Bible at random and read aloud?" He opened the Bible at the center and read. In dead silence the Court strained to hear. Nothing could be heard the length of that enormous hall.

Samuels: "Miss Gomez. Will you take these binoculars and repeat, to the Court, just what the officer is reading at the other end of the room?"

She took the binoculars and focused them expertly on the officer, who had stopped reading and was watching alertly. "I am ready."

Samuels: "Will you please read, sir?"

He did, and the Gomez woman repeated aloud, quickly and easily, a section that sounded as though it might be anything at all. I can't speak Spanish. The officer continued to read for a minute or two.

Samuels: "Thank you, sir. And thank you, Miss Gomez. Your pardon, sir, but since there are several who have been known to memorize the Bible, will you tell the Court if you have anything on your person that is written, anything that Miss Gomez has had no chance of viewing?" Yes, the officer had. "Will you read that as before? Will you, Miss Gomez—"

She read that, too. Then the officer came to the front to listen to the court reporter read Miss Gomez's words.

"That's what I read," he affirmed.

Samuels turned her over to the prosecution, who made more experiments that served only to convince that she was equally good as an interpreter and lipreader in either language.

In rapid succession Samuels put the rest of the lipreaders on the stand. In rapid succession they proved themselves as able and as capable as Miss Gomez, in their own linguistic specialty. The Russian from Ambridge generously offered to translate into his broken English any other Slavic language handy, and drew scattered grins from the press box. The Court was convinced, but failed to see the purpose of the exhibition. Samuels, glowing with satisfaction and confidence, faced the Court.

"Thanks to the indulgence of the Court, and despite the efforts of the distinguished prosecution, we have proved the almost amazing accuracy of lipreading in general, and these lipreaders in particular." One Justice absently nodded in agreement. "Therefore, our defense will be based on that premise, and on one other which we have had until now found necessary to keep hidden—the picture in question was and is definitely not a fictional representation of events of questionable authenticity. Every scene in that film contained, not polished professional actors, but the original person named and portrayed. Every foot, every inch of film was not the result of an elaborate studio reconstruction but an actual collection of pictures, an actual collection of newsreels—if they can be called that—edited and assembled in story form!"

Through the startled spurt of astonishment we heard one of the prosecution: "That's ridiculous! No newsreel—"

Samuels ignored the objections and the tumult to put me on the stand. Beyond the usual preliminary questions I was allowed to say things my own way. At first hostile, the Court became interested enough to overrule the repeated objections that flew from the table devoted to the prosecution. I felt that at least two of the Court, if not outright favorable, were friendly. As far as I can remember, I went over the maneuvers of the past years, and ended something like this:

"As to why we arranged the cards to fall as they did: both Mr. Laviada and myself were unable to face the prospect of destroying his discovery, because of the inevitable penalizing of needed research. We were, and we are, unwilling to better ourselves or a limited group by the use and maintenance of secrecy, if secrecy were possible. As to the only other alternative," and I directed this straight at Judge Bronson, the well-known liberal on the bench, "since the last war all atomic research and activity has been under the direction of a Board nominally civilian, but actually under the 'protection and direction' of the Army and Navy. This 'direction and protection,' as any competent physicist will gladly attest, has proved to be nothing but a smothering blanket serving to conceal hidebound antiquated reasoning, abysmal ignorance, and inestimable amounts of fumbling. As of right now, this country, or any country, that was foolish enough to place any confidence in the rigid regime of the military mind, is years behind what would otherwise be the natural course of discovery and progress in nuclear and related fields.

"We were, and we are, firmly convinced that even the slightest hint of the inherent possibilities and scope of Mr. Laviada's discovery would have meant, under the present regime, instant and mandatory confiscation of even a supposedly secure patent. Mr. Laviada has never applied for a patent, and never will. We both feel that such a discovery belongs not to an individual, a group, a corporation, or even to a nation, but to the world and those who live in it.

"We know, and are eager and willing to prove, that the domestic and external affairs of not only this nation, but of every nation are influenced, sometimes controlled, by esoteric groups warping political theories and human lives to suit their own ends." The Court was smothered in sullen silence, thick and acid with hate and disbelief.

"Secret treaties, for example, and vicious, lying propaganda have too long controlled human passions and made men hate; honored thieves have too long rotted secretly in undeserved high places. The machine can make treachery and untruth impossible. It *must*, if atomic war is not to sear the face and fate of the world.

"Our pictures were all made with that end in view. We needed, first, the wealth and prominence to present to an international audience what we knew to be the truth. We have done as much as we can. From now on, this Court takes over the burden we have carried. We are guilty of no treachery, guilty of no deceit, guilty of nothing but deep and true humanity. Mr. Laviada wishes me to tell the Court and the world that he has been unable till now to give his discovery to the world, free to use as it wills."

The Court stared at me. Every foreign representative was on the edge of his seat waiting for the Justices to order us shot without further ado, the sparkling uniforms were seething, and the pressmen were racing their pencils against time. The tension dried my throat. The speech that Samuels and I had rehearsed the previous night was strong medicine. Now what?

Samuels filled the breach smoothly. "If the Court pleases, Mr. Lefko has made some startling statements. Startling, but certainly sincere, and certainly either provable or disprovable. And proof it shall be!"

He strode to the door of the conference room that had been allotted us. As the hundreds of eyes followed him it was easy for me to slip down from the witness stand, and wait, ready. From the conference room Samuels rolled the machine, and Mike rose. The whispers that curdled the air seemed disappointed, unimpressed. Right in front of the Bench he trundled it.

He moved unobtrusively to one side as the television men trained their long-snouted cameras. "Mr. Laviada and Mr. Lefko will show you . . . I trust there will be no objection from the prosecution?" He was daring them.

One of the prosecution was already on his feet. He opened his mouth hesitantly, but thought better, and sat down. Heads went together in conference as he did. Samuels was watching the Court with one eye, and the courtroom with the other.

"If the Court pleases, we will need a cleared space. If the bailiff will . . . thank you, sir." The long tables were moved back, with a raw scraping. He stood there, with every eye in the courtroom glued on him. For two long breaths he stood there, then he spun and went to his table. "Mr. Lefko," and he bowed formally. He sat.

The eyes swung to me, to Mike, as he moved to his machine and stood there silently. I cleared my throat and spoke to the Bench as though I did not see the directional microphones trained at my lips.

"Justice Bronson."

He looked steadily at me and then glanced at Mike. "Yes, Mr. Lefko?"

"Your freedom from bias is well known." The corners of his mouth went down as he frowned. "Will you be willing to be used as proof that there can be no trickery?" He thought that over, then nodded slowly. The prosecution objected, and was waved down. "Will you tell me exactly where you were at any given time? Any place where you are absolutely certain and can verify that there were no concealed cameras or observers?"

He thought. Seconds. Minutes. The tension twanged, and I swallowed dust. He spoke quietly. "1918. November 11th."

Mike whispered to me. I said, "Any particular time?"

Justice Bronson looked at Mike. "Exactly eleven. Armistice time." He paused, then went on. "Niagara Falls. Niagara Falls, New York."

I heard the dials tick in the stillness, and Mike whispered again. I said, "The lights should be off." The bailiff rose. "Will you please watch the left wall, or in that direction? I think that if Justice Kassel will turn a little . . . we are ready."

Bronson looked at me, and at the left wall. "Ready."

E for Effort 43

The lights flicked out overhead and I heard the television crews mutter. I touched Mike on the shoulder. "Show them, Mike!"

We're all showmen at heart, and Mike is no exception. Suddenly out of nowhere and into the depths poured a frozen torrent. Niagara Falls. I've mentioned, I think, that I've never got over my fear of heights. Few people ever do. I heard long, shuddery gasps as we started straight down. Down, until we stopped at the brink of the silent cataract, weird in its frozen majesty. Mike had stopped time at exactly eleven, I knew. He shifted to the American bank. Slowly he moved along. There were a few tourists standing in almost comic attitudes. There was snow on the ground, flakes in the air. Time stood still, and hearts slowed in sympathy.

Bronson snapped, "Stop!"

A couple, young. Long skirts, high-buttoned army collar, dragging army overcoat, facing, arms about each other. Mike's sleeve rustled in the darkness and they moved. She was sobbing and the soldier was smiling. She turned away her head, and he turned it back. Another couple seized them gayly, and they twirled breathlessly.

Bronson's voice was harsh. "That's enough!" The view blurred for seconds.

Washington. The White House. The president. Someone coughed like a small explosion. The president was watching a television screen. He jerked erect suddenly, startled. Mike spoke for the first time in court.

"That is the president of the United States. He is watching the trial that is being broadcast and televised from this courtroom. He is listening to what I am saying right now, and he is watching, in his television screen, as I use my machine to show him what he was doing one second ago."

The president heard those fateful words. Stiffly he threw an unconscious glance around his room at nothing and looked back at his screen in time to see himself do what he just had done, one second ago. Slowly, as if against his will, his hand started toward the switch of his set.

"Mr. President, don't turn off that set." Mike's voice was curt, almost rude. "You must hear this, you of all people in the world. You must understand!"

"This is not what we wanted to do, but we have no recourse left but to appeal to you, and to the people of this twisted world." The president might have been cast in iron. "You must see, you must understand that you have in your hands the power to make it impossible for greed-born war to be bred in secrecy and rob man of his youth or his old age or whatever he prizes." His voice softened, pleaded. "That is all we have to say. That is all we want. That is all anyone could want, ever." The president, unmoving, faded into blackness. "The lights, please," and almost immediately the Court adjourned. That was over a month ago.

Mike's machine has been taken from us, and we are under military guard. Probably it's just as well we're guarded. We understand there have been lynching parties, broken up only as far as a block or two away. Last week we watched a white-haired fanatic scream about us, on the street below. We couldn't catch what he was shrieking, but we did catch a few air-borne epithets.

"Devils! Anti-Christs! Violation of the Bible! Violations of this and that!" Some, right here in the city, I suppose, would be glad to build a bonfire to cook us right back to the flames from which we've sprung. I wonder what the various religious groups are going to do now that the truth can be seen. Who can read lips in Aramaic, or Latin, or Coptic? And is a mechanical miracle a miracle?

This changes everything. We've been moved. Where, I don't know, except that the weather is warm, and we're on some type of military reservation, by the lack of civilians. Now we know what we're up against. What started out to be just a time-killing occupation, Joe, has turned out to be a necessary preface to what I'm going to ask you to do. Finish this, and then move fast! We won't be able to get this to you for a while yet, so I'll go on for a bit the way I started, to kill time. Like our clippings:

TABLOID:

. . . Such a weapon cannot, must not be loosed in unscrupulous hands. The last professional production of the infamous pair proves what distortions can be wrested from isolated and misunderstood events. In the hands of perpetrators of heretical isms, no property, no business deal, no personal life could be sacrosanct, no foreign policy could be . . .

TIMES:

. . . colonies stand with us firmly . . . liquidation of the Empire . . . white man's burden . . .

LE MATIN:

. . . rightful place . . . restore proud France .

PRAVDA:

. . . democratic imperialist plot . . . our glorious scientists ready to announce . . .

NICHI-NICHI:

. . . incontrovertibly prove divine descent . . .

LA PRENSA:

. . . oil concessions . . . dollar diplomacy . . .

DETROIT JOURNAL:

. . . under our noses in a sinister fortress on East Warren . . . under close Federal supervision . . . perfection by our production-trained technicians a mighty aid to law-enforcement agencies . . . tirades against politicians and business common-sense carried too far . . . tomorrow revelations by . . .

L'OSSERVATORE ROMANO:

Council of Cardinals . . . announcement expected hourly . . .

JACKSON STAR-CLARION:

. . . proper handling will prove the fallacy of race equality . . .

Almost unanimously the press screamed; Pegler frothed, Winchell leered. We got the surface side of the situation from the press. But a military guard is composed of individuals, hotel rooms must be swept by maids, waiters must serve food, and a chain is as strong— We got what we think the truth from those who work for a living.

There are meetings on street corners and homes, two great veterans' groups have arbitrarily fired their officials, seven governors have resigned, three senators and over a dozen representatives have retired with "ill health," and the general temper is ugly. International travelers report the same of Europe, Asia is bubbling, and transport planes with motors running stud the airports of South America. A general whisper is that a Constitutional Amendment is being rammed through to forbid the use of any similar instrument by any individual, with the manufacture and leasing by the Federal government to law-enforcement agencies or financially responsible corporations suggested; it is whispered that motor caravans are forming throughout the country for a Washington march to demand a decision by the Court on the truth of our charges; it is generally suspected that all news disseminating services are under direct Federal — Army—control; wires are supposed to be sizzling with petitions and demands to Congress, which are seldom delivered.

One day the chambermaid said: "And the whole hotel might as well close up shop. The whole floor is blocked off, there're MPs at every door, and they're clearing out all the other guests as fast as they can be moved. The whole place wouldn't be big enough to hold the letters and wires addressed to you, or the ones that are trying to get in to see you. Fat chance they have," she added grimly. "The joint is lousy with brass."

Mike glanced at me and I cleared my throat. "What's your idea of the whole thing?"

Expertly she spanked and reversed a pillow. "I saw your last picture before they shut it down. I saw all your pictures. When I wasn't working I listened to your trial. I heard you tell them off. I never got married because my boy friend never came back from Burma. Ask *him* what he thinks," and she jerked her head at the young private that was supposed to keep her from talking. "Ask him if he wants some bunch of stinkers to start him shooting at some other poor chump. See what he says, and then ask me if I want an atom bomb dropped down my neck just because some chiselers want more than they got." She left suddenly, and the soldier left with her. Mike and I had a beer and went to bed. Next week the papers had headlines a mile high.

U. S. KEEPS MIRACLE RAY
CONSTITUTION AMENDMENT
AWAITS STATES OKAY
LAVIADA-LEFKO FREED

We were freed all right, Bronson and the president being responsible for that. But the president and Bronson don't know, I'm sure, that we were rearrested immediately. We were told that we'll be held in "protective custody" until enough states have ratified the proposed constitutional amendment. The Man Without a Country was in what you might call "protective custody," too. We'll likely be released the same way he was.

* * *

We're allowed no newspapers, no radio, allowed no communication coming or going, and we're given no reason, as if that were necessary. They'll never, never let us go, and they'd be fools if they did. They think that if we can't communicate, or if we can't build another machine, our fangs are drawn, and when the excitement dies, we fall into oblivion, six feet of it. Well, we can't build another machine. But communicate?

Look at it this way. A soldier is a soldier because he wants to serve his country. A soldier doesn't want to die unless his country is at war. Even then death is only a last resort. And war isn't necessary any more, not with our machinery. In the dark? Try to plan or plot in absolute darkness, which is what would be needed. Try to plot or carry on a war without putting things in writing. O.K. Now—

The Army has Mike's machine. The Army has Mike. They call it military expediency, I suppose. Bosh! Anyone beyond the grade of moron can see that to keep that machine, to hide it, is to invite the world to attack, and attack in self-defense. If every nation, or if every man, had a machine, each would be equally open, or equally protected. But if only one nation, or only one man can see, the rest will not long be blind. Maybe we did this all wrong. God knows that we thought about it often. God knows we did our best to make an effort at keeping man out of his own trap.

There isn't much time left. One of the soldiers guarding us will get this to you, I hope, in time.

A long time ago we gave you a key, and hoped we would never have to ask you to use it. But now is the time. That key fits a box at the Detroit Savings Bank. In that box are letters. Mail them, not all at once, or in the same place. They'll go all over the world, to men we know, and have watched well: clever, honest, and capable of following the plans we've enclosed.

But you've got to hurry! One of these bright days someone is going to wonder if we've made more than one machine. We haven't, of course. That would have been foolish. But if some smart young lieutenant gets hold of that machine long enough to start tracing back our movements they'll find that safety deposit box, with the plans and letters ready to be scattered broadside. You can see the need for haste—if the rest of the world, or any particular nation, wants that machine bad enough, they'll fight for it. And they will! They must! Later on, when the Army gets used to the machine and its capabilities, it will become obvious to everyone, as it already has to Mike and me, that, with every plan open to inspection as soon as it's made, no nation or group of nations would have a chance in open warfare. So if there is to be an attack, it will have to be deadly, and fast, and sure. Please God that we haven't shoved the world into a war we tried to make impossible. With all the atom bombs and rockets that have been made in the past few years—*Joe, you've got to hurry!*

GHQ TO 9TH ATTK GRP
Report report report report report report report report report report

CMDR 9TH ATTK GRP TO GHQ

BEGINS: No other manuscript found. Searched body of Lefko immediately upon landing. According to plan Building Three untouched. Survivors insist both were moved from Building Seven previous day defective plumbing. Body of Laviada identified definitely through fingerprints. Request further instructions. ENDS

GHQ TO CMDR 32ND SHIELDED RGT

BEGINS: Seal area Detroit Savings Bank. Advise immediately condition safety deposit boxes. Afford coming technical unit complete co-operation. ENDS

LT. COL. TEMP. ATT. 32ND SHIELDED RGT

BEGINS: Area Detroit Savings Bank vaporized direct hit. Radioactivity lethal. Impossible boxes or any contents survive. Repeat, direct hit. Request permission proceed Washington Area. ENDS

GHQ. TO LT. COL. TEMP. ATT. 32ND SHIELDED RGT

BEGINS: Request denied. Sift ashes if necessary regardless cost. Repeat, regardless cost. ENDS

GHQ. TO ALL UNITS REPEAT ALL UNITS

BEGINS: Lack of enemy resistance explained misdirected atom rocket seventeen miles SSE Washington. Lone survivor completely destroyed special train claims all top officials left enemy capital two hours preceding attack. Notify local governments where found necessary and obvious cessation hostilities. Occupy present areas Plan Two. Further orders follow. ENDS

THE WEAPON SHOP
A. E. van Vogt

Peace is a complicated concept. It includes both freedom from external aggression and domestic tranquillity. At least the superficial appearance of the latter can be assured by a powerful government which simply will not tolerate crime—but most of us in this region of time and space consider peace without individual liberty meaningless.

Should individual liberty include the right to own weapons? Weapons, after all, can be used for either defense or aggression on either an individual or a national level—in wars of conquest, defense against such wars, or domestic violence.

The question has been hotly debated ever since people began to recognize that it could be a question. It has never been simple—and it could get a lot more complicated.

THE VILLAGE AT NIGHT made a curiously timeless picture. Fara walked contentedly beside his wife along the street. The air was like wine; and he was thinking dimly of the artist who had come up from Imperial City, and made what the telestats called—he remembered the phrase vividly—"a symbolic painting reminiscent of a scene in the electrical age of seven thousand years ago."

Fara believed that utterly. The street before him with its weedless, automatically tended gardens, its shops set well back among the flowers, its perpetual hard, grassy sidewalks, and its street lamps that glowed from every pore of their structure—this was a restful paradise where time had stood still.

And it was like being a part of life that the great artist's picture of this quiet, peaceful scene before him was now in the collection of the empress herself. She had praised it, and naturally the thrice-blest artist had immediately and humbly begged her to accept it.

What a joy it must be to be able to offer personal homage to the glorious, the divine, the serenely gracious and lovely Innelda Isher, one thousand one hundred eightieth of her line.

As they walked, Fara half turned to his wife. In the dim light of the nearest street lamp, her kindly, still youthful face was almost lost in shadow. He murmured softly, instinctively muting his voice to harmonize with the pastel shades of night:

"She said—our empress said—that our little village of Glay seemed to her to have in it all the wholesomeness, the gentleness, that constitutes the finest qualities of her people. Wasn't that a wonderful thought, Creel? She must be a marvelously understanding woman. I—"

He stopped. They had come to a side street, and there was something about a hundred and fifty feet along it that—

"Look!" Fara said hoarsely.

He pointed with rigid arm and finger at a sign that glowed in the night, a sign that read:

FINE WEAPONS
THE RIGHT TO BUY WEAPONS IS THE RIGHT TO BE FREE

Fara had a strange, empty feeling as he stared at the blazing sign. He saw that other villagers were gathering. He said finally, huskily:

"I've heard of these shops. They're places of infamy, against which the government of the empress will act one of these days. They're built in hidden factories, and then transported whole to towns like ours and set up in gross defiance of property rights. That one wasn't there an hour ago."

Fara's face hardened. His voice had a harsh edge in it, as he said:

"Creel, go home."

Fara was surprised when Creel did not move off at once. All their married life, she had had a pleasing habit of obedience that had made cohabitation a wonderful thing.

He saw that she was looking at him wide-eyed, and that it was a timid alarm that held her there. She said:

"Fara, what do you intend to do? You're not thinking of—"

"Go home!" Her fear brought out all the grim determination in his nature. "We're not going to let such a monstrous thing desecrate our village. Think of it"—his voice shivered before the appalling thought—"this fine, old-fashioned community, which we had resolved always to keep exactly as the empress has it in her picture gallery, debauched now, ruined by this . . . this thing— But we won't have it; that's all there is to it."

Creel's voice came softly out of the half-darkness of the street corner, the timidity gone from it: "Don't do anything rash, Fara. Remember it is not the first new building to come into Glay—since the picture was painted."

Fara was silent. This was a quality of his wife of which he did not approve, this reminding him unnecessarily of unpleasant facts. He knew exactly what she meant. The gigantic, multitentacled corporation, Automatic Atomic Motor Repair Shops, Inc., had come in under the laws of the State with their flashy building, against the wishes of the village council—and had already taken half of Fara's repair business.

"That's different!" Fara growled finally. "In the first place people will discover in good time that these new automatic repairers do a poor job. In the second place it's fair competition. But this weapon shop is a defiance of all the decencies that make life under the House of Isher such a joy. Look at the hypocritical sign: 'The right to buy weapons—' Aaaaahh!"

He broke off with: "Go home, Creel. We'll see to it that they sell no weapons in this town."

He watched the slender woman-shape move off into the shadows. She was halfway across the street when a thought occurred to Fara. He called:

"And if you see that son of ours hanging around some street corner, take him home. He's got to learn to stop staying out so late at night."

The shadowed figure of his wife did not turn: and after watching her for a moment moving along against the dim background of softly glowing street lights, Fara twisted on his heel, and walked swiftly toward the shop. The crowd was growing larger every minute, and the night pulsed with excited voices.

Beyond doubt, here was the biggest thing that had ever happened to the village of Glay.

The sign of the weapon shop was, he saw, a normal-illusion affair. No matter what his angle of view, he was always looking straight at it. When he paused finally in front of the great display window, the words had pressed back against the store front, and were staring unwinkingly down at him.

Fara sniffed once more at the meaning of the slogan, then forgot the simple thing. There was another sign in the window, which read:

THE FINEST ENERGY WEAPONS IN THE KNOWN UNIVERSE

A spark of interest struck fire inside Fara. He gazed at that brilliant display of guns, fascinated in spite of himself. The weapons were of every size, ranging from tiny little finger pistols to express rifles. They were made of every one of the light, hard, ornamental substances: glittering glassein, the colorful but opaque Ordine plastic, viridescent magnesitic beryllium. And others.

It was the very deadly extent of the destructive display that brought a chill to Fara. So many weapons for the little village of Glay, where not more than two people to his knowledge had guns, and those only for hunting. Why, the thing was absurd, fantastically mischievous, utterly threatening.

Somewhere behind Fara, a man said: "It's right on Lan Harris's lot. Good joke on that old scoundrel. Will he raise a row!"

There was a faint titter from several men, that made an odd patch of sound on the warm, fresh air. And Fara saw that the man had spoken the truth. The weapon shop had a forty-foot frontage. And it occupied the very center of the green, gardenlike lot of tight-fisted old Harris.

Fara frowned. The clever devils, the weapon-shop people, selecting the property of the most disliked man in town, coolly taking it over and giving everybody an agreeable titillation. But the very cunning of it made it vital that the trick shouldn't succeed.

He was still scowling anxiously when he saw the plump figure of Mel Dale, the mayor. Fara edged toward him hurriedly, touched his hat respectfully, and said:

"Where's Jor?"

"Here." The village constable elbowed his way through a little bundle of men. "Any plans?" he said.

"There's only one plan," said Fara boldly. "Go in and arrest them."

To Fara's amazement, the two men looked at each other, then at the ground. It was the big constable who answered shortly:

"Door's locked. And nobody answers our pounding. I was just going to suggest we let the matter ride until morning."

"Nonsense!" His very astonishment made Fara impatient. "Get an ax and we'll break the door down. Delay will only encourage such riffraff to resist. We don't want their kind in our village for so much as a single night. Isn't that so?"

There was a hasty nod of agreement from everybody in his immediate vicinity. Too hasty. Fara looked around puzzled at eyes that lowered before his level gaze. He thought: "They are all scared. And unwilling." Before he could speak, Constable Jor said:

"I guess you haven't heard about those doors or these shops. From all accounts, you can't break into them."

It struck Fara with a sudden pang that it was he who would have to act here. He said, "I'll get my atomic cutting machine from my shop. That'll fix them. Have I your permission to do that, Mr. Mayor?"

In the glow of the weapon-shop window, the plump man was sweating visibly. He pulled out a handkerchief and wiped his forehead. He said:

"Maybe I'd better call the commander of the Imperial garrison at Ferd, and ask them."

"No!" Fara recognized evasion when he saw it. He felt himself steel; the conviction came that all the strength in this village was in him. "We must act ourselves. Other communities have let these people get in because they took no decisive action. We've got to resist to the limit. Beginning now. This minute. Well?"

The mayor's "All right!" was scarcely more than a sigh of sound. But it was all Fara needed.

He called out his intention to the crowd; and then, as he pushed his way out of the mob, he saw his son standing with some other young men, staring at the window display.

Fara called: "Cayle, come and help me with the machine."

Cayle did not even turn; and Fara hurried on, seething. That wretched boy! One of these days he, Fara, would have to take firm action there. Or he'd have a no-good on his hands.

The energy was soundless—and smooth. There was no sputter, no fireworks. It glowed with a soft, pure white light, almost caressing the metal panels of the door—but not even beginning to sear them.

Minute after minute, the dogged Fara refused to believe the incredible failure, and played the boundlessly potent energy on that resisting wall. When he finally shut off his machine, he was perspiring freely.

"I don't understand it," he gasped. "Why—no metal is supposed to stand up against a steady flood of atomic force. Even the hard metal plates used inside the blast chamber of a motor take the explosions in what is called infinite series, so that each one has unlimited rest. That's the theory, but actually steady running crystallizes the whole plate after a few months."

"It's as Jor told you," said the mayor. "These weapon shops are—big. They spread right through the empire, *and they don't recognize the empress.*"

Fara shifted his feet on the hard grass, disturbed. He didn't like this kind of talk. It sounded—sacrilegious. And besides it was nonsense. It must be. Before he could speak, a man said somewhere behind him:

"I've heard it said that the door will open only to those who cannot harm the people inside."

The words shocked Fara out of his daze. With a start, and for the first time, he saw that his failure had had a bad psychological effect. He said sharply:

"That's ridiculous! If there were doors like that, we'd all have them. We—"

The Weapon Shop

The thought that stopped his words was the sudden realization that *he* had not seen anybody try to open the door; and with all this reluctance around him it was quite possible that—

He stepped forward, grasped at the doorknob, and pulled. The door opened with an unnatural weightlessness that gave him the fleeting impression that the knob had come loose into his hand. With a gasp, Fara jerked the door wide open.

"Jor!" he yelled. "Get in!"

The constable made a distorted movement—distorted by what must have been a will to caution, followed by the instant realization that he could not hold back before so many. He leaped awkwardly toward the open door—and it closed in his face.

Fara stared stupidly at his hand, which was still clenched. And then, slowly, a hideous thrill coursed along his nerves. The knob had—withdrawn. It had twisted, become viscous, and slipped amorphously from his straining fingers. Even the memory of that brief sensation gave him a feeling of unnormal things.

He grew aware that the crowd was watching with a silent intentness. Fara reached again for the knob, not quite so eagerly this time; and it was only a sudden realization of his reluctance that made him angry when the handle neither turned nor yielded in any way.

Determination returned in full force, and with it came a thought. He motioned to the constable. "Go back, Jor, while I pull."

The man retreated, but it did no good. And tugging did not help. The door would not open. Somewhere in the crowd, a man said darkly:

"It decided to let you in, then it changed its mind."

"What foolishness are you talking!" Fara spoke violently. *"It* changed its mind. Are you crazy? A door has no sense."

But a surge of fear put a half-quaver into his voice. It was the sudden alarm that made him bold beyond all his normal caution. With a jerk of his body, Fara faced the shop.

The building loomed there under the night sky, in itself bright as day, huge in width and length, and alien, menacing, no longer easily conquerable. The dim queasy wonder came as to what the soldiers of the empress would do if they were invited to act. And suddenly—a bare, flashing glimpse of grim possibility—the feeling grew that even they would be able to do nothing.

Abruptly, Fara was conscious of horror that such an idea could enter his mind. He shut his brain tight, said wildly:

"The door opened for me once. It will open again."

It did. Quite simply it did. Gently, without resistance, *with* that same sensation of weightlessness, the strange, sensitive door followed the tug of his fingers. Beyond the threshold was dimness, a wide, darkened alcove. He heard the voice of Mel Dale behind him, the mayor saying:

"Fara, don't be a fool. What will you do inside?"

Fara was vaguely amazed to realize that he had stepped across the threshold. He turned, startled, and stared at the blur of faces. "Why—" he began blankly; then he brightened; he said. "Why, I'll buy a gun, of course."

The brilliance of his reply, the cunning implicit in it, dazzled Fara for half a minute longer. The mood yielded slowly, as he found himself in the dimly lighted interior of the weapon shop.

It was preternaturally quiet inside. Not a sound penetrated from the night from which he had come; and the startled thought came that the people of the shop might actually be unaware that there was a crowd outside.

Fara walked forward gingerly on a rugged floor that muffled his footsteps utterly. After a moment, his eyes accustomed themselves to the soft lighting, which came like a reflection from the walls and ceilings. In a vague way, he had expected ultranormalness; and the ordinariness of the atomic lighting acted like a tonic to his tensed nerves.

He shook himself angrily. Why should there be anything really superior? He was getting as bad as those credulous idiots out in the street.

He glanced around with gathering confidence. The place looked quite common. It was a shop, almost scantily furnished. There were showcases on the walls and on the floor, glitteringly lovely things, but nothing unusual, and not many of them—a few dozens. There was in addition a double, ornate door leading to a back room—

Fara tried to keep one eye on that door, as he examined several showcases, each with three or four weapons either mounted or arranged in boxes or holsters.

Abruptly, the weapons began to excite him. He forgot to watch the door, as the wild thought struck that he ought to grab one of those guns from a case, and then the moment someone came, force him outside where Jor would perform the arrest and—

Behind him, a man said quietly: "You wish to buy a gun?"

Fara turned with a jump. Brief rage flooded him at the way his plan had been wrecked by the arrival of the clerk.

The anger died as he saw that the intruder was a fine-looking, silver-haired man, older than himself. That was immeasurably disconcerting. Fara had an immense and almost automatic respect for age, and for a long second he could only stand there gaping. He said at last, lamely:

"Yes, yes, a gun."

"For what purpose?" said the man in his quiet voice.

Fara could only look at him blankly. It was too fast. He wanted to get mad. He wanted to tell these people what he thought of them. But the age of this representative locked his tongue, tangled his emotions. He managed speech only by an effort of will:

"For hunting." The plausible word stiffened his mind. "Yes, definitely for hunting. There is a lake to the north of here," he went on more fulsomely, glibly, "and—"

He stopped, scowling, startled at the extent of his dishonesty. He was not prepared to go so deeply into prevarication. He said curtly:

"For hunting."

Fara was himself again. Abruptly, he hated the man for having put him so completely at a disadvantage. With smoldering eyes he watched the old fellow click open a showcase, and take out a green-shining rifle.

As the man faced him, weapon in hand, Fara was thinking grimly, "Pretty clever, having an old man as a front." It was the same kind of cunning that had made them choose the property of Miser Harris. Icily furious, taut with his purpose, Fara reached for the gun; but the man held it out of his reach, saying:

"Before I can even let you test this, I am compelled by the by-laws of the weapon shops to inform you under what circumstances you may purchase a gun."

So they had private regulations. What a system of psychological tricks to impress gullible fools. Well, let the old scoundrel talk. As soon as he, Fara, got hold of the rifle, he'd put an end to hypocrisy.

"We weapons makers," the clerk was saying mildly, "have evolved guns that can, in their particular ranges, destroy any machine or object made of what is called matter. Thus whoever possesses one of our weapons is the equal and more of any soldier of the empress. I say more because each gun is the center of a field of force which acts as a perfect screen against immaterial destructive forces. That screen offers no resistance to clubs or spears or bullets, or other material substances, but it would require a small atomic cannon to penetrate the superb barrier it creates around its owner.

"You will readily comprehend," the man went on, "that such a potent weapon could not be allowed to fall, unmodified, into irresponsible hands. Accordingly, no gun purchased from us may be used for aggression or murder. In the case of the hunting rifle, only such specified game birds and animals as we may from time to time list in our display windows may be shot. Finally, no weapon can be resold without our approval. Is that clear?"

Fara nodded dumbly. For the moment, speech was impossible to him. The incredible, fantastically stupid words were still going round and around in his head. He wondered if he ought to laugh out loud, or curse the man for daring to insult his intelligence so tremendously.

So the gun mustn't be used for murder or robbery. So only certain birds and animals could be shot. And as for reselling it, suppose—suppose he bought this thing, took a trip of a thousand miles, and offered it to some wealthy stranger for two credits—who would ever know?

Or suppose he held up the stranger. Or shot him. How would the weapon shop ever find out? The thing was so ridiculous that—

He grew aware that the gun was being held out to him stock first. He took it eagerly, and had to fight the impulse to turn the muzzle directly on the old man. Mustn't rush this, he thought tautly. He said:

"How does it work?"

"You simply aim it, and pull the trigger. Perhaps you would like to try it on a target we have."

Fara swung the gun up. "Yes," he said triumphantly, "and you're it. Now, just get over there to the front door, and then outside."

He raised his voice: "And if anybody's thinking of coming through the back door, I've got that covered, too."

He motioned jerkily at the clerk. "Quick now, move! I'll shoot! I swear I will."

The man was cool, unflustered. "I have no doubt you would. When we decided to attune the door so that you could enter despite your hostility, we assumed the capacity for homicide. However, this is our party. You had better adjust yourself accordingly, and look behind you—"

There was silence. Finger on trigger, Fara stood moveless. Dim thoughts came of all the *half-things* he had heard in his days about the weapon shops: that they had secret supporters in every district, that they had a private and ruthless hidden government, and that once you got into their clutches, the only way out was death and—

But what finally came clear was a mind picture of himself, Fara Clark, family man, faithful subject of the empress, standing here in this dimly lighted store, deliberately fighting an organization so vast and menacing that— He must have been mad.

Only—here he was. He forced courage into his sagging muscles. He said:

"You can't fool me with pretending there's someone behind me. Now, get to that door. And *fast!*"

The firm eyes of the old man were looking past him. The man said quietly: "Well, Rad, have you all the data?"

"Enough for a primary," said a young man's baritone voice behind Fara. "Type A-7 conservative. Good average intelligence, but a Monaric development peculiar to small towns. One-sided outlook fostered by the Imperial schools present in exaggerated form. Extremely honest. Reason would be useless. Emotional approach would require extended treatment. I see no reason why we should bother. Let him live his life as it suits him."

"If you think," Fara said shakily, "that that trick voice is going to make me turn, you're crazy. That's the left wall of the building. I know there's no one there."

"I'm all in favor, Rad," said the old man, "of letting him live his life. But he was the prime mover of the crowd outside. I think he should be discouraged."

"We'll advertise his presence," said Rad. "He'll spend the rest of his life denying the charge."

Fara's confidence in the gun had faded so far that, as he listened in puzzled uneasiness to the incomprehensible conversation, he forgot it completely. He parted his lips, but before he could speak, the old man cut in, persistently:

"I think a little emotion might have a long-run effect. Show him the palace."

Palace! The startling word tore Fara out of his brief paralysis. "See here," he began, "I can see now that you lied to me. This gun isn't loaded at all. It's—"

His voice failed him. Every muscle in his body went rigid. He stared like a madman. *There was no gun in his hands.*

"Why, you—" he began wildly. And stopped again. His mind heaved with imbalance. With a terrible effort he fought off the spinning sensation, thought finally, tremblingly: Somebody must have sneaked the gun from him. That meant—there was someone behind him. The voice was no mechanical thing. Somehow, they had—

He started to turn—and couldn't. What in the name of— He struggled, pushing with his muscles. And couldn't move, couldn't budge, couldn't even—

The room was growing curiously dark. He had difficulty seeing the old man and— He would have shrieked then if he could. Because the weapon shop was gone. He was—

He was standing in the sky above an immense city.

In the sky, and nothing beneath him, nothing around him but air, and blue summer heaven, and the city a mile, two miles below.

Nothing, nothing— He would have shrieked, but his breath seemed solidly embedded in his lungs. Sanity came back as the remote awareness impinged upon his terrified mind that he was actually standing on a hard floor, and that the city must be a picture somehow focused directly into his eyes.

For the first time, with a start, Fara recognized the metropolis below. It was the city of dreams, Imperial City, capital of the glorious Empress Isher— From his great height, he could see the gardens, the gorgeous grounds of the silver palace, the official Imperial residence itself—

The last tendrils of his fear were fading now before a gathering fascination and wonder; they vanished utterly as he recognized with a ghastly thrill of uncertain expectancy that the palace was drawing nearer at great speed.

"Show him the palace," they had said. Did that mean, could it mean—

The spray of tense thoughts splattered into nonexistence, as the glittering roof flashed straight at his face. He gulped, as the solid metal of it passed through him, and then other walls and ceilings.

His first sense of imminent and mind-shaking desecration came as the picture paused in a great room where a score of men sat around a table at the head of which sat—a young woman.

The inexorable, sacrilegious, limitlessly powered cameras that were taking the picture swung across the table, and caught the woman full face.

It was a handsome face, but there was passion and fury twisting it now, and a very blaze of fire in her eyes, as she leaned forward, and said in a voice at once familiar—how often Fara had heard its calm, measured tones on the telestats—and distorted. Utterly distorted by anger and an insolent certainty of command. That caricature of a beloved voice slashed across the silence as clearly as if he, Fara, was there in that room:

"I want that skunk killed, do you understand? I don't care how you do it, but I want to hear by tomorrow night that he's dead."

The picture snapped off and instantly—it was as swift as that—Fara was back in the weapon shop. He stood for a moment, swaying, fighting to accustom his eyes to the dimness; and then—

His first emotion was contempt at the simpleness of the trickery—a motion picture. What kind of a fool did they think he was, to swallow something as transparently unreal as that? He'd—

Abruptly, the appalling lechery of the scheme, the indescribable wickedness of what was being attempted here brought red rage.

"Why, you scum!" he flared. "So you've got somebody to act the part of the empress, trying to pretend that— Why, you—"

"That will do," said the voice of Rad; and Fara shook as a big young man walked into his line of vision. The alarmed thought came that people who would besmirch so vilely the character of her imperial majesty would not hesitate to do physical damage to Fara Clark. The young man went on in a steely tone:

"We do not pretend that what you saw was taking place this instant in the palace. That would be too much of a coincidence. But it was taken two weeks ago; the woman *is* the empress. The man whose death she ordered is one of her many former lovers. He was found murdered two weeks ago; his name, if you care to look it up in the news files, is Banton McCreddie. However, let that pass. We're finished with you now and—"

"But I'm not finished," Fara said in a thick voice. "I've never heard or seen so much infamy in all my life. If you think this town is through with you, you're crazy. We'll have a guard on this place day and night, and nobody will get in or out. We'll—"

"That will do." It was the silver-haired man; and Fara stopped out of respect for age, before he thought. The old man went on: "The examination has been most interesting. As an honest man, you may call on us if you are ever in trouble. That is all. Leave through the side door."

It *was* all. Impalpable forces grabbed him, and he was shoved at a door that appeared miraculously in the wall, where seconds before the palace had been.

He found himself standing dazedly in a flower bed, and there was a swarm of men to his left. He recognized his fellow townsmen and that he was—outside.

The incredible nightmare was over.

"Where's the gun?" said Creel, as he entered the house half an hour later.

"The gun?" Fara stared at his wife.

"It said over the radio a few minutes ago that you were the first customer of the new weapon shop. I thought it was queer, but—"

He was eerily conscious of her voice going on for several words longer, but it was the purest jumble. The shock was so great that he had the horrible sensation of being on the edge of an abyss.

So that was what the young man had meant: "Advertise! We'll advertise his presence and—"

Fara thought: His reputation! Not that his was a great name, but he had long believed with a quiet pride that Fara Clark's motor repair shop was widely known in the community and countryside.

First, his private humiliation inside the shop. And now this—lying—to people who didn't know why he had gone into the store. Diabolical.

His paralysis ended, as a frantic determination to rectify the base charge drove him to the telestat. After a moment, the plump, sleepy face of Mayor Mel Dale appeared on the plate. Fara's voice made a barrage of sound, but his hopes dashed, as the man said:

"I'm sorry, Fara. I don't see how you can have free time on the telestat. You'll have to pay for it. They did."

"They did!" Fara wondered vaguely if he sounded as empty as he felt.

"And they've just paid Lan Harris for his lot. The old man asked top price, and got it. He just phoned me to transfer the title."

"Oh!" The world was shattering. "You mean nobody's going to do anything. What about the Imperial garrison at Ferd?"

Dimly, Fara was aware of the mayor mumbling something about the empress' soldiers refusing to interfere in civilian matters.

"Civilian matters!" Fara exploded. "You mean these people are just going to be allowed to come here whether we want them or not, illegally forcing the sale of lots by first taking possession of them?"

A sudden thought struck him breathless. "Look, you haven't changed your mind about having Jor keep guard in front of the shop?"

With a start, he saw that the plump face in the telestat plate had grown impatient. "Now, see here, Fara," came the pompous words, "let the constituted authorities handle this matter."

"But you're going to keep Jor there," Fara said doggedly.

The mayor looked annoyed, said finally peevishly: "I promised, didn't I? So he'll be there. And now—do you want to buy time on the telestat? It's fifteen credits for one minute. Mind you, as a friend, I think you're wasting your money. No one has ever caught up with a false statement."

Fara said grimly: "Put two on, one in the morning, one in the evening."

"All right. We'll deny it completely. Good night."

The telestat went blank; and Fara sat there. A new thought hardened his face. "That boy of ours—there's going to be a showdown. He either works in my shop, or he gets no more allowance."

Creed said: "You've handled him wrong. He's twenty-three, and you treat him like a child. Remember, at twenty-three, you were a married man."

"That was different," said Fara. "I had a sense of responsibility. Do you know what he did tonight?"

He didn't quite catch her answer. For the moment, he thought she said: "No; in what way did you humiliate him first?"

Fara felt too impatient to verify the impossible words. He rushed on: "He refused in front of the whole village to give me help. He's a bad one, all bad."

"Yes," said Creel in a bitter tone, "he is all bad. I'm sure you don't realize how bad. He's as cold as steel, but without steel's strength or integrity. He took a long time, but he hates even me now, because I stood up for your side so long, knowing you were wrong."

"What's that?" said Fara, startled; then gruffly: "Come, come, my dear, we're both upset. Let's go to bed."

He slept poorly.

There were days then when the conviction that this was a personal fight between himself and the weapon shop lay heavily on Fara. Grimly, though it was out of his way, he made a point of walking past the weapon shop, always pausing to speak to Constable Jor and—

On the fourth day, the policeman wasn't there.

Fara waited patiently at first, then angrily; then he walked hastily to his shop, and called Jor's house. No, Jor wasn't home. He was guarding the weapon store.

Fara hesitated. His own shop was piled with work, and he had a guilty sense of having neglected his customers for the first time in his life. It would be simple to call up the mayor and report Jor's dereliction. And yet—

He didn't want to get the man into trouble—

Out in the street, he saw that a large crowd was gathering in front of the weapon shop. Fara hurried. A man he knew greeted him excitedly:

"Jor's been murdered, Fara!"

"Murdered!" Fara stood stock-still, and at first he was not clearly conscious of the grisly thought that was in his mind: satisfaction! A flaming satisfaction. Now, he thought, even the soldiers would have to act. They—

With a gasp, he realized the ghastly tenor of his thoughts. He shivered, but finally pushed the sense of shame out of his mind. He said slowly:

"Where's the body?"

"Inside."

"You mean, those . . . scum—" In spite of himself, he hesitated over the epithet; even now it was difficult to think of the fine-faced, silver-haired old man in such

The Weapon Shop

terms. Abruptly, his mind hardened; he flared: "You mean those scum actually killed him, then pulled his body inside?"

"Nobody saw the killing," said a second man beside Fara, "but he's gone, hasn't been seen for three hours. The mayor got the weapon shop on the telestat, but they claim they don't know anything. They've done away with him, that's what, and now they're pretending innocence. Well, they won't get out of it as easily as that. Mayor's gone to phone the soldiers at Ferd to bring up some big guns and—"

Something of the intense excitement that was in the crowd surged through Fara, the feeling of big things brewing. It was the most delicious sensation that had ever tingled along his nerves, and it was all mixed with a strange pride that he had been so right about this, that he at least had never doubted that here was evil.

He did not recognize the emotion as the full-flowering joy that comes to a member of a mob. But his voice shook, as he said:

"Guns? Yes, that will be the answer, and the soldiers will have to come, of course."

Fara nodded to himself in the immensity of his certainty that the Imperial soldiers would now have no excuse for not acting. He started to say something dark about what the empress would do if she found out that a man had lost his life because the soldiers had shirked their duty, but the words were drowned in a shout:

"Here comes the mayor! Hey, Mr. Mayor, when are the atomic cannons due?"

There was more of the same general meaning, as the mayor's sleek, all-purpose car landed lightly. Some of the questions must have reached His Honor, for he stood up in the open two-seater, and held up his hand for silence.

To Fara's astonishment, the plump-faced man looked at him with accusing eyes. The thing seemed so impossible that, quite instinctively, Fara looked behind him. But he was almost alone; everybody else had crowded forward.

Fara shook his head, puzzled by that glare; and then, astoundingly, Mayor Dale pointed a finger at him, and said in a voice that trembled:

"There's the man who's responsible for the trouble that's come upon us. Stand forward, Fara Clark, and show yourself. You've cost this town seven hundred credits that we could ill afford to spend."

Fara couldn't have moved or spoken to save his life. He just stood there in a maze of dumb bewilderment. Before he could even think, the mayor went on, and there was quivering self-pity in his tone:

"We've all known that it wasn't wise to interfere with these weapon shops. So long as the Imperial government leaves them alone, what right have we to set up guards, or act against them? That's what I've thought from the beginning, but this man . . . this . . . Fara Clark kept after all of us, forcing us to move against our wills, and so now we've got a seven-hundred-credit bill to meet and—"

He broke off with: "I might as well make it brief. When I called the garrison, the commander just laughed and said that Jor would turn up. And I had barely disconnected when there was a money call from Jor. He's on Mars."

He waited for the shouts of amazement to die down. "It'll take three weeks for him to come back by ship, and we've got to pay for it, and Fara Clark is responsible. He—"

The shock was over. Fara stood cold, his mind hard. He said finally, scathingly: "So you're giving up, and trying to blame me all in one breath. I say you're all fools."

As he turned away, he heard Mayor Dale saying something about the situation not being completely lost, as he had learned that the weapon shop had been set up in Glay because the village was equidistant from four cities, and that it was the city business the shop was after. This would mean tourists, and accessory trade for the village stores and—

Fara heard no more. Head high, he walked back toward his shop. There were one or two catcalls from the mob, but he ignored them.

He had no sense of approaching disaster, simply a gathering fury against the weapon shop, which had brought him to this miserable status among his neighbors.

The worst of it, as the days passed, was the realization that the people of the weapon shop had no personal interest in him. They were remote, superior, undefeatable. That unconquerableness was a dim, suppressed awareness inside Fara.

When he thought of it, he felt a vague fear at the way they had transferred Jor to Mars in a period of less than three hours, when all the world knew that the trip by fastest spaceship required nearly three weeks.

Fara did not go to the express station to see Jor arrive home. He had heard that the council had decided to charge Jor with half of the expense of the trip, on the threat of losing his job if he made a fuss.

On the second night after Jor's return, Fara slipped down to the constable's house, and handed the officer one hundred seventy-five credits. It wasn't that he was responsible, he told Jor, but—

The man was only too eager to grant the disclaimer, provided the money went with it. Fara returned home with a clearer conscience.

It was on the third day after that that the door of his shop banged open and a man came in. Fara frowned as he saw who it was: Castler, a village hanger-on. The man was grinning:

"Thought you might be interested, Fara. Somebody came out of the weapon shop today."

Fara strained deliberately at the connecting bolt of a hard plate of the atomic motor he was fixing. He waited with a gathering annoyance that the man did not volunteer further information. Asking questions would be a form of recognition of the worthless fellow. A developing curiosity made him say finally, grudgingly:

"I suppose the constable promptly picked him up."

He supposed nothing of the kind, but it was an opening.

"It wasn't a man. It was a girl."

Fara knitted his brows. He didn't like the idea of making trouble for women. But—the cunning devils! Using a girl, just as they had used an old man as a clerk. It was a trick that deserved to fail, the girl probably a tough one who needed rough treatment. Fara said harshly:

"Well, what's happened?"

"She's still out, bold as you please. Pretty thing, too."

The bolt off, Fara took the hard plate over to the polisher, and began patiently the long, careful task of smoothing away the crystals that heat had seared on the once shining metal. The soft throb of the polisher made the background to his next words:

"Has anything been done?"

"Nope. The constable's been told, but he says he doesn't fancy being away from his family for another three weeks, and paying the cost into the bargain."

Fara contemplated that darkly for a minute, as the polisher throbbed on. His voice shook with suppressed fury, when he said finally:

"So they're letting them get away with it. It's all been as clever as hell. Can't they see that they mustn't give an inch before these . . . these transgressors. It's like giving countenance to sin."

From the corner of his eye, he noticed that there was a curious grin on the face of the other. It struck Fara suddenly that the man was enjoying his anger. And there was something else in that grin; something—a secret knowledge.

Fara pulled the engine plate away from the polisher. He faced the ne'er-do-well, scathed at him:

"Naturally, that sin part wouldn't worry you much."

"Oh," said the man nonchalantly, "the hard knocks of life make people tolerant. For instance, after you know the girl better, you yourself will probably come to realize that there's good in all of us."

It was not so much the words, as the curious I've-got-secret-information tone that made Fara snap:

"What do you mean—if I get to know the girl better! I won't even speak to the brazen creature."

"One can't always choose," the other said with enormous casualness. "Suppose he brings her home."

"Suppose who brings who home?" Fara spoke irritably. "Castler, you—"

He stopped; a dead weight of dismay plumped into his stomach; his whole being sagged. "You mean—" he said.

"I mean," replied Castler with a triumphant leer, "that the boys aren't letting a beauty like her be lonesome. And, naturally, your son was the first to speak to her."

He finished: "They're walkin' together now on Second Avenue, comin' this way, so—"

"Get out of here!" Fara roared. "And stay away from me with your gloating. Get out!"

The man hadn't expected such an igniminious ending. He flushed scarlet, then went out, slamming the door.

Fara stood for a moment, every muscle stiff; then, with an abrupt, jerky movement, he shut off his power, and went out into the street.

The time to put a stop to that kind of thing was—now!

He had no clear plan, just that violent determination to put an immediate end to an impossible situation. And it was all mixed up with his anger against Cayle. How could he have had such a worthless son, he who paid his debts and worked hard, and tried to be decent and live up to the highest standards of the empress?

A brief, dark thought came to Fara that maybe there was some bad blood on Creel's side. Not from her mother, of course—Fara added the mental thought hastily. *There* was a fine, hard-working woman, who hung on to her money, and who would leave Creel a tidy sum one of these days.

But Creel's father had disappeared when Creel was only a child, and there had been some vague scandal about him having taken up with a telestat actress.

And now Cayle with this weapon-shop girl. A girl who had let herself be picked up—

He saw them, as he turned the corner onto Second Avenue. They were walking a hundred feet distant, and heading away from Fara. The girl was tall and slender, almost as big as Cayle, and, as Fara came up, she was saying:

"You have the wrong idea about us. A person like you can't get a job in our organization. You belong in the Imperial Service, where they can use young men of good education, good appearance, and no scruples. I—"

Fara grasped only dimly that Cayle must have been trying to get a job with these people. It was not clear; and his own mind was too intent on his purpose for it to mean anything at the moment. He said harshly:

"Cayle!"

The couple turned, Cayle with the measured unhurriedness of a young man who has gone a long way on the road to steel-like nerves; the girl was quicker, but withal dignified.

Fara had a vague, terrified feeling that his anger was too great, self-destroying, but the very violence of his emotions ended that thought even as it came. He said thickly:

"Cayle, get home—at once."

Fara was aware of the girl looking at him curiously from strange, gray-green eyes. No shame, he thought, and his rage mounted several degrees, driving away the alarm that came at the sight of the flush that crept into Cayle's cheeks.

The Weapon Shop

The flush faded into a pale, tight-lipped anger. Cayle half-turned to the girl, said: "This is the childish old fool I've got to put up with. Fortunately, we seldom see each other; we don't even eat together. What do you think of him?"

The girl smiled impersonally: "Oh, we know Fara Clark; he's the backbone of the empress in Glay."

"Yes," the boy sneered. "You ought to hear him. He thinks we're living in heaven; and the empress is the divine power. The worst part of it is that there's no chance of his ever getting that stuffy look wiped off his face."

They walked off; and Fara stood there. The very extent of what had happened had drained anger from him as if it had never been. There was the realization that he had made a mistake so great that—

He couldn't grasp it. For long, long now, since Cayle had refused to work in his shop, he had felt this building up to a climax. Suddenly, his own uncontrollable ferocity stood revealed as a partial product of that—deeper—problem.

Only, now that the smash was here, he didn't want to face it—

All through the day in his shop, he kept pushing it out of his mind, kept thinking:

Would this go on now, as before, Cayle and he living in the same house, not even looking at each other when they met, going to bed at different times, getting up, Fara at 6:30, Cayle at noon? Would *that* go on through all the days and years to come?

When he arrived home, Creel was waiting for him. She said:

"Fara, he wants you to loan him five hundred credits, so that he can go to Imperial City."

Fara nodded wordlessly. He brought the money back to the house the next morning, and gave it to Creel, who took it into the bedroom.

She came out a minute later. "He says to tell you good-by."

When Fara came home that evening, Cayle was gone. He wondered whether he ought to feel relieved or—what?

The days passed. Fara worked. He had nothing else to do, and the gray thought was often in his mind that now he would be doing it till the day he died. Except—

Fool that he was—he told himself a thousand times how big a fool—he kept hoping that Cayle would walk into the shop and say:

"Father, I've learned my lesson. If you can ever forgive me, teach me the business, and then you retire to a well-earned rest."

It was exactly a month to a day after Cayle's departure that the telestat clicked on just after Fara had finished lunch. "Money call," it sighed, "money call."

Fara and Creel looked at each other. "Eh," said Fara finally, "money call for us."

He could see from the gray look in Creel's face the thought that was in her mind. He said under his breath: "Damn that boy!"

But he felt relieved. Amazingly, relieved! Cayle was beginning to appreciate the value of parents and—

He switched on the viewer. "Come and collect," he said.

The face that came on the screen was heavy-jowled, beetle-browed—and strange. The man said:

"This is Clerk Pearton of the Fifth Bank of Ferd. We have received a sight draft on you for ten thousand credits. With carrying charges and government tax, the sum required will be twelve thousand one hundred credits. Will you pay it now or will you come in this afternoon and pay it?"

"B-but . . . b-but—" said Fara. "W-who—"

He stopped, conscious of the stupidity of the question, dimly conscious of the heavy-faced man saying something about the money having been paid out to one Cayle Clark, that morning, in Imperial City. At last, Fara found his voice:

"But the bank had no right," he expostulated, "to pay out the money without my authority. I—"

The voice cut him off coldly: "Are we then to inform our central that the money was obtained under false pretenses? Naturally, an order will be issued immediately for the arrest of your son."

"Wait . . . wait—" Fara spoke blindly. He was aware of Creel beside him, shaking her head at him. She was as white as a sheet, and her voice was a sick, stricken thing, as she said:

"Fara, let him go. He's through with us. We must be as hard—let him go."

The words rang senselessly in Fara's ears. They didn't fit into any normal pattern. He was saying:

"I . . . I haven't got— How about my paying . . . installments? I—"

"If you wish a loan," said Clerk Pearton, "naturally we will be happy to go into the matter. I might say that when the draft arrived, we checked up on your status, and we are prepared to loan you eleven thousand credits on indefinite call with your shop as security. I have the form here, and if you are agreeable, we will switch this call through the registered circuit, and you can sign at once."

"Fara, no."

The clerk went on: "The other eleven hundred credits will have to be paid in cash. Is that agreeable?"

"Yes, yes, of course, I've got twenty-five hund—" He stopped his chattering tongue with a gulp; then: "Yes, that's satisfactory."

The deal completed, Fara whirled on his wife. Out of the depths of his hurt and bewilderment, he raged:

"What do you mean, standing there and talking about not paying it? You said several times that I was responsible for him being what he is. Besides, we don't know why he needed the money. He—"

Creel said in a low, dead tone: "In one hour, he's stripped us of our life work. He did it deliberately, thinking of us as two old fools, who wouldn't know any better than to pay it."

The Weapon Shop

Before he could speak, she went on: "Oh, I know I blamed you, but in the final issue, I knew it was he. He was always cold and calculating, but I was weak, and I was sure that if you handled him in a different . . . and besides I didn't want to see his faults for a long time. He—"

"All I see," Fara interrupted doggedly, "is that I have saved our name from disgrace."

His high sense of duty rightly done lasted until midafternoon, when the bailiff from Ferd came to take over the shop.

"But what—" Fara began.

The bailiff said: "The Automatic Atomic Repair Shops, Limited, took over your loan from the bank, and are foreclosing. Have you anything to say?"

"It's unfair," said Fara. "I'll take it to court. I'll—"

He was thinking dazedly: "If the empress ever learned of this, she'd . . . she'd—"

The courthouse was a big, gray building; and Fara felt emptier and colder every second, as he walked along the gray corridors. In Glay, his decision not to give himself into the hands of a bloodsucker of a lawyer had seemed a wise act. Here, in these enormous halls and palatial rooms, it seemed the sheerest folly.

He managed, nevertheless, to give an articulate account of the criminal act of the bank in first giving Cayle the money, then turning over the note to his chief competitor, apparently within minutes of his signing it. He finished with:

"I'm sure, sir, the empress would not approve of such goings-on against honest citizens. I—"

"How dare you," said the cold-voice creature on the bench, "use the name of her holy majesty in support of your own gross self-interest?"

Fara shivered. The sense of being intimately a member of the empress' great human family yielded to a sudden chill and a vast mind-picture of the ten million icy courts like this, and the myriad malevolent and heartless men—*like this*—who stood between the empress and her loyal subject, Fara.

He thought passionately: If the empress knew what was happening here, how unjustly he was being treated, she would—

Or would she?

He pushed the crowding, terrible doubt ut of his mind—came out of his hard reverie with a start, to hear the Cadi saying:

"Plaintiff's appeal dismissed, with costs assessed at seven hundred credits, to be divided between the court and the defense solicitor in the ratio of five to two. See to it that the appellant does not leave till the costs are paid. Next case—"

Fara went alone the next day to see Creel's mother. He called first at "Farmer's Restaurant" at the outskirts of the village. The place was, he noted with satisfaction in the thought of the steady stream of money flowing in, half full, though it was only midmorning. But madame wasn't there. Try the feed store.

He found her in the back of the feed store, overseeing the weighing out of grain into cloth measures. The hard-faced old woman heard his story without a word. She said finally, curtly:

"Nothing doing, Fara. I'm one who has to make loans often from the bank to swing deals. If I tried to set you up in business, I'd find the Automatic Atomic Repair people getting after me. Besides, I'd be a fool to turn money over to a man who lets a bad son squeeze a fortune out of him. Such a man has no sense about worldly things.

"And I won't give you a job because I don't hire relatives in my business." She finished: "Tell Creel to come and live at my house. I won't support a man, though. That's all."

He watched her disconsolately for a while, as she went on calmly superintending the clerks who were manipulating the old, no longer accurate measuring machines. Twice her voice echoed through the dust-filled interior, each time with a sharp: "That's overweight, a gram at least. Watch your machine."

Though her back was turned, Fara knew by her posture that she was still aware of his presence. She turned at last with an abrupt movement, and said:

"Why don't you go to the weapon shop? You haven't anything to lose, and you can't go on like this."

Fara went out, then, a little blindly. At first the suggestion that he buy a gun and commit suicide had no real personal application. But he felt immeasurably hurt that his mother-in-law should have made it.

Kill himself? Why, it was ridiculous. He was still only a young man, going on fifty. Given the proper chance, with his skilled hands, he could wrest a good living even in a world where automatic machines were encroaching everywhere. There was always room for a man who did a good job. His whole life had been based on that credo.

Kill himself—

He went home to find Creel packing. "It's the common-sense thing to do," she said. "We'll rent the house and move into rooms."

He told her about her mother's offer to take her in, watching her face as he spoke. Creel shrugged.

"I told her 'No' yesterday," she said thoughtfully. "I wonder why she mentioned it to you."

Fara walked swiftly over to the great front window overlooking the garden, with its flowers, its pool, its rockery. He tried to think of Creel away from this garden of hers, this home of two-thirds a lifetime, Creel living in rooms—and knew what her mother had meant. There was one more hope—

He waited till Creel went upstairs, then called Mel Dale on the telestat. The mayor's plump face took on an uneasy expression as he saw who it was.

But he listened pontifically, said finally: "Sorry, the council does not loan money; and I might as well tell you, Fara—I have nothing to do with this, mind you—but you can't get a license for a shop any more."

"W-what?"

"I'm sorry!" The mayor lowered his voice. "Listen, Fara, take my advice and go to the weapon shop. These places have their uses."

There was a click, and Fara sat staring at the blank face of the viewing screen.

So it was to be—death!

He waited until the street was empty of human beings, then slipped across the boulevard, past a design of flower gardens, and so to the door of the shop. The brief fear came that the door wouldn't open, but it did, effortlessly.

As he emerged from the dimness of the alcove into the shop proper, he saw the silver-haired old man sitting in a corner chair, reading under a softly bright light. The old man looked up, put aside his book, then rose to his feet.

"It's Mr. Clark," he said quietly. "What can we do for you?"

A faint flush crept into Fara's cheeks. In a dim fashion, he had hoped that he would not suffer the humiliation of being recognized; but now that his fear was realized, he stood his ground stubbornly. The important thing about killing himself was that there be no body for Creel to bury at great expense. Neither knife nor poison would satisfy that basic requirement.

"I want a gun," said Fara, "that can be adjusted to disintegrate a body six feet in diameter in a single shot. Have you that kind?"

Without a word, the old man turned to a showcase, and brought forth a sturdy gem of a revolver that glinted with all the soft colors of the inimitable Ordine plastic. The man said in a precise voice:

"Notice the flanges on this barrel are little more than bulges. This makes the model ideal for carrying in a shoulder holster under the coat; it can be drawn very swiftly because, when properly attuned, it will leap toward the reaching hand of its owner. At the moment it is attuned to me. Watch while I replace it in its holster and—"

The speed of the draw was absolutely amazing. The old man's fingers moved; and the gun, four feet away, was in them. There was no blur of movement. It was like the door the night that it had slipped from Fara's grasp, and slammed noiselessly in Constable Jor's face. *Instantaneous!*

Fara, who had parted his lips as the old man was explaining, to protest the utter needlessness of illustrating any quality of the weapon except what he had asked for, closed them again. He stared in a brief, dazed fascination; and something of the wonder that was here held his mind and his body.

He had seen and handled the guns of soldiers, and they were simply ordinary metal or plastic things that one used clumsily like any other material substance, not like this at all, not possessed of a dazzling life of their own, leaping with an intimate eagerness to assist with all their superb power the will of their master. They—

With a start, Fara remembered his purpose. He smiled wryly, and said:

"All this is very interesting. But what about the beam that can fan out?"

The old man said calmly: "At pencil thickness, this beam will pierce any body except certain alloys of lead up to four hundred yards. With proper adjustment of the firing nozzle, you can disintegrate a six-foot object at fifty yards or less. This screw is the adjustor."

He indicated a tiny device in the muzzle itself. "Turn it to the left to spread the beam, to the right to close it."

Fara said: "I'll take the gun. How much is it?"

He saw that the old man was looking at him thoughtfully; the oldster said finally, slowly: "I have previously explained our regulations to you, Mr. Clark. You recall them, of course?"

"Eh!" said Fara, and stopped, wide-eyed. It wasn't that he didn't remember them. It was simply—

"You mean," he gasped, "those things actually apply. They're not—"

With a terrible effort, he caught his spinning brain and blurring voice. Tense and cold, he said:

"All I want is a gun that will shoot in self-defense, but which I can turn on myself if I have to or—want to."

"Oh, suicide!" said the old man. He looked as if a great understanding had suddenly dawned on him. "My dear sir, we have no objection to you killing yourself at any time. That is your personal privilege in a world where privileges grow scanter every year. As for the price of this revolver, it's four credits."

"Four cre . . . only four credits!" said Fara.

He stood, absolutely astounded, his whole mind snatched from its dark purpose. Why, the plastic alone was—and the whole gun with its fine, intricate workmanship—twenty-five credits would have been dirt cheap.

He felt a brief thrall of utter interest; the mystery of the weapon shops suddenly loomed as vast and important as his own black destiny. But the old man was speaking again:

"And now, if you will remove your coat, we can put on the holster—"

Quite automatically, Fara complied. It was vaguely startling to realize that, in a few seconds, he would be walking out of here, equipped for self-murder, and that there was now not a single obstacle to his death.

Curiously, he was disappointed. He couldn't explain it, but somehow there had been in the back of his mind a hope that these shops might, just might—what?

What indeed? Fara sighed wearily—and grew aware again of the old man's voice, saying:

"Perhaps you would prefer to step out of our side door. It is less conspicuous than the front."

There was no resistance in Fara. He was dimly conscious of the man's fingers on his arm, half guiding him; and then the old man pressed one of several buttons on the wall—so that's how it was done—and there was the door.

He could see flowers beyond the opening; without a word he walked toward them. He was outside almost before he realized it.

Fara stood for a moment in the neat little pathway, striving to grasp the finality of his situation. But nothing would come except a curious awareness of many men around him; for a long second, his brain was like a log drifting along a stream at night.

Through that darkness grew a consciousness of something wrong; the wrongness was there in the back of his mind, as he turned leftward to go to the front of the weapon store.

Vagueness transformed to a shocked, startled sound. For—he was not in Glay, and the weapon shop *wasn't* where it had been. In its place—

A dozen men brushed past Fara to join a long line of men farther along. But Fara was immune to their presence, their strangeness. His whole mind, his whole vision, his very being was concentrating on the section of machine that stood where the weapon shop had been.

A machine, oh, a machine—

His brain lifted up, up in his effort to grasp the tremendousness of the dull-metaled immensity of what was spread here under a summer sun beneath a sky as blue as a remote southern sea.

The machine towered into the heavens, five great tiers of metal, each a hundred feet high; and the superbly streamlined five hundred feet ended in a peak of light, a gorgeous spire that tilted straight up a sheer two hundred feet farther, and matched the very sun for brightness.

And it *was* a machine, not a building, because the whole lower tier was alive with shimmering lights, mostly green, but sprinkled colorfully with red and occasionally a blue and yellow. Twice, as Fara watched, green lights directly in front of him flashed unscintillatingly into red.

The second tier was alive with white and red lights, although there were only a fraction as many lights as on the lowest tier. The third section had on its dull-metal surface only blue and yellow lights; they twinkled softly here and there over the vast area.

The fourth tier was a series of signs, that brought the beginning of comprehension. The whole sign was:

WHITE	—	BIRTHS
RED	—	DEATHS
GREEN	—	LIVING

BLUE   — IMMIGRATION TO EARTH
YELLOW — EMIGRATION

The fifth tier was also all sign, finally explaining:

POPULATIONS
SOLAR SYSTEM — 19,174,463,747
EARTH — 11,193,247,361
MARS — 1,097,298,604
VENUS — 5,141,053,811
MOONS — 1,742,863,971

The numbers changed, even as he looked at them, leaping up and down, shifting below and above what they had first been. People were dying, being born, moving to Mars, to Venus, to the moons of Jupiter, to Earth's moon, and others coming back again, landing minute by minute in the thousands of spaceports. Life went on in its gigantic fashion—and here was the stupendous record. Here was—

"Better get in line," said a friendly voice beside Fara. "It takes quite a while to put through an individual case, I understand."

Fara stared at the man. He had the distinct impression of having had senseless words flung at him. "In line?" he started—and stopped himself with a jerk that hurt his throat.

He was moving forward, blindly, ahead of the younger man, thinking a curious jumble about that this must have been how Constable Jor was transported to Mars — when another of the man's words penetrated.

"Case?" said Fara violently. "Individual case!"

The man, a heavy-faced, blue-eyed young chap of around thirty-five, looked at him curiously: "You must know why you're here," he said. "Surely, you wouldn't have been sent through here unless you had a problem of some kind that the weapon shop courts will solve for you; there's no other reason for coming to Information Center."

Fara walked on because he was in the line now, a fast-moving line that curved him inexorably around the machine; and seemed to be heading him toward a door that led into the interior of the great metal structure.

So it was a building as well as a machine.

A problem, he was thinking; why, of course, he had a problem, a hopeless, insoluble, completely tangled problem so deeply rooted in the basic structure of Imperial civilization that the whole world would have to be overturned to make it right.

With a start, he saw that he was at the entrance. And the awed thought came: In seconds he would be committed irrevocably to—what?

Inside was a long, shining corridor, with scores of completely transparent hallways leading off the main corridor. Behind Fara, the young man's voice said:

"There's one, practically empty. Let's go."

Fara walked ahead; and suddenly he was trembling. He had already noticed that

The Weapon Shop

at the end of each side hallway were some dozen young women sitting at desks, interviewing men and . . . and, good heavens, was it possible that all this meant—

He grew aware that he had stopped in front of one of the girls.

She was older than she had looked from a distance, over thirty, but good-looking, alert. She smiled pleasantly, but impersonally, and said:

"Your name, please?"

He gave it before he thought and added a mumble about being from the village of Glay. The woman said:

"Thank you. It will take a few minutes to get your file. Won't you sit down?"

He hadn't noticed the chair. He sank into it; and his heart was beating so wildly that he felt choked. The strange thing was that there was scarcely a thought in his head, nor a real hope; only an intense, almost mind-wrecking excitement.

With a jerk, he realized that the girl was speaking again, but only snatches of her voice came through that screen of tension in his mind:

"—Information Center is . . . in effect . . . a bureau of statistics. Every person born . . . registered here . . . their education, change of address . . . occupation . . . and the highlights of their life. The whole is maintained by . . . combination of . . . unauthorized and unsuspected liaison with . . . Imperial Chamber of Statistics and . . . through medium of agents . . . in every community—"

It seemed to Fara that he was missing vital information, and that if he could only force his attention and hear more— He strained, but it was no use; his nerves were jumping madly and—

Before he could speak, there was a click, and a thin, dark plate slid onto the woman's desk. She took it up, and examined it. After a moment, she said something into a mouthpiece, and in a short time two more plates precipitated out of the empty air onto her desk. She studied them impassively, looked up finally.

"You will be interested to know," she said, "that your son, Cayle, bribed himself into a commission in the Imperial army with five thousand credits."

"Eh?" said Fara. He half rose from his chair, but before he could say anything, the young woman was speaking again, firmly:

"I must inform you that the weapon shops take no action against individuals. Your son can have his job, the money he stole; we are not concerned with moral correction. That must come naturally from the individual, and from the people as a whole—and now if you will give me a brief account of your problem for the record and the court."

Sweating, Fara sank back into his seat; his mind was heaving; most desperately, he wanted more information about Cayle. He began:

"But . . . but what . . . how—" He caught himself; and in a low voice described what had happened. When he finished, the girl said:

"You will proceed now to the Name Room; watch for your name, and when it appears go straight to Room 474. Remember, 474—and now, the line is waiting, if you please—"

She smiled politely, and Fara was moving off almost before he realized it. He half turned to ask another question, but an old man was sinking into his chair. Fara hurried on, along a great corridor, conscious of curious blasts of sound coming from ahead.

Eagerly, he opened the door; and the sound crashed at him with all the impact of a sledgehammer blow.

It was such a colossal, incredible sound that he stopped short, just inside the door, shrinking back. He stood then trying to blink sense into a visual confusion that rivaled in magnitude that incredible tornado of noise.

Men, men, men everywhere; men by the thousands in a long, broad auditorium, packed into rows of seats, pacing with an abandon of restlessness up and down aisles, and all of them staring with a frantic interest at a long board marked off into squares, each square lettered from the alphabet, from A, B, C and so on to Z. The tremendous board with its lists of names ran the full length of the immense room.

The Name Room, Fara was thinking shakily, as he sank into a seat—and his name would come up in the C's, and then—

It was like sitting in at a no-limit poker game, watching the jewel-precious cards turn up. It was like playing the exchange with all the world at stake during a stock crash. It was nerve-racking, dazzling, exhausting, fascinating, terrible, mind-destroying, stupendous. It was—

It was like nothing else on the face of the earth.

New names kept flashing on to the twenty-six squares; and men would shout like insane beings and some fainted, and the uproar was absolutely shattering; the pandemonium raged on, one continuous, unbelievable sound.

And every few minutes a great sign would flash along the board, telling everyone: "WATCH YOUR OWN INITIALS."

Fara watched, trembling in every limb. Each second it seemed to him that he couldn't stand it an instant longer. He wanted to scream at the room to be silent; he wanted to jump up to pace the floor, but others who did that were yelled at hysterically, threatened wildly, hated with a mad, murderous ferocity.

Abruptly, the blind savagery of it scared Fara. He thought unsteadily: "I'm not going to make a fool of myself. I—"

"Clark, Fara—" winked the board. "Clark, Fara—"

With a shout that nearly tore off the top of his head, Fara leaped to his feet. "That's me!" he shrieked. "Me!"

No one turned; no one paid the slightest attention. Shamed, he slunk across the room to where an endless line of men kept crowding into a corridor beyond.

The silence in the long corridor was almost as shattering as the mind-destroying noise it replaced. It was hard to concentrate on the idea of a number—474.

It was completely impossible to imagine what could lie beyond—474.

* * *

The room was small. It was furnished with a small, business-type table and two chairs. On the table were seven neat piles of folders, each pile a different color. The piles were arranged in a row in front of a large, milky-white globe, that began to glow with a soft light. Out of its depths, a man's baritone voice said:

"Fara Clark?"

"Yes," said Fara.

"Before the verdict is rendered in your case," the voice went on quietly, "I want you to take a folder from the blue pile. The list will show the Fifth Interplanetary Bank in its proper relation to yourself and the world, and it will be explained to you in due course."

The list, Fara saw, was simply that: a list of the names of companies. The names ran from A to Z, and there were about five hundred of them. The folder carried no explanation: and Fara slipped it automatically into his side pocket, as the voice came again from the shining globe:

"It has been established," the words came precisely, "that the Fifth Interplanetary Bank perpetrated upon you a gross swindle, and that it is further guilty of practicing scavengery, deception, blackmail and was accessory in a criminal conspiracy.

"The bank made contact with your son, Cayle, through what is quite properly known as a scavenger, that is, an employee who exists by finding young men and women who are morally capable of drawing drafts on their parents or other victims. The scavenger obtains for this service a commission of eight percent, which is always paid by the person making the loan, in this case your son.

"The bank practiced deception in that its authorized agents deceived you in the most culpable fashion by pretending that it had already paid out the ten thousand credits to your son, whereas the money was not paid over until your signature had been obtained.

"The blackmail guilt arises out of the threat to have your son arrested for falsely obtaining a loan, a threat made at a time when no money had exchanged hands. The conspiracy consists of the action whereby your note was promptly turned over to your competitor.

"The bank is accordingly triple-fined, thirty-six thousand three hundred credits. It is not in our interest, Fara Clark, for you to know how this money is obtained. Suffice to know that the bank pays it, and that of the fine the weapon shops allocate to their own treasury a total of one half. The other half—"

There was a *plop;* a neatly packaged pile of bills fell onto the table. "For you," said the voice; and Fara, with trembling fingers, slipped the package into his coat pocket. It required the purest mental and physical effort for him to concentrate on the next words that came:

"You must not assume that your troubles are over. The re-establishment of your motor repair shop in Glay will require force and courage. Be discreet, brave and determined, and you cannot fail. Do not hesitate to use the gun you have purchased in defense of your rights. The plan will be explained to you. And now, proceed through the door facing you—"

Fara braced himself with an effort, opened the door and walked through.

It was a dim, familiar room that he stepped into, and there was a silver-haired, fine-faced man who rose from a reading chair, and came forward in the dimness, smiling gravely.

The stupendous, fantastic, exhilarating adventure was over; and he was back in the weapon shop of Glay.

He couldn't get over the wonder of it—this great and fascinating organization established here in the very heart of a ruthless civilization, a civilization that had in a few brief weeks stripped him of everything he possessed.

With a deliberate will, he stopped that glowing flow of thought. A dark frown wrinkled his solidly built face; he said:

"The . . . judge—" Fara hesitated over the name, frowned again, annoyed at himself, then went on: "The judge said that, to re-establish myself I would have to—"

"Before we go into that," said the old man quietly, "I want you to examine the blue folder you brought with you."

"Folder?" Fara echoed blankly. It took a long moment to remember that he had picked up a folder from the table in Room 474.

He studied the list of company names with a gathering puzzlement, noting that the name Automatic Atomic Motor Repair Shops was well down among the A's, and the Fifth Interplanetary Bank only one of several great banks included. Fara looked up finally:

"I don't understand," he said; "are these the companies you have had to act against?"

The silver-haired man smiled grimly, shook his head. "That is not what I mean. These firms constitute only a fraction of the eight hundred thousand companies that are constantly in our books."

He smiled again, humorlessly: "These companies all know that, because of us, their profits on paper bear no relation to their assets. What they don't know is how great the difference really is; and, as we want a general improvement in business morals, not merely more skillful scheming to outwit us, we prefer them to remain in ignorance."

He paused, and this time he gave Fara a searching glance, said at last: "The unique feature of the companies on this particular list is that they are every one wholly owned by Empress Isher."

He finished swiftly: "In view of your past opinions on that subject, I do not expect you to believe me."

Fara stood as still as death, for—he did believe with unquestioning conviction, completely, finally. The amazing, the unforgivable thing was that all his life he had watched the march of ruined men into the oblivion of poverty and disgrace—and blamed *them*.

Fara groaned. "I've been like a madman," he said. "Everything the empress and her officials **did** was right. No friendship, no personal relationship could survive with me that did not include belief in things as they were. I suppose if I started to talk against the empress I would receive equally short shrift."

"Under no circumstances," said the old man grimly, "must you say anything against her majesty. The weapon shops will not countenance any such words, and will give no further aid to anyone who is so indiscreet. The reason is that, for the moment, we have reached an uneasy state of peace with the Imperial government. We wish to keep it that way; beyond that I will not enlarge on our policy.

"I am permitted to say that the last great attempt to destroy the weapon shops was made seven years ago, when the glorious Innelda Isher was twenty-five years old. That was a secret attempt, based on a new invention; and failed by purest accident because of our sacrifice of a man from seven thousand years in the past. That may sound mysterious to you, but I will not explain.

"The worst period was reached some forty years ago when every person who was discovered receiving aid from us was murdered in some fashion. You may be surprised to know that your father-in-law was among those assassinated at that time."

"Creel's father!" Fara gasped. "But—"

He stopped. His brain was reeling; there was such a rush of blood to his head that for an instant he could hardly see.

"But," he managed at last, "it was reported that he ran away with another woman."

"They always spread a vicious story of some kind," the old man said; and Fara was silent, stunned.

The other went on: "We finally put a stop to their murders by killing the three men from the top down, *excluding* the royal family, who gave the order for the particular execution involved. But we do not again want that kind of bloody murder.

"Nor are we interested in any criticism of our toleration of so much that is evil. It is important to understand that *we do not interfere in the mainstream of human existence.* We right wrongs; we act as a barrier between the people and their more ruthless exploiters. Generally speaking, we help only honest men; that is not to say that we do not give assistance to the less scrupulous, but only to the extent of selling them guns—which is a very great aid indeed, and which is one of the reasons why the government is relying almost exclusively for its power on an economic chicanery.

"In the four thousand years since the brilliant genius, Walter S. DeLany, invented the vibration process that made the weapon shops possible, and laid down the first principles of weapon shop political philosophy, we have watched the tide of government swing backward and forward between democracy under a limited monarchy to complete tyranny. And we have discovered one thing:

"People always have the kind of government they want. When they want change, they must change it. As always we shall remain an incorruptible core—and I mean that literally; we have a psychological machine that never lies about a man's character—I repeat, an incorruptible core of human idealism, devoted to relieving the ills that arise inevitably under any form of government.

"But now—your problem. It is very simple, really. You must fight, as all men have fought since the beginning of time for what they valued, for their just rights. As you know, the Automatic Repair people removed all your machinery and tools within an hour of foreclosing on your shop. This material was taken to Ferd, and then shipped to a great warehouse on the coast.

"We recovered it, and with our special means of transportation have now replaced the machines in your shop. You will accordingly go there and—"

Fara listened with a gathering grimness to the instructions, nodded finally, his jaw clamped tight.

"You can count on me," he said curtly. "I've been a stubborn man in my time; and though I've changed sides, I haven't changed *that.*"

Going outside was like returning from life to—death; from hope to—reality.

Fara walked along the quiet streets of Glay at darkest night. For the first time it struck him that the weapon shop Information Center must be halfway around the world, for it had been day, brilliant day.

The picture vanished as if it had never existed, and he grew aware again, preternaturally aware of the village of Glay asleep all around him. Silent, peaceful—yet ugly, he thought, ugly with the ugliness of evil enthroned.

He thought: The right to buy weapons—and his heart swelled into his throat; the tears came to his eyes.

He wiped his vision clear with the back of his hand, thought of Creel's long-dead father, and strode on, without shame. Tears were good for an angry man.

The shop was the same, but the hard, metal padlock yielded before the tiny, blazing, supernal power of the revolver. One flick of fire; the metal dissolved—and he was inside.

It was dark, too dark to see, but Fara did not turn on the lights immediately. He fumbled across to the window control, turned the wndows to darkness vibration, and then clicked on the lights.

He gulped with awful relief. For the machines, his precious tools that he had seen carted away within hours after the bailiff's arrival, were here again, ready for use.

Shaky from the pressure of his emotion, Fara called Creel on the telestat. It took a little while for her to appear; and she was in her dressing robe. When she saw who it was she turned a dead white.

"Fara, oh, Fara, I thought—"

He cut her off grimly: "Creel, I've been to the weapon shop. I want you to do this:

go straight to your mother. I'm here at my shop. I'm going to stay here day and night until it's settled that I *stay*. . . . I shall go home later for some food and clothing, but I want you to be gone by then. Is that clear?"

Color was coming back into her lean, handsome face. She said: "Don't you bother coming home, Fara. I'll do everything necessary. I'll pack all that's needed into the carplane, including a folding bed. We'll sleep in the back room at the shop."

Morning came palely, but it was ten o'clock before a shadow darkened the open door; and Constable Jor came in. He looked shamefaced.

"I've got an order here for your arrest," he said.

"Tell those who sent you," Fara replied deliberately, "that I resisted arrest—with a gun."

The deed followed the words with such rapidity that Jor blinked. He stood like that for a moment, a big, sleepy-looking man, staring at that gleaming, magical revolver; then:

"I have a summons here ordering you to appear at the great court of Ferd this afternoon. Will you accept it?"

"Certainly."

"Then you will be there?"

"I'll send my lawyer," said Fara. "Just drop the summons on the floor there. Tell them I took it."

The weapon shop man had said: "Do not ridicule by word any legal measure of the Imperial authorities. Simply disobey them."

Jor went out, and seemed relieved. It took an hour before Mayor Mel Dale came pompously through the door.

"See here, Fara Clark," he bellowed from the doorway. "You can't get away with this. This is defiance of the law."

Fara was silent as his honor waddled farther into the building. It was puzzling, almost amazing, that Mayor Dale would risk his plump, treasured body. Puzzlement ended as the mayor said in a low voice:

"Good work, Fara; I knew you had it in you. There's dozens of us in Glay behind you, so stick it out. I had to yell at you just now, because there's a crowd outside. Yell back at me, will you? Let's have a real name-calling. But, first, a word of warning: the manager of the Automatic Repair Shop is on his way here with his bodyguards, two of them—"

Shakily, Fara watched the mayor go out. The crisis was at hand. He braced himself, thought: "Let them come, let them—"

It was easier than he had thought—for the men who entered the shop turned pale when they saw the holstered revolver. There was a violence of blustering, nevertheless, that narrowed finally down to:

"Look here," the man said, "we've got your note for twelve thousand one hundred credits. You're not going to deny you owe that money."

"I'll buy it back," said Fara in a stony voice, "for exactly half, not a cent more."

The strong-jawed young man looked at him for a long time. "We'll take it," he said finally, curtly.

Fara said: "I've got the agreement here—"

His first customer was old man Miser Lan Harris. Fara stared at the long-faced oldster with a vast surmise, and his first, amazed comprehension came of how the weapon shop must have settled on Harris's lot—by arrangement.

It was an hour after Harris had gone that Creel's mother stamped into the shop. She closed the door.

"Well," she said, "you did it, eh? Good work. I'm sorry if I seemed rough with you when you came to my place, but we weapon-shop supporters can't afford to take risks for those who are not on our side.

"But never mind that. I've come to take Creel home. The important thing is to return everything to normal as quickly as possible."

It was over; incredibly it was over. Twice, as he walked home that night, Fara stopped in mid-stride, and wondered if it had not all been a dream. The air was like wine. The little world of Glay spread before him, green and gracious, a peaceful paradise where time had stood still.

THE WABBLER
Murray Leinster

The stories of war are, by usual popular assumption, the stories of warriors, warmongers, and victims. Not so long ago, the idea that the weapon itself might be a character—a being that perceives and acts and is acted upon—seemed wildly fantastic. It seems much less so now.

THE WABBLER WENT WESTWARD, with a dozen of its fellows, by night and in the belly of a sleek, swift-flying thing. There were no lights anywhere save the stars overhead. There was a sustained, furious roaring noise, which was the sound the sleek thing made in flying. The Wabbler lay in its place, with its ten-foot tail coiled neatly about its lower end, and waited with a sort of deadly patience for the accomplishment of its destiny. It and all its brothers were pear-shaped, with absurdly huge and blunt-ended horns, and with small round holes where eyes might have been, and shielded vents where they might have had mouths. They looked chinless, somehow. They also looked alive, and inhuman, and filled with a sort of passionless hate. They seemed like bodiless demons out of some metallic hell. It was not possible to feel any affection for them. Even the men who handled them felt only a sort of vengeful hope in their capacities.

The Wabblers squatted in their racks for long hours. It was very cold, but they gave no sign. The sleek, swift-flying thing roared on and roared on. The Wabblers waited. Men moved somewhere in the flying thing, but they did not come where the Wabblers were until the very end. But somehow, when a man came and inspected each one of them very carefully and poked experimentally about the bottoms of the racks in which the Wabblers lay, they knew that the time had come.

The man went away. The sleek thing tilted a little. It seemed to climb. The air grew colder, but the Wabblers—all of them—were indifferent. Air was not their element. Then, when it was very, very cold indeed, the roaring noise of the flying thing ceased abruptly. The cessation of the noise was startling. Presently little whistling, whispering noises took the place of the roar, as hearing adjusted to a new level of sound. That whistling and whining noise was wind, flowing past the wings of the flying thing. Presently the air was a little warmer—but still very cold. The flying thing was gliding, motors off, and descending at a very gradual slant.

The Wabbler was the fourth in the row of its brothers on the port side of the flying thing. It did not stir, of course, but it felt an atmosphere of grim and savage anticipation. It seemed that all the brothers coldly exchanged greetings and farewell. The time had definitely come.

The flying thing leveled out. Levers and rods moved in the darkness of its belly. The feeling of anticipation increased. Then, suddenly, there were only eleven of the Wabblers. Wind roared where the twelfth had been. There were ten. There were nine, eight, seven, six—

The Wabbler hurtled downward through blackness. There were clouds overhead, now. In all the world there was no speck of actual light. But below there was a faint luminosity. The Wabbler's tail uncurled and writhed flexibly behind it. Wind screamed past its ungainly form. It went plunging down and down and down, its round holes—which looked so much like eyes—seeming incurious and utterly impassive. The luminosity underneath separated into streaks of bluish glow, which were phosphorescences given off by the curling tips of waves. Off to westward there was a brighter streak of such luminosity. It was surf.

The Wabbler

Splash! The Wabbler plunged into the water with a flare of luminescence and a thirty-foot spout of spume and spray rising where it struck. But then that spouting ceased, and the Wabbler was safely under water. It dived swiftly for twenty feet. Perhaps thirty. Then its falling checked. It swung about, and its writhing tail settled down below it. For a little while it seemed almost to intend to swim back to the surface. But bubbles came from the shielded opening which seemed to be a mouth. It hung there in the darkness of the sea—but now and then there were little fiery streaks of light as natives of the ocean swam about it—and then slowly, slowly, slowly it settled downward. Its ten-foot tail seemed to waver a little, as if groping.

Presently it touched. Ooze. Black ooze. Sea bottom. Sixty feet overhead the waves marched to and fro in darkness. Somehow, through the still silence, there came a muffled vibration. That was the distant surf, beating upon a shore. The Wabbler hung for an instant with the very tip of its tail barely touching the bottom. Then it made small sounds inside itself. More bubbles came from the round place like a mouth. It settled one foot; two feet; three. Three feet of its tail rested on the soft ooze. It hung, pear-shaped, some seven feet above the ocean bottom, with the very tip of its horns no more than four feet higher yet. There was fifty feet of empty sea above it. This was not its destiny. It waited passionlessly for what was to happen.

There was silence save for the faint vibration from the distant surf. But there was an infinitesimal noise, also, within the Wabbler's bulk. A rhythmic, insistent, hurried *tick-tick-tick-tick—* It was the Wabbler's brain in action.

Time passed. Above the sea the sleek, swift-flying thing bellowed suddenly, far away. It swerved, and went roaring back in the direction from which it had come. Its belly was empty, now, and somewhere in the heaving sea there were other Wabblers, each one now waiting as the fourth Wabbler did, for the thing that its brain expected. Minutes and minutes passed. The seas marched to and fro. The faraway surf rumbled and roared against the shore. And higher yet, above the clouds, a low-hanging and invisible moon dipped down toward a horizon which did not show anywhere. But the Wabbler waited.

The tide came. Here, so far from the pounding surf, the stirring of the lower levels of the sea was slight indeed. But the tide moved in toward the land. Slowly, the pressure of water against one of the Wabbler's sides became evident. The Wabbler leaned infinitesimally toward the shore. Presently its flexible tail ceased to be curved where it lay upon the ooze. It straightened out. There were little bluish glows where it stirred the phosphorescent mud. Then the Wabbler moved. Shoreward. It trailed its tail behind it and left a little glowing track of ghostly light.

Fish swam about it. Once there was a furry purring sound, and propellers pushed an invisible floating thing across the surface of the sea. But it was far away and the Wabbler was impassive. The tide flowed. The Wabbler moved in little jerks. Sometimes three feet or four, and sometimes eight or ten. Once, where the sea bottom slanted downward for a space, it moved steadily for almost a hundred yards. It came to rest, then, swaying a little. Presently it jerked onward once more. Somewhere an indefinite distance away were its brothers, moving in the same fashion. The Wabbler went on and on, purposefully, moved by the tide.

Before the tide turned, the Wabbler had moved two miles nearer to the land. But it did not move in a straight line. Its trailing, flexible tail kept it in the deepest water and the strongest current. It moved very deliberately and almost always in small jerks, and it followed the current. The current was strongest where it moved toward a harbor entrance. In moving two miles shoreward, the Wabbler also moved more than two miles nearer to a harbor.

There came a time, though, when the tide slackened. The Wabbler ceased to move. For half an hour it hung quite still, swaying a little and progressing not at all, while the *tick-tick-tick-tick* of its brain measured patience against intent. At the end of the half-hour there were small clanking noises within its body. Its shielded mouth emitted bubbles. It sank, and checked, and gave off more bubbles, and sank again. It eased itself very cautiously and very gently into the ooze. Then it gave off more bubbles and lay at rest.

It waited there, its brain ticking restlessly within it, but with its appearance of eyes impassive. It lay in the darkness like some creature from another world, awaiting a foreordained event.

For hours it lay still with no sign of any activity at all. Toward the end of those hours, a very faint graying of the upper sea became manifest. It was very dim indeed. It was not enough, in all likelihood, for even the Wabbler to detect the slight movement of semifloating objects along the sea floor, moved by the ebb tide. But there came a time when even such movements ceased. Again the sea was still. It was full ebb. And now the Wabbler stirred.

It clanked gently, and wavered where it lay in the ooze. There was a cloud of stirred-up mud, as if it had emitted jets of water from its under parts. It wabbled to one side and the other, straining, and presently its body was free, and a foot or two and then four or five feet of its tail—but it still writhed and wabbled spasmodically—and then suddenly it left the sea floor and floated free.

But only for a moment. Almost immediately its tail swung free, the Wabbler spat out bubbles and descended gently to the bottom again. It rested upon the tip of its tail. It spat more bubbles. One—two—three feet of its tail rested on the mud. It waited. Presently the flood tide moved it again.

It floated always with the current. Once it came to a curve in the deeper channel to which it had found its way, and the tide tended to sweep it up and out beyond the channel. But its tail resisted the attempt. In the end, the Wabbler swam grandly back to the deeper water. The current was stronger there. It went on and on at a magnificent two knots.

But when the current slowed again as the time of tide-change neared, the Wabbler stopped again. It swung above the yard-length of its tail upon the mud. Its brain went *tick-tick-tick-tick* and it made noises. It dribbled bubbles. It sank, and checked, and dribbled more bubbles, and sank cautiously again— It came cautiously to rest in the mud.

During this time of waiting, the Wabbler heard many sounds. Many times during slack tide, and during ebb tide, too, the water brought humming, purring noises of engines. Once a boat came very near. There was a curious hissing sound in the water. Something—a long line—passed very close overhead. A mine-sweeper and a mine-sweep patrolled the sea, striving to detect and uproot submarine mines. But the Wabbler had no anchor cable for the sweep to catch. It lay impassively upon the bottom. But its eyes stared upward with a deadly calm until the mine-sweeper passed on its way.

Once more during the light hours the Wabbler shook itself free of the bottom ooze and swam on with the tide. And once more—with another wait on the mud while the tide flowed out—at night. But day and night meant little to the Wabbler. Its ticking brain went on tirelessly. It rested, and swam, and swam, and rested, with a machinelike and impassive pertinacity, and always it moved toward places where the tide moved faster and with channels more distinct.

At last it came to a place where the water was no more than forty feet deep, and a distinct, greenish-blue light came down from the surface sunshine. In that light the Wabbler was plainly visible. It had acquired a coating of seaweed and slime which seemed to form a sort of aura of wavering greenish tentacles. Its seeming of eyes appeared now to be small and snakelike and very wise and venomous. It was still chinless, and its trailing tail made it seem more than ever like some bodiless demon out of a metallic hell. And now it came to a place where for a moment its tail caught in some minor obstruction, and as it tugged at the catch, one of its brothers floated by. It passed within twenty feet of the fourth Wabbler, and they could see each other clearly. But the fourth Wabbler was trapped. It wavered back and forth in the flood tide, trying to pull free, as its fellow swam silently and implacably onward.

Some twenty minutes after that passage there was a colossal explosion somewhere, and after that very many fuzzy, purring noises in the sea. The Wabbler may have known what had happened, or it may not. A submarine net across a harbor entrance is not a thing of which most creatures have knowledge, but it was a part of the Wabbler's environment. Its *tick-tick-tick*ing brain may have interpreted the explosion quite correctly as the destiny of its brother encountering that barrier. It is more likely that the brain only noted with relief that the concussion had broken the grip of the obstruction in the mud. The Wabbler went onward in the wake of its fellow. It went sedately, and solemnly, and with a sort of unholy purposefulness, following the tidal current. Presently there was a great net that stretched across the channel, far beyond any distance that the Wabbler could be expected to see. But right where the Wabbler would pass, there was a monstrous gaping hole in that net. Off to one side there was the tail of another Wabbler, shattered away from that other Wabbler's bulk.

The fourth Wabbler went through the hole. It was very simple indeed. Its tail scraped for a moment, and then it was inside the harbor. And then the *tick-tick-tick*ing of the Wabbler's brain was very crisp and incisive indeed, because this was its chance for the accomplishment of its destiny. It listened for sounds of engines, estimating their loudness with an uncanny precision, and within its rounded brainpan it measured things as abstract as variations in the vertical component of terrestrial magnetism. There were many sounds and many variations to note, too, because surface craft swarmed about the scene of a recent violent explosion. Their engines purred and rumbled, and their steel hulks made marked local changes in magnetic force. But none of them came quite close enough to the Wabbler to constitute its destiny.

It went on and on as the flood tide swept in. The harbor was a busy one, with many small craft moving about, and more than once in these daylight hours flying things alighted upon the water and took off again. But it happened that none came sufficiently near. An hour after its entrance into the harbor the Wabbler was in a sort of eddy, in a basin, and it made four slow, hitching circuits about the same spot—during one of which it came near to serried ranks of piling—before the time of slack water. But even here the Wabbler, after swaying a little without making progress for perhaps twenty minutes, made little clanking noises inside itself and dribbled out bubbles and eased itself down in the mud to wait.

It lay there, canted a little and staring up with its small round, seeming eyes with a look of unimpassioned expectancy. Small boats roved overhead. Once engines rumbled, and a wooden-hulled craft swam on the surface of the water to the very dock whose pilings the Wabbler had seen. Then creaking sounds emanated from those pilings. The Wabbler may have known that unloading-cranes were at work. But this was not its destiny, either.

There came other sounds of greater import. Clankings of gears. A definite, burbling rush of water. It continued and continued. The Wabbler could not possibly be expected to understand, of course, that such burbling underwater sounds are typical of a drydock being filled—the filling beginning near low tide when a great ship is to leave at high. Especially, perhaps, the Wabbler could not be expected to know that a great warship had occupied a vastly important drydock and that its return to active service would restore much power to an enemy fleet. Certainly it could not know that another great warship waited impatiently to be repaired in the same basin. But the restless *tick-tick-tick-tick* which was the Wabbler's brain was remarkably crisp and incisive.

When flood tide began once more, the Wabbler jetted water and wabbled to and fro until it broke free of the bottom. It hung with a seeming impatience—wreathed in seaweed and coated with greenish slime—above the tail which dangled down to the harbor mud. It looked alive, and inhuman, and chinless, and it looked passionately demoniac, and it looked like something out of a submarine Gehenna. And presently, when the flood tide began to flow and the eddy about the docks and the drydock gates began, the Wabbler inched as if purposefully toward the place where water burbled through flooding valves.

Sounds in the air did not reach the Wabbler. Sounds under water did. It heard the grinding rumble of steam winches, and it heard the screeching sound as the drydock gates swung open. They were huge gates, and they made a considerable eddy of their own. The Wabbler swam to the very center of that eddy and hung there, waiting. Now, for the first time, it seemed excited. It seemed to quiver a little. Once when it seemed that the eddy might bring it to the surface, it bubbled impatiently from the vent which appeared to be a mouth. And its brain went *tick-tick-tick-tick* within it, and inside its brainpan it measured variations in the vertical component of terrestrial magnetism, and among such measurements it noted the effect of small tugs which came near but did not enter the drydock. They only sent lines within, so they could haul the warship out. But the tugs were not the Wabbler's destiny, either.

It heard their propellers thrashing, and they made, to be sure, a very fine noise. But the Wabbler quivered with eagerness as somewhere within itself it noted a vast variation in the vertical magnetic component, which increased and increased steadily. That was the warship moving very slowly out of its place in the drydock. It moved very slowly but very directly toward the Wabbler, and the Wabbler knew that its destiny was near.

Somewhere very far away there was the dull, racking sound of an explosion. The Wabbler may have realized that another of its brothers had achieved its destiny, but paid no heed. Its own destiny approached. The steel prow of the battleship drew nearer and nearer, and then the bow plates were overhead, and something made a tiny click inside the Wabbler. Destiny was certain, now. It waited, quivering. The mass of steel within the range of its senses grew greater and greater. The strain of restraint grew more intense. The *tick-tick-tick-tick*ing of the Wabbler's brain seemed to accelerate to a frantic—to an intolerable—pace. And then—

The Wabbler achieved its destiny. It turned into a flaming ball of incandescent gasses—three hundred pounds of detonated high explosive—squarely under the keel of a thirty-five-thousand-ton battleship which at the moment was only halfway out of a drydock. The watertight doors of the battleship were open, and its auxiliary power was off, so they could not be closed. There was much need for this drydock, and repairs were not completed in it. But it was the Wabbler's destiny to end all that. In three minutes the battleship was lying crazily on the harbor bottom, half in and half out of the drydock. She careened as she sank, and her masts and fighting tops demolished sheds by the drydock walls. Battleship and dock alike were out of action for the duration of the war.

And the Wabbler—

A long, long time afterward—years afterward—salvage divers finished cutting up the sunken warship for scrap. The last irregularly cut mass of metal went up on the salvage slings. The last diver down went stumbling about the muddy harbor water. His heavy, weighted shoes kicked up something. He fumbled to see if anything remained to be salvaged. He found a ten-foot, still-flexible tail of metal. The rest of the Wabbler had ceased to exist. Chronometer, tide-time gear, valves, compressed-air tanks, and all the balance of its intricate innards had been blown to atoms when the Wabbler achieved its destiny. Only the flexible metal tail remained intact.

The salvage diver considered that it was not worth sending the sling down for, again. He dropped it in the mud and jerked on the life line to be hauled up to the surface. ■

CONQUEST BY DEFAULT
Vernor Vinge

At least among humans in historic times, wars have been conflicts of governments. Might something inherent in the very concept of "government" be a fundamental cause of war? For us, the concept is so deeply ingrained that government and civilization tend to seem inseparable, and it's hard to imagine alternatives. But when we meet other intelligences, they may begin to show us just how narrow our preconceptions are—and vice versa.

THIS ALL HAPPENED A LONG TIME AGO, and almost twenty light-years from where we're standing now. You honor me here tonight as a humanitarian, as a man who has done something to bring a temporary light to the eternal darkness that is our universe. But you deceive yourselves. I made the situation just civilized enough so that its true brutality, shed of bloody drapery, can be seen.

I see you don't believe what I say. In this whole audience I suspect that only aMelmwn truly understands—and she better than I. Not one of you has ever been kicked in the teeth by these particular facts of life. Perhaps if I told you the story as it happened to me—I could make you *feel* the horror you hear me describe.

Two centuries ago, the Pwrlyg Spice & Trading Company completed the first interstellar flight. They were thirty years ahead of their nearest competitors. They had a whole planet at their disposal, except for one minor complication . . .

The natives were restless.

My attention was unevenly divided between the beautiful girl who had just introduced herself, and the ancient city that shimmered in the hot air behind her.

Mary Dahlmann. That was a hard name to pronounce, but I had studied Australian for almost two years, and I was damned if I couldn't say a name. I clumsily worked my way through a response. "Yes, ah, Miss, ah, Dahlmann, I am Ron Melmwn, and I am the new Company anthropologist. But I thought the Vice President for Aboriginal Affairs was going to meet me."

Ngagn Chev dug me in the ribs, "Say, you really can speak that gabble, can't you, Melmwn?" he whispered in Mikin. Chev was vice president for violence—an O.K. guy, but an incurable bigot.

Mary Dahlmann smiled uncertainly at this exchange. Then she answered my question. "Mr. Horlig will be right along. He asked me to meet you. My father is Chief Representative for Her Majesty's Government." I later learned that Her Majesty was two centuries dead. "Here, let me show you off the field." She grasped my wrist for a second—an instant. I guess I jerked back. Her hand fell away and her eagerness vanished. "This way," she said icily, pointing to a gate in the force fence surrounding the Pwrlyg landing field. I wished very much I had not pulled away from her touch. Even though she was so blond and pale, she was a woman, and in a weird way, pretty. Besides, *she* had overcome whatever feelings she had against *us*.

There was an embarrassed silence, as the five of us cleared the landing craft and walked toward the gate.

The sun was bright—brighter than ours ever shines over Miki. It was also very dry. There were no clouds in the sky. Twenty or thirty people worked in the field. Most were Mikin, but here and there were clusters of Terrans. Several were standing around a device in the corner of the field where the fence made a joint to angle out toward the beach. The Terrans knelt by the device.

Orange fire flickered from the end of the machine, followed by a loud *guda-bam-*

Conquest by Default 91

bam-bam. Even as my conscious mind concluded that we were under fire, I threw myself on the ground and flattened into the lowest profile possible. You've heard the bromide about combat making life more real. I don't know about that, but it's certainly true that when you are flat against the ground with your face in the dirt, the whole universe looks different. That red-tan sand was *hot*. Sharp little stones bit into my face. Two inches before my face a clump of sage had assumed the dimensions of a vola tree.

I cocked my head microscopically to see how the others were doing. They were all down, too. Correction: that idiot Earthgirl was still standing. More than a second after the attack she was still working toward the idea that someone was trying to kill her. Only a dement or a Little Sister brought up in a convent could be so dense. I reached out, grabbed her slim ankle, and jerked. She came down hard. Once down, she didn't move.

Ngagn Chev and some accountant, whose name I didn't remember, were advancing toward the slug-thrower. That accountant had the fastest low-crawl I have ever seen. The Terrans frantically tried to lower the barrels of their gun—but it was really primitive and couldn't search more than five degrees. The little accountant zipped up to within twenty meters of the gun, reached into his weapons pouch, and tossed a grenade toward the Earthmen and their weapon. I dug my face into the dirt and waited for the explosion. There was only a muffled thud. It was a gas bomb—not frag. A green mist hung for an instant over the gun and the Terrans.

When I got to them, Chev was already complimenting the accountant on his throw.

"A private quarrel?" I asked Chev.

The security chief looked faintly surprised. "Why no. These fellows"—he pointed at the unconscious Terrans—"belong to some conspiracy to drive us off the planet. They're really a pitiful collection." He pointed to the weapon. It was composed of twenty barrels welded to three metal hoops. By turning a crank, the barrels could be rotated past a belt cartridge feeder. "That gun is hardly more accurate than a shrapnel bomb. This is nothing very dangerous, but I'm going to catch chaos for letting them get within the perimeter. And I can tell you, I am going to scorch those agents of mine that let these abos sneak in. Anyway, we got the pests alive. They'll be able to answer some questions." He nudged one of the bodies over with his boot. "Sometimes I think it would be best to exterminate the race. They don't occupy much territory but they sure are a nuisance.

"See," he picked up a card from the ground and handed it to me. It was lettered in neat Mikin: MERLYN SENDS YOU DEATH. "Merlyn is the name of the 'terrorist' organization—it's nonprofit, I think. Terrans are a queer lot."

Several Company armsmen showed up then and Chev proceeded to bawl them out in a very thorough way. It was interesting, but a little embarrassing, too. I turned and started toward the main gate. I still had to meet my new boss—Horlig, the Vice President for Abo Affairs.

Where was the Terran girl? In the fuss I had completely forgotten her. But now she was gone. I ran back to where we stood when the first shots were fired. I felt cold and a little sick as I looked at the ground where she had fallen. Maybe it had been a superficial wound. Maybe the medics had carried her off. But whatever the explanation, a pool of blood almost thirty centimeters wide lay on the sand. As I watched, it soaked into the sand and became a dark brown grease spot, barely visible against the reddish-tan soil. As far as appearances go, it could have been human blood.

Horlig was a Gloyn. I should have known from his name. As it was, I got quite a surprise when I met him. With his pale gray skin and hair, Herul Horlig could easily be mistaken for an Earthman. The vice president for aboriginal affairs was either an Ostentatious Simplist or very proud of his neolithic grandparents. He wore wooden shin plates and a black breech-clout. His only weapon was a machine dartgun strapped to his wrist.

It quickly became clear that the man was unhappy with me as an addition to his staff. I could understand that. As a professional, my opinions might carry more weight with the board of directors and the president than his. Horlig did his best to hide his displeasure, though. He seemed a hard-headed, sincere fellow who could be ruthless, but nevertheless believed whatever he did was right. He unbent considerably during our meal at Supply Central. When I mentioned I wanted to interview some abos, he surprised me by suggesting we fly over to the native city that evening.

When we left Central, it was already dark. We walked to the parking lot, and got into Horlig's car. Three minutes later we were ghosting over the suburbs of Adelaide-west. Horlig cast a practiced eye upon the queer rectangular street pattern below, and brought us down on the lawn of a two-story wood house. I started to get out.

"Just a minute, Melmwn," said Horlig. He grabbed a pair of earphones and set the TV on pan. I didn't say anything as he scanned the quiet neighborhood for signs of hostile activity. I was interested: usually a Simplist will avoid using advanced defense techniques. Horlig explained as he set the car's computer on SENTRY and threw open the hatch:

"Our illustrious board of directors dictates that we employ 'all security precautions at our disposal.' Bunk. Even when these Earth creatures attack us, they are less violent than good-natured street brawlers back home. I don't think there have been more than thirty murders in this city since Pwrlyg landed twenty years ago."

I jumped to the soft grass and looked around. Things really were quiet. Gas lamps lit the cobblestone street and dimly outlined the wood buildings up and down the lane. Weak yellow light emerged from windows. From down the street came faint laughter of some party. Our landing had gone unnoticed.

Demoneyes. I stepped back sharply. The twin yellow disks glittered maniacally, as the cat turned to face us, and the lamps' light came back from its eyes. The little animal turned slowly and walked disdainfully across the lawn. This was a bad omen indeed. I would have to watch the Signs very carefully tonight. Horlig was not disturbed at all. I don't think he knew I was brought up a witch-fearer. We started up the walk toward the nearest house.

"You know, Melmwn, this isn't just any old native we're visiting. He's an anthropologist, Earth style. Of course, he's just as insipid as the rest of the bunch, but our staff is forced to do quite a bit of liaison work with him."

An anthropologist! This was going to be interesting, both as an exchange of information and of research procedures.

"In addition, he's the primary representative chosen by the Australian *gowernmen'* . . . a *gowernmen'* is sort of a huge corporation, as far as I can tell."

"Uh-huh." As a matter of fact, I knew a lot more about the mysterious *government* concept than Horlig. My Scholarate thesis was a theoretical study of macro organizations. The paper was almost rejected because my instructors claimed it was an analysis of a patent impossibility. Then came word that three macro organizations existed on Earth.

We climbed the front porch steps. Horlig pounded on the door. "The fellow's name is Nalman."

I translated his poor pronunciation back to the probable Australian original: Dahlmann! Perhaps I could find out what happened to the Earthgirl.

There were shuffling steps from within. Whoever it was did not even bother to look us over through a spy hole. Earthmen were nothing if not trusting. We were confronted by a tall, middle-aged man with thin, silvery hair. His hand quavered slightly as he removed the pipe from his mouth. Either he was in an extremity of fear or he had terrible coordination.

But when he spoke, I knew there was no fear. "Mr. Horlig. Won't you come in?" The words and tone were mild, but in that mildness rested an immense confidence. In the past I had heard that tone only from Umpires. It implied that neither storm, nor struggle, nor crumbling physical prowess could upset the mind behind the voice. That's a lot to get out of six quiet words—but it was all there.

When we were settled in Scholar Dahlmann's den, Horlig made the introductions. Horlig understood Australian fairly well, but his accent was atrocious.

"As you must surely know, Scholar Dahlmann, the objective voyage time to our home planet, Epsilon Eridani II, is almost twelve years. Three days ago the third Pwrlyg Support Fleet arrived and assumed a parking orbit around the Earth. At this instant, they soar omnipotent over the lands of your people." Dahlmann just smiled. "In any case, the first passengers have been unfrozen and brought down to the Pwrlyg Ground Base. This is Scholar Ron Melmwn, the anthropologist that the Company has brought in with the Fleet."

From behind his thick glasses, Dahlmann inspected me with new interest. "Well, I certainly am happy to meet a Mikin anthropologist. Our meeting is something of a first, I believe."

"I think so, too. Your institutions are ill-reported to us on Miki. This is natural, since Pwrlyg is primarily interested in the commercial and immigration prospects of your northern hemisphere. I want to correct the situation. During my stay I hope to use you and other Terrans for source material in my study of your history and, uh, government. It's especially good luck that I meet a professional like yourself."

Dahlmann seemed happy to discuss his people and soon we were immersed in Terran history and cultures. Much of what he told me I knew from reports received, but I let him tell the whole story.

It seems that two hundred years before, there was a high-technology culture in the northern hemisphere. The way Dahlmann spoke, it was very nearly Mikin caliber—the North People even had some primitive form of space flight. Then there was a war. A war is something like a fight, only much bigger, bigger even than an antitrust action. They exploded more than 12,500 megatons of bombs on their own cities. In addition, germ cultures were released to kill anybody who survived the fusion bombs. Without radiation screens and panphagic viruses, it was a slaughter. Virtually all the mammals in the northern hemisphere were destroyed and, according to Dahlmann, there was, for a while, the fear that the radiation poisons and disease strains would wipe out life in the South World, too.

It is very difficult to imagine how anything like that could get started in the first place—the cause of "war" was one of the objects of my research. Of course the gross explanation was that the Terrans never developed the Umpire System or the Concept of Chaos. Instead they used the gargantuan organizations called "governments." But the underlying question was why they chose this weird governmental path at all. Were the Terrans essentially subhuman—or is it just luck that we Mikins discovered the True Way?

The war didn't discourage the Terrans from their fundamental errors. Three governments rose from the ashes of war. The Australian, the Sudamerican, and the Zulunder. Even the smallest nation, Australia, had one thousand times as many people as the Pwrlyg Spice & Trading Company. And remember that Pwrlyg is already as a big as a group can get without being slapped with an antitrust ruling by the Umpires.

I forgot my surroundings as Dahlmann went on to explain the present power structure, the struggle of the two stronger nations to secure colonies in portions of the northern hemisphere where the war poisons had dissipated. This was a very dangerous situation, according to the Terran anthropologist, since there were many disease types dormant in the northern hemisphere that could start hellish plagues in the South World, for the Terrans were still more than a century behind the technology they had achieved before the blowup.

Through all this discussion, Horlig maintained an almost contemptuous silence, not listening to what we were saying so much as observing us as specimens. Finally he interrupted. "Well, I'm glad to see you both hit it off so well. It's getting too late for me, though. I'll have to take your leave. No, you don't have to come back just yet, Melmwn. I'll send the car back here on auto after I get to Base."

"You don't have to bother with that, Horlig. Things look pretty tame around here. I can walk back."

"No," Horlig said definitely. "We have regulations. And there is always this Merlyn, you know."

The Merlyn bunglers didn't frighten me, but I remembered that cat's Demoneyes. Suddenly I was happy to fly back. After Horlig had left, we returned to the den and its dim gas mantle lamps. I could understand why Dahlmann's eyesight was so bad—you try reading at night without electric lights for a couple decades and you'll go blind, too. He rummaged around in his desk and drew out a pouch of "tobacco." He fumbled the ground leaves into the bowl of his pipe and tamped them down with a clumsy forefinger. I thought he was going to burn his face when he lit the mixture. Back home, anyone with coordination that poor would be dead in less than two days, unless he secluded himself in a pacific enclave. This Terran culture was truly alien. It was different along a dimension we had never imagined, except in a few mathematical theories of doubtful validity.

The Terran sat back and regarded me for a long moment. Behind those thick lenses his eyes loomed large and wise. Now I was the one who seemed helpless. Finally he pulled back the curtains and inspected the lawn and the place where the car had rested. "I believe, Scholar Melmwn, that you are a reasonable and intelligent individual. I hope that you are even more than that. Do you realize that you are attending the execution of a race?"

This took me completely by surprise. "What! What do you mean?"

He appeared to ignore my question. "I knew when you people first landed and we saw your machines: our culture is doomed. I had hoped that we could escape with our lives—though in our own history, few have been so lucky. I hoped that your social sciences would be as advanced as your physical. But I was wrong.

"Your vice president for aboriginal affairs arrived with the Second 'wrlyg Fleet. Is genocide the 'wrlyg policy or is it Horlig's private scheme?"

This was too much. "I find your questions insulting, Terran! The Pwrlyg Company intends you no harm. Our interests are confined to reclaiming and colonizing areas of your planet that you admit are too hot for you to handle."

Now Dahlmann was on the defensive. "I apologize, Scholar Melmwn, for my discourtesy. I dived into the subject too hastily. I don't mean to offend you. Let me describe my fears and the reasons for them. I believe that Herul Horlig is not content with the cultural destruction of Earth. He would like to see all Terrans dead. Officially his job is to promote cooperation between our races and to eliminate possible frictions. In fact, he has played the opposite role. Since he arrived, his every act has increased our mutual antagonism. Take, for instance, the 'courtesy call' he made to the Zulunder capital. He and that armed forces chief of yours, Noggin Chem—is that how you pronounce the name?"

"Ngagn Chev," I corrected.

"They breezed into Pret armed to the teeth—fifteen air tanks and a military airspace craft. The Zulunder government requested that Horlig return the spaceship to orbit before they initiate talks. In reponse, the Mikins destroyed half the city. At the time I hoped that it was just the act of some demented gunner, but Horlig staged practically the same performance at Buenos Aires, the capital of Sudamerica. And this time he had no pretext whatsoever, since the Americans bent over backwards trying to avoid a clash. Every chance he gets, the man tries to prove how vicious Mikins can be."

I made a note to check on these events when I returned to Base. Aloud I said: "Then you believe that Horlig is trying to provoke terrorist movements like this Merlyn thing, so he'll have an excuse to kill all Terrans?"

Dahlmann didn't answer immediately. He carefully pulled back the curtain again and looked into the yard. The aircar had not yet returned. I think he realized that the mikes aboard the car could easily record what we were saying. "That's not quite what I mean, Scholar Melmwn. I believe that Horlig *is* Merlyn."

I snorted disbelief.

"I know it sounds ridiculous—but everything fits. Just take the word 'Merlyn.' In Australian this refers to a magician who lived ages ago in England—that was one of the great pre-war nations in the northern hemisphere. At the same time it is a word that easily comes to the lips of a Mikin since it is entirely pronounceable within your phoneme system—it contains no front oral stops. With its magical connotations, it is designed to set fear in Mikins. The word Merlyn is a convenient handle for the fear and hatred that Mikins will come to associate with Terran activities. But note—we Terrans are a very unsuperstitious lot, especially the Australians and the Zulunders. And very few Terrans realize how superstitious many Mikins—the witch-fearers and the demon-mongers—are. The Merlyn concept is the invention of a Mikin mind."

Dahlmann rushed on to keep me from interrupting. "Consider also: When terrorist attacks are thwarted and the Terrans captured, they turn out to be ill-equipped rumdums—not the skilled agents of some world-wide plot. But whenever great damage is done—say the detonation of the Company ammo stores last year—no one is caught. In fact, it is almost impossible to imagine how the job could be pulled off without Mikin technology. At first I discounted this theory, because so many Mikins were killed in the ammo blast, but I have since learned that you people do not regard such violence as improper business procedure."

"It depends on who you are working for. There are plenty of Violent Nihilists on Miki, and occasionally they have their own companies. If Pwrlyg is one such, he's been keeping the fact a secret."

"What it adds up to is that Horlig is creating an artificial threat, which he believes will eventually justify genocide. One last element of proof. You came in on a Fleet landing craft this afternoon, did you not? Horlig was supposed to greet you. He invited me out to meet you on the field, as the chief representative of Her Majesty's Government in Australia. This is the first friendly gesture the man has made in three years. As it happened, I couldn't go. I sent my daughter, Mary. But when you actually landed, Horlig got a sliver from his shin board, or something equally idiotic, and so couldn't go onto the field—where just five minutes later a group of 'Merlyn's Men' tried to shoot the lot of you."

Mary Dahlmann. I stuttered over the next question. "How . . . how is your daughter, Scholar Dahlmann?"

Dahlmann was nonplussed for a moment. "She's fine. Apparently someone pulled her out of the line of fire. A bloody nose was the sum total of her 'injuries.' "

For some reason I felt great relief at this news. I looked at my watch; it was thirty minutes to midnight, the witching hour. Tonight especially I wanted to get back to Base before Demonsloose. And I hadn't known that Merlyn was the name of a wizard. I stood up. "You've certainly given me something to think about, Dahlmann. Of course you know where my sympathies ultimately lie, but I'll be alert for signs of the plot you speak of, and I won't tell anyone what you've told me."

The Terran rose. "That's all I ask." He led me out of the den, and into the darkened mainroom. The wood floor creaked comfortably beneath the thick carpet. Crystal goblets on wood shelving were outlined in faint glistening reflection from the den light. To the right a stairway led to the second floor. Was *she* up there sleeping, or out with some male? I wondered.

As we approached the door, something much more pertinent occurred to me. I touched Dahlmann's elbow; he stopped, ready to open the door. "A moment, Scholar Dahlmann. All the facts you present fit another theory: namely, that some Terran, expert in Mikin ways, yourself perhaps, has manufactured Merlyn and the rumor that members of the Pwrlyg Company are responsible for the conspiracy."

I couldn't tell for sure, but I think he smiled. "Your counter-proposal does indeed fit the facts. However, I am aware of the power that you Mikins have at your disposal, and how futile resistance would be." He opened the door. I stepped out onto the porch. "Good night," he said.

"Good night." I stood there for several seconds, listening to his retreating footsteps, and puzzling over our last exchange.

I turned and was halfway across the porch when a soft voice behind me asked, "And how did you like Daddy?" I jumped a good fifteen centimeters, spun around with my wrist gun extended. Mary Dahlmann sat on a wooden swing hung from the ceiling of the porch. She pushed the swing gently back and forth. I walked over and sat down beside her.

"He's an impressive and intelligent man," I answered.

"I want to thank you for pulling me down this afternoon." Her mind seemed to jump randomly from one topic to another.

"Uh, that's O.K. There really wasn't too much danger. The gun was so primitive that I imagine it's almost as unpleasant to be behind it as in front. I would've thought you'd be the first to recognize it as an attack. You must be familiar with Australian weapons."

"Are you kidding? The biggest gun I've ever seen was a 20mm rifle in a shooting exhibition."

"You mean you've never been under fire until today?" I saw that she hadn't. "I didn't mean to be insulting, Miss Dahlmann. I haven't really had much first-hand information about Terrans. That's one reason why I'm here."

She laughed. "If you're puzzled about us, then the feeling is mutual. Since my father became chief representative, he's been doing everything he can to interview Mikins and figure out the structure of your culture. I'll bet he spent half the night pumping you. As an anthropologist, you should be the best source he can find."

Apparently she wasn't aware of her father's true concerns.

"In the last three years we've managed to interview more than fifteen of you Mikins. It's crazy. You're all so different from one another. You claim you are all from the same continent, and yet each individual appears to have an entirely different cultural background. Some of you don't wear clothes at all, while others go around with every inch of their skin covered. Some, like Horlig, make a fetish of primitiveness. But we had one fellow here who had so many gadgets with him that he had to wear powered body armor. He was so heavy, he busted my father's favorite chair. We can't find any common denominator. Mikins believe in one god, or in many, or in none. At the same time, many of you are dreadfully superstitious. We've always wondered what aliens might be like, but we never guessed that— What's the matter?"

I pointed shakily at the creature in the street. She placed a reassuring hand on my arm. "Why, that's just a cat. Don't you have catlike creatures on Miki?"

"Certainly."

"Why the shock then? Are your cats poisonous or something?"

"Of course not. Many people keep them as pets. It's just that it's a bad sign to see one at night—an especially bad sign if it looks at you and its eyes glow." I was sorry when she withdrew her hand.

She looked at me closely. "I hope you won't be angry, Mr. Melmwn, but this is exactly what I mean. How can a race that travels between the stars believe in ill or good omens? Or have you developed magic as a science?"

"No, that's not it. Many Mikins don't believe in signs at all, and depending on whether you are a demon-monger or a witch-fearer, you recognize different signs. As for how I personally can believe in nonempirical, nonscientific signs—that's easy. There are many more causal relations in this universe than Mikin science will ever discover. I believe that witch-fearers have divined a few of these. And though I am quite a mild witch-fearer, I don't take any chances."

"But you are an anthropologist. I should think in your studies you would see so many different attitudes and superstitions that you would disregard your own."

I watched carefully as the cat went round the corner of the house. Then I turned to look at Mary Dahlmann. "Is that how it is with Terran anthropologists? Perhaps then I should not translate my occupation as 'anthropology.' Before Pwrlyg, I was employed by the Anavog Pacific Enclave & Motor Corporation. A fine group. As anthropologist, my job was to screen the background attitudes of prospective employees. For instance, it just wouldn't do to have a Cannibal and a Militant Vegetarian work next to each other on the production line—they'd kill each other inside of three hours, and the corporation would lose money."

She pushed the swing back with an agitated kick. "But now we're back where we started. How can a single culture produce both cannibals and 'militant' vegetarians?"

I thought about it. Her question really seemed to go beyond cultures entirely—right to the core of reality. I had practiced my specialty within the Mikin framework—where such questions never came up. Maybe I should start with something basic.

"Our system is founded on the Concept of Chaos. The universe is basically a dark and unhappy place—a place where evil and injustice and randomness rule. The ironic thing is that the very act of organization creates the potential for even greater ruin. Social organizations have a natural tendency to become monopolistic and inflexible. When they finally break down, it is a catastrophic debacle. So, we must accept a great deal of disorder and violence in our lives if we are to avoid a complete blowup later.

"Every Mikin is free to *try* anything. Naturally, in order to survive, groups of people cooperate—and from this you get the tens of thousands of organizations, corporations, and convents that make our civilization. But no group may become monopolistic. This is why we have Umpires. I don't think you have anything comparable. Umpires see that excessively large organizations are never formed. They keep our society from becoming rigid and unresponsive to the natural world. Our system has lasted a very long time." *Much longer than yours*, I added to myself.

She frowned. "I don't understand. Umpires? Is this some sort of police force? How do they keep governments from forming? What's to keep the Umpires from becoming a government themselves?"

If I didn't watch out, I was going to learn more about Miki than I did about Earth. Mary's questions opened doors I never knew existed. My answer was almost as novel to me as it was to her. "I suppose it's because the Umpire tradition is very old with us. With one minor exception, all Mikins have had this tradition for almost four thousand years. The Umpires probably originated as a priest class serving a number of different nomad tribes. There never were many Umps. They go unarmed. They have bred for intelligence and flexibility. There's quite a bit of, uh, mystery—which we take for granted—surrounding them. I believe that they live under the influence of some rather strange drugs. You might say that they are brainwashed. In all history, there is no period in which they have sought power. Though they spend most of their lives in the abstract study of behavior science, their real task is to watch society for signs of bigness.

"There's one watching Pwrlyg right now. If he decides that Pwrlyg is too big—and that's a distinct possibility, since there are almost twelve thousand Pwrlyg employees altogether—the Ump will issue an, uh, antitrust ruling, describing the situation and ordering certain changes. There is no appeal. Defiance of an antitrust ruling is the only deed that is recognized by all Mikins as a sin. When there is such defiance, all Mikins are bound to take antitrust action—that is, to destroy the criminal. Some antitrust actions have involved fusion bombs and armies—they're the closest thing we have to wars."

She didn't look convinced. "Frankly, I can't imagine how such a system could avoid becoming a dictatorship of 'Umpires.' "

"I feel the same incredulity about your civilization."

"How big are your 'organizations'?"

"It might be a single person. More than half the groups on Miki are just families or family groups. Anything goes unless it threatens stability—or becomes too large. The largest groups allowed are some of the innocuous religious types—the Little Brother Association, for instance. They preach approximately the principles I read of in your Christianity. But they don't proselytize, and so manage to avoid antitrust rulings. The largest 'hardware' organizations have about fifteen thousand employees."

"And how can a company support interstellar operations?"

"Yes, that's a very tricky point. Pwrlyg had to cooperate with several hundred industrial groups to do it. They came mighty close to antitrust."

She sat silently, thinking all this over. Then she asked, "When can we expect an antitrust ruling against the Australian government?"

I laughed, "You don't have to worry about that. No offense, but antitrust can only apply to human groupings."

She didn't like that at all, but she didn't argue it either. Instead she came back with, "Then that means we also don't have Umpire protection if Pwrlyg commits genocide upon us."

That was a nasty conclusion, but it fitted the letter of custom. Killing millions of humans would warrant antitrust, but Terrans weren't human.

For an instant I thought she was laughing, low and bitter. Then her face seemed to collapse and I knew she was crying. This was an unpleasant turn of events. Awkwardly, I put my arm around her shoulders and tried to comfort her. She no longer seemed to me an abo, but simply a person in pain. "Please, Mary Dahlmann. My people aren't monsters. We only want to use places on your planet that are uninhabited, that are too dangerous for you. Our presence will actually make Earth safer. When we colonize the North World, we'll null the radiation poisons and kill the war viruses."

That didn't stop the tears, but she did move close into my arms. Several seconds passed and she mumbled something like, "History repeats." We sat like that for almost half an hour.

It wasn't until I got back to Base that I remembered that I had been out between Demonsloose and Dawn without so much as a Hexagram.

I got my equipment installed the next day. I was assigned an office only fifty-four hundred meters from the central supply area. This was all right with me since the site was also quite near the outskirts of Adelaide-west. Though the office was made entirely of local materials, the style was old *vimwv*. The basement contained my sleeping and security quarters, and the first floor was my office and business machines. The surface construction was all hand-polished hardwood. The roof was tiled with rose marble and furnished with night chairs and a drink mixer. At the center of the roof was a recoilless rifle and a live map of the mine field around the building. It was all just like home—which is what I had specified when I had signed the contract back on Miki. I had expected some chiseling on the specifications once we got out in the boondocks, but Pwrlyg's integrity was a pleasant surprise.

After I checked out the equipment, I called Horlig and got a copy of his mission log. I wanted to check on Dahlmann's charges. Horlig was suspiciously unhappy about parting with the information, but when I pointed out that I was without a job until I got background info, he agreed to squirt me a copy. The incidents were more or less as Dahlmann had described them. At Pret, though, the Zulunders attacked the air tanks with some jury-rigged antiaircraft weapon—so the retaliation seemed justified. There was also one incident that Dahlmann hadn't mentioned. Just five days before, Chev—on Horlig's orders—burned the food supplies of the Sudamerican colony at Panama, thus forcing the Terran explorers to return to the inhabited portions of their continent. I decided to keep a close watch on these developments. There could be something here quite as sinister as Dahlmann claimed.

Later that day, Horlig briefed me on my first assignment. He wanted me to record and index the Canberra Central Library. The job didn't appeal at all. It was designed to keep me out of his hair. I spent the next couple weeks getting equipment together. I found Robert Dahlmann especially helpful. He telegraphed his superiors in Canberra and they agreed to let us use Terran clerical help in the recording operation. (I imagine part of the reason was that they were eager to study our equipment.) I never actually flew to Canberra. Horlig had some deputy take the stuff out and instruct the natives on how to use it. It turned out the Canberra library was huge—almost as big as the Information Services library at home. Just supervising the indexing computers was a full-time job. It was a lot more interesting than I thought it would be. When the job was done I would have many times the source material I could have collected personally.

A strange thing: as the weeks went by, I saw more and more of Mary Dahlmann.

Even at this point I was still telling myself that it was all field work for my study of Terran customs. One day we had a picnic in the badlands north of Adelaide. The next she took me on a tour of the business district of the city—it was amazing how so many people could live so close together day after day. Once we even went on a train ride all the way to Murray Bridge. Railroads are stinking, noisy and dirty, but they're fun—and they transport freight almost as cheaply as a floater does. Mary had that spark of intelligence and good humor that made it all the more interesting. Still I claimed it was all in the cause of objective research.

About six weeks after my landing I invited her to visit the Pwrlyg Base. Though Central Supply is only four or five kilometers from Adelaide-west, I took her in by air, so she could see the whole base at once. I think it was the first time she had ever flown.

The Pwrlyg Primary Territory is a rectangular area fifteen by thirty kilometers. It was ceded by the Australian government to the Company in gratitude for our intercession in the Battle of Hawaii, seventeen years before. You might wonder why we didn't just put all our bases in the northern hemisphere, and ignore the Terrans entirely. The most important reason was that the First and Second Fleets hadn't had the equipment for a large-scale decontamination job. Also, every kilogram of cargo from Miki requires nearly 100,000 megatons of energy for the voyage to Earth: this is expensive by any reckoning. We needed all the labor and materials the locals could provide. Since the Terrans inhabited the Southern Hemisphere only, that's where our first base had to be.

By native standards, Pwrlyg paid extremely good wages. So good that almost thirty thousand Terrans were employed at the Ground Base. Many of these individuals lived in an area just off the base, which Mary referred to as Clowntown. Its inhabitants were understandably enamored with the advantages of Mikin technology. Though their admiration was commendable, the results were a little ludicrous. Clowntowners tried to imitate the various aspects of Mikin life. They dressed eccentrically—by Terran standards—and adopted a variety of social behaviors. But their city was just as crowded as regular Australian urban areas. And though they had more scraps of our technology than many places in Australia, their city was filthy. Anarchy just isn't practical in such close quarters. They had absorbed the superficial aspects of our society without ever getting down to the critical matters of Umpires and antitrust. Mary had refused to go with me into Clowntown. Her reason was that police protection ceased to exist in that area. I don't think that was her real reason.

Below us, the blue sea and white breakers met the orange and gray-green bluffs of the shore. The great Central Desert extended right up to the ocean. It was difficult to believe that this land had once supported grass and trees. Scattered randomly across the sand and sage were the individual offices and workshops of Company employees. Each of these had its own unique appearance. Some were oases set in the desert.

Others were squat gray forts. Some even looked like Terran houses. And, of course, a good number were entirely hidden from sight, the property of Obscurantist employees who kept their location secret even from Pwrlyg. Taken as a whole, the Base looked like a comfortable metropolitan area on the A1 W1 peninsula. But, if the Company had originally based in the Northern Hemisphere, none of the amenities would have been possible. We would have had to live in prefab domes.

I swung the car in a wide arc and headed for the central area. Here was the robot factory that provided us with things like air tanks and drink mixers—things that native labor couldn't construct. Now we could see the general landing area, and the airy columns of Supply Central. Nearby was housing for groups that believed in living together: the sex club, the Little Brothers. A low annex jutted off from the Little Brothers building—the creche for children born of Non-Affective parents. They even had some half-breed Terran-Human children there. The biologists had been amazed to find that the two species could interbreed—some claimed that this proved the existence of a prehistoric interstellar empire.

I parked the car and we took the lift to the open eating area at the top of Supply Central. The utilitarian cafeteria served the Extroverts on the Company staff. The position afforded an excellent view of the sailing boats and surfers as well as three or four office houses out in the sea.

We were barely seated when two Terran waiter-servants came over to take our order. One of them favored Mary with a long, cold look, but they took my order courteously enough.

Mary watched them go, then remarked, "They hate my guts, do you know that?"

"Huh? Why should they hate you?"

"I'm, uh, 'consorting' with the Greenies. That's you. I knew one of those two in college. A real nice guy. He wanted to study low-energy nuclear reactions; prewar scientists never studied that area thoroughly. His life ended when he discovered that you people know more than he'll ever discover, unless he starts over from the beginning on your terms. Now he's practically a slave, waiting on tables."

"A slave he's not, girl. Pwrlyg just isn't that type of organization. That fellow is a trusted and well-cared-for servant—an employee, if you will. He can pack up and leave any time. With the wages we pay, we have Terrans begging for jobs."

"That's exactly what I mean," Mary said opaquely. Then she turned the question around. "Don't you feel any hostility from your friends, for running around with an 'Earthie' girl?"

I laughed. "In the first place, I'm not running around. I'm using you in my studies. In the second place, I don't know any of these people well enough yet to have friends. Even the people I came out with were all in deep freeze, remember.

"Some Mikins actually support fraternization with the natives—the Little Brothers, for instance. Every chance they get, they tell us to go out and make love—or is that verb just plain 'love'?—to the natives. I think there are some Company people who are definitely hostile toward you people—Horlig and Chev, for example. But I didn't ask their permission and, if they want to stop me, they'll have to contend with this,'' I tapped the dart gun on my wrist.

"Oh?" I think she was going to say something more when the servants came out and placed the food on our table. It was good, and we didn't say anything for several minutes. When we were done we sat and watched the surfers. A couple on a powered board were racing a dolphin across the bay. Their olive skins glistened pleasantly against the blue water.

Finally she spoke. "I've always been puzzled by that Horlig. He's odd even for a Mikin—no offense. He seems to regard Terrans as foolish and ignorant cowards. Yet as a person, he looks a lot more like a Terran than a Mikin."

"Actually, he's a different subspecies from the rest of us. It's like the difference between you and Zulunders. His bone structure is a little different and his skin is pale gray instead of olive green. His ancestors lived on a different continent than mine. They never developed beyond a neolithic culture there. About four hundred years ago, my race colonized his continent. We already had firearms then. Horlig's people just shriveled away. Whenever they fought us, we killed them; and whenever they didn't, we set them away in preserves. The last preserve, Gloyn, died about fifty years ago, I think. The rest interbred with the mainstream. Horlig is the nearest thing to a full-blooded Gloyn I've seen. Maybe that's why he affects primitiveness."

Mary said, "If he weren't out to get us Terrans, I think I could feel sorry for him."

I couldn't understand that comment. Horlig's race may have been mistreated in the past, but he was a lot better off than his ancestors ever were.

Three tables away, another couple was engaged in an intense conversation. Gradually it assumed the proportions of an argument. The man snapped an insult and the woman returned it with interest. Without warning, a knife appeared in her hand, flashed at the other's chest. But the man jumped backward, knocking over his chair. Mary gasped, as the man brought his knife in a grazing slash across the woman's middle. Red instantly appeared on green. They danced around the tables, feinting and slashing.

"Ron, do something! He's going to kill her."

They were fighting in a meal area, which is against Company regs, but on the other hand, neither was using power weapons. "I'm not going to do anything, Mary. This is a lovers' quarrel."

Mary's jaw dropped. "A lovers' quarrel? What—"

"Yeah," I said, "they both want the same woman." Mary looked sick. As soon as the fight began, a Little Brother at the other end of the roof got up and sprinted toward the combatants. Now he stood to one side, pleading with them to respect the holiness of life, and to settle their differences peacefully. But the two weren't much for religion. The man hissed at the Little Brother to get lost before he got spitted. The woman took advantage of her opponent's momentary inattention to pink his arm. Just then a Company officer arrived on the roof and informed the two just how big a fine they would be subject to if they continued to fight in a restricted area. That stopped them. They backed away from each other, cursing. The Little Brother followed them to the lift as he tried to work out some sort of reconciliation.

Mary seemed upset. "You people lead sex lives that make free love look like monogamy."

"No, you're wrong, Mary. It's just that every person has a different outlook. It's as if all Earth's sex customs coexisted. Most people subscribe to some one type." I decided not to try explaining the sex club.

"Don't you have marriage?"

"That's just what I'm saying. A large proportion of us do. We even have a word analogous to your *missus: a*. For instance, Mrs. Smith is aSmith. I would say that nearly fifteen percent of all Mikins are monogamous in the sense you mean it. And a far greater percentage never engage in the activities you regard as perversions."

She shook her head. "Do you know—if your group had appeared without a superior technology, you would have been locked up in an insane asylum? I like you personally, but most Mikins are so awfully weird."

I was beginning to get irritated. "You're the one that's nuts. The Pwrlyg employees here on Earth were deliberately chosen for their intelligence and compatibility. Even the mildly exotic types were left at home."

Mary's voice wavered slightly as she answered. "I . . . I guess I know that. You're all just so terribly different. And soon all the ways I know will be destroyed, and my people will all be dead or like you—more probably dead. No, don't deny it. More than once in our history we've had episodes like the colonization of Gloyn. Six hundred years ago, the Europeans took over North America from the stone-age Indians. One group of Indians—a tribe called the Cherokee—saw that they could never overcome the invaders. They reasoned that the only way to survive was to adopt European ways—no matter how offensive those ways appeared. The Cherokee built schools and towns; they even printed newspapers in their own language. But this did not satisfy the Europeans. They coveted the Cherokee lands. Eventually they evicted the Indians and force-marched the tribe halfway across the continent into a desert preserve. For all their willingness to adapt, the Cherokee suffered the same fate that your Gloyn did.

"Ron, are you any different from the Europeans—or from your Mikin ancestors? Will my people be massacred? Will the rare survivor be just another Mikin with all your aw— . . . all your alien customs? Isn't there any way you can save us from yourselves?" She reached out and grasped my hand. I could see she was fighting back tears.

There was no rationalizing it: I had fallen for her. I silently cursed my moralistic

Little Brother upbringing. At that moment, if she had asked it, I would have run right down to the beach and started swimming for Antarctica. The feel of her hand against mine and the look in her eyes would have admitted to no other response. For a moment, I wondered if she was aware of the awful power she had. Then I said, "I'll do everything I can, Mary. I don't think you have to worry. We've advanced a long way since Gloyn. Only a few of us wish you harm. But I'll do anything to protect your people from massacre and exploitation. Is that enough of a commitment?"

She squeezed my hand. "Yes. It's a greater commitment than has been made in all the past."

"Fine," I said, standing up. I wanted to get off this painful subject as fast as possible. "Let me show you some of our equipment."

I took her over to the Abo Affairs Office. The AAO wasn't a private residence-office, but it did bear Horlig's stamp. Even close up, it looked like a Gloyn rock-nest—a huge pile of boulders set in a marshy—and artificial—jungle. It was difficult, even for me, to spot the location of the recoilless rifles and machine guns. Inside, the neolithic motif was maintained. The computing equipment and TV screens were hidden behind woven curtains, and lighting came indirectly through chinks in the boulders. Horlig refused to employ Terrans, and his Mikin clerks and techs hadn't returned from lunch.

At the far end of the "room" a tiny waterfall gushed tinkling into a pool. Beyond the pool was Horlig's office, blocked from direct view by a rock partition. I noticed that the pool gave us an odd, ripply view into his office. That's the trouble with these "open" architectural forms: they have no real rooms, or privacy. In the water I could see the upside-down images of Horlig and Chev. I motioned Mary to be quiet, and knelt down to watch. Their voices were barely audible above the sound of falling water.

Chev was saying—in Mikin, of course: "You've been sensible enough in the past, Horlig. My suggestion is just a logical extension of previous policy. Once he's committed I'm sure that Pwrlyg won't have any objections. The Terrans have provided us with almost all the materials we needed from them. Their usefulness is over. They're vermin. It's costing the Company two thousand man-hours a month to provide security against their attacks and general insolence." He waved a sheaf of papers at Horlig. "My plan is simple. Retreat from Ground Base for a couple weeks and send orbital radiation bombs over the three inhabited areas. Then drop some lethal viruses to knock off the survivors. I figure it would cost one hundred thousand man-hours total, but we'd be permanently rid of this nuisance. And our ground installations would be undamaged. All you have to do is camouflage some of our initial moves so that the Company officers on the Orbital Base don't catch—"

"Enough!" Horlig exploded. He grabbed Chev by the scruff of his cape and pulled him up from his chair. "You putrid bag of schemings. I'm reporting you to Orbit. And if you ever even *think* of that plan again, I personally will kill you—if Pwrlyg doesn't do it first!" He shoved the vice president for violence to the floor. Chev got up, ready to draw and fire, but Horlig's wrist gun pointed directly at the other's middle. Chev spat on the floor and backed out of the room.

"What was that all about?" Mary whispered. I shook my head. This was one conversation I wasn't going to translate. Horlig's reaction amazed and pleased me. I almost liked the man after the way he had handled Chev. And unless the incident had been staged for my benefit, it shattered Robert Dahlmann's theory about Merlyn and Horlig. Could Chev be the one masquerading as a Terran rebel? He had just used Terran sabotage as an excuse for genocide.

Or was Merlyn simply what it appeared to be: a terrorist group created and managed by deranged Terrans? Things were all mixed up.

Ngagn Chev stalked out of the passage that led to Horlig's office. He glared murderously at Mary and me as he swept past us toward the door hole.

I looked back into the pool, and saw the reflection of Horlig's face looking back out at me. Perhaps it was the ripple distortion from the waterfall, but he seemed just as furious with my eavesdropping as he had been with Chev. If it had been a direct confrontation, I would've expected a fight. Then Horlig remembered his privacy field and turned it on, blanking out my view.

My library project proceeded rapidly to a conclusion. Everything was taped, and I had 2×10^7 subjects cross-indexed. The computerized library became my most powerful research tool. Dahlmann hadn't been kidding when he said that the pre-war civilization was high class. If the North Americans and Asians had managed to avoid war, they probably would have sent an expedition to Miki while we were still developing the fission bomb. Wouldn't that have been a switch—the Terrans colonizing our lands!

In the two hundred years since the North World War, the Australians had spent a great deal of effort in developing social science. They hadn't given up their government mania, but they had modified the concept so that it was much less malevolent than in the past. Australia now supported almost eleven million people, at a fairly high standard of living. In fact, I think there was probably less suffering in Australia than there is in most parts of Miki. Too bad their way of life was doomed. The Terrans were people—they were human. (And that simple conclusion was the answer to the whole problem, though I did not see it then.) In all my readings, I kept in mind the solution I was looking for: some way to save the Terrans from physical destruction, even if it was impossible to save their entire culture.

As the weeks passed, this problem came to overshadow my official tasks. I even looked up the history of the Cherokee and read about Elias Boudinot and Chief Sequoyah. The story was chillingly similar to the situation that was being played out now by the Mikins and the Terrans. The only way that the Terrans could hope for physical safety was to adopt Mikin institutions. But even then, wouldn't we eventually wipe them out the same way President Andrew Jackson did the Cherokee? Wouldn't we eventually covet all the lands of Earth?

While I tried to come up with a long-term solution, I also kept track of Chev's activities. Some of his men were pretty straight guys, and I got to know one platoon leader well. Late one evening about ten weeks after my landing, my armsman friend tipped me off that Chev was planning a massacre the next day in Perth.

I went over to see Horlig that night. From his reaction to Chev's genocide scheme, I figured he'd squash the massacre plan. The Gloyn was working late. I found him seated behind his stone desk in the center of the AAO rock-nest. He looked up warily as I entered. "What is it, Melmwn?"

"You've got to do something, Horlig. Chev is flying three platoons to Perth. I don't know exactly what type of mayhem he's planning, but—"

"Rockingham."

"Huh?"

"Chev is flying to Rockingham, not Perth." Horlig watched me carefully.

"You knew? What's he going to do—"

"I know because he's doing the job at my suggestion. I've identified the abos who blew up our ammo warehouse last year. Some of the ringleaders are Rockingham city officials. I'm going to make an example of them." He paused, then continued grimly, as if daring me to object. "By tomorrow at this time, every tenth inhabitant of Rockingham will be dead."

I didn't say anything for a second. I couldn't. When I finally got my mouth working again, I said with great originality, "You just can't do this, Horlig. We've had a lot more trouble from the Sudamericans and the Zulunders than we've ever had from the Australians. Killing a bunch of Aussies will just prove to everyone that Mikins don't want peace. You'll be encouraging belligerence. If you really have proof that these Rockingham officials are Merlyn's Men, you should send Chev out to arrest just those men and bring them back here for some sort of Company trial. Your present action is entirely arbitrary."

Horlig sat back in his chair. There was a new frankness and a new harshness in his face. "Perhaps I just made it all up. I'll fabricate some proof too, when necessary."

I hadn't expected this admission. I answered, "Pwrlyg's Second Son himself is coming down from Orbit tomorrow morning. Perhaps you thought he wouldn't know of your plans until they were executed. I don't know why you are doing this, but I can tell you that the Second Son is going to hear about it the minute he gets off the landing craft."

Horlig smiled pleasantly. "Get out."

I turned and started for the door. I admit it: I was going soft in the brain. My only excuse is that I had been associating with the natives too long. They generally say what they think because they have the protection of an impartial and all-powerful police force. This thought occurred to me an instant before I heard the characteristic sound of wrist gun smacking into palm. I dived madly for the floor as the first 0.07-mm dart hit the right boulder of the door hole. The next thing I knew I was lying in the cubbyhole formed by two or three large boulders knocked loose by the blast. My left arm was numb; a rock splinter had cut through it to the bone.

In the next couple seconds, Horlig fired about twenty darts wildly. The lights went out. Rocks weighing many tons flew about. The rock nest had been designed for stability, but this demolition upset the balance and the whole pile was shifting into a new configuration. It was a miracle I wasn't crushed. Horlig screamed. The shooting stopped. Was he dead? The man was nuts to fire more than a single dart indoors. He must have wanted me pretty bad.

As the horrendous echoes faded away, I could hear Horlig swearing. The pile was unrecognizable now. I could see the sky directly between gaps in the rocks. Moonlight came down in silvery shafts through suspended rock dust. Half-human shapes seemed to lurk in the rubble. I realized now that the nest was much bigger than I had thought. To my left an avalanche of boulders had collapsed into some subterranean space. The surface portion of the nest was only a fraction of the total volume. Right now Horlig could be right on the other side of a nearby rock or one hundred meters away—the pile shift had been that violent.

"You still kicking, Melmwn, old man?" Horlig's voice came clearly. The sound was from my right, but not too close. Perhaps if I moved quietly enough I could sneak out of the pile to my air car. Or I could play dead and wait for morning when Horlig's employees came out. But some of those might be partners in Horlig's scheme—whatever it was. I decided to try the first plan. I crawled over a nearby boulder, made a detour around an expanse of moonlit rock. My progress was definitely audible—there was too much loose stuff. Behind me, I could hear Horlig following. I stopped. This was no good. Even if I managed to make it out, I would then be visible from the pile, and Horlig could shoot me down. I would have to get rid of my opponent before I could escape. Besides, if he got away safely, Horlig could have Chev's sentries bar me from the landing field the next day. I stopped and lay quietly in the darkness. My arm really hurt now, and I could feel from the wetness on the ground that I had left a trail of blood.

"Come, Melmwn, speak up. I know you're still alive." I smiled. If Horlig thought I was going to give my position away by talking, he was even crazier than I thought. Every time he spoke, I got a better idea of his position.

"I'll trade information for the sound of your voice, Melmwn." Maybe he was not quite so nuts after all. He knew my greatest failing: curiosity. If Horlig should die this night, I might never know what his motives were. And I was just as well armed as he. If I could keep him talking I stood to gain just as much as he.

"All right, Horlig. I'll trade." I had said more than I wanted to. The shorter my responses the better. I listened for the sound of movement. But all I heard was Horlig's voice.

"You see, Melmwn, I am Merlyn." I heard a slithering sound as he moved to a new position. He was revealing everything to keep me talking. Now it was my turn to say something.

"Say on, O Horlig."

"I should have killed you before. When you overheard my conversation with Chev, I thought you might have guessed the truth."

I had received a lot of surprises so far, and this was another. Horlig's treatment of Chev's genocide scheme had seemed proof that Horlig couldn't be Merlyn. "But why, Horlig? What do you gain? What do you want?"

My opponent laughed, "I'm an altruist, Melmwn. And I'm a Gloyn; maybe the last full-blooded Gloyn. The Terrans are not going to be taken over by you the way you took over my people. The Terrans are people; they are human—and they must be treated as such."

I guess the idea must have been floating around in my mind for weeks. The Terrans were human, and should be treated as such. Horlig's statement triggered the whole solution in my mind. I saw the essential error of the Cherokee and of all my previous plans to save the Terrans. Horlig's motive was a complete surprise, but I could understand it. In a way he seemed to be after the same thing as I—though his methods couldn't possibly work. Maybe we wouldn't have to shoot it out.

"Listen Horlig. There's a way I can get what you want without bloodshed. The Terrans can be saved." I outlined my plan. I talked for almost two minutes.

As I finished, a dart smashed into a boulder thirty meters from my position. Then Horlig spoke. "I will not accept your plan. It is just what I'm fighting against." He seemed to be talking to himself, repeating a cycle that played endlessly, fanatically in his own brain. "Your plan would make the Terrans carbon-copy Mikins. Their culture would be destroyed as thoroughly as mine was. It is far better to die fighting you monsters than to lie down and let you take over. That's why I became Merlyn. I give the rebellious Terran elements a backbone, secret information, supplies. In my capacity as a Mikin official, I provoke incidents to convince the spineless ones of the physical threat to their existence. The Australians are the most cowardly of the lot. Apparently their government will accept any indignity. That's why I must be especially brutal at Rockingham tomorrow."

"Your plan's insane," I blurted without thinking. "Pwrlyg could destroy every living thing on Earth without descending from orbit."

"Then that is better than the cultural assassination you intend! We will die fighting." I think he was crying. "I grew up on the last preserve. I heard the last stories. The stories of the lands and the hunting my people once had, before you came and killed us, drove us away, talked us out of everything of value. If we had stood and fought then, I at least would never have been born into the nightmare that is your world." There was silence for a second.

I crept slowly toward the sound of his voice. I tucked my left arm in my shirt to keep it from dragging on the ground. I guessed that Horlig was wounded too, from the slithery sound he made when he moved.

The man was so involved in his own world that he kept on talking. It's strange, but now that I had discovered a way to save the Terrans, I felt doubly desperate to get out of the rock-nest alive. "And don't, Melmwn, be so sure that we will lose to you this time. I intend to provoke no immediate insurrection. I am gathering my forces. A second robot factory was brought in with the Third Fleet. Pwrlyg's Second Son is coming down with it tomorrow. With Chev's forces on the West Coast it will be an easy matter for Merlyn's Men to hijack the factory and its floater. I already have a hidden place, in the midst of all the appropriate ore fields, to set it up. Over the years, that factory will provide us with all the weapons and vehicles we need. And someday, someday we will rise and kill all the Mikins."

Horlig sounded delirious now. He was confusing Gloyn and Terran. But that robo-factory scheme was not the invention of a delirious mind—only an insane one. I continued across the boulders—under and around them. The moon was directly overhead and its light illuminated isolated patches of rock. I knew I was quite near him now. I stopped and inspected the area ahead of me. Just five meters away a slender beam of moonlight came down through a chink in the rock overhead.

"Tomorrow, yes, tomorrow will be Merlyn's greatest coup."

As Horlig spoke I thought I detected a faint agitation in the rock dust hung in that moonbeam. Of course it might be a thermal effect from a broken utility line, but it could also be Horlig's breath stirring the tiny particles.

I scrambled over the last boulder to get a clear shot that would not start an avalanche. My guess was right. Horlig sprang to his feet, and for an instant was outlined by the moonlight. His eyes were wide and staring. He was a Gloyn warrior in shin boards and breechclout, standing in the middle of his wrecked home and determined to protect his way of life from the alien monsters. He was only four hundred years too late. He fired an instant before I did. Horlig missed. I did not. The last Gloyn disappeared in an incandescent flash.

I was in bad shape by the time I got out to my car and called a medic. The next couple hours seem like someone else's memories. I woke the Ump at 0230. He wasn't disturbed by the hour; Umpires can take anything in stride. I gave him the whole story and my solution. I don't think I was very eloquent, so either the plan was sharp or the Ump was especially good. He accepted the whole plan, even the ruling against Pwrlyg. To be frank, I think it was a solution that he would have come to on his own, given time—but he had come down from the Orbital Base the week before, and had just begun his study of the natives. He told me he'd reach an official decision later in the day and tell me about it.

I flew back to my office, set all the protection devices on auto, and blacked out. I didn't wake until fifteen hours later, when Ghuri Kym—the Ump—called and asked me to come with him to Adelaide.

Just twenty-four hours after my encounter with Horlig, we were standing in Robert Dahlmann's den. I made the introductions. "Umpire Kym can read Australian but he hasn't had any practice with speaking, so he's asked me to interpret. Scholar Dahlmann, you were right about Herul Horlig—but for the wrong reasons." I explained Horlig's true motives. I could see Dahlmann was surprised. "And Chev's punitive expedition to the West Coast has been called off, so you don't have to worry about Rockingham." I paused, then plunged into the more important topic, "I think I've come up with a way to save your species from extinction. Ghuri Kym agrees."

Kym laid the document on Dahlmann's desk and spoke the ritual words. "What's this?" asked Dahlmann, pointing at the Mikin printing.

"The English is on the other side. As the representative of the Australian government, you have just been served with an antitrust ruling. Among other things, it directs your people to split into no fewer than one hundred thousand autonomous organizations. Ngagn Chev is delivering similar documents to the Sudamerican and Zulunder governments. You have one year to effect the change. You may be interested to know that Pwrlyg has also been served and must split into at least four competitive groups."

Pwrlyg had been served with the antitrust ruling that morning. My employers were very unhappy with my plan. Kym told me that the Second Son had threatened to have me shot if I ever showed up on Company property again. I was going to have to lay low for a while, but I knew that Pwrlyg needed all the men they could get. Ultimately, I would be forgiven. I wasn't worried; the risk-taking was worth while if it saved the Terrans from exploitation.

I had expected an enthusiastic endorsement from Dahlmann, but he took the plan glumly. Kym and I spent the next hour explaining the details of the ruling to him. I felt distinctly deflated when we left. From the Terran's reaction you'd think I had ordered the execution of his race.

Mary was sitting on the porch swing. As we left the house, I asked Kym to return to the base without me. If her father hadn't been appreciative, I thought that at least Mary would be. She was, after all, the one who had given me the problem. In a way I had done it all for her.

I sat down on the swing beside her.

"Your arm! What happened?" She passed her hand gently over the plastic web dressing. I told her about Horlig. It was just like the end of a melodrama. There was admiration in her eyes, and her arms were around me—boy gets girl, et cetera.

"And," I continued, "I found a way to save all of you from the fate of the Cherokee."

"That's wonderful, Ron. I knew you would." She kissed me.

"The fatal flaw in the Cherokee's plan was that they segregated themselves from the white community, while they occupied lands that the whites wanted. If they had been citizens of the United States of America, it would not have been legal to confiscate their lands and kill them. Of course we Mikins don't even have a word for 'citizen,' but Umpire law extends to all humans. I got the Umpire to declare that Terrans are a human species. I know it sounds obvious, but it just never occurred to us before.

"Genocide is now specifically barred, because it would be monopolistic. An antitrust ruling has already been served on Australia and the other Earth governments."

Mary's enthusiasm seemed to evaporate somewhat. "Then our governments will be abolished?"

"Why, yes, Mary."

"And in a few decades, we will be the same as you with all your . . . perversions and violence and death?"

"Don't say it that way, Mary. You'll have Mikin cultures, with some Terran enclaves. Nothing could have stopped this. But at least you won't be killed. I've saved—"

For an instant I thought I'd been shot in the face. My mind did three lazy loops, before I realized that Mary had just delivered a roundhouse slap. "You green-faced thing," she hissed. "You've saved us nothing. Look at this street. Look! It's quiet. No one's killing anyone. Most people are tolerably happy. This suburb is not old, but its way of life is—almost five hundred years old. We've tried very hard in that time to make it better, and we've succeeded in many ways. Now, just as we're on the verge of discovering how all people can live in peace, you monsters breeze in. You'll rip up our cities. 'They are too big,' you say. You'll destroy our police forces. 'Monopolistic enterprise,' you call them. And in a few years we'll have a planet-wide Clowntown. We'll have to treat each other as animals in order to survive on these oh-so-generous terms you offer us!" She paused, out of breath, but not out of anger.

And for the first time I saw the real fear she had tried to express from the first. She was afraid of dying—of her race dying; everybody had those fears. But what was just as important to her was her home, her family, her friends. The shopping center, the games, the theaters, the whole concept of courtesy. My people weren't going to kill her body, that was true, but we were destroying all the things that give meaning to life. I hadn't found a solution—I'd just invented murder without bloodshed. Somehow I had to make it right.

I tried to reach my arm around her. "I love you, Mary." The words came out garbled, incomprehensible. "I love you, Mary," more clearly this time.

I don't think she even heard. She pushed away hysterically. "Horlig was the one who was right. Not you. It is better to fight and die than—" she didn't finish. She hit frantically and inexpertly at my face and chest. She'd never had any training, but those were hard, determined blows and they were doing damage. I knew I couldn't stop her, short of injuring her. I stood up under the rain of blows and made for the steps. She followed, fighting, crying.

I stumbled off the steps. She stayed on the porch, crying in a low gurgle. I limped past the street lamp and into the darkness. ■

WARRIOR
Gordon R. Dickson

Wars are waged by governments, using armies and navies and weapon systems. All of which are ultimately composed of, built by, and operated by individual human beings—who are, in turn, shaped and molded by the jobs they do.

THE SPACELINER COMING IN from New Earth and Freiland, worlds under the Sirian sun, was delayed in its landing by traffic at the spaceport in Long Island Sound. The two police lieutenants, waiting on the bare concrete beyond the shelter of the Terminal buildings, turned up the collars of their cloaks against the hissing sleet, in this unweatherproofed area. The sleet was turning into tiny hailstones that hit and stung all exposed areas of skin. The gray November sky poured them down without pause or mercy, the vast, reaching surface of concrete seemed to dance with their white multitudes.

"Here it comes now," said Tyburn, the Manhattan Complex police lieutenant, risking a glance up into the hailstorm. "Let me do the talking when we take him in."

"Fine by me," answered Breagan, the spaceport officer, "I'm only here to introduce you—and because it's my bailiwick. You can have Kenebuck, with his hood connections, and his millions. If it were up to me, I'd let the soldier get him."

"It's him," said Tyburn, "who's likely to get the soldier—and that's why I'm here. You ought to know that."

The great mass of the interstellar ship settled like a cautious mountain to the concrete two hundred yards off. It protruded a landing stair near its base like a metal leg, and the passengers began to disembark. The two policemen spotted their man immediately in the crowd.

"He's big," said Breagan, with the judicious appraisal of someone safely on the sidelines, as the two of them moved forward.

"They're all big, these professional military men off the Dorsai world," answered Tyburn, a little irritably, shrugging his shoulders against the cold, under his cloak. "They breed themselves that way."

"I know they're big," said Breagan. "This one's bigger."

The first wave of passengers was rolling toward them now, their quarry among the mass. Tyburn and Breagan moved forward to meet him. When they got close they could see, even through the hissing sleet, every line of his dark, unchanging face looming above the lesser heights of the people around him, his military erectness molding the civilian clothes he wore until they might as well have been a uniform. Tyburn found himself staring fixedly at the tall figure as it came toward him. He had met such professional soldiers from the Dorsai before, and the stamp of their breeding had always been plain on them. But this man was somehow more so, even than the others Tyburn had seen. In some way he seemed to be the spirit of the Dorsai, incarnate.

He was one of twin brothers, Tyburn remembered now from the dossier back at his office. Ian and Kensie were their names, of the Graeme family at Foralie, on the Dorsai. And the report was that Kensie had two men's likability, while his brother Ian, now approaching Tyburn, had a double portion of grim shadow and solitary darkness.

Staring at the man coming toward him, Tyburn could believe the dossier now. For a moment, even, with the sleet and the cold taking possession of him, he found himself believing in the old saying that, if the born soldiers of the Dorsai ever cared to pull back to their own small, rocky world, and challenge the rest of humanity, not all the thirteen other inhabited planets could stand against them. Once, Tyburn had laughed at that idea. Now, watching Ian approach, he could not laugh. A man like this would live for different reasons from those of ordinary men—and die for different reasons.

Tyburn shook off the wild notion. The figure coming toward him, he reminded himself sharply, was a professional military man—nothing more.

Ian was almost to them now. The two policemen moved in through the crowd and intercepted him.

"Commandant Ian Graeme?" said Breagan. "I'm Kaj Breagan of the spaceport police. This is Lieutenant Walter Tyburn of the Manhattan Complex Force. I wonder if you could give us a few minutes of your time?"

Ian Graeme nodded, almost indifferently. He turned and paced along with them, his longer stride making more leisurely work of their brisk walking, as they led him away from the route of the disembarking passengers and in through a blank metal door at one end of the Terminal, marked *Unauthorized Entry Prohibited*. Inside, they took an elevator tube up to the offices on the Terminal's top floor, and ended up in chairs around a desk in one of the offices.

All the way in, Ian had said nothing. He sat in his chair now with the same indifferent patience, gazing at Tyburn, behind the desk, and at Breagan, seated back against the wall at the desk's right side. Tyburn found himself staring back in fascination. Not at the granite face, but at the massive, powerful hands of the man, hanging idly between the chair-arms that supported his forearms. Tyburn, with an effort, wrenched his gaze from those hands.

"Well, Commandant," he said, forcing himself at last to look up into the dark, unchanging features, "you're here on Earth for a visit, we understand."

"To see the next-of-kin of an officer of mine." Ian's voice, when he spoke at last, was almost mild compared to the rest of his appearance. It was a deep, calm voice, but lightless—like a voice that had long forgotten the need to be angry or threatening. Only . . . there was something sad about it, Tyburn thought.

"A James Kenebuck?" said Tyburn.

"That's right," answered the deep voice of Ian. "His younger brother, Brian Kenebuck, was on my staff in the recent campaign on Freiland. He died three months back."

"Do you," said Tyburn, "always visit your deceased officers' next of kin?"

"When possible. Usually, of course, they die in line of duty."

"I see," said Tyburn. The office chair in which he sat seemed hard and uncomfortable underneath him. He shifted slightly. "You don't happen to be armed, do you, Commandant?"

Ian did not even smile.

Warrior

"No," he said.

"Of course, of course," said Tyburn, uncomfortable. "Not that it makes any difference." He was looking again, in spite of himself, at the two massive, relaxed hands opposite him. "Your . . . extremities by themselves are lethal weapons. We register professional karate and boxing experts here, you know—or did you know?"

Ian nodded.

"Yes," said Tyburn. He wet his lips, and then was furious with himself for doing so. Damn my orders, he thought suddenly and whitely, I don't have to sit here making a fool of myself in front of this man, no matter how many connections and millions Kenebuck owns.

"All right, look here, Commandant," he said, harshly, leaning forward. "We've had a communication from the Freiland-North Police about you. They suggest that you hold Kenebuck—James Kenebuck—responsible for his brother Brian's death."

Ian sat looking back at him without answering.

"Well," demanded Tyburn, raggedly after a long moment, "do you?"

"Force-leader Brian Kenebuck," said Ian calmly, "led his Force, consisting of thirty-six men at the time, against orders farther than was wise into enemy perimeter. His Force was surrounded and badly shot up. Only he and four men returned to the lines. He was brought to trial in the field under the Mercenaries Code for deliberate mishandling of his troops under combat conditions. The four men who had returned with him testified against him. He was found guilty and I ordered him shot."

Ian stopped speaking. His voice had been perfectly even, but there was so much finality about the way he spoke that after he finished there was a pause in the room while Tyburn and Breagan stared at him as if they had both been tranced. Then the silence, echoing in Tyburn's ears, jolted him back to life.

"I don't see what all this has to do with James Kenebuck, then," said Tyburn. "Brian committed some . . . military crime, and was executed for it. You say you gave the order. If anyone's responsible for Brian Kenebuck's death then, it seems to me it'd be you. Why connect it with someone who wasn't even there at the time, someone who was here on Earth all the while, James Kenebuck?"

"Brian," said Ian, "was his brother."

The emotionless statement was calm and coldly reasonable in the silent, brightly lit office. Tyburn found his open hands had shrunk themselves into fists on the desk top. He took a deep breath and began to speak in a flat, official tone.

"Commandant," he said, "I don't pretend to understand you. You're a man of the Dorsai, a product of one of the splinter cultures out among the stars. I'm just an old-fashioned Earthborn—but I'm a policeman in the Manhattan Complex and James Kenebuck is . . . well, he's a taxpayer in the Manhattan Complex."

He found he was talking without meeting Ian's eyes. He forced himself to look at them—they were dark unmoving eyes.

"It's my duty to inform you," Tyburn went on, "that we've had intimations to the effect that you're to bring some retribution to James Kenebuck, because of Brian Kenebuck's death. These are only intimations, and as long as you don't break any laws here on Earth, you're free to go where you want and see whom you like. But this *is* Earth, Commandant.''

He paused, hoping that Ian would make some sound, some movement. But Ian only sat there, waiting.

"We don't have any Mercenaries Code here, Commandant," Tyburn went on harshly. "We haven't any feud-right, no *droit-de-main*. But we do have laws. Those laws say that, though a man may be the worst murderer alive, until he's brought to book in our courts, under our process of laws, no one is allowed to harm a hair of his head. Now, I'm not here to argue whether this is the best way or not; just to tell you that that's the way things are." Tyburn stared fixedly into the dark eyes. "Now," he said, bluntly, "I know that if you're determined to try to kill Kenebuck without counting the cost, I can't prevent it."

He paused and waited again. But Ian still said nothing.

"I know," said Tyburn, "that you can walk up to him like any other citizen, and once you're within reach you can try to kill him with your bare hands before anyone can stop you. *I* can't stop you in that case. But what I can do is catch you afterwards, if you succeed, and see you convicted and executed for murder. And you *will* be caught and convicted, there's no doubt about it. You can't kill James Kenebuck the way someone like you would kill a man, and get away with it here on Earth—do you understand that, Commandant?"

"Yes," said Ian.

"All right," said Tyburn, letting out a deep breath. 'Then you understand. You're a sane man and a Dorsai professional. From what I've been able to learn about the Dorsai, it's one of your military tenets that part of a man's duty to himself is not to throw his life away in a hopeless cause. And this cause of yours, to bring Kenebuck to justice for his brother's death, is hopeless."

He stopped. Ian straightened in a movement preliminary to getting up.

"Wait a second," said Tyburn.

He had come to the hard part of the interview. He had prepared his speech for this moment and rehearsed it over and over again—but now he found himself without faith that it would convince Ian.

"One more word," said Tyburn. "You're a man of camps and battlefields, a man of the military; and you must be used to thinking of yourself as a pretty effective individual. But here, on Earth, those special skills of yours are mostly illegal. And without them you're ineffective and helpless. Kenebuck, on the other hand, is just the opposite. He's got money—millions. And he's got connections, some of them nasty. And he was born and raised here in Manhattan Complex." Tyburn stared emphatically at the tall, dark man, willing him to understand. "Do you follow me? If you, for example, should suddenly turn up dead here, we just might not be able to bring Kenebuck to book for it. Where we absolutely could, and would, bring you to book if the situation were reversed. Think about it."

He sat, still staring at Ian. But Ian's face showed no change, or sign that the message had gotten through to him.

"Thank you," Ian said. "If there's nothing more, I'll be going."

"There's nothing more," said Tyburn, defeated. He watched Ian leave. It was only when Ian was gone, and he turned back to Breagen, that he recovered a little of his self-respect. For Breagan's face had paled.

Ian went down through the Terminal and took a cab into Manhattan Complex, to the John Adams Hotel. He registered for a room on the fourteenth floor of the transient section of that hotel and inquired about the location of James Kenebuck's suite in the resident section; then sent his card up to Kenebuck with a request to come by to see the millionaire. After that, he went on up to his own room, unpacked his luggage, which had already been delivered from the spaceport, and took out a small, sealed package. Just at that moment there was a soft chiming sound and his card was returned to him from a delivery slot in the room wall. It fell into the salver below the slot and he picked it up, to read what was written on the face of it. The penciled note read:

Come on up—   K.

He tucked the card and the package into a pocket and left his transient room. And Tyburn, who had followed him to the hotel, and who had been observing all of Ian's actions from the second of his arrival, through sensors placed in the walls and ceilings, half rose from his chair in the room of the empty suite directly above Kenebuck's, which had been quietly taken over as a police observation post. Then, helplessly, Tyburn swore and sat down again, to follow Ian's movements in the screen fed by the sensors. So far there was nothing the policeman could do legally—nothing but watch.

So he watched as Ian strode down the softly carpeted hallway to the elevator tube, rose in it to the eightieth floor and stepped out to face the heavy, transparent door sealing off the resident section of the hotel. He held up Kenebuck's card with its message to a concierge screen beside the door, and with a soft sigh of air the door slid back to let him through. He passed on in, found a second elevator tube, and took it up thirteen more stories. Black doors opened before him—and he stepped one step forward into a small foyer to find himself surrounded by three men.

They were big men—one, a lantern-jawed giant, was even bigger than Ian—and they were vicious. Tyburn, watching through the sensor in the foyer ceiling that had been secretly placed there by the police the day before, recognized all of them from his files. They were underworld muscle hired by Kenebuck at word of Ian's coming; all armed, and brutal and hair-trigger—mad dogs of the lower city. After that first step into their midst, Ian stood still. And there followed a strange, unnatural cessation of movement in the room.

The three stood checked. They had been about to put their hands on Ian to search him for something, Tyburn saw, and probably to rough him up in the process. But something had stopped them, some abrupt change in the air around them. Tyburn, watching, felt the change as they did; but for a moment he felt it without understanding. Then understanding came to him.

The difference was in Ian, in the way he stood there. He was, saw Tyburn, simply . . . waiting. That same patient indifference Tyburn had seen upon him in the Terminal office was there again. In the split second of his single step into the room he had discovered the men, had measured them, and stopped. Now, he waited, in his turn, for one of them to make a move.

A sort of black lightning had entered the small foyer. It was abruptly obvious to the watching Tyburn, as to the three below, that the first of them to lay hands on Ian would be the first to find the hands of the Dorsai soldier upon him—and those hands were death.

For the first time in his life, Tyburn saw the personal power of the Dorsai fighting man, made plain without words. Ian needed no badge upon him, standing as he stood now, to warn that he was dangerous. The men about him were mad dogs; but, patently, Ian was a wolf. There was a difference with the three, which Tyburn now recognized for the first time. Dogs—even mad dogs—fight, and the losing dog, if he can, runs away. But no wolf runs. For a wolf wins every fight but one, and in that one he dies.

After a moment, when it was clear that none of the three would move, Ian stepped forward. He passed through them without even brushing against one of them, to the inner door opposite, and opened it and went on through.

He stepped into a three-level living room stretching to a large, wide window, its glass rolled up, and black with the sleet-filled night. The living room was as large as a small suite in itself, and filled with people, men and women, richly dressed. They held cocktail glasses in their hands as they stood or sat, and talked. The atmosphere was heavy with the scents of alcohol, and women's perfumes and cigarette smoke. It seemed that they paid no attention to his entrance, but their eyes followed him covertly once he had passed.

He walked forward through the crowd, picking his way to a figure before the dark window, the figure of a man almost as tall as himself, erect, athletic-looking with a handsome, sharp-cut face under whitish-blond hair that stared at Ian with a sort of incredulity as Ian approached.

"Graeme . . . ?" said this man, as Ian stopped before him. His voice in this moment of off-guardedness betrayed its two levels, the semi-hoodlum whine and harshness underneath, the polite accents above. "My boys . . . you didn't—" he stumbled, "leave anything with them when you were coming in?"

"No," said Ian. "You're James Kenebuck, of course. You look like your brother." Kenebuck stared at him.

"Just a minute," he said. He set down his glass, turned and went quickly through the crowd and into the foyer, shutting the door behind him. In the hush of the room, those there heard first silence, then a short, unintelligible burst of sharp voices, then silence again. Kenebuck came back into the room, two spots of angry color high on his cheekbones. He came back to face Ian.

"Yes," he said, halting before Ian. "They were supposed to . . . tell me when you came in." He fell silent, evidently waiting for Ian to speak, but Ian merely stood, examining him, until the spots of color on Kenebuck's cheekbones flared again.

"Well?" he said, abruptly. "Well? You came here to see me about Brian, didn't you? What about Brian?" He added, before Ian could answer, in a tone suddenly brutal, "I know he was shot, so you don't have to break that news to me. I suppose you want to tell me he showed all sorts of noble guts—refused a blindfold and that sort of—"

"No," said Ian. "He didn't die nobly."

Kenebuck's tall, muscled body jerked a little at the words, almost as if the bullets of an invisible firing squad had poured into it.

"Well . . . that's fine!" he laughed angrily. "You come light-years to see me and then you tell me that! I thought you liked him—liked Brian."

"Liked him? No," Ian shook his head. Kenebuck stiffened, his face for a moment caught in a gape of bewilderment. "As a matter of fact," went on Ian, "he was a glory-hunter. That made him a poor soldier and a worse officer. I'd have transferred him out of my command if I'd had time before the campaign on Freiland started. Because of him, we lost the lives of thirty-two men in his Force, that night."

"Oh." Kenebuck pulled himself together, and looked sourly at Ian. "Those thirty-two men. You've got them on your conscience, is that it?"

"No," said Ian. There was no emphasis on the word as he said it, but somehow to Tyburn's ears above, the brief short negative dismissed Kenebuck's question with an abruptness like contempt. The spots of color on Kenebuck's cheeks flamed.

"You didn't like Brian and your conscience doesn't bother you—what're you here for, then?" he snapped.

"My duty brings me," said Ian.

"Duty?" Kenebuck's face stilled, and went rigid.

Ian reached slowly into his pocket as if he were surrendering a weapon under the guns of an enemy and did not want his move misinterpreted. He brought out the package from his pocket.

"I brought you Brian's personal effects," he said. He turned and laid the package on a table beside Kenebuck. Kenebuck stared down at the package and the color over his cheekbones faded until his face was nearly as pale as his hair. Then slowly, hesitantly, as if he were approaching a booby-trap, he reached out and gingerly picked it up. He held it and turned to Ian, staring into Ian's eyes, almost demandingly.

"It's in here?" said Kenebuck, in a voice barely above a whisper, and with a strange emphasis.

"Brian's effects," said Ian, watching him.

"Yes . . . sure. All right," said Kenebuck. He was plainly trying to pull himself together, but his voice was still almost whispering. "I guess . . . that settles it."

"That settles it," said Ian. Their eyes held together, "Good-by," said Ian. He turned and walked back through the silent crowd and out of the living room. The three muscle-men were no longer in the foyer. He took the elevator tube down and returned to his own hotel room.

Tyburn, who with a key to the service elevators had not had to change tubes on the way down as Ian had, was waiting for him when Ian entered. Ian did not seem surprised to see Tyburn there, and only glanced casually at the policeman as he crossed to a decanter of Dorsai whisky that had since been delivered up to the room.

"That's that, then!" burst out Tyburn, in relief. "You got in to see him and he ended up letting you out. You can pack up and go, now. It's over."

"No," said Ian. "Nothing's over yet." He poured a few inches of the pungent, dark whisky into a glass, and moved the decanter over another glass. "Drink?"

"I'm on duty," said Tyburn, sharply.

"There'll be a little wait," said Ian, calmly. He poured some whisky into the other glass, took up both glasses, and stepped across the room to hand one to Tyburn. Tyburn found himself holding it. Ian had stepped on to stand before the wall-high window. Outside, night had fallen; but—faintly seen in the lights from the city levels below—the sleet here above the weather shield still beat like small, dark ghosts against the transparency.

"Hang it, man, what more do you want?" burst out Tyburn. "Can't you see it's you I'm trying to protect—as well as Kenebuck? I don't want *anyone* killed! If you stay around here now, you're asking for it. I keep telling you, here in Manhattan Complex you're the helpless one, not Kenebuck. Do you think he hasn't made plans to take care of you?"

"Not until he's sure," said Ian, turning from the ghost-sleet, beating like lost souls against the windowglass, trying to get in.

"Sure about what? Look, Commandant," said Tyburn, trying to speak calmly, "half an hour after we hear from the Freiland-North Police about you, Kenebuck called my office to ask for police protection." He broke off, angrily. "Don't look at me like that! How do I know how he found out you were coming? I tell you he's rich, and he's got connections! But the point is, the police protection he's got is just a screen—an excuse—for whatever he's got planned for you on his own. You saw those hoods in the foyer!"

"Yes," said Ian, unemotionally.

"Well, think about it!" Tyburn glared at him. "Look, I don't hold any brief for

Warrior 123

James Kenebuck! All right—let me tell you about him! We knew he'd been trying to get rid of his brother since Brian was ten—but blast it, Commandant, Brian was no angel, either—"

"I know," said Ian, seating himself in a chair opposite Tyburn.

"All right, you know! I'll tell you anyway!" said Tyburn. "Their grandfather was a local kingpin—he was in every racket on the eastern seaboard. He was one of the mob, with millions he didn't dare count because of where they'd come from. In their father's time, those millions started to be fed into legitimate businesses. The third generation, James and Brian, didn't inherit anything that wasn't legitimate. Hell, we couldn't even make a jaywalking ticket stick against one of them, if we'd ever wanted to. James was twenty and Brian ten when their father died, and when he died the last bit of tattle-tale gray went out of the family linen. But they kept their hoodlum connections, Commandant!"

Ian sat, glass in hand, watching Tyburn almost curiously.

"Don't you get it?" snapped Tyburn. "I tell you that, on paper, in law, Kenebuck's twenty-four-carat gilt-edge. But his family was hoodlum, he was raised like a hoodlum, and he thinks like a hood! He didn't want his young brother Brian around to share the crown prince position with him—so he set out to get rid of him. He couldn't just have him killed, so he set out to cut him down, show him up, break his spirit, until Brian took one chance too many trying to match up to his older brother, and killed himself off."

Ian slowly nodded.

"All right!" said Tyburn. "So Kenebuck finally succeeded. He chased Brian until the kid ran off and became a professional soldier—something Kenebuck wouldn't leave his wine, women and song long enough to shine at. And he can shine at most things he really wants to shine at, Commandant. Under that hood attitude and all those millions, he's got a good mind and a good body that he's made a hobby out of training. But, all right. So now it turns out Brian was still no good, and he took some soldiers along when he finally got around to doing what Kenebuck wanted, and getting himself killed. All right! But what can you do about it? What can anyone do about it, with all the connections, and all the money and all the law on Kenebuck's side of it? And, why should you think about doing something about it, anyway?"

"It's my duty," said Ian. He had swallowed half the whisky in his glass, absently, and now he turned the glass thoughtfully around, watching the brown liquor swirl under the forces of momentum and gravity. He looked up at Tyburn. "You know that, Lieutenant."

"Duty! Is duty that important?" demanded Tyburn. Ian gazed at him, then looked away, at the ghost-sleet beating vainly against the glass of the window that held it back in the outer dark.

"Nothing's more important than duty," said Ian, half to himself, his voice thoughtful and remote. "Mercenary troops have the right to care and protection from their own officers. When they don't get it, they're entitled to justice, so that the same thing is discouraged from happening again. That justice is a duty."

Tyburn blinked, and unexpectedly a wall seemed to go down in his mind.

"Justice for those thirty-two dead soldiers of Brian's!" he said, suddenly understanding. "That's what brought you here!"

"Yes." Ian nodded, and lifted his glass almost as if to the sleet-ghosts to drink the rest of his whisky.

"But," said Tyburn, staring at him, "You're trying to bring a civilian to justice. And Kenebuck has you out-gunned and out-maneuvered—"

The chiming of the communicator screen in one corner of the hotel room interrupted him. Ian put down his empty glass, went over to the screen, and depressed a stud. His wide shoulders and back hid the screen from Tyburn, but Tyburn heard his voice.

"Yes?"

The voice of James Kenebuck sounded in the hotel room.

"Graeme—listen!"

There was a pause.

"I'm listening," said Ian, calmly.

"I'm alone now," said the voice of Kenebuck. It was tight and harsh. "My guests have gone home. I was just looking through that package of Brian's things . . ." He stopped speaking and the sentence seemed to Tyburn to dangle unfinished in the air of the hotel room. Ian let it dangle for a long moment.

"Yes?" he said, finally.

"Maybe I was a little hasty . . ." said Kenebuck. But the tone of his voice did not match the words. The tone was savage. "Why don't you come up, now that I'm alone, and we'll . . . talk about Brian, after all?"

"I'll be up," said Ian.

He snapped off the screen and turned around.

"Wait!" said Tyburn, starting up out of his chair. "You can't go up there!"

"Can't?" Ian looked at him. "I've been invited, Lieutenant."

The words were like a damp towel slapping Tyburn in the face, waking him up.

"That's right . . ." he stared at Ian. "Why? Why'd he invite you back?"

"He's had time," said Ian, "to be alone. And to look at that package of Brian's."

"But . . ." Tyburn scowled. "There was nothing important in that package. A watch, a wallet, a passport, some other papers . . . Customs gave us a list. There wasn't anything unusual there."

"Yes," said Ian. "And that's why he wants to see me again."

"But what does he want?"

"He wants me," said Ian. He met the puzzlement of Tyburn's gaze. "He was always jealous of Brian," Ian explained, almost gently. "He was afraid Brian would grow up to outdo him in things. That's why he tried to break Brian, even to kill him. But now Brian's come back to face him."

"Brian . . . ?"

"In me," said Ian. He turned toward the hotel door.

Tyburn watched him turn, then suddenly—like a man coming out of a daze, he took three hurried strides after him as Ian opened the door.

"Wait!" snapped Tyburn. "He won't be alone up there! He'll have hoods covering you through the walls. He'll definitely have traps set for you . . ."

Easily, Ian lifted the policeman's grip from his arm.

"I know," he said. And went.

Tyburn was left in the open doorway, staring after him. As Ian stepped into the elevator tube, the policeman moved. He ran for the service elevator that would take him back to the police observation post above the sensors in the ceiling of Kenebuck's living room.

When Ian stepped into the foyer the second time, it was empty. He went to the door to the living room of Kenebuck's suite, found it ajar, and stepped through it. Within the room was empty, with glasses and overflowing ashtrays still on the tables; the lights had been lowered. Kenebuck rose from a chair with its back to the far, large window at the end of the room. Ian walked toward him and stopped when they were little more than an arm's length apart.

Kenebuck stood for a second, staring at him, the skin of his face tight. Then he made a short, almost angry gesture with his right hand. The gesture gave away the fact that he had been drinking.

"Sit down!" he said. Ian took a comfortable chair and Kenebuck sat down in the one from which he had just risen. "Drink?" said Kenebuck. There was a decanter and glasses on the table beside and between them. Ian shook his head. Kenebuck poured part of a glass for himself.

"That package of Brian's things," he said, abruptly, the whites of his eyes glinting as he glanced up under his lids at Ian, "there was just personal stuff. Nothing else in it!"

"What else did you expect would be in it?" asked Ian, calmly.

Kenebuck's hands clenched suddenly on the glass. He stared at Ian, and then burst out into a laugh that rang a little wildly against the emptiness of the large room.

"No, no . . ." said Kenebuck, loudly. "I'm asking the questions, Graeme. I'll ask them! What made you come all the way here, to see me, anyway?"

"My duty," said Ian.

"Duty? Duty to whom—Brian?" Kenebuck looked as if he would laugh again, then thought better of it. There was the white, wild flash of his eyes again. "What was something like Brian to you? You said you didn't even like him."

"That was beside the point," said Ian, quietly. "He was one of my officers."

"One of your officers! He was my brother! That's more than being one of your officers!"

"Not," answered Ian in the same voice, "where justice is concerned."

"Justice?" Kenebuck laughed. "Justice for Brian? Is that it?"

"And for thirty-two enlisted men."

"Oh—" Kenebuck snorted laughingly. "Thirty-two men . . . those thirty-two men!" He shook his head. "I never knew your thirty-two men, Graeme, so you can't blame me for them. That was Brian's fault; him and his idea—what was the charge they tried him on? Oh, yes, that he and his thirty-two or thirty-six men could raid enemy Headquarters and come back with the enemy Commandant. Come back . . . covered with glory." Kenebuck laughed again. "But it didn't work. Not my fault."

"Brian did it," said Ian, "to show you. You were what made him do it."

"Me? Could I help it if he never could match up to me?" Kenebuck stared down at his glass and took a quick swallow from it, then went back to cuddling it in his hands. He smiled a little to himself. "Never could even *catch* up to me." He looked whitely across at Ian. "I'm just a better man, Graeme. You better remember that."

Ian said nothing. Kenebuck continued to stare at him; and slowly Kenebuck's face grew more savage.

"Don't believe me, do you?" said Kenebuck, softly. "You better believe me. I'm not Brian, and I'm not bothered by Dorsais. You're here, and I'm facing you—alone."

"Alone?" said Ian. For the first time Tyburn, above the ceiling over the heads of the two men, listening and watching through hidden sensors, thought he heard a hint of emotion—contempt—in Ian's voice. Or had he imagined it?

"Alone— Well!" James Kenebuck laughed again, but a little cautiously. "I'm a civilized man, not a hick frontiersman. But I don't have to be a fool. Yes, I've got men covering you from behind the walls of the room here. I'd be stupid not to. And I've got this . . ." He whistled, and something about the size of a small dog, but made of smooth, black metal, slipped out from behind a sofa nearby and slid on an aircushion over the carpeting to their feet.

Ian looked down. It was a sort of satchel with an orifice in the top from which two metallic tentacles protruded slightly.

Ian nodded slightly.

"A medical mech," he said.

"Yes," said Kenebuck, "cued to respond to the heartbeats of anyone in the room with it. So you see, it wouldn't do you any good, even if you somehow knew where all my guards were and beat them to the draw. Even if you killed me, this could get to me in time to keep it from being permanent. So, I'm unkillable. Give up!" He laughed and kicked at the mech. "Get back," he said to it. It slid back behind the sofa.

"So you see . . ." he said. "Just sensible precautions. There's no trick to it. You're a military man—and what's that mean? Superior strength. Superior tactics. That's all. So I outpower your strength, outnumber you, make your tactics useless—and what are you? Nothing." He put his glass carefully aside on the table with the decanter. "But I'm not Brian. I'm not afraid of you. I could do without these things if I wanted to."

Ian sat watching him. On the floor above, Tyburn had stiffened.

"Could you?" asked Ian.

Kenebuck stared at him. The white face of the millionaire contorted. Blood surged up into it, darkening it. His eyes flashed whitely.

"What're you trying to do—test me?" he shouted suddenly. He jumped to his feet and stood over Ian, waving his arms furiously. It was, recognized Tyburn overhead, the calculated, self-induced hysterical rage of the hoodlum world. But how would Ian Graeme below know that? Suddenly, Kenebuck was screaming. "You want to try me out? You think I won't face you? You think I won't face you? You think I'll back down like that brother of mine, that . . ." he broke into a flood of obscenity in which the name of Brian was freely mixed. Abruptly he whirled about to the walls of the room, yelling at them. "Get out of there. All right, out! Do you hear me? All of you! Out—"

Panels slid back, bookcases swung aside, and four men stepped into the room. Three were those who had been in the foyer earlier when Ian had entered for the first time. The other was of the same type.

"Out!" screamed Kenebuck at them. "Everybody out. Outside, and lock the door behind you. I'll show this Dorsai, this . . ." almost foaming at the mouth, he lapsed into obscenity again.

Overhead, above the ceiling, Tyburn found himself gripping the edge of the table below the observation screen so hard his fingers ached.

"It's a trick!" he muttered between his teeth to the unhearing Ian. "He planned it this way! Can't you see that?"

"Graeme armed?" inquired the police sensor technician at Tyburn's right. Tyburn jerked his head around momentarily to stare at the technician.

"No," said Tyburn. "Why?"

"Kenebuck is." The technician reached over and tapped the screen, just below the left shoulder of Kenebuck's jacket image. "Slugthrower."

Tyburn made a fist of his aching right fingers and softly pounded the table before the screen in frustration.

"All right!" Kenebuck was shouting below, turning back to the still-seated form of Ian, and spreading his arms wide. "Now's your chance. Jump me! The door's locked. You think there's anyone else near to help me? Look!" He turned and took five steps to the wide, knee-high to ceiling window behind him, punched the control button and watched as it swung wide. A few of the whirling sleet-ghosts outside drove from out of ninety stories of vacancy, into the opening—and fell dead in little drops of moisture on the windowsill as the automatic weather shield behind the glass blocked them out.

He stalked back to Ian, who had neither moved nor changed expression through all this. Slowly, Kenebuck sank back down into his chair, his back to the night, the blocked-out cold and the sleet.

"What's the matter?" he asked, slowly, acidly. "You don't do anything? Maybe *you* don't have the nerve, Graeme?"

"We were talking about Brian," said Ian.

"Yes, Brian . . ." Kenebuck said, quite slowly. "He had a big head. He wanted to be like me, but no matter how he tried—how I tried to help him—he couldn't make it." He stared at Ian. "That's just the way, he never could make it—the way he decided to go into enemy lines when there wasn't a chance in the world. That's the way he was—a loser."

"With help," said Ian.

"What? What's that you're saying?" Kenebuck jerked upright in his chair.

"You helped him lose." Ian's voice was matter of fact. "From the time he was a young boy, you built him up to want to be like you—to take long chances and win. Only your chances were always safe bets, and his were as unsafe as you could make them."

Kenebuck drew in an audible, hissing breath.

"You've got a big mouth, Graeme!" he said, in a low, slow voice.

"You wanted," said Ian, almost conversationally, "to have him kill himself off. But he never quite did. And each time he came back for more, because he had it stuck into his mind, carved into his mind, that he wanted to impress you—even though by the time he was grown, he saw what you were up to. He knew, but he still wanted to make you admit that he wasn't a loser. You'd twisted him that way while he was growing up, and that was the way he grew."

"Go on," hissed Kenebuck. "Go on, big mouth."

"So, he went off-Earth and became a professional soldier," went on Ian, steadily and calmly. "Not because he was drafted like someone from Newton or a born professional from the Dorsai, or hungry like one of the ex-miners from Coby. But to show you you were wrong about him. He found one place where you couldn't compete with him, and he must have started writing back to you to tell you about it—half rubbing it in, half-asking for the pat on the back you never gave him."

Kenebuck sat in the chair and breathed. His eyes were all one glitter.

"But you didn't answer his letters," said Ian. "I suppose you thought that'd make him desperate enough to finally do something fatal. But he didn't. Instead he succeeded. He went up through the ranks. Finally, he got his commission and made Force-Leader, and you began to be worried. It wouldn't be long, if he kept on going up, before he'd be above the field officer grades, and out of most of the actual fighting."

Warrior

Kenebuck sat perfectly still, a little leaning forward. He looked almost as if he were praying, or putting all the force of his mind to willing that Ian finish what he had started to say.

"And so," said Ian, "on his twenty-third birthday—which was the day before the night on which he led his men against orders into the enemy area—you saw that he got this birthday card . . ." He reached into a side pocket of his civilian jacket and took out a white, folded card that showed signs of having been savagely crumpled but was now smoothed out again. Ian opened it and laid it beside the decanter on the table between their chairs, the sketch and legend facing Kenebuck. Kenebuck's eyes dropped to look at it.

The sketch was a crude outline of a rabbit, with a combat rifle and battle helmet discarded at its feet, engaged in painting a broad yellow stripe down the center of its own back. Underneath this picture was printed in block letters, the question—"WHY FIGHT IT?"

Kenebuck's face slowly rose from the sketch to face Ian, and the millionaire's mouth stretched at the corners, and went on stretching into a ghastly version of a smile.

"Was that all . . . ?" whispered Kenebuck.

"Not all," said Ian. "Along with it, glued to the paper by the rabbit, there was this—"

He reached almost casually into his pocket.

"No, you don't!" screamed Kenebuck triumphantly. Suddenly he was on his feet, jumping behind his chair, backing away toward the darkness of the window behind him. He reached into his jacket and his hand came out holding the slug-thrower, which cracked loudly in the room. Ian had not moved, and his body jerked to the heavy impact of the slug.

Suddenly, Ian had come to life. Incredibly, after being hammered by a slug, the shock of which should have immobilized an ordinary man, Ian was out of the chair on his feet and moving forward. Kenebuck screamed again—this time with pure terror—and began to back away, firing as he went.

"Die, you—! Die!" he screamed. But the towering Dorsai figure came on. Twice it was hit and spun clear around by the heavy slugs, but like a football fullback shaking off the assaults of tacklers, it plunged on, with great strides narrowing the distance between it and the retreating Kenebuck.

Screaming finally, Kenebuck came up with the back of his knees against the low sill of the open window. For a second his face distorted itself out of all human shape in a grimace of its terror. He looked, to right and to left, but there was no place left to run. He had been pulling the trigger of his slugthrower all this time, but now the firing pin clicked at last upon an empty chamber. Gibbering, he threw the weapon at Ian, and it flew wide of the driving figure of the Dorsai, now almost upon him, great hands outstretched.

Kenebuck jerked his head away from what was rushing toward him. Then, with a howl like a beaten dog, he turned and flung himself through the window before those hands could touch him, into ninety-odd stories of unsupported space. And his howl carried away down into silence.

Ian halted. For a second he stood before the window, his right hand still clenched about whatever it was he had pulled from his pocket. Then, like a toppling tree, he fell.

—As Tyburn and the technician with him finished burning through the ceiling above and came dropping through the charred opening into the room. They almost landed on the small object that had come rolling from Ian's now-lax hand. An object that was really two objects glued together. A small paintbrush and a transparent tube of glaringly yellow paint.

"I hope you realize, though," said Tyburn, two weeks later on an icy, bright December day as he and the recovered Ian stood just inside the Terminal waiting for the boarding signal from the spaceliner about to take off for the Sirian worlds, "what a chance you took with Kenebuck. It was just luck it worked out for you the way it did."

"No," said Ian. He was as apparently emotionless as ever; a little more gaunt from his stay in the Manhattan hospital, but he had mended with the swiftness of his Dorsai constitution. "There was no luck. It all happened the way I planned it."

Tyburn gazed in astonishment.

"Why . . ." he said, "if Kenebuck hadn't had to send his hoods out of the room to make it seem necessary for him to shoot you himself when you put your hand into your pocket that second time—or if you hadn't had the card in the first place—" He broke off, suddenly thoughtful. "You mean . . . ?" he stared at Ian. "Having the card, you planned to have Kenebuck get you alone . . . ?"

"It was a form of personal combat," said Ian. "And personal combat is my business. You assumed that Kenebuck was strongly entrenched, facing my attack. But it was the other way around."

"But you had to come to him—"

"I had to appear to come to him," said Ian, almost coldly, "otherwise he wouldn't have believed that he had to kill me—before I killed him. By his decision to kill me, he put himself in the attacking position."

"But he had all the advantages!" said Tyburn, his head whirling. "You had to fight on his ground, here where he was strong . . ."

"No," said Ian. "You're confusing the attack position with the defensive one. By coming here, I put Kenebuck in the position of finding out whether I actually had the birthday card, and the knowledge of why Brian had gone against orders into enemy territory that night. Kenebuck planned to have his men in the foyer shake me down for the card—but they lost their nerve."

Warrior 131

"I remember," murmured Tyburn.

"Then, when I handed him the package, he was sure the card was in it. But it wasn't," went on Ian. "He saw his only choice was to give me a situation where I might feel it was safe to admit having the card and the knowledge. He had to know about that, because Brian had called his bluff by going out and risking his neck after getting the card. The fact Brian was tried and executed later made no difference to Kenebuck. That was a matter of law—something apart from hoodlum guts, or lack of guts. If no one knew that Brian was braver than his older brother, that was all right; but if I knew, he could only save face under his own standards by killing me."

"He almost did," said Tyburn. "Any one of those slugs—"

"There was the medical mech," said Ian, calmly. "A man like Kenebuck would be bound to have something like that around to play safe—just as he would be bound to set an amateur's trap." The boarding horn of the spaceliner sounded. Ian picked up his luggage bag. "Good-by," he said, offering his hand to Tyburn.

"Good-by . . ." he muttered. "So you were just going along with Kenebuck's trap, all of it. I can't believe it . . ." He released Ian's hand and watched as the big man swung around and took the first two strides away toward the bulk of the ship shining in the winter sunlight. Then, suddenly, the numbness broke clear from Tyburn's mind. He ran after Ian and caught at his arm. Ian stopped and swung half-around, frowning slightly.

"I can't believe it!" cried Tyburn. "You mean you went up there, *knowing* Kenebuck was going to pump you full of slugs and maybe kill you—all just to square things for thirty-two enlisted soldiers under the command of a man you didn't even like? I don't believe it—you can't be that cold-blooded! I don't care how much of a man of the military you are!"

Ian looked down at him. And it seemed to Tyburn that the Dorsai face had gone away from him, somehow become as remote and stony as a face carved high up on some icy mountain's top.

"But I'm not just a man of the military," Ian said. "That was the mistake Kenebuck made, too. That was why he thought that stripped of military elements, I'd be easy to kill."

Tyburn, looking at him, felt a chill run down his spine as icy as wind off a glacier.

"Then, in heaven's name," cried Tyburn. "What are you?"

Ian looked from his far distance down into Tyburn's eyes and the sadness rang as clear in his voice finally, as iron-shod heels on barren rock.

"I am a man of war," said Ian, softly.

With that, he turned and went on; and Tyburn saw him black against the winter-bright sky, looming over all the other departing passengers, on his way to board the spaceship. ■

HAWK AMONG THE SPARROWS
Dean McLaughlin

When we look at the spectacle of weapons growing ever bigger and more effective and fearsome, it is well to remember that effectiveness and fearsomeness can be defined only in terms of a historical context. That fact can have surprising implications, as this latter-day "Connecticut Yankee" found out. . . .

THE MAP-POSITION SCOPE on the left side of *Pika-Don*'s instrument panel showed where he was, but it didn't show airfields. Right now, Howard Farman needed an airfield. He glanced again at the fuel gauge. Not a chance of making it to Frankfurt, or even into West Germany. Far below, white clouds like a featureless ocean sprawled all the way to the horizon.

Those clouds shouldn't have been there. Less than four hours ago, before he lifted off the *Eagle*, he'd studied a set of weather satellite photos freshly televised down from orbit. Southern France had been almost clear—only a dotting of cottonboll tufts. It shouldn't have been possible for solid overcast to build up so fast. For the dozenth time, he flipped through the meteorological data on his clipboard. No, nothing that could have created such a change.

That made two things he hadn't been able to figure out. The other was even stranger. He'd lifted from the *Eagle*'s deck at midmorning. The French bomb test he'd been snooping had blinded him for a while—how long he didn't know—and *Pika-Don* was thrown out of control. The deadman circuit had cut in; control was re-established. When his sight came back—and it couldn't have been terribly long—the sun had been halfway down in the west.

It wasn't possible. *Pika-Don* didn't carry enough fuel to stay up that long.

Just the same, she'd stayed up, and she still had almost half her load. When he couldn't find the *Eagle* near Gibraltar, he'd thought there was enough to take him to the American airbase at Frankfurt. (And where could the *Eagle* have gone? What could have happened to her radar beacon? Could the French blast have smashed *Pika-Don*'s reception equipment? Everything else seemed to work all right. But he'd made an eyeball search, too. Aircraft tenders didn't just vanish.)

On the map scope, the Rhone valley crawled slowly southward under the north-moving central piplight that marked *Pika-Don*'s inertially computed position. It matched perfectly the radar-scanned terrain displayed on the airspace viewscope on the right-hand side of the instrument panel. Frankfurt was still beyond the horizon, more than four hundred miles off. *Pika-Don* didn't have fuel to cover half that distance.

Well, he wouldn't find an airfield by staying up here, above the carpet of cloud. He eased the throttles back and put *Pika-Don*'s nose down. She'd burn fuel a lot faster down close to the deck, but at mach 1.5 he could search a lot of ground before the tanks went dry.

Not that he absolutely had to find an airfield. *Pika-Don* could put down almost anywhere if she had to. But an airfield would make it a lot simpler to get a new load of fuel, and it would make less complicated the problems that would come from putting down in a technically still friendly nation.

It was a long way down. He watched the radar-echo altimeter reel downward like a clock thrown into panicked reverse; watched the skin temperature gauge edge up, level out, edge up again as *Pika-Don* descended into thicker air. For the first eighty thousand feet, visibility was perfect, but at twelve thousand feet *Pika-Don* went into the clouds; it was like being swallowed by gray night. Uneasily, Farman watched the radar horizon; these clouds might go down all the way to the ground, and at mach 1.5 there wouldn't be anything left but a smear if *Pika-Don* hit. She was too sweet an airplane for that. Besides, he was inside.

He broke out into clear air a little under four thousand feet. A small city lay off to his right. He turned toward it. Beaufort, the map scope said. There'd be some sort of airfield near it. He pulled the throttles back as far as he dared—just enough to maintain air-speed. The machmeter slipped back to 1.25.

He passed north of the town, scanning the land. No sign of a field. He circled southward, careful to keep his bearing away from the town's center. There'd be trouble enough about his coming down in France—aerial trespass by a nuclear-armed warplane, to start with—without half the townspeople screaming about smashed windows, cracked plaster, and roosters that stopped laying eggs. The ambassador in Paris was going to earn his paycheck this week.

Still no airfield. He went around again, farther out. Dozens of villages flashed past below. He tore his flight plan, orders, and weather data off their clipboard—crammed the papers into the disposal funnel; wouldn't do to have nosy Frenchmen pawing that stuff, not at all. He substituted the other flight plan—the one they'd given him just in case he had to put down in French or French-friendly territory.

He was starting his third circuit and the fuel gauge was leaning against the red mark when he saw the field. It wasn't much of a place—just a grassy postage stamp with a few old planes in front of three ramshackle sheds and a windsock flopping clumsily over the middle one. He put around, aimed for it, and converted to vertical thrust. Airspeed dropped quickly—there was a momentary surge of wing-surface heating—and then he was hovering only a few miles from the field. He used the deflectors to cover the distance, losing altitude as he went. He jockeyed to a position near the hangars, faced *Pika-Don* into the wind, and let her down.

The engines died—starved of fuel—before he could cut them off.

It took a while to disconnect all the umbilici that linked him into *Pika-Don*'s control and environment systems. Some of the connections were hard to reach. It took a while longer to raise the canopy, climb over the side, and drop to the ground. Two soldiers were waiting for him. They had rifles.

The bigger one—the one with the bushy moustache—spoke dangerously. Farman didn't know French, but their gestures with rifle muzzles were a universal language. He raised his hands. "I'm an American," he said. "I ran out of fuel." He hoped they weren't disciples of the late *le grand Charles*. They looked nasty enough.

The two exchanged glances. "Americaine?" the smaller one asked. He was clean-shaved. His eyes had a deep, hollow look. He didn't sound at all displeased.

Farman nodded vigorously. "Yes. American." He pointed to the fifty-one-star flag on his coverall sleeve. Their faces broke into delighted smiles and they put down their weapons. The small one—he made Farman think of a terrier, and his rifle was absurdly big for him—pointed to a shack beyond the hangars. "Come."

Farman went. The area in front of the hangars had been paved—an uneven spread of asphalt. Half a dozen rattletrap airplanes stood in a line, facing out toward the field. Where the pavement met unpaved ground, it was one mud puddle after another. Farman had to be careful where he put his feet; his flight boots had been clean when he took off this morning. The soldiers didn't seem to mind. They splashed cheerfully through the wet and scuffed their heels on the tufts of grass.

The planes were all the same type—biplanes with open cockpits and two-bladed wooden propellers and radial-type piston engines. The kind of planes, Farman thought, that shouldn't even be flying any more. Nevertheless, they were obviously working airplanes, with oil stains on their cowls and the smell of gasoline and patches glued over holes in the fabric of wings and fuselage. A crop-dusting outfit? Did the French have crop-dusting outfits? Then he realized those things in front of the cockpits were machine guns. Air-cooled machine guns rigged to shoot through the propeller. And those odd, oval-shaped tail assemblies . . .

Some kind of museum?

"That is a strange aeroplane you have," the moustached soldier said. His accent was as thick as the grass on the field. "I have not seen one like it."

Farman hadn't known either of them spoke English. "I'll need to make some phone calls," he said, thinking of the ambassador in Paris. A mechanic was working on one of the planes they passed; he was standing on a wooden packing crate, tinkering with the engine.

A movie outfit, doing a period flick? But he didn't see any cameras.

Another biplane taxied in from the field—a Nieuport, like the others. Its engine racketed like a lawnmower. It joggled and bounced in the chuckholes. There were a lot of chuckholes in the mud at the pavement's fringe. The plane came up on the pavement and the engine cut out. As the propeller turned around to a spasmodic stop, Farman realized that not just the propeller but the whole engine had been spinning. What kind of crazy way to build airplanes was that?

The Nieuport's pilot climbed up out of the cockpit and dropped to the ground. "Guns jammed again!" he yelled loudly, hellishly mad. He flung a small hammer on the ground at his feet.

Three men came out of the hangar carrying packing crates. They set them down around the Nieuport's nose, got up on them, and started working on the guns. The flier pulled off his scarf and draped it over the cockpit's side. He turned away, spoke a few French words to the mechanics over his shoulder, and walked off.

"*Monsieur* Blake!" the big soldier hailed. When the flier didn't seem to hear, the soldier ran to him, caught his shoulder. "*Monsieur* Blake. A countryman." The soldier beside Farman pointed to the flag on Farman's sleeve.

Blake came over, stuffing a goggled cloth helmet into a pocket of his heavy overcoat as he approached. His hand was out in welcome.

"This one has teach all my *Anglais* to me," the big trooper grinned. "Is good, *non?*"

Farman scarcely heard him. All his attention was on this American. "Harry Blake," the man introduced himself. " 'Fraid I won't be able to hear you too good for a while." He swung a glance at his Nieuport's motor and raised hands to his ears to signify deafness. He was young—not more than twenty-two or three—but he had the mature poise of a man much older. "I'm a Lafayette with this outfit. From Springfield, Illinois. You?"

Farman accepted the hand in numb silence. Calling himself a Lafayette, he'd obliterated Farman's last incredulous doubt. It wasn't possible—not real. Things like this didn't happen.

"Hey, you don't look so good," Blake said, grabbing his arm with a strong hand.

"I'll be all right," Farman said, but he wasn't really sure.

"Come on," Blake said. He steered Farman into the passageway between two of the hangars. "We've got what you need back there."

The troopers came after them. "*Monsieur* Blake. This man has only now arrived. He has not reported."

Blake waved them away. "I haven't either. We'll report later. Can't you see when a man's breathed too much oil?"

The soldiers turned back. Blake's hand steered Farman onward. Puddles slopped under Blake's boots.

Behind the hangars, the path split in two directions. One way led to a latrine whose door swung loose in the breeze. The other led to a shack huddled up to the back of a hangar. It was hard to guess which path was more frequently used. Blake paused at the parting of the ways. "Think you can make it?"

"I'm all right." He wasn't, really. It takes more than a deep breath and a knuckling of the eyes to adjust a man to having lost six decades. Between books about aerial combat he'd devoured as a kid—two wars and all those brushfire skirmishes—he'd read some Heinlein and Asimov. If it wasn't for that, he'd have had nothing to hang on to. It was like a kick in the belly.

"I'll be all right," he said.

"You're sure? You breathe castor oil a few hours a day and it doesn't do a man's constitution much good. Nothin' to be embarrassed about."

Every now and then, Farman had heard castor oil mentioned, mostly in jokes, but he'd never been sure what it did to a man. Now he remembered it had been used in aircraft engines of this time. Suddenly, he understood all. "That's one problem I don't have."

Blake laughed. "It's a problem we all have." He pushed open the shack's door. Farman went inside at his nod. Blake followed. "On-ree!" Blake called out. "Two double brandies."

A round little bald-pated Frenchman got up from a stool behind the cloth-draped trestle that served as a bar. He poured two glasses almost full of something dark. Blake picked up one in each hand. "How many for you?"

Whatever it was, it looked evil. "One," Farman said, "for a start." Either this youngster was showing off—which didn't seem likely—or it wasn't as deadly as it looked. "A double, that is."

Blake led the way to a table in the far corner, next to a window. It was a plain wood table, stained and scarred. Farman set his glass down and took a chair before he tried a small taste. It was like a trickle of fire all the way down. He looked at the glass as if it had fangs. "What is this stuff?"

Blake had sampled from each glass on the way to the table, to keep them from spilling. Now he was almost halfway through one of them and the other was close to his hand. "Blackberry brandy," he said with a rueful grin. "It's the only cure we've found. Would you rather have the disease?"

Flight medicine, Farman thought, had a long way to go. He put his glass carefully aside. "My plane doesn't use that kind of oil."

Blake was on him right away. "Something new? I thought they'd tried everything."

"It's a different kind of engine," Farman said. He had to do something with his hands. He took a sip of the brandy, choked, regretted it.

"How long you been flying?" Blake asked.

"Ten, twelve years."

Blake had been about to finish his first glass. He set it down untouched, looked straight at Farman. Slowly, a grin came. "All right. A joke's a joke. You going to be flying with us?"

"Maybe. I don't know," Farman said, holding his brandy glass in both hands, perfectly steady—and all the time, deep inside him, the small trapped being that was himself screamed silently, *What's happened to me? What's happened?*

It had been a tricky mission, but he'd flown a lot of tricky ones. Ostensibly, he'd been taking part in a systems-test/training exercise off the northwest coast of Africa. High altitude mach 4 aircraft, their internal equipment assisted by the tracking and computer equipment on converted aircraft carriers, were attempting to intercept simulated ballistic warheads making re-entry into the atmosphere. He'd lifted from the deck of the airplane tender *Eagle* in the western Mediterranean. Half an hour later he was circling at Big Ten—one-oh-oh thousand feet—on-station north of the Canary Islands when the signal came that sent him on his true mission.

A guidance system had gone wrong at the Cape, said the talker aboard the *Iwo Jima,* and the range-safety system had failed. The misdirected warhead was arching over the Atlantic, farther and higher than programmed. Instead of splashing in the Atlantic, its projected impact-point was deep in the Sahara. It carried only a concrete block, not thermonuclear weaponry, but diplomatic relations with France—which still maintained military bases in this land it had once governed—were troublesome. Standing orders for such an eventuality were that, as a good-faith demonstration, an attempt should be made to intercept it.

Operation Skeetshoot's master computer said Farman's *Pika-Don* was the only plane able to make the interception. No other plane was in the right position. No other plane had enough altitude, or fuel load. No other plane had such an advantageous direction of flight at that moment. Farman sent *Pika-Don* streaking toward interception point at full thrust.

As planned.

Nothing had really gone wrong at the Cape. It was a pretext. Washington knew the French were about to test a new model nuclear bomb. They would explode it above the atmosphere, in the radiation belt; the rocket would be launched from their main testing site, the Saharan oasis of Reggan; they would select the moment of launch to coincide with the arrival of a solar proton storm, when subnuclear particles from the storm would blend with the bomb's fission products, rendering surveillance by other nations more difficult and the findings less certain.

The proton storm had been already on its way when Farman left the *Eagle*'s deck. It was being tracked, not only by American installations around the world, but French stations also. Code message traffic was high between New Caledonia and Reggan. The time of the storm's arrival was known to within five seconds.

Farman hadn't paid much attention to why Washington wanted to snoop the test; the French were, after all, still allies in spite of the frictions between Paris and Washington. Asking questions like that wasn't Farman's job; he was just the airplane driver. But they'd told him anyway, when they gave him the mission. Something about Washington wanting to have up-to-date knowledge of France's independent nuclear capability. Such information was needed, they said, for accurate judgment of how dependent France might still be on America's ability to wage modern war. To Farman, the explanation didn't mean much; he didn't understand much about international politics.

But a warhead dropping into the atmosphere, sheathed in the meteor-flame of its fall—*that* he could understand. And a multi-megaton fireball a hundred miles up, blazing like the sun brought suddenly too close—that, too, he could understand. And a mach 4 airplane riding her shock-wave across the sky, himself inside watching instruments and flight-path guide scopes, and his thumb on the button that would launch the Lance rockets sheathed against her belly. Those were things he understood. They were his job.

Nor did the mission call for him to do more than that. All that was really necessary was to have *Pika-Don* somewhere in the sky above Reggan when the French bomb went off. *Pika-Don* would do everything else, automatically.

All the planes in Operation Skeetshoot were equipped the same as *Pika-Don*. All of them carried elaborate flight recorders; and because they were fitted to intercept thermonuclear warheads, and their own Lance rockets had sub-kiloton fission tips, those recorders included all the instruments needed to monitor a nuclear explosion—even a unit to measure the still-not-fully-understood magnetohydrodynamic disturbances that played inside a nuclear fireball. (And, it was known from previous tests, there was something unusual about the magnetic fields of French bombs.)

Nor would there be much risk if *Pika-Don* were forced down on French or French-friendly territory. All *Pika-Don* carried was standard equipment—equipment the French already knew about, in configurations and for purposes they also understood. There would be nothing the French could find to support a charge of deliberate snooping, no matter how much they might suspect. Not that the possibility was large; the explosion, after all, would be out in space. There'd be no blast effects, certainly, and very little radiation. Enough to tickle the instruments, was all.

And already the hot line between Washington and Paris would be explaining why an American plane was intruding on French-controlled airspace. Everything had been planned.

Farman watched his instruments, his flight-path guide scopes, his radar. *Pika-Don* slashed the thin air so fast she drew blood. She was up to one-thirty thousand now; rocket launch point lay five thousand higher, two hundred miles ahead. Reggan moved onto the edge of the inertial-guide map-position scope, ahead and off to the south. The projected trajectory of the warhead was a red line striking downward on the foreview guide scope. An X-slash marked Skeetshoot Control's computed interception point.

Something flared on the radar near Reggan. It rose, slowly for a moment, then asymptotically faster and faster, shining on the radar screen like a bright, fierce jewel. The French rocket. It had to be. Farman's breath caught as he watched it. The thing was going up. The test was on.

It rose, was level with him, then higher. Suddenly, it quivered like a water drop, and suddenly it was gone from the screen in an expanding black blindness like a hole in the universe; and simultaneously the cockpit was full of unendurable white light. The sky was flaming, so bright Farman couldn't look at it, didn't dare. He had just time enough to think, terrified, *Not in the radiation belt!* and then *Pika-Don* was spinning, spinning, spinning like a spindle—light flashing into the cockpit, then blackness, brightness, then blackness again, repeating and repeating faster and faster and faster until light and darkness merged to a flickering brilliance that dazzled not only the eyes but the whole brain. Farman battled the controls, but it was like fighting the Almighty's wrath. The flickering blaze went on and on.

And slowed, finally. Stopped, like the last frame of a halted movie projector, and it was only daylight again, and *Pika-Don*'s disabled pilot circuit had cut in. She was flying level, northwestward if the compass could be trusted, and the sun was more than halfway down in the west, although Farman was sure that much time hadn't passed.

The map scope confirmed the compass. So did the airspace radar view. The controls felt all right now, and *Pika-Don* seemed to fly without difficulty. He turned straight north toward the Mediterranean and came out over it not far from Oran. He curved west then, toward the spot he'd left the *Eagle*. He watched the foreview guide scope for the *Eagle*'s homing beacon. It didn't come on. He spoke on the radio, got no answer. Equipment damage?

He took *Pika-Don* down to fifty thousand. He used the telescopeview scope on the ships his radar picked out. None were the *Eagle*; old freighters, mostly, and two small warships of a type he'd thought weren't used any more except by the Peruvian Navy.

His orders said, if he couldn't find his base ship, go to Frankfurt. The big base there could take him. He turned *Pika-Don* northwestward. He crossed the French coast. Overcast covered the land. It shouldn't have been there. Fuel began to run low. It was going into the engines faster than the distance to Frankfurt was narrowing. He tried to cut fuel consumption, but he couldn't cut it enough. He had no choice but to put down in France.

"Look, Mister. Either you've got orders to fly with us, or you don't," Blake said. "What outfit are you with?"

It was restricted information, but Farman didn't think it mattered much. "The CIA, I think."

He might as well have said the Seventh Cavalry with General Custer. "Where's your base?" Blake asked.

Farman took another swallow of brandy. He needed it, even if not for the reason Blake thought. It wasn't so bad, this time. He tried to think of a way to explain the thing that had happened to him. "Did you ever read *The Time Machine*?" he asked.

"What's that? A book about clocks?"

"It's a story by H.G. Wells."

"Who's H.G. Wells?"

He wasn't going to make much explanation by invoking H.G. Wells. "It's about a man who . . . who builds a machine that moves through time the way an airplane moves in the air."

"If you're having fun with me, you're doing it good," Blake said.

Farman tried again. "Think of a building—a tall building, with elevators in it. And suppose you don't know about elevators—can't even imagine how they work. And suppose you were on the ground floor, and suppose I came up and told you I was from the twentieth floor."

"I'd say that's doing a lot of supposing," Blake said.

"But you get the idea?"

"Maybe. Maybe not."

"All right. Now imagine that the ground floor is now. Today. And the basement is yesterday. And the second floor is tomorrow, and the third floor is the day after tomorrow, and so on."

"It's a way of thinking about things," Blake said.

Hawk Among the Sparrows

Give thanks the elevator was invented. "Take it one step more, now. Suppose you're on the ground floor, and someone comes down from the twentieth floor."

"He'd of come from somewhere the other side of next week," Blake said.

"That's the idea," Farman said. He took more of the brandy. He needed it. "What if I told you I . . . just fell down the elevator shaft from sixty years up?"

Blake appeared to consider while he started on his second glass. He permitted himself a smile and a chuckle. "I'd say a man's got to be a bit crazy if he wants to fly in this war, and if you want to fight Huns you've come to the right place."

He didn't believe. Well, you couldn't expect him to. "I was born in 1946," Farman told him. "I'm thirty-two years old. My father was born in 1920. Right now, it's nineteen . . . seventeen?"

"Nineteen *eighteen*," Blake said. "June tenth. Have another brandy."

Farman discovered his glass was empty. He didn't remember emptying it. Shakily, he stood up. "I think I'd better talk to your commanding officer."

Blake waved him back to his chair. "Might as well have another brandy. He hasn't come back yet. My guns jammed and I couldn't get them unjammed, so I came home early. He'll be back when he runs out of bullets or fuel, one or the other."

His back was to the door, so he had to twist around while still talking, to see who came in. The small, razor-moustached man draped his overcoat on a chair and accepted the brandy the barman had poured without having to be asked. "Today, *M'sieu* Blake, it was a small bit of both." His English had only a flavor of accent. "On coming back, I find I am left with one bullet."

"How was the hunting?"

The Frenchman gave a shrug that was as much a part of France as the Eiffel tower. "Ah, that man has the lives of a cat, the hide of an old bull elephant, and the skills of a magician."

"Keyserling?" Blake asked.

The newcomer took a chair at the table. "Who else? I have him in my sights. I shoot, and he is gone. It would be a shame to kill this man—he flies superbly!—and I would love to do it very much." He smiled and sipped his brandy.

"This is our CO," Blake said. "Philippe Deveraux. Thirty-three confirmed kills and maybe a dozen not confirmed. The only man on this part of the front with more is Keyserling." He turned to Farman. "I don't think I got your name."

Farman gave it. "He's just over from the States," Blake said. "And he's been funning me with the craziest story you ever heard."

Farman didn't bother to protest. In similar shoes, he'd be just as skeptical. "This Keyserling," he said. "That's Bruno Keyserling?"

He'd read about Keyserling; next to Richthofen, Bruno Keyserling had been the most hated, feared, and respected man in the German air force.

"That's him," Blake said. "There's not a one of us that wouldn't like to get him in our sights." He set his empty glass down hard. "But it won't happen that way. He's gotten better men than us. Sooner or later, he'll get us all."

Deveraux had been delicately sipping his drink. Now he set it down. "We shall talk of it later, *M'sieu* Blake," he said firmly. He addressed Farman. "You have been waiting for me?"

"Yes. I . . ." Suddenly, he realized he didn't know what to say.

"Don't give him the same you gave me," Blake warned. "Now it's business."

"You are a pilot, *M'sieu* Farman?" Deveraux asked.

Farman nodded. "And I've got a plane that can fly faster and climb higher than anything you've got. I'd like a try at this Keyserling."

"That could possibly be arranged. But I should warn you, *M'sieu* . Farman, did you say?"

"Howard Farman."

"I should warn you, the man is a genius. He had done things his aeroplane should not be possible to do. He has shot down forty-six, perhaps more. Once three in a day. Once two in five minutes. It has been said the man came from nowhere—that he is one of the gods from the *Nibelungenleid,* come to battle for his fatherland. He . . ."

"You might say I'm from nowhere, too," Farman said. "Me and my plane."

When Deveraux had finished his brandy and when Blake had downed his fourth, they went out in front of the hangars again. Farman wanted them to see *Pika-Don*. *Pika-Don* would be sixty years ahead of any plane they'd ever seen.

Her skids had cut into the turf like knives. Blake and Deveraux examined her from end to end. They walked around her, their boottips whipping the grass. "Don't touch anything," Farman told them. "Even a scratch in the wrong place could wreck her." He didn't add that the rockets concealed under her belly could vaporize everything within a hundred yards. The false-skin strips that sealed them from the slipstream were supposed to be tamper-proof, but just to be safe Farman placed himself where the men would have to go past him to investigate *Pika-Don*'s underside.

Pika-Don was eighty-nine feet long. Her shark-fin wings spanned less than twenty-five. She was like a needle dart, sleek and shiny and razor-sharp on the leading edge of her wings. Her fuselage was oddly flat-bodied, like a cobra's hood. Her airscoops were like tunnels.

Blake crouched down to examine the gear that retracted the skids. Farman moved close, ready to interrupt if Blake started to fool with the rockets. Instead, Blake discovered the vertical thrust vents and lay down to peer up into them. Deveraux put his head inside one of the tail pipes. It was big enough to crawl into. Slowly, Blake rolled out from under and got to his feet again.

"Do you believe me now?" Farman asked.

"Mister," Blake said, looking at him straight, "I don't know what this thing is, and I don't know how you got it here. But don't try to tell me it flies."

"How do you think I got it here?" Farman demanded. "I'll show you. I'll . . ." He stopped. He'd forgotten he was out of fuel. "Ask your ground crews. They saw me bring her down."

Blake shook his head, fist on hips. "I know an aeroplane when I see one. This thing can't possibly fly."

Deveraux tramped toward them from the tail. "This is indeed the strangest zeppelin I have ever been shown, *M'sieu*. But obviously, a zeppelin so small—so obviously heavy . . . it can hardly be useful, *M'sieu*."

"I tell you, this is a *plane*. An *air*plane. It's faster than anything else in the air."

"But it has no wings, *M'sieu*. No propeller. It does not even have wheels on the undercarriage. How can such a thing as this gain airspeed if it has no wheels?"

Farman was speechless with exasperation. Couldn't they see? Wasn't it obvious?

"And why does it have so strong the scent of paraffin?" Deveraux asked.

A Nieuport buzzed over the hangars in a sudden burst of sound. It barrel-rolled twice, turned left, then right, then came down onto the grass. Its engine puttered. Its wires sang in the wind. It taxied across the field toward them.

"That'll be Mermier," Blake said. "He got one."

Two more planes followed. They did no acrobatics—merely turned into the wind and set down. They bounced over the turf toward the hangars. One had lost part of its upper wing. Shreds of cloth flickered in the wind.

Blake and Deveraux still watched the sky beyond the hangars, but no more planes came. Blake's hand clapped Deveraux's shoulder. "Maybe they landed somewhere else."

Deveraux shrugged. "And perhaps they did not live that long. Come. We shall find out."

They walked to the other end of the flight line where the three planes straggled up on the hardstand. Deveraux hurried ahead and Mermier and then the other two fliers climbed out of their cockpits. They talked in French, with many gestures. Farman recognized a few of the gestures—the universal language of air combat—but others were strange or ambiguous. Abruptly, Deveraux turned away, his face wearing the look of pain nobly borne.

"They won't come back," Blake told Farman quietly. "They were seen going down. Burning." His fist struck the hangar's wall. "Keyserling got Michot. He was the only one of us that had a hope of getting him."

Deveraux came back. His face wore a tight, controlled smile. "*M'sieu* Farman," he said. "I must ask to be shown the abilities of your machine."

"I'll need five hundred gallons of kerosine," Farman said. That would be enough for a lift-off, a quick crack through the barrier, and a landing. Ten minutes in the air, if he didn't drive her faster than mach 1.4. Enough to show them something of the things *Pika-Don* could do.

Deveraux frowned, touched his moustache. "Kero-sine?"

"Paraffin," Blake said. "Lamp oil." He turned to Farman. "They call it paraffin over here. But five hundred gallons—are you nuts? There isn't an aeroplane flying that needs that much lubricating. Shucks, this whole *escadrille* doesn't use that much *gas* in a week. Besides, it's no good as a lubricant—if it was, you think we'd be using the stuff we do?"

"It's not a lubricant," Farman said. "She burns it. It's fuel. And she burns it fast. She delivers a lot of thrust."

"But . . . five hundred gallons!"

"I'll need that much just for a demonstration flight." He looked straight and firm into Blake's incredulous eyes, and decided not to add that, fully loaded, *Pika-Don* took fifty thousand gallons.

Deveraux smoothed his moustache. "In liters, that is how much?"

"You're going to let him . . . ?"

"*M'sieu* Blake, do you believe this man a fraud?"

Challenged like that, Blake didn't back down. "I think he's funning us. He says he'll show us an aeroplane, and he showed us that . . . that thing over there. And when you want to see how it flies, he says it's out of fuel and asks for kerosine —*kerosine* of all things! Enough to go swimming in! Even if that's what she burns, he doesn't need anywhere near that much. And who ever heard of flying an aeroplane with lamp oil?"

Farman took Blake's arm, joggled it, made him turn. "I know," he said. "I'm telling you things it's hard to believe. In your shoes, I wouldn't believe me, either. All right. But let me have a chance to show you. I want to fight the Germans as much as you do." In his thoughts was the picture of a whole jagdstaffel of Albatrosses being engulfed by the fireball of one of *Pika-Don*'s rockets. They'd never even see him coming, he'd come at them so fast; even if they saw him, they wouldn't have a chance to get away. Sitting ducks. Fish in a barrel.

"Mister," Blake said, "I don't know what you want all that kerosine for, but I'm sure of one thing—you don't need it to fly. Because if I was ever sure of anything, I know that thing can't fly."

"*M'sieu* Blake," Deveraux said, moving in front of the American. "This man may perhaps be mistaken, but I do not think he lies. He has a faith in himself. We have need of such men in this war. If he cannot use the paraffin when we have obtained it for him, it will be given to the chef for his stoves. We shall have lost nothing. But we must let him prove his abilities, if he can, for if there is some portion of truth in his claims, why, it is possible that we have before us the man and the machine that shall hurl Bruno Keyserling from the sky."

Blake gave way grudgingly. "If you're funning us, watch out."

"You'll see," Farman promised, grim. And to Deveraux: "Make it a high-grade kerosine. The best you can get." A jet engine could burn kerosine if it had to, but

Hawk Among the Sparrows 145

kerosine wasn't a perfect jet fuel any more than wood alcohol could make good martinis. Kerosine was just the nearest thing to jet fuel he could hope to find in 1918. "And we'll have to put it through some kind of filters."

"*M'sieu,*" Deveraux said. "There is only one kind of paraffin. Either it is paraffin, or it is not."

Two days later, while they were waiting for the kerosine to come, Blake took him up in a Caudron two-seater to show him the landmarks. It was a clear day, with only a little dust haze in the direction of the front. Farman didn't think much of learning the landmarks—*Pika-Don*'s map scope was a lot more accurate than any amount of eyeball knowledge. But the scope wouldn't show him the front-line trenches twisting across the landscape, nor the location of the German airfields. It might be useful to know such things. Farman borrowed flying clothes, and they were off.

The Caudron looked like nothing so much as a clumsy box kite, or a paleolithic ancestor of the P-38. Its two racketing engines were suspended between the upper and lower wings, one on either side of the passenger nacelle. The tail empennage was joined to the wings by openwork frames of wire-braced wood that extended back from behind the engines. It had a fragile appearance, but it held together sturdily as it lurched across the field like an uncontrolled baby carriage. Finally, after what seemed an interminable length of bumping and bouncing, it lofted into the air at a speed that seemed hardly enough to get a feather airborne. A steady windblast tore at Farman's face. Hastily, he slipped the goggles down over his eyes. The climb to six thousand feet seemed to take years.

Blake didn't turn out of their spiral until they reached altitude, then headed east. The air seemed full of crests and hollows, over which the Caudron rode like a boat on a slow-swelled sea. Now and then, woozily, it swayed. A queasy feeling rooted itself in Farman's midsection, as if his stomach was being kneaded and squeezed.

Airsick? No, it couldn't be that. Anything but that. He was an experienced flier with more than ten thousand hours in the air. He couldn't possibly be airsick now. He swallowed hard and firmly held down.

Blake, in the forward cockpit, yelled and pointed over the side. Farman leaned over. The rush of air almost ripped his goggles off. Far below, small as a diorama, the trench systems snaked across a strip of barren ground—two lattice-work patterns cut into the earth, roughly parallel to each other, jaggedly angular like toothpick structures that had been crushed. Between them, naked earth as horribly pocked as the surface of the moon.

The Caudron had been following a rivercourse. The trenchlines came down from the hills to the south, crossed the river, and continued northward into the hills on that side. Ahead, over the German trenches, black puffs of anti-aircraft fire blossomed in spasmodic, irregular patterns. Blake banked the Caudron and turned south, yelling something over his shoulder about the Swiss border. The antiaircraft barrage slacked off.

Recognizing the front would be no problem, Farman decided. He tried to tell Blake, but the slipstream ripped the words away. He reached forward to tap Blake's shoulder. Something whipped his sleeve.

He looked. Something had gashed the thick fabric, but there was nothing in sight that could have done it. And for some unaccountable reason Blake was heeling the Caudron over into a dive. The horizon tilted crazily, like water sloshing in a bowl. The Caudron's wire rigging snarled nastily.

"Use the gun!" Blake yelled.

There was a machine gun mounted behind Farman's cockpit, but for a shocked moment Farman didn't grasp what Blake was talking about. Then a dark airplane shape flashed overhead, so close the buzz of its motor could be heard through the noise of the Caudron's own two engines. The goggled, cruel-mouthed face of its pilot turned to look at them. Blake threw the Caudron into a tight turn that jammed Farman deep in his cockpit. Farman lost sight of the German plane, then found it again. It was coming at them.

It was purple—a dark, royal purple with white trim around the edges of wing and tail, and around the engine cowl. Little flashes of light sparked from its nose, and Farman heard something—it sounded like thick raindrops—spattering the upper wing close to the passenger nacelle. Tracer bullets flashed past like quick fireflies.

"Use the gun!" Blake yelled again. They were climbing now. They leveled off, turned. The German plane came after them. "Use the gun!"

He was being shot at. It was appalling. Things like that didn't happen. In a moment, Farman was too busy to think about it. He got turned around in the cockpit, fumbled with the machine gun's unfamiliar handles. He'd never handled a gun like this before in his life. He found the trigger before he knew what it was. The gun chattered and bucked in his grasp. He looked all over the sky for the purple airplane. It was nowhere in sight. Blake hurled the Caudron through another violent maneuver, and suddenly there were three German planes behind them, high, the one with the white trim in front and the others trailing. The one with the white trim shifted a little to the left, turned inward again. It nosed down, gun muzzles flickering.

Farman swung the machine gun to bear on the German. He pressed the trigger. The gun stuttered and a spray of tracers streamed aft as if caught in the slipstream. They passed under the German, not even close.

Aerial gunnery wasn't something Farman ever had to learn. Combat was done with guidance systems, computers, and target-seeking missiles, not antique .30-caliber popguns. He raised the gun and fired another burst. Still too low, and passing behind the German, who was boring close in, weaving up, sidewise, and down as he came. The gun didn't have any sights worth mentioning—no target-tracking equipment at all. Farman wrestled with the clumsy weapon, trying to keep its muzzle pointed at the German. It should have been easy, but it wasn't. The German kept dodging. Farman emptied the machine gun without once touching the other plane. He spent an eternity dismounting the empty magazine and clipping another into place while Blake hurled the Caudron through a wild series of gut-wrenching acrobatics.

A section of the cockpit coaming at Farman's elbow shattered and disappeared in the wind. He got the gun working again—fired a burst just as the German sidled behind the Caudron's right rudder. The rudder exploded in a spray of chips and tatters. The German swung out to the right, gained a few feet altitude, turned in again and down again. His guns hurled blazing streaks. Blake sent the Caudron into a dive, a turn, a twist that almost hurled Farman out of his cockpit. Abruptly, then, the German was gone. Little scraps were still tearing loose from the rudder, whipped away by the slipstream.

"Where?" Farman shouted. He meant, where had the German gone, but his thoughts weren't up to asking a question that complicated.

"Skedaddled," Blake yelled back. "We've got friends. Look."

Farman twisted around, saw Blake point upward, and looked. Five hundred feet above them five Nieuports cruised in neat formation. After a moment, the formation leader waggled his wings and they curved off eastward. Farman looked down and saw they were far behind the French lines, headed northwest. They were flying level and smooth—only the slow, gentle lift and descent of random air currents, like silence at the end of a storm. "You all right?" Blake asked.

"I think so," Farman said. But suddenly, as the Caudron slipped into a downdraft, he wasn't. His stomach wrenched, and he had time enough only to get his head over the cockpit's side before the first gush of vomit came. He was still there, gripping the coaming with both hands, his stomach squeezing itself like a dry sponge, when Blake circled the airfield and slowly brought the Caudron down to a three-point landing. All Farman could think—distantly, with the part of his brain not concerned with his own terrible miseries—was how long it had been since anyone, anywhere in the world, had even thought about making a three-point landing.

He wouldn't admit—even to himself—it had been airsickness. But after a while the horizon stopped wheeling around him and he could stand without needing a hand to steady him. He discovered he was very hungry. Blake went down to the mess hall and came back with a half-loaf of black bread and a dented tin of *paté*. They went to the shack behind the hangars. Henri gave Blake a bottle of peasants' wine and two glasses. Blake put them down in the middle of the table and sat down across from Farman. He poured, and they went to work on the bread and *paté*.

"He was trying to kill us," Farman said. It just came out of him. It had been there ever since the fight. "He was trying to *kill* us."

Blake cut himself another slice of the bread. He gnawed on the leathery crust. "Sure. And I'd of killed him, given the chance. That's what we're supposed to do—him and us, both. Nothing personal at all. I've got to admit I wasn't expecting him, though. They don't often come this side of the lines. But . . ." He made a rueful grimace. "He's a tough one to outguess."

"He?"

Blake stopped gnawing, frowned. "You know who it was, don't you?"

The idea of knowing an enemy's name after such a brief acquaintance was completely strange to Farman. He couldn't even think it. His mouth made motions, but no words came out.

"Bruno Keyserling," Blake said. "He's the only man with an aeroplane painted that way."

"I'm going to get him," Farman said.

"Easier said than done," Blake said. His mouth turned grim. "You'll have to sharpen up your gunnery quite a bit, if you're going to make good on that."

"I'm going to get him," Farman repeated, knuckles white on the table.

The next day it rained. Thick, wet, gray clouds crouched low to the ground and poured down torrents. All patrols were canceled, and the fliers sat in the shack behind the hangars, drinking and listening to the storm as it pelted the shingles. At first light, when he woke and heard the rain, Farman had borrowed a slicker and gone out to *Pika-Don*. She was all right. He'd left her buttoned up tight, and the rain was doing her no harm.

Blake was still the only man Farman could talk with, except for Deveraux. None of the other fliers had more than a smattering of English. When they left the mess hall after a drab lunch, instead of returning to the drinking shack, Blake led him to one of the hangars. There, in a back corner, were stacked wooden boxes of ammunition and others full of the bentmetal sections of disintegrating-link machine-gun belts. Blake showed Farman how to assemble the links and how to check both the links and the cartridges for manufacturing defects. He handed Farman a gauge into which a properly shaped cartridge should fit perfectly, and they spent the next several hours inspecting cartridges and assembling belts of ammunition. It was tedious work. Each cartridge looked just like the one before it. The imperfections were small.

"Do you always do this yourself?" Farman inspected his grimy hands, his split cuticles. He wasn't accustomed to this kind of work.

"Every chance I get," Blake said. "There're enough reasons for a gun to jam without bad ammunition being one of 'em. When you're up there with Keyserling's circus flying rings around you, all you've got are your guns and your engine and your wings, and if any of those go, you go. And it's a long way down."

Farman said nothing for a while. Rain drummed on the roof. Now and then came the clang of tools being used in another part of the hangar. "How come you're here?" he asked finally. "What's in it for you?"

Blake's busy hands paused. He looked at Farman. "Say that again, slower."

"This here's a French squadron. You're an American. What are you doing here?"

Blake snorted—not quite a chuckle. "Fighting Germans."

Hawk Among the Sparrows

Farman wondered if Blake was making fun of him. He tried again. "Sure—but why with a bunch of Frenchmen?"

Blake inspected a cartridge, fitted it into the belt. He picked up another. "Didn't care to transfer," he said. "Could have, when they started bringing U.S. squadrons over. But I like the plane I've got. If I transferred, they'd give me a plane the French don't want and the British don't want, because that's all the American squadrons are getting. Well, I don't want 'em, either." He dropped a cartridge in the reject pile.

"I didn't mean that," Farman said. "You joined before America got into the war—right?"

"Came over in '16."

"All right. That's what I mean. Why help France?" He couldn't understand why an American would do anything to help the personal kingdom of *le grand Charles*. "You weren't involved," he said. "Why?"

Blake went on inspecting cartridges. "Depends what you mean, involved. I figure I am. Everyone is. The Germans started this war. If we can show the world it doesn't pay to start a war, then there won't be any more. I want that. This is going to be the last war the human race will ever have."

Farman went back to inspecting cartridges. "Don't get your hopes too high," he said. It was as near as he could bring himself to telling Blake how doomed his optimism was. The rain made thunder on the roof like the march of armies.

Late in the afternoon, two days later, three lorries sputtered into the supply area behind the hangars. They brought fuel for the *escadrille,* but also, crowded among the drums of gasoline, were twenty hundred-liter barrels of kerosine which were carefully put aside and trucked down to the mess hall's kitchen and then—when the error was discovered—had to be reloaded and trucked back up to the hangars again.

Farman had managed to rig a crude filtration system for the kerosine. The stuff they cooked with was full of junk. He'd scrounged sheets of silk, and enlisted a crew of mechanics to scrub empty petrol drums until their innards gleamed like the insides of dairy cans. He even managed to test the rig with a bucket of kerosine cadged from the kitchens. The process was glacially slow, and the end product neither looked nor smelled any different from the stuff he started with. But when he tried it in one of *Pika-Don*'s engines, the engine had started and—at low RPM—had delivered thrust and had functioned as it should until the tank was sucked dry. More important, when he inspected, none of the injectors had fouled.

He started the filtering process, and stayed with it through the night and all the next day. He had a mechanic to help him, but he had no confidence in the mechanic's understanding of how vital fuel quality was to an engine. It wasn't a thing an airplane mechanic of this time could be expected to know. Deveraux came around once, inspected the raw material and sniffed the filtered product, and went away again, having said nothing.

Once, between missions, Blake came and sat to watch. Farman showed him the sludge the filters had taken out of the kerosine. Blake scowled. "It's still kerosine," he said. "You can't fly an aeroplane on kerosine any more than you can feed it birdseed. I don't know what you really want it for, but don't expect me to believe it's for flying."

Farman shrugged. "I'll take *Pika-Don* up tomorrow morning. You can tell me what you think tomorrow afternoon. Fair enough?"

"Maybe," Blake said.

"You think I'm a cushmaker, don't you."

"Possible. What's a cushmaker?"

Blake hadn't heard the story. Maybe it hadn't been invented yet. Farman explained it—the ultra-shaggy joke about the cushmaker who, obliged by an admiral to demonstrate his specialty, after commandeering a battleship and tons of elaborate equipment, and after arduous technological efforts, finally dropped a white-hot sphere of steel amid the ice floes of the Antarctic Ocean, where it went *kussh*.

Blake went away, then. "I'll say this. If you're pulling a deal, you're a cool one." He shook his head. "I just don't know about you."

Morning brought high, ragged clouds. They'd make no trouble for the demonstration flight. Farman waited beside *Pika-Don* while Blake took off and slowly climbed to ten thousand feet, circling over the field the whole time. "I think we are ready, *M'sieu*," Deveraux said, fingering his trim moustache.

Farman turned to his plane. "Better make everybody stand back," he said. Turbine scream wasn't gentle to unprotected ears. He climbed up on the packing crate—pulled himself up *Pika-Don*'s sloped side and dropped into the cockpit. Looking back, he saw the onlookers had retreated about twenty-five feet. He had quite an audience. He grinned. They'd back off a lot farther when he got the engines going.

He got the cockpit hatch down. He checked the seal; it was tight. He went through the pre-ignition cockpit check. He began the engine start-up cycle, felt the momentary vibration and saw the twitch of instruments coming alive. Engine One caught, ragged for an instant, then steady as the tachometer wound around like a clock gone wild. Its scream of power drilled through the cockpit's insulation. Farman started Engine Two, then Engine Three. He brought them up to standby idle. They burned smooth.

Good enough. He didn't have fuel to waste on all the pre-takeoff operations; some were necessary, some not. He did all the necessary ones, turned the jets into the lift vents, and brought them up to full power. By that time, *Pika-Don* was already off the ground. She bobbled momentarily in the light breeze, and rose like a kite on a string. The sprawling fuselage surface prevented him from looking down at the airfield; it didn't matter. They'd be watching, all right—and probably holding shriek-filled ears. He grinned at the trembling instruments in front of him. He wished he could see their eyes, their open mouths. You'd think they'd never seen a plane fly before.

He took *Pika-Don* up to ten thousand feet. Hovering, he tried to find the image of Blake's Nieuport on the airspace view scope. It didn't show. For a worried moment, Farman wondered if something had gone wrong and Blake had gone down. Then the Nieuport flew past him on the left, a little above. It turned to pass in front of him. He could see Blake's goggled face turned toward him.

Even then, there wasn't an image on the radar. Farman swore. Something was wrong with the equipment.

No time to fiddle with the dials now, though. *Pika-Don* was guzzling the kerosine like a sewer. He converted to lateral flight. As always, it was like the floor dropping out from under him. He moved all three throttles forward, felt the thrust against his back. For a frightened instant, he saw Blake had turned back—was coming straight at him, head-on. He'd warned Blake not to get ahead of him like that. But *Pika-Don* was dropping fast. At speeds less than mach 0.5 she had the glide capability of a bowling ball. She slashed underneath the Nieuport with a hundred feet to spare. The altimeter began to unwind, faster and faster. The horizon lifted on the forward view scope like a saucer's rim.

He watched the machmeter. It was edging up. He could feel the drive of the engines, full thrust now, exciting him like they always did, hurling him across the sky. The altimeter steadied, began to rise again. He tipped *Pika-Don*'s prow upward and cracked the barrier in a rocketing fifty-degree climb. Blake's Nieuport was nowhere in sight.

At forty thousand he cut the engines back, leveled off, and started down. He had to search hard for the airfield; without the map scope he couldn't have found it. It was just another green field in a countryside of green fields. At five thousand feet he converted back to vertical thrust and let *Pika-Don* drop to a landing—quickly for most of the distance to save fuel, with a heavy retarding burst in the last thousand feet. He hovered a moment two hundred feet up, picked out a landing spot, and put down. According to the gauges, less than thirty seconds' fuel was left in the tanks.

He dropped to the ground without waiting for a packing crate to be brought. He stood and looked around in disbelief. There was hardly a man in sight, and none of the *escadrille*'s planes remained on the field. He saw them, finally, small specks flying off eastward. He walked back to the hangars, perplexed. Was that all the impression he'd made? He grabbed the first man he found—a mechanic. "What happened?"

The mechanic grinned and made gestures and gabbled in French. Farman shook him and asked again—or tried to—in pidgin French. All he got was more of the same jabber and some gestures in the general direction of the front lines. "I know they went that way," Farman growled and flung the man away. He stalked back to the shack behind the hangars and asked Henri for a Scotch. He drank it, waited five minutes, and had another. He was deep into his fourth when the men came back.

They trooped into the shack, and Henri set a row of glasses on the counter and went down the line with the brandy bottle. As soon as a glass had been filled, a hand snatched it away. Blake came to Farman's table, a brimful glass in his hand, sat down.

"Howard," he said, "I don't know how that thing of yours works. I don't even know if you can call it an aeroplane. But I've got to admit you got it off the ground, and the only thing I ever saw go past me faster was a bullet. Now, if you'll just tell me one thing . . ."

"Anything you want to know," Farman said, abruptly raised from dejection to smugness.

"How can you fly when you don't have the wind on your face?"

Farman started to laugh, but Blake wasn't even smiling. To him, it wasn't an old joke. He was serious.

With effort, Farman controlled his amusement. "I don't need the wind. In fact, if the window broke, I'd probably be killed. I've got instruments that tell me everything I need to know."

He could see the skeptical expression shaping itself on Blake's face. He started to get up, not quite steady because of the Scotches he'd downed. "Come on. I'll show you the cockpit."

Blake waved him down. "I saw the cockpit. You've got so many things in there you don't have time to look outside. I don't know if I'd call it flying. You might as well be sitting at a desk."

Sometimes, Farman had thought the same thought. But all those instruments were necessary to fly a thing like *Pika-Don*. He wondered if he'd have taken up flying if he'd known it would be like that. "Or maybe a submarine?" he asked, not entirely sarcastic. "The thing is, did I fly circles around you, or didn't I?"

Blake's reply was a rueful shrug. "First, you hung there like a balloon. If I hadn't seen you, I wouldn't believe it. Then all of a sudden you were coming at me like something out of a cannon. I got to admit you had me scared. I never saw anything move like that thing of yours. By the time I got turned around you were out of sight. If we'd been dogfighting, you could of put a string of bullets through me from end to end, and I couldn't of got a shot off."

A shadow intruded onto the table between them. They looked up. "Indeed, *M'sieu* Farman," Deveraux said, "your machine's speed gives it the ability to attack without the risk of being attacked itself. I will not pretend to understand how it can fly with such small wings, nor how it can rise directly into the air, but I have seen it do these things. That is enough. I must apologize that we could not be here to applaud you when you landed."

So he'd made an impression after all. "Where'd you go? I thought you didn't have any patrols scheduled until this afternoon."

Deveraux pulled out a chair and sat down beside Blake. With delicate care, he placed a half-full wineglass in front of him. "That is true, *M'sieu*. But we heard the sound of big guns at the front, and our duty is to be in the air at such times, until the matter is clarified, doing such things as will assist our men in the trenches."

"I didn't hear any guns," Farman said. "When I got back here, it was as quiet as a bar mitzvah in Cairo."

He realized almost at once, seeing their faces, the metaphor had no meaning for them. Well, they hadn't heard of Social Security, either.

"It is curious," Deveraux said. "When we are come to the front, it is as you say—most quiet. The guns have stopped, and we see no aircraft but our own. We search for fifty kilometers along the front. There is no evidence of even small actions. When we come back, I message to commanders at the front, and they tell me there has been no action. Nor have guns in their sectors been made use of—theirs or the Boche—though it is curious . . . some do say that they have heard guns being used in other sectors. And you can see . . ." He pointed to the window—the clear sky. "It could not have been thunder."

He said it all with the innocent mystification of a small boy, still not sure of all the things in the universe. Farman suddenly laughed and Deveraux blinked, startled.

"Sorry," Farman said. "I just realized. It wasn't guns you heard. It was me."

"You, *M'sieu?* What jest is this?"

"No joke. What you heard was my plane. It makes a shock wave in the air, just like an explosion's." He looked at their faces. "You don't believe me."

Deveraux's wineglass was empty. Blake stood up, empty brandy glass in hand. He reached for Deveraux's glass, but the Frenchman put his hand in the way. Blake went to the bar with only his own glass. Farman nursed his drink.

"I do not pretend to understand this aeroplane of yours," Deveraux said. "But now that you have shown its abilities . . ."

"Some of them," Farman said. They'd only seen an iceberg tip of what *Pika-Don* could do.

"Yes. But now we have seen," Deveraux said. "I will agree, it is possible your machine could outmatch Bruno Keyserling."

"I know she can," Farman said.

"Perhaps," Deveraux said with a small smile, but very firm. "But I agree—it should be tried. If you will tell us where to mount the guns on your machine . . ."

"I don't need guns," Farman said. "Don't want them."

"But *M'sieu*, an aeroplane *must* have guns. Without guns, it is like a tiger without teeth and claws."

The thought of machine guns stuck on *Pika-Don*'s prow was a horror. "I've got my own weapons," Farman said. Blake came back, sat down heavily. His glass slopped a little on the table. "Machine guns would . . . they'd destroy her aerodynamic integrity. They'd . . . she probably couldn't even fly with them sticking out in the wind."

"Aerody . . . what integrity?" Blake snorted. "What are you talking about?"

Farman leaned forward. "Look. You've seen my plane. All right. Now—you've seen those overlapping strips along her belly, between the ports the skids retract into?"

"I have noticed," Deveraux said.

"There's a rocket under each one of them," Farman said. "Just one of those can wipe out a whole squadron."

"Ah? How many rockets? Eight?"

"Six," Farman said. "How many squadrons have the Germans got in this sector?"

"Two *jagdstaffels*," Deveraux said. "They are quite enough." He shook his head. "But *M'seiu*, the men who planned the equipping of your aeroplane did not understand the needs of combat. It is assuming a marksman's skill beyond human abilities to believe that with only six of these rockets you could expect to be effective against enemy aircraft. One must remember, they are not motionless targets, like balloons. It is difficult enough to strike a balloon with rockets—balloons do not move—but to destroy an aeroplane . . . that cannot be done. Often I have expended all my ammunition—hundreds of rounds—without so much as touching my opponent. That you would imagine going into combat with a mere six possibilities of striking your target . . . this is folly. It is not worth the effort."

"They're not just things I shoot off," Farman said. Did he have to explain everything? "In fact, my plane's so fast any weapons system that depends on human senses couldn't possibly work. My rockets find their targets themselves. They are . . ."

He saw the utter disbelief on their faces. "Look," he said, "I've shown you my plane can do everything I told you it could. It flies faster and climbs faster than anything you ever saw. Now, if you'll give me enough fuel to take her up against Keyserling, I'll show you what my rockets can do. They'll wipe him out of the sky like a blob of smoke in a high wind."

"Bruno Keyserling is a very skilled and deadly man," Deveraux said. "A man impossible to kill. We have tried—all of us. He has killed many of our men, and he will send more of us down in flames before this war ends. I would suggest you be not so confident of yourself and your equipment."

"Just give me enough kerosine for a mission," Farman said. "One mission. Let me worry about the rest of it." He wasn't worried at all. A dogfight between World War I model planes and something from 1975 would be like a wrestling match between a man and a gorilla.

"But *M'sieu*, you *have* the paraffin," Deveraux said, mildly puzzled. "You have almost two thousand liters.*"*

Farman shook his head. "I burned that. There's just about enough left to fill that glass of yours."

Deveraux looked down at his empty wineglass. "*M'sieu,* you must be joking."

"No joke," Farman said. "*Pika-Don* flies fast and climbs like a rocket, but you don't get something for nothing—law of conservation of energy, if you know what that is. She drinks fuel like a sewer."

There was a silence—a silence, Farman realized, not only at their own table, but all through the shack. Maybe these fliers understood more English than he thought. Blake downed a large swallow of brandy.

"How much do you need for a mission?" he asked.

"Ten thousand gallons will do for a short one," Farman said. "An hour—hour and a half."

There was another long silence. *"M'sieu,"* Deveraux said at last, "I have wide discretion in the requisition of the usual materials. I am trying to balance in my mind the possible destruction of Bruno Keyserling—which is a thing we all desire—against the difficulty I must expect in explaining my request for so much kitchen fuel. And I remain in doubt you will be able to accomplish as successful as you claim. So I must ask—have I your word of honor as an American that you must have this paraffin to fly your machine?"

"You've got it, on a stack of Bibles."

"The good old U.S.A. is alive with con men," Blake said.

"M'sieu Blake," Deveraux said reproachfully, "we must not assume that a man tell lies because he claims ability to do a thing we cannot do ourselves. He is optimistic, yes. But that is a fault of almost all the young men who come to us. If we do not put him to the test, we shall not know if he could do the thing he claims or not."

Blake made a sour twist of his mouth. "All right. But how are you going to explain wanting forty thousand liters of kerosine?"

Deveraux cocked his head to one side, as if listening to a voice no one else could hear. "I think I shall merely tell a part of the truth. That we wish to try a weapon suggested by one of our men, a weapon which makes use of paraffin."

"Such as?" Blake asked.

"If they want details," Farman said, leaning forward, "tell them you're putting it in old winebottles and cramming a rag in the neck. And before you drop the bottle on the Germans you set fire to the rag. The bottle breaks when it hits, and spills burning kerosine over everything."

Blake and Deveraux looked at each other. Delight animated their faces. "Now that's something I think might work," Blake said, rubbing his jaw. "Why didn't somebody think of it before?"

It was the first time Farman had heard him enthusiastic about something. This, at least, was a weapon they could understand. "It might work," he said. "But gasoline does it better. It's called a Molotov cocktail."

"M'sieu Farman," Deveraux said, "I think we shall try that, also." He stood up, wineglass in hand. "Henri!" he called. "More wine!"

Early that afternoon, two men came to the airfield fresh from training school. Boys, really; neither could have been more than seventeen. They were eager to get into the war—looked disconsolate as they came away from reporting to Deveraux. "They'll have to spend a day or two learning their way around," Blake said, a twisty smile curling his mouth. "Some guys just can't wait to get killed."

Their Nieuports were straight from the factory, new as pennies. The smell of dope and varnish surrounded them like an aura. Blake worked his way around them, a point by point inspection. The new men would be assigned to his flight. He peered intently at struts and wires and fabric surfaces. "Good aeroplanes," he said finally. Then it was time for him to go out on patrol. Three other men went with him. Farman watched them take off. They disappeared eastward. He went back and saw about readying his jerrybuilt filtration plant for the job of turning ten thousand gallons of cooking oil into aviation fuel.

At first light next morning, the new men stood beside their planes and watched the *escadrille* fly out on dawn patrol. They looked like children not invited to play. Farman went and checked *Pika-Don*; there was sign of a gummy deposit in her tailpipes, but a close inspection of her compressor blades showed they were clean, and none of the fuel injectors were fouled. He buttoned her up again and headed for the drinking shack. Until he got a shipment of kerosine, he'd have nothing to do.

The *escadrille* came back three hours later. If there'd been any Germans in the sky that morning, they'd made themselves hard to find. There'd been no action. Six planes refueled at once and went out again. Deveraux took the new men out on an orientation flight. In the afternoon, Blake and another pilot took the new men out for a mock dogfight. When they came back, Farman was waiting at the edge of the field; he'd had an idea he felt foolish for not having thought of sooner—to make a start on the long kerosine-upgrading job by borrowing a barrel or two of the raw material from the mess hall. He needed Blake to translate and haggle for him.

As Blake taxied up onto the hardstand, Farman saw the tattered fabric fluttering from the right upper wing. He ran over as Blake cut the motor. "Hey! You've been in a fight!"

Blake dropped down from the cockpit. He stripped off helmet and goggles and gloves. Farman repeated his question. Blake grinned and pointed to his ears and shook his head. Farman pointed at the shredded wing.

"Yeh. I've been in a fight," he said, his voice loud as if he was trying to talk through the noise his motor had made.

Farman looked out at the other planes taxiing in from the field. "They're all right," Blake said. "We jumped a Pfalz—what he was doing way off there behind the lines, don't ask me. I got the observer interested in me"—he nodded at the damaged wing—"and Jacques moved in and put a few in the engine. Simple enough."

The other planes of the flight came up on the hardstand, and the mechanics moved in to turn them around and chock the wheels. The pilots climbed out, and the new men crowded around the other veteran—Jacques, Farman assumed. They pumped his arm and slapped his back and jabbered jubilantly. Jacques managed to break free of them long enough to reach Blake. He grabbed both Blake's arms and spoke with a warm grin. Blake looked a little embarrassed by the attention and managed, finally, to shrug Jacques's hands without offending. By then the new men had closed in again. A rapid four-way conversation broke out.

Blake got loose again after a minute. "They never saw an aeroplane shot down before." He grinned. "Wasn't much of a shoot-down, really. Jacques put a few in the engine, and it just sort of went into a glide." He nodded at the three men; they were still talking energetically. "I guess they liked the show, even if they don't understand some of it. They're wanting to know why we didn't go on shooting after Jacques got their engine."

It sounded like a reasonable thing to ask. "Well, why didn't you?" He remembered to speak loud.

Blake shrugged. "Why kill 'em? There's enough people getting killed. They were out of the war as soon as their propeller stopped."

"Well, yes. Sure. But . . ."

"Oh, we made sure they landed close to a convoy on the road, so they'd be captured all right," Blake said. "Didn't want a pair of Huns running loose behind the lines."

"But they were Germans. The enemy."

Blake punched a finger into Farman's ribs. "Once Jacques got their engine, they were just a couple of poor guys in an aeroplane that couldn't fly any more. We got no fight with guys like that. It's the man they worked for we're against. The Kaiser. Besides, that guy in the rear cockpit still had a lot of bullets in his machine gun, and he was sort of mad at us. I figure we were smart to keep our distance."

The new men had a few more training flights the next day, and the day after that they went out with the dawn patrol. The patrol met a flight of German machines led by Keyserling's white-trimmed purple Albatross. It was a fast, cruel scrap. Only one of the new men came back.

"We shouldn't of put 'em on service so quick," Blake said, nodding across the shack toward where the survivor was slowly drinking himself into numbness; he'd been in shock ever since he climbed out of his cockpit. "But we've got to have men. It takes three months to train a man enough so he's got a chance in the air—and Keyserling and his circus kill 'em in five minutes. Like swatting a fly." He picked up his brandy and downed it whole.

Deveraux came and put a hand on Blake's shoulder. "It is true," he said. "One might wish we did not so desperately need men to fight. But we fight a war to preserve civilization, and for that it is necessary that some good men die. And so we have lost one man today. And one other machine is damaged. Do not forget, Keyserling has lost two men in this morning's battle, and three of his aeroplanes will need considerable work before they fly again. We have done well, this day."

"Yeh. Sure. But he was just a kid," Blake said. His open hand banged on the table. Glasses rattled. "A poor, dumb kid. As green as—"

"To keep a civilization is worth a few lives, *M'sieu* Blake." Deveraux squeezed Blake's shoulder, held the grip a moment, let his hand slip away. He moved off to talk with the men at another table.

"Civilization," Blake muttered.

"Stick around," Farman said. If he lived long enough, Blake would know of Dachau, Bataan, Hiroshima, and the bloody mess France herself would make of her African colonies. And lots more.

"You haven't seen anything yet," Farman said.

The kerosine began to come two days later. It came spasmodically, in odd-sized lots: one day a demijohn arrived, the next—half a lorry load. Kerosine wasn't, to these people, a strategically vital petrochemical; it was a fluid used in lamps and stoves. It couldn't just be commanded up from the nearest supply dump in anything like the quantities a supersonic jet had to have. Genghis Khan's army might have been similarly inept at meeting a sudden, inexplicable demand for a few thousand pounds of gunpowder.

June became July. The summer sun burned warm. There was talk of heavy fighting to the north, in a place called *Bois de Belleau*. Farman worked at the makeshift filters day after day. The smell of warm kerosine was a weight in his lungs, an ache in his brain. Some evenings, he was too sickened to eat.

The weeks blended into each other. He didn't have much idle time; there was always more kerosine to be poured into the system, or a filter to be changed and the clogged filter to be scraped and scrubbed and carefully examined for flaws before being used again. After a while, he stopped looking up when he heard the sound of airplane motors.

But in that time he saw airplanes lose power as they left the ground, stall, and nose stiffly into the turf. Their wings snapped like jackstraws. He saw a tattered plane coming back from a dogfight; it fell apart over the field and its pilot died in the wreck. He saw a man bring his plane down, taxi off the field, and die from loss of blood with the engine still running. And there were many times when he saw men watch the sky, searching for planes that would not come back, ever.

Some nights, he heard the big guns thunder at the front, like a grumbling storm just beyond the horizon. Muzzle flash and shellburst blazed in the sky.

Several days came when no new loads of kerosine arrived. He used that time to learn what he could about the Germans—their tactics, their formations, the capabilities of their planes. Not much of the information was useful—he'd expected that; matched against *Pika-Don*, they'd be almost motionless targets. But with only ten thousand gallons to fly on, it would be a good idea to know where he'd be most likely to find them. He wouldn't have much more time in the air than just enough to lift off, aim and launch rockets, and return to base. He started planning the mission.

"They stay mostly on their own side of the lines," he said to Deveraux. "All right. When I go up, I don't want you to have any planes on that side. I want to be sure any planes I find over there are theirs, not yours. I'll be going too fast to look at 'em close."

"You ask more than is possible, or even wise," Deveraux said. Breeze ruffled grass on the field. The Frenchman's scarf flapped and fluttered. "It is necessary always to have patrols in all sectors to protect our reconnaissance aeroplanes. If we do not patrol, the reconnaissance aeroplanes would be attacked. They could not do their missions. Perhaps it would be possible to remove patrols from one sector for a few hours—one in which none of our observation missions will be flying. Is not that as much as you shall need?"

"Not quite," Farman said. "I don't think you've thought it all the way through. You cover the front between the Swiss border and the Vosges Mountains. Right?"

"There are several *escadrilles* with which we share that duty."

"Yeah. Well, that's not important except they'll have to be warned off, too. What I'm asking now is, how many miles of front are you covering? Fifty? Seventy-five?"

"It is fifty kilometers," Deveraux said.

"All right. I'll be flying at about mach 2. At that speed, I can cover that much distance in three minutes. It takes me twenty miles just to get turned around. I can patrol the whole front, all by myself. You don't need to have anybody else out there."

Deveraux's face wore a scowlish mask. "So fast? I must assume you do not exaggerate, *M'sieu*."

"At sixty thousand feet, I could do it twice that fast," Farman said. "But I'm going to cruise at forty. Air's too thick for full-power flying that low down. I'd burn like a meteor."

"Of course, *M'sieu*."

Farman couldn't be sure if Deveraux believed him or not.

"But I must say, it would seem you have not considered all the necessities," the Frenchman went on. "Even if you are able to patrol all the sectors, that would be true only should you not find a Boche patrol. Then you would move to attack it, and *voila*, you would be engaged in combat, *M'sieu*. You would cease to patrol. And it is not uncommon for the Boche to have four or five flights in the air at one time. Who would be protecting our observation missions while you are fighting?"

"I don't even want any observation flights on that side of the lines while I'm flying," Farman said. "Because I'm going to wipe that sky clean like a blackboard. If you have observation planes over there, they might get it, too. So you don't need to have any patrols out to protect 'em. Anyway, it won't take me more than five minutes from the time I've spotted a flight until I've launched rockets, and then I'll be free to go back on patrol. That's not much more than if I'd took time out for a smoke."

They heard, then, very faint but growing, the sound of aircraft motors. Deveraux turned to search the eastward sky for the approaching planes. "And have you thought, *M'sieu,* what the Boche would be doing while you are shooting these rockets of yours? Bruno Keyserling and his men are aviators of consummate skill. They would not fly calmly, doing nothing, while you attack them. And even should your rockets each find a target, that would still be only one of their aeroplanes for each rocket. You have, I believe you said, only six."

"They won't even see me coming, I'll jump 'em so fast," Farman said. "They won't have time to do anything but look surprised. And one of my rockets can . . ." He made a wipe-out gesture. "Look. All I'm asking—keep your planes on this side of the lines for a couple of hours. With only ten thousand gallons, I won't be able to stay out even that long. Am I asking too much? Two hours?"

The returning planes were in sight now. There were three of them, strung out, the one in the rear far behind the other two, losing altitude, regaining it, losing it again. Farman didn't know how many had gone out on that particular patrol—he hadn't been paying much attention to such things—but it was rare for a patrol of only three planes to go out. There would be some empty chairs in the mess, this evening.

The first plane came in to land. Its lower wing was shredded close to the fuselage—loose fabric fluttered like torn flags—and the landing gear wheel on that side wobbled oddly. As it touched down, the whole gear collapsed. The wing dipped—caught the ground—and flung the machine into a tangle of broken struts, tail high in the air. Men ran across the field. Farman caught a glimpse of the pilot's arm, waving for help. A thin black thread of smoke began to rise. A moment later it was a fierce inferno. No one could get near it. There wasn't a sign of the man. The second plane landed and taxied across the grass unheeded.

Deveraux turned to Farman again. "No, *M'sieu,*" he said. "You do not ask too much. It is we, who ask too much of men."

Farman boosted *Pika-Don* from the field while dawn was still a growing light in the east and all the land was gray. She lifted sluggishly; well, the gunk he was feeding her was a poor substitute for her usual diet. He took her to eight thousand feet before converting to lateral flight. She was down to four before she cracked the barrier and down to three and a half before she bottomed out and started to climb. The machmeter moved past 1.25. He raised *Pika-Don*'s nose and drove her at the sky.

She broke into sunlight at twenty thousand feet. The sun was gold and the air was as clean as clear ice. Somewhere in the darkness below two armies faced each other as they'd faced each other for four years. At forty thousand feet he leveled off and began his loiter pattern—a slim-waisted figure-eight course, looping first to the south, then to the north—overflying the German lines from the Swiss border to the Vosges

Mountains. He watched the airspace viewscope for the pip that would be German aircraft.

Almost always, on good flying days, the Germans sent up patrols a few minutes before sunrise, to intercept the reconnaissance planes the French almost always sent over on good flying days. Bruno Keyserling would be leading one of those patrols. Farman watched particularly the area surrounding the German airfield. The Germans would climb quickly to fighting altitude; as soon as their altitude and motion dissociated them from the ground, *Pika-Don*'s radars would pick them out. He watched the scope, followed his loiter pattern, and waited for the German planes to appear.

Two circuits later, he was still up there. The scope showed the shaded contours of the land, but that was all. Not one German plane—no planes at all, even though the whole *escadrille* had flown out ahead of him to watch the fight he'd promised. He had fuel enough for six or eight more circuits—it was going faster than he'd counted on—before there'd be only enough to get him back to the field.

And more weeks of filtering kerosine? Not if he could help it. He made two more circuits—still nothing. He put *Pika-Don*'s needle prow downward. If they wouldn't come up and fight, he'd go after them. He checked the German field's position on the map scope. He could fly down straight to the end of its runway, and he had six rockets. One would be enough. Two would destroy it utterly.

He was down below twenty thousand feet when he saw the airplanes. They were flying on a northerly course, as he was, patrolling above the German lines in a Junck's row formation—each plane above, behind, and to the side of the one below it; an upright, diagonal line. A quick glance at the radar scope: not a hint of those planes.

Nuts with the airfield. Not with those planes over there. Flying where they were, using that formation, they had to be Germans. Farman pulled out of this attack dive, immelmanned into a corkscrew turn that would take him back and place him behind their formation. He lost sight of them in that maneuver, but the map scope showed him where they had to be; they didn't have the speed to move far while he was getting into position.

Behind them now, he turned again and drove toward them. Still nothing on the airspace scope, but he knew where they were. He tried the target-tracking radar—the one in the middle of the instrument panel. They didn't show there, either.

But he knew where they were, and in another moment he saw them again. Little black specks, like gnats, only gnats didn't fly in formation. And one rocket anywhere near them . . .

Still they didn't show on the target-tracking scope. It would have to be an eyeball launch, then. He primed the proximity detonators on rockets one and six. There still wasn't a sign they'd seen him. They didn't even seem to move against the sky.

He launched the rockets at four miles. The distance was a guess—without help from his radars, a guess was all he could do—but the German planes were still only specks.

It didn't matter. The rockets were built to heat-seek a target from ten times that distance. He felt the shock as the rockets struck from their sheaths even as he sent *Pika-Don* screaming straight up, engines suddenly at full thrust, and over on her back, and a half-roll, and he was at forty-five thousand feet. Rockets one and six sketched their ionized tracks on the airspace scope, all the way to the edge.

The edge was somewhere beyond the crest of the Vosges Mountains. Farman couldn't understand it. He'd sent those rockets straight as bullets into that formation, proximities primed and warheads armed. They should have climbed right up those Germans' tailpipes and fireballed and wiped those planes from the sky like tinder touched by flame. It hadn't happened.

He brought *Pika-Don* around. On the map scope he found again the position where the German planes had been. They still didn't show on the airspace view—what could possibly be wrong with the radar—but they'd still be close to where he'd seen them last, and he still had four rockets left. On the airspace scope, the tracks of rockets one and six ended in tiny sparks as their propellants exhausted and their automatic destructs melted them to vapor. He turned *Pika-Don*'s nose down. He armed the warheads, primed the proximities. This time he wouldn't miss.

He saw the German planes from ten miles away. He launched rockets two and five from a distance of five miles. Two seconds later, he launched three and four and turned away in a high-G immelmann. His G-suit seized him like a hand—squeezed, relaxed, and squeezed again as he threw *Pika-Don* into a long, circling curve. The airspace scope flickered, re-oriented itself. His four rockets traced bright streaks across its face.

Explode! he thought. *Explode!*

They didn't. They traced their paths out to the scope's edge. Their destruct mechanisms turned them to vapor. Ahead of him now, again, he could see the disorganized swarm of the *jagdstaffel*. He hadn't touched one of them. And they still didn't show on the airspace scope.

Farman swore with self-directed disgust. He should have thought of it. Those planes were invisible to radar. They didn't have enough metal to make a decent tin can, so his radar equipment rejected the signals they reflected as static. For the same reason, the proximities hadn't worked. The rockets could have passed right through the formation—probably had—without being triggered. As far as the proximities were concerned, they'd flown through empty air. He might as well have tried to shoot down the moon.

He turned west, back to base. He located the field with the map scope. He had enough fuel to get there, and some to spare. A thought trickled through his mind about the dinosaurs—how their bodies had been perfectly adapted to the world they lived in, and when the world changed their bodies hadn't been able to adjust to the changes. So they died.

Pika-Don was like that—a flying *Tyrannosaurus rex* whose world now provided only insects for food.

* * *

"Yeh. We saw the whole action," Blake said. He sat with his back against the hangar wall, a wine bottle close to his hand. The sun was bright and the fields were green. A light breeze stirred.

The *escadrille* had come back a half hour after Farman landed. Farman had hesitated, but then went out to face Deveraux. He wasn't eager for the confrontation.

Deveraux was philosophically gentle. "You have seen now, *M'sieu*, the rockets you carried were not an adequate armament for combat situations. Now, if you will show our mechanics where you think it would be best to mount the machine guns they . . ."

"*Pika-Don* flies faster than bullets," Farman said. He kicked at a ridge of dirt between wheel ruts. The dirt was hard, but it broke on the third try. "I even heard of a guy that got ahead of his own bullets and shot himself down. And his plane was a lot slower than mine." He shook his head—looked back toward where *Pika-Don* crouched low to the ground, sleek and sinister-looking, totally useless. "Might as well let her rot there."

He kicked the loosened clod off into the grass.

About eleven o'clock, Blake got a bottle of wine from Henri. It was plain peasant's wine, but that was all right. They sat in the narrow noontide shade of a hangar and worked on it.

"You've got to get in close before you shoot," Blake said. "I don't know where you learned combat, but it didn't look like you learned much. You flew at their formation so fast they wouldn't of seen you until you broke right through 'em, but you shot those rockets from a couple of miles away. You can't hit anything at that kind of range."

"I thought I could," Farman said. "And with the kind of warheads they had, it's a good idea to be a few miles away when they go off."

"You don't think you're funning me with that, do you?" Blake said. He sat up straight—looked at Farman. "Nothing scatters shrapnel that wide."

Farman helped himself from the bottle. "My rockets would have done more than just scatter shrapnel, if they'd gone off."

"Not much good if you've got to shoot 'em from so far off you can't hit the target," Blake said.

It was no use trying again to explain target-seeking missiles. Anyway, they hadn't worked. He'd finally figured that out, too. Their heat-seeking elements had been designed to track on a hot jet's exhaust, or the meteor-flame of a ballistic warhead. All the German planes were putting out was the feeble warmth of piston engine. That wasn't enough. If he was going to do any good in this war, it wasn't going to be with *Pika-Don*. "Harry, I want you to check me out on your plane."

"Huh?"

"My plane's useless. She hasn't any teeth left," Farman said. "If I'm going to do any more fighting, it's going to be in a plane like yours. I've got more flying hours than all of you put together, but I don't have any cockpit time in your—" He almost called them box kites. "I want you to show me how it flies."

Blake shrugged. "One plane's pretty much like another. They've all got their tricks—like these Nieuports: you don't want to do much diving in them; takes the fabric off the top wings every time. But aside from that the only way you get the feel is by flying 'em."

They walked out to Blake's Nieuport. It looked about as airworthy as a model T Ford. Farman had a little trouble climbing up until Blake showed him the footholds. It was cramped in the cockpit, and the wicker seat was hard. Blake stood on a packing crate and leaned over the coaming.

Farman put his hand on the stick. That was what it was—an erect rod sticking up between his knees. He'd never seen one like it before. He tried moving it, and it moved with the smoothness of a spoon in a gluepot. "Do you have to fight it like this all the time?" he asked.

"Takes some getting used to," Blake said. "It's easier when she's flying, though."

Farman turned his attention to the instruments. They were a haphazard assortment of circular dials, unevenly distributed, and except for one big dial straight in front of him there wasn't any apparent priority of position given to the more important ones—whichever ones they were. They were all identified, the words lettered across their faces, but the words were French.

"That's the oil pressure," Blake said, tapping the glass in front of a dial. "And that's RPM, and that's fuel mixture."

"Oil pressure. Is that important?"

Blake looked at him strangely. "You say you've been flying—*how* long? And you don't know oil pressure?"

"I've never flown a piston engine craft," Farman said. "*Pika-Don* has a different kind. Is it important?"

"Your engine doesn't work too good without it."

"And—fuel mixture, did you say?" Farman asked, putting his finger to the dial Blake had indicated. He was careful not to ask if it was important, though he wasn't sure what difference it made. Mixed with what, he wondered to himself.

"Right," Blake said. "And this here's your compass—don't trust it too far—and that's the altimeter, and here's the gas gauge."

At least those were instruments Farman understood. But he frowned at the altimeter. "Is that the highest this can fly?"

"Those are meters, not feet," Blake said. "This crate can go up as high as I can breathe. Sixteen . . . eighteen thousand feet." He pointed into the cockpit again. "This here's the switch, and that's the throttle, and that's the mixture control."

Hawk Among the Sparrows

Farman touched them, one by one, trying to get their feel. His hand encountered a small plumb bob dangling from a cord. "That's a funny good-luck charm," he said.

Blake laughed. "Yeh, it's good luck all right. Without it I could be flying upside down and not know it."

"Don't you have a turn-and-bank indicator?" Farman wondered.

"Mister—that *is* my turn-and-bank indicator."

"Oh," Farman said, feeling foolish. But how could he have known.

"And these here," Blake went on, unnoticing, "that one tightens the flying wires, and that one the landing wires."

"What kind of wires?"

"Some wires you want tight when you're flying, and some others when you're coming in to land. If you don't, you stand a good chance of coming apart at the wrong time."

"Oh." Flying a Nieuport wasn't going to be as easy as he'd thought. It would be like trying to ride horseback after driving cars all your life. "My plane doesn't have wires."

"What holds it together?" Blake asked.

Farman ignored him. He was thinking about driving a car, and some of his confidence came back. This Nieuport was a lot different from *Pika-Don,* but her engine wasn't too much different from the one in his 1972 Chevy—more primitive, maybe, but it worked on the same principles. He could handle a gasoline engine all right.

"How do I start it?" he asked.

Half a minute later he was looking forward through the blur of a spinning propeller. He felt the blast of air on his face, and the stench of exhaust made him want to retch. The oil-pressure gauge worked up. He experimented with throttle settings and fuel-mixture adjustments, trying to learn something about how it handled. It occurred to him that his Chevy had two or three times the horsepower this thing had.

Blake handed him a helmet and goggles. Farman put them on. "Taxi her around a bit, until you get the feel," Blake yelled through the engine's blatting. Farman nodded, and Blake bent to pull the chocks from in front of the wheels; one side and then—slipping quickly underneath—the other. The Nieuport lurched forward even before Farman advanced the throttle. It bumped clumsily over the grass.

The thing had no brakes, so when he advanced the throttle again she hurtled forward, bumping and thumping across the field. The airspeed indicator began to show readings. The bumping got worse. He edged the throttle forward a little more. Except for the jouncing and that awful smell, it wasn't much different from driving a car.

The tail came up. It startled him, and it was almost by reflex—seeing the horizon lift in front of him—that Farman pulled the stick back. The bumping stopped as if it were shut off. The engine's sound changed, and airspeed began to slacken. The silly model T was airborne. He shoved the throttle forward and tried to level out. It shouldn't have been flying at this speed—he'd driven his Chevy faster than this, and his Chevy was a lot more streamlined.

He was beyond the field's edge now, with a rise of ground ahead of him. He tried to turn, but the Nieuport resisted. He pulled the stick back to clear the hill's crest. The airspeed meter started to unwind. He got over the hill with a few yards to spare, but airspeed was falling back toward zero. He tried to level out again; it wasn't easy to do without an artificial horizon on the instrument panel. The real horizon was rocking back and forth, up and down, and drifting sidewise. He tried turning the other way, and she turned easily but she also nosed down. He hauled back on the stick, swearing loudly. How any man could fly a crazy, contrary thing like this was more than he could understand.

The ground wheeled under him. The engine's sound changed, became a snarl, then a sputter. Wildly, he looked for a place to put down, but there was nothing but orchard under him as far as he could see—which wasn't far because the plane had nosed down again. A queasy, liquid feel began in his stomach, and the stench from the engine didn't help it any.

The engine chose that moment to quit. For a long time—it couldn't really have been more than a few seconds—the only sound was the whisper of air against the wings. Then the Nieuport stalled and plunged down among the trees. Branches snapped and the wings buckled. The Nieuport came to rest midway between the treetops and the ground. It dangled there, swaying a little in the gentle breeze. After a while, Farman thought to turn off the ignition, to reduce the danger of fire. After another while, he began to think about how to climb down.

He met Blake and half a dozen other men before he got out of the orchard. They went back to the Nieuport. Blake looked up at the wreck among the tree branches, made an angry noise that might have been a word, or it might not, and walked away.

Farman started to go after him, but then thought better of it. Another tree branch cracked and the Nieuport sagged a few feet closer to the ground. Farman looked up at the mess one more time, then turned away and followed Blake. It was a long walk back to the field.

Blake was given another Nieuport. The *escadrille* had several replacements ready—craft that had been sent down from an *escadrille* in the Somme region that had switched to Spads. The older Nieuports were still good enough for this less active section of the front. Blake spent the rest of the day and all the next with the mechanics, checking it out.

Farman spent the time poking around *Pika-Don,* trying to figure a way she could still be used. There was a space where a Vickers gun could be fitted if he took out the infrared sensor unit, but working out a trigger linkage was beyond him; every cubic inch inside *Pika-Don* was occupied by one or another piece of vital equipment.

And at mach 2 an orifice the size of a .30-caliber muzzle might be enough to blow the plane apart.

The only other thing he could think of was that the radars were powerful enough to fry a man dead, but it didn't seem likely that Bruno Keyserling would hold still for the hour or two needed for the job.

He gave up. *Pika-Don* was useless. Reluctantly, he resigned himself to asking Deveraux for assignment to a flight school. It would mean swallowing a lot of pride, but if he was going to shoot Keyserling out of the sky, he'd have to learn how to fly a Nieuport.

When the *escadrille* came back from a patrol, he went out to talk with the Frenchman. Deveraux came toward him, helmet bunched in a still-gloved hand. "I am sorry, *M'sieu*," he said gravely. He laid his empty hand on Farman's shoulder. "Your friend . . . your countryman . . ."

The patrol had run into a flock of Albatrosses, Keyserling in the lead. No one had seen Blake go down, but several planes had been seen falling, burning like meteors. When the dogfight broke off and the flight had reformed, Blake wasn't with them.

Farman's mind became like cold iron as he heard Deveraux recite the plain, inclusive facts. It shouldn't have struck him so hard, but Blake was a man he'd known, a man he'd talked with. All the other men here, even Deveraux, were strangers.

"Did anyone see a parachute?"

"*M'sieu*, such things do not work," Deveraux said. "We do not use them. They catch on the wires. For men in the balloons, perhaps such things can be used, but for us, our aeroplane is hit in its vitals, we go down."

"You shouldn't build 'em with so many wires, then."

Deveraux's reply was a Gallic shrug. "Perhaps not, *M'sieu*. But they are what hold our aeroplanes together."

"The German planes, too?" Farman asked in a suddenly different voice.

"Of course, *M'sieu*."

"Get me some kerosine," Farman said.

"Paraffin? Of course, *M'sieu*. And if you will show the mechanics where to fasten the machine guns they . . ."

Farman shook his head. "I don't need guns. Just get me the kerosine. I'll do the rest. And when I'm done with 'em on this front, I'll go up the line and clean out the rest of 'em."

"Of course, *M'sieu*," Deveraux said without irony.

Not that Farman cared. This time he'd do what he said he could do. He knew it. "Ten thousand gallons," he said.

Mid-August came, and *Pika-Don* was fueled again. Reports and rumors had been coming down from other sectors of the front that American troops were somewhere in the fighting.

Pika-Don lifted into a sky as clean as polished glass. Later in the day there might be a scatter of cumulus tufts, but it was not yet midmorning. "It is not a good day for fighting," Deveraux had said. "One can make use of the clouds."

It would be a good day for observation planes, though, so the German patrols would be out. And, Farman thought savagely, there'd be fighting enough. He'd see to that.

Once he'd shifted to lateral flight, he didn't try for altitude. *Pika-Don* would guzzle fuel faster at low levels, but he didn't figure the mission to take long. The German field was less than thirty miles away. He fixed its location on the map scope and sent *Pika-Don* toward it at full thrust. *Pika-Don* began to gain altitude, but at ten thousand feet, with the machmeter moving up past 1.75, he leveled her off and turned her downward along a trajectory that would bring her to ground level just as he reached the German field.

It was almost perfectly calculated. He saw the field ahead of him. It was small—he'd seen pastures that were bigger—and he started to pull out of his descent. He passed over the field with just enough altitude to clear the trees on the far side. It took less than a second—the machmeter said 2.5, and skin temperature was going up fast. He took *Pika-Don* a few hundred feet up and brought her around—lined her up on the field with the map scope's help—and brought her down again for another pass. This time she flew straight at the open mouth of a hangar in the middle of a row of hangars on the far side of the field.

He brought *Pika-Don* around one more time, but this time he stayed a thousand feet up, and kept off to one side of the field. He looked down and felt the satisfaction of a kid who'd just stomped an anthill. Wreckage was still flying through the air. He didn't need rockets. He didn't need machine guns. All he had to have was *Pika-Don* herself.

He turned her south toward the Swiss border. He'd seen only a few planes on the ground, which meant that most of them were out on patrol.

Heading south, he took *Pika-Don* up to eighteen thousand feet. On a day like this, with no clouds to hide in, the best altitude for a German patrol would be up close to the operational ceiling. Even if no altitude advantage could be gained, at least the advantage would not be lost to a higher-flying French patrol.

The map scope showed the Swiss border. Farman brought *Pika-Don* around. The front was not hard to find. It was a sinuous gash across the land, like a bloodless wound. He followed it north, staying to the German side. He watched the sky ahead of him.

He flew the course to the Vosges Mountains at mach 1.5, partly to save fuel and to minimize the skin temperature problem; flying this low, the air was a lot thicker than *Pika-Don* was built to fly in. His main reason, though, was that even at mach 1.5 he was flying through a lot of airspace. With no more sophisticated target-finding equipment than his own eyes, he could pass within a mile or less of a German patrol without seeing it. Flying as slowly as he could improved his chances.

Hawk Among the Sparrows

The mountains rose ahead of him. They weren't very high mountains; their crests lay well below him. He caught sight of the German patrol as he turned *Pika-Don* for another run south.

They were a few hundred yards higher than he was, and so small with distance he'd have thought they were birds except that birds didn't fly this high, nor did they fly in a neatly stacked Junck's row formation. They hung suspended in the sky, like fleck-marks on a window, and if it hadn't been for their formation he wouldn't have known their direction of flight. They were flying south, as he was now—patrolling the front, as he was.

And they were close—too close. If he turned toward them, they'd be inside the radius of his turn. He'd cross their path in front of them like a black cat, warning them. He mind-fixed their position on the map scope and turned away.

Come at them from eight o'clock, he decided. That would be the best angle. On the outward arc of his circle he took *Pika-Don* up to thirty thousand feet. Then, as *Pika-Don* started to come around for the approach, he started down, full thrust in all three engines. The machmeter climbed to 2.0, then 2.5. It edged toward 3.0, trembling. It would mean a heating problem in this soup-thick air, but it wouldn't be for long.

The patrol was almost exactly where he'd seen it before. There hadn't been time for it to go far. With only a small correction *Pika-Don* was driving down toward it like a lance, target-true. The insect-speck planes became recognizable shapes, then rapidly expanded. They ballooned to their full size in a flash and he was almost on top of them.

At the last instant, he moved the controls just enough to avoid collision—passed behind them so close he had a glimpse of round knobs bulging from the cockpits just behind the upper wings—pilots' helmeted heads—and yes! at the bottom of the stack, leading the fight, the purple Albatross of Bruno Keyserling.

Then the whole flight was somewhere behind him. Farman reduced thrust and put *Pika-Don* into a steep climb, over on her back, and down again to level out into the airspace he'd flown through before.

It was all changed. The sky was full of junk, as if someone had emptied a barrel of trash. Fluttering wing sections, bashed fuselages, masses of twisted wreckage without any shape he could recognize. He saw a wingless fuselage falling a-tumble, like a crippled dragonfly. It was all purple, with bits of white on the shattered engine cowl. *Got him!*

And there wasn't a whole plane left in the sky. They hadn't been built to survive the impact of *Pika-Don*'s shock wave. Just like the hangars at their field which had exploded when he buzzed them.

He started to curve southward again. He'd tasted blood, wanted more. He'd hardly started the turn before a whump shook *Pika-Don* and the sky wheeled crazily and the engine function instruments erupted with a Christmas tree of red lights as if engine two had gobbled something that didn't digest too well. (Part of an airplane? Part of a man?) Some of the lights flashed panic, others glared firmly at his eyes. The horizon outside was tipping up on edge, falling over, tipping up again. The controls felt numb in his hands.

Farman knew the drill. When a plane as hot as this one went bad, you got out if you could. At mach 2 you could hit the ground in less than thirty seconds. He slapped the eject button—felt the rockets blast him upward. A moment later the instrument panel broke away and the seat's firm pressure on his back and thighs was gone. He was tumbling like a wobbling top in midair, suddenly no longer enclosed in several million dollars' worth of airplane. There was the teeth-cracking shock of his chute coming open, and abruptly the confusion of too many things happening too fast stopped. He looked all around for some sign of *Pika-Don,* but there wasn't any.

He tugged at the shrouds to spill air from the chute and drift him westward toward the French lines. The wind was doing some of it, but not enough. A line of planes came toward him. He held his breath, thinking of a school of sharks nosing in toward a man cast overboard. But then he saw the French markings on their wings and sides. They were Nieuports, and the pilot of the leading plane waved. Farman waved back. The flight came on. It circled him once and then curved off. They stayed in sight, though, following him down. When flak bursts started to puff around him, they went down to strafe the German trenches.

He spilled another dollop of air from his chute. He was over the French lines now. He could see the men in the trenches looking up at him. He floated down toward them, closer and closer. Then, very abruptly, he was down—down among the trenches and barbed wire of the French Seventh Army. He sprawled in the greasy mud of a shell hole. The chute started to drag him, but it caught on a tangle of wire and deflated.

He got to his hands and knees, fumbling with the parachute harness. A bullet snapped past his ear. He flattened. The Nieuports dove on the German trenches again.

He struggled out of the harness and started to crawl in the direction of the nearest trench. It wasn't far. He scraped the dirt with his belt buckle all the way. Bullets whipped past him like deadly mosquitoes. The soldiers in the trench reached out to pull him down.

They hugged him. They mobbed around him. There must have been thousands of men in that trench to celebrate the man who'd downed Bruno Keyserling. Someone pressed a cup of wine into his hands—a soldier in dirty clothes, with mud on his brow and a matted beard. Farman drank gratefully.

After a while, he sat down and just sat there, dead inside. He looked at the dirt wall a few inches from his eyes. The empty cup dangled from his hand. *Pika-Don* was gone, and nothing he could do would rebuild her. Suddenly, he was just an ordinary man. He couldn't even fly any more. *Pika-Don* was the only plane in this age that he knew how to fly, and *Pika-Don* was gone.

He wasn't aware of the passage of time, but only of the heat and dust and the smell of a trench that had been occupied too long by unwashed men. He didn't know what he was going to do. But after a time, the wine began to have its effect. A trickle of life came back into him.

Slowly, he got to his feet. The start of a smile quirked his mouth. On second thought, no, he wasn't just an ordinary man.

The war would be over in a few months. Maybe he didn't know what he'd do, but . . .

The soldier who'd given him the wine was standing a few feet away. Farman held himself crisply erect. It occurred to him the man probably didn't know a word of English.

"How do I get back to America?" he asked, and grinned at the soldier's incomprehension.

A man from the future ought to have *some* advantage over the natives! ■

THE MERCENARY
Jerry Pournelle

Peace and internal order are closely linked, but they are not the same thing. A person or organization with the problem of maintaining either or both might attempt to solve it by considering it a job to be done and hiring professionals to do it. But there's more than one very deep pitfall in that. . . .

THE LANDING BOAT FELL AWAY from the orbiting warship, drifted to a safe distance and fired retros. When it entered the thin reaches of the planet's upper atmosphere, scoops opened in the bows, drew in air until the stagnation temperature in the ramjet chambers was high enough for ignition. Engines lit with a roar of flame. Wings swung out slightly, enough to provide lift at hypersonic speeds, and the spaceplane turned, streaked over empty ocean toward the continental land mass two thousand kilometers away.

It circled over craggy mountains twelve kilometers high, dropped low over thickly forested plains, slowing until the craft posed no danger to the thin strip of inhabited lands along the ocean shores. The planet's great ocean was joined to a nearly landlocked channel no more than five kilometers across at its widest point, and nearly all of the colonists lived near the junction of the waters. Hadley's capital city nestled on a long peninsula at the mouth of that channel, the two natural harbors, one in the sea, the other in the ocean, giving the city the fitting name of Refuge.

The ship extended its wings to their fullest reach, floated low over the calm water of the channel harbor until it touched, settled in. Tugboats raced across clear blue water. Sweating seamen threw lines, secured the landing craft and warped it to dock.

A long line of CoDominium marines in garrison uniform marched out of the boat, were gathered on the gray concrete piers into bright lines of color by cursing officers and sergeants. Two men in civilian clothes followed the marines from the flier. They blinked at the unaccustomed blue-white of Hadley's sun, a sun so far away that it would have been a small point if either of them were foolish enough to look directly at it.

Both men were tall and stood as straight as the marines in front of them, so that except for their clothing they might have been mistaken for a part of the disembarking battalion. The shorter of the two carried luggage for both of them and stood respectfully behind; although older, he was obviously a subordinate. They watched as two younger men came uncertainly along the pier. The newcomers' unadorned blue uniforms contrasted sharply with the bright reds and golds of the CoDominium marines who milled around them. Already the marines were scurrying back into the flier, carrying out barracks bags, weapons, the personal gear of a light infantry battalion.

The taller of the two civilians faced the uniformed newcomers. "I take it you're here to meet us?" he asked pleasantly. His voice rang through the noise on the pier, carrying easily although he had not shouted. The accent was neutral, the nearly universal English of American officers in CoDominium service, marking his profession almost as certainly as did his posture and the tone of command.

The newcomers were uncertain, however. There were a lot of ex-officers of the CoDominium Space Navy on the beach with CD budgets lower every year. "I think so," one finally said. "John Christian Falkenberg?"

His name was actually John Christian Falkenberg III, he thought amusedly. His grandfather would probably have insisted on the distinction. "Right. And Sergeant-Major Calvin."

"Pleasure to meet you, sir. I'm Lieutenant Banners, this is Ensign Mowrer. We're on President Budreau's staff." Banners looked around as if expecting other men, but there were none except the marines. He gave Falkenberg a slightly puzzled look, then added, "We have transportation for you, but I'm afraid your men will have to walk. It's about eleven miles."

"Miles." Falkenberg smiled to himself. This *was* out in the boondocks. "I see no reason why ten healthy mercenaries can't march eighteen kilometers, Lieutenant." He turned to the black shape of the landing boat's entry port, called to someone still inside. "Captain Fast. There's no transportation, but someone here will show you where to march the men. Have them carry all gear."

"Uh, sir, that won't be necessary," the lieutenant protested. "We can get—well, we have horse-drawn transport for baggage." He looked at Falkenberg as if he expected the man to laugh, then went on. "Ensign Mowrer will attend to it." He paused again, looked thoughtful, his youthful features knotted in a puzzled expression as if he were uncertain of how to tell Falkenberg something. Finally he shook his head. "I think it would be wise if you issued your men their personal weapons, sir. There shouldn't be any trouble on their way to barracks, but—anyway, ten armed men certainly won't have any problems."

"I see. Perhaps I should go with my troops, Lieutenant. I hadn't known things were quite that bad on Hadley." Falkenberg's voice was calm and even, but he looked intently at the junior man.

"No, sir. They aren't, really . . . just that, well, there's no point in taking chances." He waved Ensign Mowrer to the landing craft, turned to Falkenberg again. A large black shape rose from the water outboard of the landing craft, splashed, and vanished. Banners seemed not to notice, but the marines shouted excitedly. "I'm sure the ensign and your officers can handle the disembarkation . . . the president would like to see you, sir."

"No doubt. All right, Banners. Lead on. I'll bring Sergeant-Major Calvin with me." No point in continuing this farce, Falkenberg thought. Anyone seeing ten armed men conducted by a presidential ensign would know they were troops, civilian clothes or not. Another case of wrong information; he'd been told to keep their status secret. He wondered whether this was going to make it more difficult to keep his own secrets.

Banners ushered them quickly through the bustling CoDominium marine barracks, past bored guards who half-saluted the Presidential Guard uniform. The marine fortress was a blur of activity, every open space crammed with packs and weapons, the signs of a military force about to move on to another station.

As they were leaving the building, Falkenberg saw an elderly naval officer. "Excuse me a moment, Banners," he muttered, and turned to the CoDominium Navy captain. "They sent someone for me. Thanks, Ed."

The Mercenary 175

"No problem. I'll report your arrival to the admiral; he wants to keep track of you. Unofficially, of course. Good luck, John. God knows you need some right now. Sorry about everything else."

"Way it goes," Falkenberg said. He shook the offered hand warmly. "Pay my respects to the rest of your officers. You run a good ship."

The captain smiled thinly. "You ought to know . . . look, we pull out of here in a couple of days, John. No more than that. If you need a ride out, I can arrange it. The Senate won't have to know. We can fix you a hitch to anywhere in CD territory. Just in case, I mean. It might be rough here."

"And it won't be everywhere else in the CoDominium? Thanks again, Ed." He gave a half salute, checked himself, and strode back to where Banners stood with his sergeant. Calvin lifted three personal effects bags as if they were empty, pushed the door open in a smooth motion.

"The car's here." Banners opened the rear door of a battered ground-effects vehicle of no discoverable make. It had been cannibalized from a dozen other machines, and some parts were obviously cut-and-try jobs done by an uncertain machinist. Banners climbed into the driver's seat and started the engine, which coughed twice, then ran smoothly. They moved away in a cloud of black smoke.

They drove past another dock where a landing craft with wings as large as the entire marine landing boat was unloading an endless stream of civilian passengers. Children screamed, men and women stared about uncertainly until they were ungently hustled along by guards in uniforms matching Banners's. The sour smell of unwashed humanity mingled with the crisp clean salt air from the ocean beyond. Banners rolled up the windows with an expression of distaste.

"Always like that," Calvin commented to no one in particular. "Water discipline on them CoDominium prison ships being what it is, takes weeks dirtside to get clean again."

"Have you ever been inside one of those ships?" Banners asked.

"No, sir," Calvin replied. "Been in marine assault boats just about as bad, I reckon. But I can't say I fancy being stuffed into no cubicles with ten, fifteen thousand civilians for six months."

"We may all see the inside of one of those," Falkenberg commented. "And be glad of the chance. Tell me about the situation here, Banners."

"I don't even know where to start, sir," the young man answered. "I—you know about Hadley?"

"Assume I don't," John Falkenberg told him. Might as well see what kind of estimate of the situation the president's officers could make. The fleet intelligence report bulged in the inner pocket of his tunic, but those reports always left out important details.

"Yes, sir. Well, to begin with, we're a long way from the nearest shipping lanes—but I guess you knew that. The only real reason we had any merchant trade was the mines. Thorium, richest veins known for a while, until they started to run out. For the first few years, that's all we had. The mines are up in the hills, about eighty miles over that way." He pointed to a thin blue line just visible at the horizon.

"Must be pretty high mountains," Falkenberg said. "What's the diameter of Hadley? About sixty percent of Earth? Something like that. Horizon ought to be pretty close."

"Yes, sir. They are high mountains. Hadley is small, but we've got bigger and better everything here." There was pride in the young officer's voice.

"Them bags seem pretty heavy for a planet this small," Calvin said.

"Hadley's very dense," Banners answered. "Gravity nearly ninety percent standard. Anyway, the mines are over there. Have their own spaceport. Refuge—that's this city—was founded by the American Express Company. Brought in colonists, quite a lot of them, all volunteers. The usual misfits. I suppose my father was typical enough, an engineer who couldn't keep up with the knowledge explosion, got tired of the rat race. That was the first wave, and they took the best land, founded the city, got an economy going. Paid back American Express in twenty years." Banners's pride was evident, and Falkenberg knew it had been a difficult job.

"That was, what, fifty years ago?" Falkenberg asked. They were driving through crowded streets lined with wooden houses, some stone buildings. Rooming houses, bars, sailors' brothels, the usual for a dock street, but there were no other cars on the roads. They could see horses and oxen pulling carts. The sky above Refuge was clear, no trace of smog or industrial wastes. Out in the harbor, tugboats moved with the silent efficiency of electric power, but there were also wind-driven sailing ships, lobster boats powered by oars, a tops'l schooner lovely against clean blue water throwing up white spume as she raced out to sea. A three-masted, full-rigged ship was drawn up to a wharf where men loaded it by hand with huge bales of what might have been cotton.

They passed a wagonload of melons. A gaily dressed young couple waved cheerfully at them, then the man snapped a long whip at the team of horses which pulled them. Falkenberg studied the primitive scene, said, "It doesn't look like you've been here fifty years."

"No." Banners gave them a bitter look, swerved to avoid several shapeless teenagers lounging in the dockside street, swerved again to avoid a barricade of paving stones which they had masked. A shower of stones banged against the vehicle. The car jounced wildly, leaped over a low place in the wall, and Banners accelerated rapidly.

Falkenberg carefully took his hand from inside his shirt, noted that Calvin was now inspecting an automatic rifle that appeared from the oversized barracks bag he'd brought into the car with him. When Banners said nothing about the incident, Fal-

The Mercenary 177

kenberg knitted his brows and sat back, listening. The intelligence reports mentioned lawlessness, but this was as bad as a Welfare Island on Earth.

"No, we're not much industrialized," Banners continued. "At first there wasn't any need to develop basic industries. The mines made everyone rich, so rich we imported everything we needed. The farmers sold fresh food to the miners for enormous prices. Refuge was a service-industry town. People who worked here could soon afford farm animals, and they scattered out across the plains, into the forest. Those people didn't want industry; they'd come here to escape it. Then some blasted CoDominium bureaucrat read the ecology reports about Hadley. The Population Control Bureau in Washington decided this was a perfect world for involuntary colonization. The ships were coming here for the thorium anyway, so instead of luxuries and machinery they were ordered to carry convicts. Hundreds of thousands of them, Colonel Falkenberg. For the last ten years, it's been better than fifty thousand people a year dumped in here."

"And you couldn't support them all," John said carefully.

"No, sir." Banners's face tightened. He seemed to be fighting tears. "Every erg the fusion generators can make has to go into basic protocarb just to feed them. These weren't like the original colonists. They didn't know anything, they wouldn't *do* anything . . . oh, not really, of course. Some of them work. Some of our best citizens are transportees. But there were so many of the other kind."

"Why'n't you let 'em work or starve?" Calvin asked bluntly. Falkenberg gave him a cold look, and the sergeant nodded slightly, sank back into his seat.

"Because the CD wouldn't let us!" Banners shouted. "Damn it, we didn't have self-government. CD Bureau of Relocation people told us what to do, ran everything . . ."

"We know," Falkenberg said gently. "We've seen the results of Humanity League influence over BuRelock. My sergeant-major wasn't asking you a question, he was expressing an opinion. I'm surprised though—won't your farms support the urban population?"

"They should, sir." Banners drove in grim silence for long moments. "But there's no transportation. The people are here, and most of the agricultural land is five hundred miles inland. There's arable land closer, but it isn't cleared . . . our settlers wanted to get away from Refuge and BuRelock. We have a railroad, but bandit gangs keep blowing it up, so we can't rely on Hadley's produce to keep Refuge alive. With about a million people on Hadley, half of them are crammed into this one ungovernable city."

They were approaching an enormous bowl-shaped structure attached to a massive square stone fortress. Falkenberg inspected the buildings carefully, then asked what they were.

"Our stadium," Banners replied. There was no pride in his voice now. "The CD built it for us. We'd rather have had a new fusion plant, but we got a stadium that can hold a hundred thousand people. For recreation. We have very fine sports teams and racehorses," he added bitterly. "The building next to it is the Palace. Its architecture is quite functional."

The city was even more thickly populated as they approached the fortress-like palace. Now the buildings were mostly stone and concrete instead of wood. Few were more than three stories high, so that Refuge spread as far as the eye could see along the shore, the population density increasing beyond the stadium-palace complex. Banners was watchful as he drove along the wide streets, but seemed less nervous.

Refuge was a city of contrasts. The streets were straight and wide, and there was evidently a good waste disposal system, but the lower floors of the buildings were open shops, the sidewalks were clogged with market stalls, crowds of pedestrians; there were still no motor traffic, no moving pedways. Horse troughs and hitching posts had been constructed at frequent intervals, along with starkly functional street lights and water distribution towers. The few signs of technology contrasted strongly with the general primitive air of the city.

A uniformed contingent of men thrust their way through the crowd at a street crossing. Falkenberg looked at them closely, then at Banners. "Your troops?"

"No, sir. That's the livery of Glenn Foster's household. Officially they're unorganized reserves of the President's Guard, but they're household troops all the same." Banners laughed bitterly. "Sounds like something out of a history book, doesn't it? We're nearly back to feudalism, Colonel Falkenberg. Anyone rich enough keeps hired bodyguards. They *have* to. The criminal gangs are so strong the police don't try to catch anyone under organized protection, and the judges wouldn't punish them if they were caught."

"And the private bodyguards become gangs in their own right, I suppose?"

"Yes, sir." Banners looked at him sharply. "Have you seen it happen before?"

"Yes. I've seen it before." Banners was unable to make out the expression on Falkenberg's lips.

They drove into the Presidential Palace, were saluted by blue-uniformed troopers. Falkenberg noted the polished weapons, precise drill of the Presidential Guard. There were some well-trained men on duty here, although there probably weren't too many of them. He wondered if they could fight as well as stand guard.

He was conducted through a series of rooms in the heavy stone fortress. Each had heavy metal doors, and several seemed to be guardrooms. Falkenberg saw no signs of governmental activity until they had passed through the outer layers of the enormous palace to an open courtyard, through that to an inner building where clerks bustled through halls, girls in the draped togas fashionable two years before on Earth sat at desks in offices. Most seemed to be packing desk contents into boxes, and all around the palace people were scurrying about. Some offices were empty: desks covered with fine dust, plastiboard moving boxes stacked outside them.

There were two anterooms to the president's office. President Budreau was a tall thin man with a red pencil moustache and quick gestures. As they were ushered into the overly ornate room the president looked up from a sheaf of papers, but his eyes didn't focus on his visitors for long seconds. Slowly the worried concentration left his face and he rose.

"Colonel John Christian Falkenberg, sir," Lieutenant Banners said. "And Sergeant-Major Calvin."

"Pleased to see you, Falkenberg," the president said. His expression told them differently; he looked at his visitors with faint distaste, said nothing else until Banners had left the room. When the door closed he asked, "How many men did you bring with you?"

"Ten, Mister President. All we could get on board the carrier without arousing suspicion. We were lucky to get those. The Senate had an inspector at the loading docks to check for violation of the antimercenary codes. If we hadn't bribed a port official to distract him we wouldn't be here at all. Calvin and I would be on Tanith as involuntary colonists."

"I see." From his expression he was not surprised. John thought he might have been as happy if the inspector had caught them. Budreau tapped the desk nervously. "Perhaps it will be enough. I understand the ship you came on carried the marines who have volunteered to settle on Hadley. They should provide the nucleus of an excellent constabulary for us. Good troops?"

"It was a demobilized battalion," Falkenberg replied. "Those are usually the scrapings of every guardhouse on twenty planets. We'll be lucky if there's a real trooper in the lot." Falkenberg saw Budreau's face relax into a mask of depression, every trace of hope draining out. "Surely you have troops of your own?"

Budreau picked up a sheaf of papers. "It's all here, I was just looking it over when you came in." He handed the report to Falkenberg. "There's not much encouragement in it, Colonel. There's no military solution to Hadley's problems. I never thought there could be, but if you have only ten men plus a battalion of forced labor marines, the military answer isn't worth considering." Budreau gave Falkenberg a thin smile, moved his hands rapidly over the sea of papers on his desk. "If I were you, I'd get back on that Navy boat and forget Hadley."

"Why don't you?" Falkenberg asked.

"Because Hadley's my home!" Budreau snapped. "And no rabble is going to drive me off the plantation my grandfather built with his own hands. They won't make me run out."

Falkenberg took the report, flipped the pages and handed it to Calvin. "We've come a long way, Mister President. You might as well tell me what the problem is before I leave."

Budreau nodded sourly. The red moustache twitched, and he ran the back of his hand across it. "It's simple enough. The ostensible reason you're here, the reason we gave the Colonial Office for letting us recruit a planetary constabulary, is the bandit gangs out in the hills. Nobody knows how many of them there are, but they're strong enough to raid farms, cut communications between Refuge and the countryside whenever they want to. They're serious enough but they're not the real problem, as I presume Vice-President Bradford told you."

Falkenberg nodded. Budreau paused, but when John said nothing, continued. The president's voice was strong, but there was a querulous note in it, as if he were accustomed to having his conclusions argued. "Actually, the bandits aren't my worst problem. But they get support from the Freedom Party, which makes them hard to fight. My Progressive Party is larger than the Freedom Party, but the Progressives are scattered all over the planet and the FP is concentrated right here in Refuge, with God knows how many voters and about forty thousand people they can concentrate when they want to stage a riot."

"Do you have riots very often?" John asked.

"Too often. There's not much to control them with. I have three hundred men in the Presidential Guard, but they're CD recruited and trained like young Banners. Loyal to the job, not to me. And the FP's got men inside it. So scratch the President's Guard when it comes to controlling the Freedom Party."

Budreau smiled without amusement. "Then there's my police force. My police were all commanded by CoDominium officers who are pulling out. My administrative staff was recruited and trained by the CD and all the competent people have been recalled to Earth. There's nobody left who *can* govern, but I've got the job and everybody else wants it. I might be able to scrape up a thousand Progressive partisans, another fifteen thousand loyalists who would fight in a pinch but have no training, to face the FP's forty thousand. And the Freedom Party's demanded a constitutional convention after the CoDominium governor leaves. If we don't give them a convention, they'll rebel. If we do, they'll drag things out until there's nobody left but their people, throw the Progressives out of office, and ruin the planet. Under the circumstances, I don't see what a military man can do for us, but Bradford insisted we hire you."

"I take it the Progressive Party is mostly old settlers," Falkenberg said casually.

"Yes and no. It's extremely complicated. The Progressive Party wants to industrialize Hadley, which some of our farm families oppose. But we want to do it slowly. We'll close most of the mines, take out only as much thorium as we have to sell to get basic industrial equipment, keep the rest for our own fusion generators. We'll need it later. We want to develop agriculture and transportation, cut the basic rations so that we can have fusion power for industry. Close out the convenience industries and keep them closed until we can afford them." Budreau's voice rose steadily, his eyes shone. "We want to build the tools of a self-sustaining world and get along without the CoDominium until we can rejoin the human race as equals!" The president caught himself, frowned. He seemed angry with John for witnessing his emotional speech.

Falkenberg leaned back in the heavy leather chair, seemingly relaxed, but his eyes darted around the room, noting the ornate furnishings. The office decor must have cost a fortune to bring from Earth, but most of it was tasteless, chosen for the spectacular rather than for beauty. He waited until Budreau was seated again, then asked, "What does the opposition want?"

"Do you really need to know all this in order—I suppose you do." Budreau's moustache twitched nervously. "The Freedom Party's slogan is 'Service to the People.' They want strip mining—that's got them the miners' support, you can bet. They'll rape the planet to buy goods from other systems. Introduce internal combustion engines—God knows how, there's no technology for them, no heavy industry to make them even if the ecology could absorb them, but they promise cars for everyone, instant modernization. More food, robotic factories, entertainment, all the benefits of immediate industrialization."

"They mean it, or is that just slogans?"

"I think most of them mean it," Budreau answered. "It's hard to believe, but I think they do. Their people have no idea of the realities of our situation, and their leaders are ready to blame anything on the Progressive Party, CoDominium administrators, anything but admit that what they promise isn't possible. Some of the party leaders may know better." Budreau poured brandy into two glasses, waited for Falkenberg to lift one, and muttered a perfunctory "Cheers." He drained the glass at one gulp. "Some of the oldest families on Hadley have joined the Freedom Party. They're worried about the taxes I've proposed, joined the opposition hoping to make a deal . . . you don't look surprised."

"No, sir. It's an old story . . . a military man reads history; if he's smart he'll look for the causes of wars. After all, war is the normal state of affairs, isn't it? Peace is the name of an ideal we deduce from the fact that there have been interludes between wars." Before Budreau could answer, Falkenberg caught himself. "No matter. I take it you expect armed resistance from the Freedom Party after the CD pulls out."

"I hope to prevent it," Budreau snapped. "I do have some gifts at the art of persuasion . . . but they don't want to compromise. They see total victory. As to fighting, the FP partisans claim credit for driving the CoDominium out, Colonel."

Falkenberg laughed. The CD was leaving because the mines weren't worth enough to make it pay to govern Hadley. If the mines were as good as they'd been in the past, no partisans would drive the marines away . . .

Budreau nodded as if reading his thoughts. "They've got people believing it anyway. There was a campaign of terrorism for years, nothing very serious to the CD or the marines would have put a stop to it, but they've demoralized the capital police. Out in the bush people administer their own justice. In Refuge, FP gangs control a lot of the city. I don't even know how many police I'll have left when the CD pulls out." He pointed to a stack of papers. "These are resignations from the force."

Budreau sat very still, gathering his thoughts with an effort, the faraway look in his eyes again. "I'm president by courtesy of the CoDominium," he said bitterly.

"They installed me and now they're leaving! Sometimes I wish Bradford hadn't been so successful in talking to the Colonial Office. Bureau of Relocation wanted to leave a Freedom Party president in charge, you know. I wonder if that wouldn't have been better."

"I thought you said their policies would ruin Hadley," Falkenberg mused. He had little use for weaklings, and Budreau seemed to be one.

"They would. But—the policy issues came after the split, I think," Budreau said slowly. He was talking to himself as much as to John. "Now they hate us so much, they oppose anything we want out of spite. And we do the same thing."

"Sounds like CoDominium politics. Russki senators versus United States senators. Just like home," Falkenberg said. There was no trace of humor in the polite laugh that followed. "You say Vice-President Bradford arranged for the Colonial Office to install you as president against the advice of BuRelock?"

Budreau nodded. "Yes . . . the public relations campaign was expensive, more expensive than I'd have ever dreamed, but once we were in office we had the Ministry of Information funds . . . well, you see the situation, Colonel. If you stay, I'll keep the agreement, you'll be Commander of Constabulary. Your commission's already signed. But really, I think it would be better if you didn't take the post. Hadley's problems can't be solved by military consultants."

"Perhaps you're right." Falkenberg said. He suppressed the impulse to grin at the euphemism for mercenaries and finished his drink.

"Now, Mr. Bradford wants to see you," Budreau said. "Lieutenant Banners will show you to his office. And please let me know your decision."

"I will, sir." Falkenberg strode from the big room. As he did, President Budreau buried his face in his hands.

Vice-President Earnest Bradford was a small man with a perpetual half smile on a round face that might have been cherubic if it weren't so haggard. Falkenberg was conducted into the small office, waited until Calvin and Lieutenant Banners left before speaking. As the others were leaving John glanced around the room. In contrast to Budreau's richly furnished suite, the first vice-president's office was starkly functional, desk and chairs made of local woods with an indifferent finish. A solitary rose in a crystal vase provided the only color.

"Thank God you're here," Bradford said. "But I'm told you only brought ten men! We can't do anything with just ten men! You were supposed to bring a hundred men loyal to us!" He bounced up excitedly, stopped, then sat again. "Can you do something?"

"There were ten men in the Navy ship with me," Falkenberg said. "My staff. When you show me where I'm to train the regiment, I'll find the rest of the mercenaries."

"Others—" Bradford gave him a broad wink, beamed. "Then you did get more to come! We'll show them, all of them . . . What did you think of Budreau?"

"He seems sincere enough. Worried, though. Think I would be in his place."

Bradford shook his head. "He can't make up his mind. About anything! Good man, but he has to be forced to every decision. Why did the Colonial Office pick him? I thought you were going to arrange for me to be president."

"One thing at a time," Falkenberg said. "The permanent under-secretary couldn't justify you to the minister. It was hard enough for Whitlock to get them to approve Budreau with all his experience, let alone a newcomer like you. We sweated blood on this, Ernie."

Bradford's head bobbed up and down. "Good work, too," he said, but he looked at Falkenberg closely. "You kept your part of the bargain, John. I just wish you could have . . . well, we'll get to it." His smile expanded confidentially, then he grimaced. "We have to let Mr. Hamner meet you now. Then we can go to the Warner estate. I've arranged for your troops to be quartered there; it's got what you wanted for a training ground. Perfect place, nobody will bother you. You can say your other men are volunteers from the countryside."

Falkenberg nodded slightly. "Let me handle that, will you? I'm getting rather good at cover stories."

"Sure." Bradford beamed again. "By God, we'll win this yet." He touched a button on his desk. "Send Mr. Hamner in, please."

"Wait until you see this Hamner," he told John while they were waiting. "He's the second vice-president. Budreau trusts him, so he's dangerous. Represents the technocracy people in the Progressive Party; we can't do without him, but his policies are ridiculous. He wants to let go of everything. There wouldn't be a planetary government if he was in charge. And his people take credit for everything, as if technology was all there was to government. He doesn't know about the meetings, the intrigues, all the people I've had to see, speeches. . . . He thinks you build a party by working like an engineer."

"Doesn't understand the political realities," Falkenberg finished for him. "Just so. You say he has to be eliminated?"

Bradford shuddered slightly, but kept the thin smile on his face. "Eventually. We do need his influence with the technicians at the moment. And of course he doesn't know anything at all about . . . about . . ."

"Of course." Falkenberg sat easily, looking about the office, studied maps on the walls until the intercom announced that Hamner was outside.

George Hamner was a large man, taller than Falkenberg and even heavier than Sergeant-Major Calvin. He had the relaxed movements of a big man, and much of the easy confidence that such massive size usually wins. People didn't pick fights with George Hamner, drunk or sober. His grip was gentle, but he closed his hand relentlessly, testing Falkenberg carefully. As he felt answering pressure he looked surprised, and the two men stood in silence for long moments before Hamner relaxed and waved at Bradford.

"So you're our new Colonel of Constabulary," Hamner said. "Hope you know what you're getting into. I should say I hope you *don't* know. If you know about our problems and take the job anyway, we'll have to wonder if you're sane."

"I keep hearing a lot about how severe Hadley's problems are, but nobody's briefed me," Falkenberg replied. "I gather we're outnumbered by the Freedom Party people and you expect trouble. What kind of weapons do they have to make trouble with?"

Hamner laughed. "Direct son of a gun, aren't you? Nothing spectacular in the weapons, just a lot of them . . . enough small problems is a big problem, right? But the CD hasn't permitted big stuff. No tanks or armored cars . . . hell, there aren't enough cars of any kind to make any difference. No fuel or power distribution network ever built, so no way cars would be useful. We've got a subway, couple of monorails for in-city stuff, and what's left of the railroad . . . you didn't ask for a lecture on our transport, did you? My pet worry at the moment. Let's see, weapons . . ." The big man sprawled into a chair, hooked one leg over the arm and ran his fingers through thick hair just receding from his large brows. "No military aircraft, hardly any aircraft at all. No artillery, machine guns, heavy weapons in general. Mostly light caliber hunting rifles and shotguns. Some police weapons. Military rifles and bayonets, a few, and we have almost all of them. Out in the streets you can find anything, Colonel, and I mean literally anything. Bows and arrows, knives, swords, axes, hammers, you name it."

"He doesn't need to know about obsolete things like that," Bradford said contemptuously.

"No weapon is ever obsolete," Falkenberg said carefully, "not in the hands of a man who'll use it. What about armor? Enemy and our own. How good a supply of Nemourlon do you have?"

Hamner looked thoughtful for a second. "There's some body armor in the streets, and the police . . . the President's Guard doesn't use the stuff. I can supply you with Nemourlon, but you'll have to make your own armor out of it. Can you do that?"

Falkenberg nodded. "I brought men and equipment for that. Well, the situation's about what I expected. I can't see why everyone's so worried. We have a battalion of CD marines, not the best marines but they're trained soldiers. With the weapons of a light infantry battalion and the training I can give the recruits, I'll undertake to face your forty thousand Freedom Party people. The guerrilla problem will be a lot more severe, but we control the food distribution system in the city. Ration cards, identity papers . . . it shouldn't be hard to set up controls."

Hamner laughed, a bitter laugh. "You want to tell him, Ernie?" When Bradford looked confused, Hamner laughed again. "Not doing your homework. It's in the morning report for a couple of days ago. The Colonial Office has decided, on the advice of BuRelock, that Hadley doesn't need any military weapons. The CD marines will be lucky to keep their rifles and bayonets, because all the rest of their gear is being taken back to Earth."

"I see," Falkenberg said slowly. His lips compressed into a tight line, and he cursed to himself. "Hadn't counted on that. Means that if we do tighten up control through food rationing, we face armed rebellion. . . . How well organized are these FP types, anyway?"

"Well organized and well financed," Hamner said. "And I can't agree about ration cards being the answer to the guerrilla problem. The CoDominium was able to put up with a lot of sabotage, since all they were really interested in was the mines, but we can't live with the level of terror we have in this city. Some way we're going to have to restore order—and justice for that matter."

"Justice isn't a commodity soldiers generally deal with," Falkenberg said grimly. "Order's another matter. *That* I think we can supply."

"With five hundred men?" Hamner's voice was incredulous. "But I like your attitude. At least you don't sit around and whine for somebody to help you, the way some of our officials do." He looked significantly at Bradford. "Well, I wanted to meet you, Colonel. Now I have. *I've* got work to do." He didn't look at them again as he strode briskly from the room.

"You see," Bradford said as soon as Hamner was out of sight. "The man's no good. We'll find someone to deal with the technicians as soon as you've got everything else under control."

"He seemed to be right on some points," John said slowly. "For example, he knows as well as I do that it won't be easy to get proper police protection established. I saw an example of what goes on in Refuge on the way here, and if it's that bad everywhere . . ."

"You'll find a way," Bradford said reassuringly. "Lot of it's just teenage street gangs. Not loyal to anything—FP, us, CD, or anything else. They call it defending their turf or something . . . and forget Hamner. His whole group is . . . well, they're just not real Progressives, that's all." He was emphatic, then lowered his voice and leaned forward. "He used to be in the Freedom Party, you know. Claims to have broken with them over technology policies, but you can never trust a man like that." Then he smiled again, stood. "Let's get you started. And don't forget your agreement to train some men for me, too. . . ."

Falkenberg woke to a soft rapping on the door of his room. He opened his eyes, put his hand on the pistol under his pillow, but made no other movement. "Yes," he called softly.

"I'm back, Colonel," Calvin answered.

"Right. Come on in." John swung his feet out of the bunk, put on his boots. Otherwise he was fully dressed. Sergeant-Major Calvin came in, dressed in the light leather tunic and trousers of the CD marine battle dress. Falkenberg could see the total black of a night combat coverall protruding from Calvin's war bag. A short wiry man came in with the sergeant.

"Glad to see you," Falkenberg said. "Have any trouble?"

"Gang of toughs tried to stir up something as we was coming through the city, Colonel," Calvin replied. "Didn't last long enough to set any records." He grinned wolfishly.

"What about at the relocation barracks?"

"No, sir," Calvin replied. "They don't guard them places. Anybody wants to get away from BuRelock's charity, they let 'em go. Without citizens' basic supply cards, of course."

Falkenberg was inspecting the man who had entered with Calvin. Major Jeremy Savage looked tired, older than his forty-five standard years, and thinner than John remembered him. "Was it as bad as I've heard?" he asked.

"No picnic," Savage replied in the clipped accents he'd learned as a boy on Churchill. "Didn't expect it to be. We're here, John Christian."

"Good. Nobody spotted you? Men behave all right?"

"Yes, sir, we were treated no differently from any other involuntary colonists. The men behaved splendidly, and a week of hard exercise and good food ought to have us back in shape. Sergeant-Major tells me the battalion arrived intact."

"I sort of filled the major in while we was coming out," Calvin said. "I think he sees the score, sir."

Falkenberg nodded. "But keep your eyes open, Jerry, and be careful with the men until the CD pulls out. Yes, and I've hired Dr. Whitlock to check things for us. He hasn't reported in yet, but I assume he's on Hadley."

"Whitlock?" Savage sat in the room's single chair, accepted whiskey from Calvin with a nod of thanks. "My, that's good. Heard of Whitlock. Best in the field, although he puts on as a hillbilly. Very appropriate man for us, don't you know?"

John nodded. "Until he reports we won't have a full staff meeting. Just stay with the original plan. Bradford brings the battalion of marines out tomorrow, and a few hundred volunteers from the Progressive Party's little private army for us to train. More recruits coming, supposedly. Now tell me a bit about those toughs you fought on the way out here."

"Street gang, Colonel," Calvin replied. "Not bad at individual fightin', but no organization. Hardly no match for near a hundred of us."

"Street gang." John pulled his lower lip speculatively, then grinned. "How many of our battalion used to be punks just like them, Sergeant-Major?"

"Half, maybe more, sir."

Falkenberg nodded. "I think it might be a good thing if the marines got to meet some of those kids, Sergeant-Major. Informally, you know . . ."

"Sir!" Calvin's faced beamed with comprehension.

The Mercenary

"Now," Falkenberg continued. "Recruits will be our real problem. You can bet some of them will try to get chummy with the troops, pump the men about their backgrounds and outfits. We can't have that, of course. Anticipate any problems there, Top Soldier?"

Calvin looked thoughtful. "No, sir, not for a while. Won't be no trick to keep the recruits away from the men until they've passed through training; till then all they'll meet'll be drillmasters. We can do it, sir."

"Right." Falkenberg turned to Major Savage. "That's it, then."

"Yes, sir," Savage answered crisply. He drew himself erect and saluted. "Damned if it doesn't feel good to be doing this again, sir," he grinned. Years fell away from his face.

"Good to have you aboard," Falkenberg replied. He stood to return the salute. "And thanks, Jerry. For everything . . ."

The Warner estate was large, nearly four kilometers on a side, located in low hills outside the city of Refuge but no more than a day's march from the Palace and stadium. Falkenberg's troops found themselves in a partly wooded bowl in the center of the estate. At John's request there were no cooking services or other support activities other than food and fuel and basic military equipment. The troops spent the first week constructing a base camp.

The marines relearned lessons of their basic training. Each maniple of five men cooked for itself, did its own laundry, made tents from woven synthetics and ropes, and contributed men for work on the encampment revetments and palisade. When the recruits arrived they were forced to do the same things under the supervision of Falkenberg's mercenary officers and NCO's. Most of the men who had come with Savage on the BuRelock colony transport were officers, sergeants, and technicians, while there seemed to be an unusual number of monitors and corporals within the marine battalion, so that there were more than enough leaders for a regiment. Some Progressive Party stalwarts selected by Bradford were given junior commissioned rank and trained separately.

The men learned to sleep in their military greatcloaks, to live under field conditions with no uniform but synthileather battle dress and boots, cooking their own food and constructing their own quarters, dependent on no one outside the regiment. They were also taught to fashion their own body armor from Nemourlon; when it was completed they lived in it, and any man selected for punishment found his armor weighted with a calculated quantity of lead. Maniples, squads, and whole sections of recruits on punishment marches lasting late into the night became a common sight around the estate.

The volunteers had little time to fraternize with the marines as Savage and Calvin and the other cadres relentlessly drove them through drills, field problems, combat exercises, and maintenance work. The number of recruits fell every day as men were driven to leave the service, but from somewhere there was a steady supply of new troops. These were younger men, who came in small groups directly to the camp, appearing before the regimental orderly room at reveille, often in the company of a section of marine veterans. There was attrition in their numbers as well as among the Party volunteers, but the proportion was much smaller, and they were eager for combat training.

One of the regiment's main problems was the commissioned Progressives. They had to be taught basic military arts, yet they were officers by courtesy and couldn't be driven out of the regiment without protest from Bradford. The worst of them were summarily dismissed, but Falkenberg was forced to keep many men as officers who he wouldn't have had as private soldiers if given free choice.

Twice a week John went to the estate house two kilometers from the camp to report to Bradford, Hamner and, infrequently, President Budreau. Budreau had made it clear that he considered the military force as an evil whose necessity was not established, and only Bradford's insistence kept the regiment supplied. After six weeks, Bradford raised the question of the decreasing numbers of Progressive volunteers in training.

"You're letting those men go too easily, Colonel," he protested. "Those are loyal men! Loyalty is important here!"

"Sir, I'd rather have one battalion of good men I can trust than a regiment of troops who might break under fire," Falkenberg answered stiffly. "After we have the bare minimum of first-class troops, we can consider taking on others for garrison duties. For now I want men who can fight."

"You don't have them yet," Bradford sniffed. "And where are you getting those new recruits? Jailbirds, kids with police records. I notice you're keeping them when you let my Progressives go!"

"It takes time to train green men. The recruits are all treated the same, Mister Vice-President, and if those street warriors stand up better than your party toughs, I can't help it."

"We'll discuss this later," Bradford said coldly. "There's another thing." He indicated a large man with a fat jowl seated down the table from him. "This is Chief Horgan of the Refuge police. He has some complaints, Colonel."

Falkenberg faced the chief of police, stood silently until the other man spoke.

"Your marines, Colonel." Horgan rubbed his chin carefully. "They're raising hell in the city at night. Never hauled any of them in, but I'm not saying we couldn't have if we'd wanted to. But they've taken over a couple of taverns, won't let anybody in without their permission. Have fights with street gangs there every night. And they go out into the toughest parts of town, start fights whenever they can find anyone to mix with."

"How are they doing?" Falkenberg asked interestedly.

Horgan grinned, caught himself. "Pretty well. I understand they've never been beaten . . . but it raises hell with the citizens, Colonel. And another trick of theirs is driving people crazy! They march through the streets fifty strong at all hours of the night playing bagpipes! Bagpipes in the small hours, Colonel, can be a frightening thing." Falkenberg thought he saw a tiny flutter to Horgan's left eye. The man was holding back a wry smile.

"I wanted to ask you about that, Colonel," Second Vice-President Hamner added. "This is hardly a Scots outfit; why do they have bagpipes?"

"Pipes are standard with many marine regiments," Falkenberg answered easily. "Very stimulating to the troops. Since the Russki CD outfits started taking up Cossack customs, the Western Bloc regiments looked around for something equally impressive. A lot of them like the pipes." John grinned openly at the Chief of Police. "I'll try to keep the pipers off the streets at night, though. I can imagine they're not good for civilian morale. As to keeping the marines in camp, how do I do it? We need every one of them, and they're volunteers. They can get back on that CD carrier and ship out, and there's not one thing we can do."

"It's only a couple of weeks until they haul down the CoDominium flag," Bradford added with satisfaction. He glanced at the CD banner on the wall behind him, an eagle with a red shield, black sickle and hammer on its breast. The flag meant little to the people of Hadley, but on Earth it was enough to cause riots in nationalistic cities in both the U.S. and the Soviet Union. To Earth the CoDominium Alliance represented peace at a high price, too high for many. For Falkenberg it represented nearly thirty years of service ended by court martial.

A week before the departure of the CoDominium governor and the official independence of Hadley, Bradford visited the camp to make a speech to the recruits. He told them of the value of loyalty to the government, and the rewards they would get as soon as the Progressive Party was completely in power. Better pay, more liberties, and the opportunities for promotion in an expanding army were all promised. When he had finished, Falkenberg took the vice-president into his cabin and slammed the door.

"Damn you, you don't *ever* make offers to my troops without my permission!" John's face was cold with anger.

"I'll do as I please with *my* troops," Bradford replied smugly. The little smile was on his face, a smile without warmth. "Don't get snappy with me, *Colonel* Falkenberg. Without my influence Budreau would dismiss you in an instant." Then, with a sudden change of mood, Bradford took a flask of brandy from his pocket, poured two drinks. The little smile faded, was replaced by something more genuine. "We have to work together, John. There's too much to do, with both of us working we won't get it all done. Sorry, I'll ask in future. But don't you think the troops should know me? I'll be president soon." He looked at Falkenberg closely.

"Yes, sir," John said. He took the drink, held it up for a toast. "To the new president of Hadley. I shouldn't have snapped at you, but don't make offers to troops who haven't proved themselves. If you give men reason to think they're good when they're not, you'll never have an army worth its pay. Work them until they've nothing more to give, let them know that's just barely satisfactory, and one day they'll give you more than they thought they had in them. That's the day you offer rewards, only by then you won't have to."

Bradford nodded agreement, but then frowned. "That's all very well, but I insist on keeping my loyalists, Colonel. In future you will dismiss no Progressive without my approval. Is that understood?"

Falkenberg nodded. He'd seen this coming for some time. "In that case, sir, I will transfer all of your people into the fourth battalion and place your appointed officers in command of their training. Will that be satisfactory?"

"Provided that you continue to supervise their training, yes." Bradford thought for a moment, then smiled. "I will also expect you to consult me about any promotions in that battalion, in that case. You agree to that, of course?"

"Yes, sir. There may be some problems about finding locals to fill the senior NCO slots. You've got potential monitors and corporals, but they haven't the experience to be sergeants and centurions."

"You'll find a way, I'm sure," Bradford said carefully. "I have some rather, uh, special duties for the fourth battalion, Colonel. I'd prefer it to be completely staffed by Party loyalists. Is this agreed?"

"Yes, sir."

Bradford's smile was genuine as he left the camp.

Day after day the troops sweated in the bright blue-tinted sunlight. Riot control, bayonet drill, use of armor in defense and attacks against men with body armor, more complex exercises, and forced marches under the relentless direction of Major Savage, the harsh shouts of their sergeants and centurions, Captain Fast with his tiny swagger stick and biting sarcasm . . . but the number of men leaving the regiment was smaller now, while there was still a flow of recruits from the marines' nocturnal expeditions. Falkenberg was able to be more selective in his recruiting.

Each night groups of marines sneaked past sentries, drank and caroused with the fieldhands of nearby ranchers, gambled and shouted and paid little attention to their officers. But they always came back, and when Bradford protested their lack of discipline off duty he would get the same answer. "They don't have to stay here," Falkenberg told him. "How would you suggest I control them? Flogging?"

The constabulary army had a definite split personality. And the fourth battalion grew larger each day.

II

George Hamner tried to get home for dinner every day, no matter what that might cost in night work later. His walled estate just outside the Palace district was originally built by his grandfather with money borrowed from American Express and paid back before it was due, a big comfortable place which cunningly combined local materials and imported luxuries. George was always glad to return there, feel the pride of mastery. It was the only place in Refuge where he felt at home in the last few years.

It was less than a week until the CoDominium governor departed, one week before complete independence for Hadley. That should be a time of hope, but George Hamner dreaded it. Problems of public order weren't officially part of his Ministry of Technology assignment, but he couldn't ignore them. Already half the city of Refuge was nearly untouched by government, an area where police went in squads and maintenance crews performed their work as quickly as possible under the protection of CD marines. What was it going to be like when the CD was gone?

Hamner sat in the paneled study watching lengthening shadows in the groves outside make dancing patterns across neatly clipped lawns. The outside walls spoiled the view of Raceway Channel below, and Hamner cursed them, cursed the necessity for walls and a dozen armed men patroling them, remembering a time as a boy when he'd sat in this room with his father, listened to the great plans for Hadley. A paradise planet, and Lord, Lord, what have we made of it? An hour's work didn't help. There weren't any solutions, only a chain of problems that brought him back to the same place each time. A few years—that's all they needed, but he didn't see how they could get them.

The farms could support the urban population if they could move the people out to the agricultural interior and get them working, but they wouldn't leave Refuge. If only they would—if the city's population could be thinned, the power now diverted to food manufacture could be used to build a transportation net to keep people in the interior or bring food from there to the city. They could manufacture the things needed to make country life so pleasant that people would be willing to leave Refuge and go there. But there was no way to the first step. The people wouldn't move and the Freedom Party promised them they wouldn't have to.

George shook his head, thought about Falkenberg's army. If there were enough soldiers, could they forcibly evacuate part of the city? But there'd be resistance, civil war, slaughter. Budreau wouldn't let Hadley's independence be built on a foundation of blood. Hamner laughed bitterly. Not only Budreau. I can't do it either, he thought. I can see what's got to be done, but I can't do it. Bradford would . . . but what then? Besides, there weren't enough soldiers. There was no military answer.

His other problems were of the same kind. He could see that all the government was doing was putting bandages on Hadley's wounds, treating symptoms because there was never enough control over events to treat causes. He picked up an engineering report on the fusion generators.

Spare parts needed . . . how long can we keep things running even at this crazy standoff, he wondered. A few years. After that, famine, because the transportation net couldn't be built fast enough, and when the generators failed, the city's food supplies would be gone. Sanitation services would be crippled too; there would be plague despite the BuRelock inoculations.

He set his slide rule down on the desk, wishing for one of the pocket computers that were common on planets closer to Earth. The Freedom Party leader had one. George had talked to him about the fusion generators only two days before, and it seemed as if the Freedom Party didn't care that the generators wouldn't last forever. The FP leader's attitude was that Earth wouldn't allow famine, that Hadley could use her own helplessness as a weapon against the CoDominium. The concept of real independence from the CD didn't interest him. Hamner thought about that and swore, went back to engineering. He liked problems he could get his hands on and know he'd solved them, not political troubles that kept coming back no matter what he did.

Laura came in with a pack of shouting children. Was it already time for them to go to bed? The four-year-old picked up his father's slide rule, played with it carefully before climbing into his lap. George kissed the boy, hugged the others and sent them out, wondering as he did every night what would happen to them. Get out of politics, he told himself. You can't do Hadley any good, and you're not cut out for the game. You'll only get Laura and the kids finished along with yourself. But what happens if we let go, if we can't succeed, another part of his mind asked, and he had no answer to that.

But it doesn't matter . . . you'll get your family killed, and for what? Debts, inadequate pay, temptation after temptation to give in, compromise, look after Number One, swim with the stream until you become somebody you don't even want to know . . .

"You look worried," Laura said after she'd seen the children to bed. "It's only a few days . . . What happens, George? What really happens when CoDominium leaves for good? It's going to be bad, isn't it?"

He pulled her to him, feeling her warmth, tried to draw comfort from her nearness and at the same time distract her, but she knew that trick. "Shouldn't we take what we can and go east?" she asked. "We wouldn't have much, but you'd be alive."

"It won't be *that* bad," he told her. He tried to chuckle, as if she had said something funny, but the sound was hollow. "We've got a planetary constabulary . . . at the worst it should be enough to protect the government. But I am moving all of you into the Palace in a couple of days."

"The army," she said with plenty of contempt. "Some army, General Bradford's volunteers who'd kill you just to make that horrible little man happy . . . and those marines! You said yourself they were the scrapings."

"I said it. I wonder if I believe it. There's something strange happening here, Laura, something I don't understand. I went to see Karantov the other day, thought I'd presume on an old friend to get a little information about this man Falkenberg. Boris wasn't in his office but one of the junior lieutenants was. The kid was green, only been on Hadley a couple of months. . . . We got into a conversation about what happens after independence. Discussed street fighting, mob suppression, and how I wished I had some reliable marines instead of the people they were getting here. He looked funny and asked just what I wanted, the Grand Admiralty Guard? But then Boris came in and when I asked what the lieutenant meant, he said the kid was new and didn't know what he was talking about."

"And you think he did?" Laura asked. "But what could he have meant? Stop that!" she added hastily. "You have an appointment."

"It can wait."

"With only a couple of dozen cars on this whole planet and one of them coming for you, you will not keep it waiting while you make love to your wife, George Hamner!" Her eyes flashed, but not with anger. "Besides, I want to know what Boris told you." She danced away from him, sat on the other side of the desk. "What *do* you think he meant?"

"I don't know . . . but those troops don't look like misfits to me. Not on training exercises. Off duty they drink and shout and they've got the fieldhands locking up their daughters but come morning they muster out on that parade ground like . . . And there's more. The officers. They're not from Hadley, and I don't know who they are!"

"Why don't you ask?"

"I took it up with Budreau, and he gave me a stall about it being in Bradford's Ministry, so I asked him, and Ernie told me they were Progressive volunteers. I'm not that stupid, Laura. I may not notice everything, but if there were fifty men with military experience in the Party I'd know. So why would Bradford lie?"

Laura looked thoughtful, pulled her lower lip in a gesture so familiar that Hamner hardly noticed it any longer. He'd kidded her about it before they were married. . . . "He lies just for practice," she said finally. "But his wife has been talking about independence, and she seems to think Earnest will be president. Not some day, but soon . . . Why would she think that?"

George shook his head. "Maybe—no, he hasn't the guts for that, Ernie would never oust Budreau. He knows half the party wouldn't stand for it. . . . The technicians would walk out in a second; they can't stand him and he knows it."

"Earnest Bradford has never yet admitted any limitations," Laura reminded him. She glanced at the clock behind George. "It's getting late and you haven't told me what Boris said about Falkenberg."

"Said he was a good marine commander. Started out as a navy man, transferred to marines, became a regimental commander with a good combat record. That's all in the reports we have . . . I got the scoop on the court martial. There weren't any slots for promotion. But when a review board passed Falkenberg over for a promotion that the admiral couldn't have given in the first place, Falkenberg made such a fuss about it that he was dismissed for insubordination."

"Can you trust him to command here?" she asked. "His men may be the only thing keeping you alive . . ."

"I know." And keeping you alive, and Jimmy, and Christie, and Peter . . . "I asked Boris. He said there's not a better man available. You can't hire CD men from active duty, or even retired officers . . . Boris said that Falkenberg's really better than anyone we could get anyway. Troops love him, brilliant tactician, experience in troop command and staff work as well . . . Laura, if he's all that good, why did they boot him out? My God, fussing about promotion should be pretty trivial, and besides, it's not smart, Falkenberg would have to know it couldn't get him anywhere. None of it . . ."

The interphone buzzed, and Hamner answered it absently. It was the butler to announce that his car and driver were waiting. "I'll be late, sweetheart. Don't wait up for me. But you might think about . . . I swear that Falkenberg is the key to something, I wish I knew what."

"Do you like him?" Laura asked.

"He isn't a man who tries to be liked."

"I said, do *you* like him?"

"Yes. And there's no reason to. I like him, but can I trust him?" As he went out he thought about that. Could he trust Falkenberg. With Laura's life . . . and the kids', for that matter . . . with a whole planet that seemed headed for hell with no way out . . .

The troops were camped in an orderly square, earth ramparts thrown up around the perimeter, tents in lines that might have been laid with a transit. Equipment was scrubbed and polished, blanket rolls tight, each item in the same place inside the two-man tents . . . yet the men were milling about, shouting, gambling openly in front of the campfires. There were plenty of bottles in evidence even from the outer gates.

"Halt! Who's there?"

Hamner started. He hadn't seen the sentry. This was his first visit to the camp at night, and he was edgy. "Vice-President Hamner," he answered.

A strong light played on his face from the opposite side of the car. Two sentries, then, and both invisible until he'd come on them. "Good evening, sir," the first sentry said. "I'll pass the word you're here. Corporal of the Guard, Post Number Five!" The call rang clearly in the night. A few heads around campfires turned toward the gate, then went back to their other activities.

Hamner was escorted across the camp to officers' row. The huts and tents stood across a wide parade ground from the densely packed company streets of the troops, and Hamner saw another set of guards posted around these tents. Falkenberg came out of his hut. "Good evening, sir. What brings you here?"

I'll just bet you'd like to know, Hamner thought. "I have a few things to discuss with you, Colonel. About the organization of the constabulary."

"Certainly." Falkenberg was crisp, and he seemed slightly nervous. "Let's go to the mess, shall we? More comfortable there. Haven't got my quarters made up for visitors."

The Mercenary 195

Or you've got something there I shouldn't see, George thought. . . . God, can I trust him? Can I trust anyone? Falkenberg led the way to a building in the center of officer's row. There were troops milling around the parade ground, most wearing the blue and yellow duty uniforms Falkenberg had designed, but others trotted past in synthileather battle dress carrying heavy packs.

"Punishment detail," Falkenberg commented. "Not so many of those as there used to be."

Sound crashed from the officers' mess building, drums and bagpipes, a wild sound of war mingled with shouted laughter. Inside, two dozen men sat at a long table as white-coated stewards moved briskly about with whiskey bottles and glasses. Kilted bandsmen marched around the table with pipes, drummers stood in one corner. The deafening noise stopped as Falkenberg entered, and everyone got to his feet, some unsteadily.

"Carry on," Falkenberg said automatically, but no one did. They eyed Hamner nervously, and at a wave from the mess president at the head of the table the pipers went outside, followed by the drummers and several stewards with bottles.

"We'll sit over here, shall we?" the colonel asked. He led Hamner to a small table in one corner. A steward brought a whiskey bottle and two glasses.

George looked at the officers carefully. Most of them were strangers, but he recognized half-a-dozen Progressives, the highest rank a first lieutenant. Hamner waved at the ones he knew, received a brief smile that almost seemed guilty before they turned back to their companions.

"Yes, sir," Falkenberg prompted.

"Who are these men?" George demanded. "I know they're not native to Hadley. Where did they come from?"

"CoDominium officers on the beach," Falkenberg answered simply. "Reduction in force. Lots of good men riffed into early retirement. Some of them heard I was coming here, chose to give up their reserve ranks and come out on the colony ship on the chance I'd hire them. Naturally I jumped at the opportunity to get experienced men at prices we could afford. Vice-President Bradford knows all about it."

I'm sure he does, Hamner thought. I wonder what else that little snake knows about. Without his support Falkenberg would be out of here tomorrow . . . but then what would we do? "I see. I've been looking at the organization of the troops, Colonel. You've kept your marines in one battalion with, uh, with these newly hired officers. Then you've got three battalions of locals, but all the Party stalwarts are in the fourth; your second and third are locals but again under your own men."

"Yes, sir?" Falkenberg nodded agreement, gave Hamner a look of puzzlement. Hamner had noticed that particular trick of Falkenberg's before.

And you know my question, George thought. "Why, Colonel? A suspicious man would say you've got your own little army here, with a structure set so that you can take complete control if there's ever a difference of opinion between you and the government."

"A suspicious man might say that," Falkenberg agreed. He lifted one glass of whiskey, waited for George, then drained it. A steward immediately brought freshly filled glasses.

"But a practical man might say something else," Falkenberg continued. "You wouldn't expect me to put green officers in command of guard-house troops, would you? Or put your good-hearted Progressives in command of green troops? By Mr. Bradford's orders I've kept the fourth battalion as free of my mercenaries as possible, which isn't helping their training any. He seems to have the same complaint as you do, and wants his own Party force, I suspect to control me. Which is silly, Mr. Hamner. You have the purse strings. Without your supplies and money to pay these men, I couldn't hold them an hour."

"Troops have found it easier to rob the paymaster than fight before now," Hamner observed. "Cheers." He drained the glass, then suppressed a cough. The stuff was strong and he wasn't used to neat whiskey.

Falkenberg shook his head. "I might have expected that remark from Bradford, but not you."

Hamner nodded. Bradford was always suspicious of something. There were times when George wondered if the vice-president were quite sane, but that was absurd. Still, when the pressure was on, Ernie did manage to get on people's nerves, always trying to control everything. Bradford would rather have nothing done than allow action he didn't control.

"Just how am I supposed to organize this coup?" Falkenberg asked. "You can see that I've no more than a handful of men loyal directly to me. The rest are mercenaries, and your locals make up the majority of our forces. Mr. Hamner, you have paid a large price to bring my staff and me to your planet. We're expected shortly to fight impossible odds with nonexistent equipment. If you also insist on your own organization of the forces, I cannot accept the responsibility. . . . If President Budreau so orders, I'll turn over command to anyone he names."

Neatly said, Hamner thought. And predictable too. Who would Budreau name? Bradford, of course, and George trusted Falkenberg more than Ernie. Nothing wrong with Falkenberg's answers, nothing you could put your finger on. . . . "What do you want out of this, Colonel Falkenberg?"

"Money. A little glory, perhaps, although that's a word not much used outside the military nowadays. A position of responsibility commensurate with my abilities. I've always been a soldier, Mr. Hamner. You do know why I'm no longer in CD service."

"No I don't." Hamner was calm, but the whiskey was enough to make him bold, even in this camp surrounded by Falkenberg's men. . . . Who is this man we're going to entrust our lives to? For that matter, haven't we already done that? "I don't know at all. It makes no sense for you to have complained about promotion, Colonel, and

The Mercenary 197

the admiral wouldn't have let you be dismissed if you hadn't wanted. Why did you have yourself cashiered?"

Falkenberg inspected him closely, his lips tight, gray eyes boring into Hamner. "I suppose you are entitled to an answer. Grand Senator Bronson has sworn to ruin me, Mr. Hamner, for reasons I won't tell you. If I hadn't been dismissed for the trivial charge of technical insubordination, I'd have had to face an endless series of trumped-up charges. This way I'm out with a clean record."

"And that's all there is to it?"

"That's all."

It was plausible. So was everything else. And Hamner was sure that the story would check out. Yet—yet the man was lying, for no reason George could imagine. Not lying directly, not refusing to answer, but not telling it all . . . if he only knew the right questions.

The pipers came back in, looked at Falkenberg. "Something more?"

"No."

"Thank you." The colonel nodded to the pipe major, who raised his baton. The pipers marched to the crash of drums, an incredibly martial sound, and the younger officers glanced around, picked up their drinks again. Someone shouted and the party was on.

The Progressives were drinking with Falkenberg's mercenaries . . . and every one of the partisans in the mess was one of his own wing, George realized. There wasn't one of Bradford's people in the lot. He rose, signalled to a Progressive lieutenant to follow him. "I'll let Farquahar escort me out, Colonel," Hamner shouted.

"As you please."

The noise followed them outside, along the regimental street. "All right, Jamie, what's going on here?" Hamner demanded.

"Going on, sir? Nothing that I know of . . . you mean the party? Ah, we're celebrating the men's graduation from elementary training; tomorrow they start advanced work. Major Savage thought a regimental dining-in would help knit the troops together, be good for morale . . ."

"I do not mean the party." They were at the edge of officers' row now, and Hamner stopped their stroll. Hadley's third moon, the bright one called Klum, cast weird shadows around them. "Maybe I do mean the party. Where are the other officers? Mr. Bradford's people?"

"Ah, they had a field problem that kept them out of camp until late, sir. Mr. Bradford came around about dinnertime and took them with him to the ranch house. He spends a lot of time with them, sir."

"You've been around the marines, Jamie. Where are the men from? What CD outfits?"

"I really don't know, sir. Colonel Falkenberg has forbidden us to ask. He told the men that no matter what their record before, they start new here. I get the impression that some of them have served with the colonel before. They don't like him, curse him quite openly. But they're afraid of that big sergeant-major of his. . . . Calvin has offered to whip any two men in the camp, they choose the rules. None of the marines would try it. After the first couple of times, none of the recruits would either."

"Not popular." Hamner brushed his hair back from his brows with both hands, remembered what Major Karantov had told him. Whiskey buzzed in his head. "Who is popular?"

"Major Savage, sir. The men like him. And Captain Fast, the marines particularly respect him. He's the colonel's adjutant."

"All right. Look, can this outfit fight? Have we got a chance?" They stood and watched the scene around the campfires, men drinking, shouting. There was a fist fight in front of one tent, and no officer moved to stop it. "Do you permit that?"

"Not—we stop the men only if we officially see something, sir. See, the sergeants have broken up the fight. As to their abilities, really, how would I know? The men are tough, Mr. Hamner, and they obey orders."

Hamner nodded. "All right, Jamie. Go back to your party." He strode to his car. As he was driven away, he knew something was wrong, but he still had no idea what.

The stadium had been built to hold 100,000 people. There were at least that many jammed inside, and an equal number swarmed about the market squares and streets adjacent to it. The full CoDominium marine garrison was on duty to keep order, but they weren't needed. The celebration was boisterous but peaceful, with Freedom Party gangs as anxious to avoid an incident as the marines on this, the greatest day for Hadley since the planet's discovery.

Hamner and Falkenberg watched from the upper tiers of the stadium. Row after row of plastisteel seats like a giant staircase cascaded down from their perch to the central grassy field below. Across from them President Budreau and Governor Flaherty stood in the Presidential Box surrounded by the blue-uniformed President's Guard. Vice-President Bradford, Freedom Party leaders, Progressive officials, officers of the retiring CoDominium government were also there, and George knew what some of them were thinking: Where did Hamner get off to? Bradford would particularly notice his absence, probably thought Hamner was out stirring up rebellion. Lately Bradford had accused George of every kind of disloyalty to the Progressive Party.

The devil with the little man, George thought. He hated crowds, and the thought of having to stand there and listen to all those speeches, be polite to the party officials, was appalling. When he'd suggested watching from another vantage point, Falkenberg quickly agreed. As George suspected, the soldier disliked civilian ceremonies too.

The ritual was almost over. The CD marine bands had marched through the field, the speeches had been made, presents delivered and accepted. A hundred thousand people had cheered, an awesome sound, frightening in its potential power. Hamner glanced at his watch, and as he did the marine band broke into a roar of drums. The massed drummers ceased their beat one by one until there was but a single drum roll that went on and on and on, until it too, stopped. The entire stadium waited.

One trumpet, no more. A clear call, plaintive but triumphant, the final salute to the CoDominium banner above the Palace. The notes hung in Hadley's crystal air like something tangible, and slowly, deliberately, the crimson and blue banner floated down the flagpole as Hadley's blazing gold and green arose.

Across the city uniformed men saluted these flags, one rising, the other setting. The blue uniforms of Hadley saluted with smiles, the red-uniformed marines with indifference. The CoDominium banner rose and fell across two hundred light-years and seventy worlds in this Year of Grace 2079; what difference would one minor planet make?

Hamner glanced at John Falkenberg. The colonel had no eyes for the rising banners of Hadley. His rigid salute was given to the CD flag, and as the last note of the final trumpet salute died away Hamner saw Falkenberg wipe his eyes. The gesture was so startling that George looked again, but there was nothing more to see.

"That's it, then," Falkenberg snapped. His voice was crisp, gruff even. "I suppose we ought to join the party. Can't keep His Nibs waiting."

Hamner nodded. The Presidential Box connected directly to the Palace, and the officials would arrive at the reception quickly while Falkenberg and Hamner had the entire width of the stadium to traverse. People were streaming out to join festive crowds outside and it would be impossible to cross directly. "Let's go this way," George said. He led Falkenberg to the top of the stadium and into a small alcove where he used a key to open an inconspicuous door. "Tunnel system takes us right into the Palace, across and under the stadium," he told Falkenberg. "Not exactly secret, but we don't want the people generally to know about it because they'll demand we open it to the public. Designed for maintenance crews, mostly." He locked the door behind him, looked around at the wide interior corridor. "Building was designed pretty well, actually."

The grudging tone of admiration wasn't natural to him. If a thing was well done, it was well done . . . but lately he found himself talking more and more that way, especially when the CoDominium was discussed. He resented the whole CD administration, the men who'd dumped the job of government after creating problems that no one could solve.

They wound down stairways, through more passages, up to another set of locked doors, finally emerged into the Palace courtyard. The celebrations were already under way, and it would be a long night; and what after that? Tomorrow the last CD boat would rise, and the CoDominium would be gone. Tomorrow, Hadley would be alone with her problems.

"Tensh-hut!" Sergeant-Major Calvin's crisp command cut through the babble.

"Please be seated, gentlemen," Falkenberg said. He took his place at the head of the long table in the command room of what had been the central headquarters for the CoDominium marines. Except for the uniforms and banners there were as yet few changes from what people already called the old days. The officers were seated in the usual places for a regimental staff meeting, maps displayed on the walls behind them, white-coated stewards brought coffee and discreetly retired past the sentries outside. The constabulary had occupied the marine headquarters barracks for two days, and the marines had been there twenty years.

There was another difference from the usual protocol of a council of war. A civilian lounged in the seat usually taken by the regimental intelligence officer, his tunic a riot of colors. He was dressed in current Earth fashions, brilliant cravat and baggy sleeves, long sash in place of a belt. Hadley's upper classes were only beginning to acquire such finery. When he spoke it was with the lazy drawl of the American South, not the more clipped accents of Hadley.

"You all know why we're here," Falkenberg told the assembled group. "Those of you who served with me before know I don't hold many staff councils, but they are customary among mercenaries. Sergeant Calvin will represent the enlisted men of the regiment."

There were faint titters. Calvin had been associated with John Falkenberg for eighteen standard years. Presumably they had differences of opinion, but no one could remember one. The idea of the RSM opposing his colonel in the name of the troops was amusing.

Falkenberg's frozen features relaxed slightly, as if he appreciated his own joke. He looked around the room at his officers. They were all men who had come with him, all former marines. The Progressives were on duty elsewhere—it had taken careful planning by the adjutant to accomplish that.

"Dr. Whitlock, you've been on Hadley sixty-seven days. That's not very long to make a planetary study, but you had access to Fleet data as well. Have you reached any conclusions?"

"Yeah. No different from Fleet evaluation, Colonel. Cain't think why you went to the expense of bringin' me out here. Your intelligence people know their jobs 'bout as well as any professor." Whitlock leaned back in his seat, relaxed and casual in the midst of military formality, but there was no contempt in his manner. The military had one set of rules, he had another, both probably right for the jobs they did.

"Your conclusions are similar to Fleet's, then?" Falkenberg prompted.

"Within the limits of analysis, yes, suh. Doubt any competent man *could* reach a different conclusion. This planet's headed for barbarism within a generation." Whitlock produced a cigar from a sleeve pocket, inspected it carefully. "You want the analysis or just the conclusion?"

There was no sound from the assembled officers, but Falkenberg knew that some of them were startled. Good training kept them from showing it. He examined each face in turn. Major Savage knew. Captain Fast was too concerned with regimental

The Mercenary 201

affairs to care. . . . Calvin knew, of course. Who else? "If you could summarize your efforts briefly, Dr. Whitlock?"

"Simple enough. There's no self-sustaining technology for a population half this size. Without imports the standard of livin's going to fall, and when that happens, 'stead of working, the people here in Refuge will demand that the Guv'mint do something about it. Guv'mint's in no position to refuse. Not strong enough. Have to divert investment resources into consumption goods. Be a decrease in technological efficiency, fewer goods, more demands, lead to a new cycle of the same. Hard to predict just what comes after that, but it can't be good. Afore long they won't have the technological resources even if they get better organized. Not a new pattern, Colonel. Surprised you didn't just take Fleet's word for it."

Falkenberg nodded. "I did. But with something this important I thought I better get an expert. You've met the Freedom Party leaders, Dr. Whitlock. Is there any chance they could, ah, save civilization here?"

Whitlock laughed. It was a long, drawn-out laugh, relaxed, totally out of place in a military council. "'Bout as much chance as for a 'gator to turn loose of a hog, Colonel. Even did they want to, what are they goin' to do? Suppose they get a vision, try to change their policies? Somebody'll start a new party 'long the lines of the one they got now. You *never* going to convince all them people that there's things the Guv'mint just *cain't* do, Colonel. They don't want to believe that, and there's always going to be slick talkers willing to say it's a plot. Now if the Progressive Party was able to set up along the lines of the Communists, *they* might keep something going for a while longer."

"Do you think they can?" Major Savage asked.

"Nope. They might have fun tryin'," Whitlock answered. "Problem is the countryside's pretty independent. Not enough support for that kind of thing in the city, either. Eventually it'll happen, but the revolution that gives this planet a real powerful government's going to be one bloody mess, I can tell you. And a long, drawn-out, bloody mess at that."

Whitlock sighed. "No matter where you look, you see problems, gentlemen. City's vulnerable to any sabotage that stops the food plants . . . and you know them fusion generators ain't exactly eternal; I don't give them a lot of time before they slow down the way they're runnin' 'em. This place is operating on its capital, not its income, and pretty soon that's going to be gone." Whitlock sat up, stretched elaborately. "I can give you a dozen more reasons, but they always come out the same. This place ain't about to be self-sufficient without a lot of blood spilled."

"Could they ask for help from American Express?" The question was from a junior officer near the foot of the table.

"Sure they could," Whitlock drawled. "Wouldn't get it, but they could ask. Son, the Russians ain't going to let a U.S. company get hold of a planet and add it to the U.S. sphere, same as the States won't let the Commies come in and set up shop.

Grand Senate would order a quarantine on this system like that." The historian snapped his fingers. "Whole purpose of the CoDominium."

"One thing bothers me," Captain Fast said. "You've been assuming that the CD will simply let Hadley revert to barbarism. Won't BuRelock and the Colonial Office come back if things get that desperate?"

"Might, if they was around to do it," Whitlock answered. This time there was a startled gasp from several junior officers. "Haven't told them about that, Colonel? Sorry."

"Sir, what does he mean?" the lieutenant asked. "What could happen to the Bureau of Relocation?"

"No budget," Falkenberg answered. "Gentlemen, you've seen the tensions back on Earth. Kaslov's people are gaining influence in the Presidium, Harmon's gang have won minor elections in the States, and both want to abolish the CD. They've had enough influence to get appropriations cut to the bone—I shouldn't have to tell you that, you've seen what's happening to the Navy and the civilian agencies get the same. Population control has to ship people to worlds closer to Earth whether they can hold them or not. Marginal exploitation ventures like Hadley's mines are to be shut down. This isn't the only planet the CD's abandoning this year—excuse me, granting independence," he added ironically. "No, Hadley can't rely on CoDominium help. If this world's to reach takeoff, it's going to have to do it on its own."

"Which Dr. Whitlock says is impossible," Major Savage observed. "John, we've got ourselves into a cleft stick, haven't we?"

"Ah said it wasn't likely, not that it was impossible," Whitlock reminded them. "It'll take a guv'mint stronger than anything Hadley's liable to get, and some pretty smart people making the right moves. Or maybe there'll be some luck. Like a good, selective plague. Now that'd do it. Plague to kill off about a hundred thousand, leave just the right ones . . . course if it killed a lot more'n that, probably wouldn't be enough left to take advantage of the technology. Reckon a plague's not the answer at that."

Falkenberg nodded grimly. "Thank you, Dr. Whitlock. Now, gentlemen, I want battalion commanders and the headquarters officers to read Dr. Whitlock's report carefully. Meanwhile, we have other actions. Major Savage will shortly make a report to the Cabinet. I want you to pay attention to that report. Jerry?"

Savage stood, strode briskly to the wall chartboard, uncovered briefing charts. "Gentlemen. The regiment consists of approximately two thousand officers and men. Of these, five hundred are former marines. Another five hundred, approximately, are Progressive partisans, who are organized under officers appointed by Mr. Bradford. The other thousand are general recruits including youngsters who want to play soldier. All locals have received basic training comparable to CD marine ground basic without assault, fleet, or jump schooling. Their performance has been somewhat better than we might expect from a comparable number of marine recruits in CD service.

"This morning, Mr. Bradford ordered the colonel to remove the last of our officers and noncoms from the fourth battalion. As of retreat this P.M. the fourth will be totally under the control of the first vice-president, for what purpose he has not informed us."

Falkenberg nodded. "In your estimate, Major, are the troops ready for combat duties?" John sipped his coffee, listened idly. The briefing was rehearsed, and he knew what Savage would answer. The men were trained but not yet a combat unit. He waited until Savage had completed that part of the presentation. "Recommendations?"

"Recommend that the second battalion be integrated with the first, sir. Normal practice is to have one recruit, three privates, and a monitor to each maniple. With equal numbers of new men and veterans we'll have a much higher proportion of recruits, of course, but this will give us two battalions of men under our veteran marines, with marine privates for leavening. We will thus break up the provisional training organization and set up the regiment with a new permanent structure: first and second battalions for combat duties, third composed of locals with former marine officers and some noncoms to be held in reserve. The fourth will not be under our command."

"Your reasons for this organization?" Falkenberg asked.

"Morale, sir. The new troops feel discriminated against. They're under harsher discipline than the former marines, and they resent it. Putting them in the same maniples with the marines will stop that."

"You have the new organization plan there, Major?"

"Yes, sir." Savage turned the charts from their wall recess. The administrative structure was a compromise between the permanent garrison organization of CD marines and the national army of Churchill, so arranged that all of the key positions had to be held by Falkenberg's mercenaries. The best officers of the Progressive forces were in either the third or fourth battalions, and there were no locals with the proper experience. . . .

John looked at it carefully, listened to Savage's explanation. It ought to work. It looked very good, and there was no sound military reason to question the structure. . . . He didn't think the president could object. Bradford would be pleased about the fourth, hardly interested in the other battalions now, although give him time.

When Savage was finished, Falkenberg thanked him and stood again at the head of the table. "All right. You've heard Major Savage give the briefing. If you have critiques, let's hear them now. We want this smooth, without problems from the civilians. Another thing. Sergeant-Major!"

"Sir!"

"As of reveille tomorrow, this entire regiment is under normal discipline. Tell the 42nd the act's over, we want them back on behavior. From here on the recruits and the old hands will be treated the same, and the next man who gives me trouble will wish he hadn't been born."

"Sir!" Calvin smiled happily. The last months had been a strain for everyone. Now the old man was taking over again, thank God. The men had lost some of the edge, but he'd soon put it back again. It was time to take off the masks, and Calvin for one was glad of it.

III

The sound of fifty thousand people shouting in unison can be terrifying. It raises fears at a level below thought, a panic older than the fear of nuclear weapons and the whole panoply of technology, raw naked power, a cauldron of sound. Everyone in the Palace listened to the chanting crowd, and if most of the government officials were able to appear calm, they were afraid nonetheless.

The cabinet meeting started at dawn, went on until late in the morning, on and on without settling anything. It was growing close to noon when Vice-President Bradford stood at his place at the council table, the thin smile gone, his lips tight with rage. He pointed a trembling finger at Hamner.

"It's your fault!" Bradford shouted. "Now the technicians have joined in the demand for a new constitution, and you control them! I've always said you were a traitor to the Progressive Party!"

"Gentlemen, please," President Budreau insisted tiredly. "Come now, that sort of language . . ."

"Traitor?" Hamner demanded. "If your blasted officials would pay a little attention to the technicians this wouldn't have happened. In three months you've managed to convert the techs from the staunchest supporters of this Party into allies of the rebels, despite everything I could do." George made a conscious effort to control his own anger. "You've herded them around the city like cattle, worked them overtime for no increase in pay, and set those damned soldiers of yours on them when they protested. It's worth a man's life to have your constabulary mad at him, I know of cases where your troops have beaten my people to death! And you've got the nerve to call me a traitor! I ought to wring your goddam neck."

"This isn't getting us anywhere," Budreau protested. There was a roar from the stadium. The Palace seemed to vibrate to the shouts of the constitutional convention. Wearily, Budreau rose to his feet. The others remained sitting, something they wouldn't have done even a month earlier. "We will adjourn for half an hour to allow tempers to cool," Budreau insisted. "And I want no more accusations when we convene again."

Bradford left the room with a handful of his close supporters. Other ministers followed him, afraid not to be seen with the first vice-president. It could be dangerous to oppose him.

Outside in the hall he was joined by Lieutenant Colonel Cordova, commander of the fourth battalion of constabulary, a fanatic Bradford supporter. They whispered together until they were out of Hamner's sight.

"Buy you some coffee?" The voice behind him startled George. He turned to see Falkenberg.

"Sure. Not that it's going to do any good . . . we're in trouble, Colonel."

"Anything decided?" Falkenberg asked. "It's been a long wait."

"And a useless one. They ought to invite you into the cabinet meetings or let you go; there's certainly no reason to make you wait in the anteroom while we yell at each other. I've tried to change the policy, but I'm not too popular right now . . ." There was another shout from the stadium.

"Whole government's not too popular," Falkenberg observed. "And when that convention gets through . . ."

"Another thing I tried to stop last week," George told him. "But Budreau didn't have the guts to stand up to them. So now we've got fifty thousand drifters with nothing better to do sitting as an assembly of the people. That ought to produce quite a constitution."

Falkenberg shrugged. He seemed about to say something, changed his mind. They reached the executive dining room, took seats near one wall. Bradford's group had a table across the room from them. All of Bradford's people looked at them suspiciously.

"You'll get tagged as a traitor for sitting with me, Colonel." Hamner laughed, then grew serious. "I think I meant that, you know. Bradford's blaming me for our problems with the techs, and between us he's also insisting that you aren't doing enough to restore order in the city."

Falkenberg ordered coffee, waited until the waitress had left the table. "Do I need to explain to you why we haven't?"

"No." George shook his head slowly. "God knows you've been given almost no support the last two months. Impossible orders, never allowed to do anything decisive . . . I see you've stopped the raids on rebel headquarters."

Falkenberg nodded. "We weren't catching anyone. Too many leaks in the Palace, too often the fourth battalion had already muddied the waters. If they'd let us do our job instead of having to ask permission through channels for each operation we undertake, maybe the enemy wouldn't know as much about what we're going to do. I've quit asking."

"You've done pretty well with the railroad."

Falkenberg nodded. "That's one success, anyway. Things are pretty calm out in the country where we're on our own. Odd, isn't it, that the closer we are to the expert supervision of the government, the less effective my men seem to be?"

"But can't you control Cordova's men? They're causing more people to join the Freedom Party than you can count. I can't believe unrestrained brutality is useful."

"Mr. Bradford has removed all command over the fourth from me," Falkenberg answered. "Expanded it pretty well, too. That battalion's nearly as big as the rest of the regiment."

"He's accused me of being a traitor," Hamner said carefully. "With his own army, he might have something planned . . ."

Falkenberg smiled grimly. "I wouldn't worry about it too much."

"You wouldn't. Well, I'm scared, Colonel. And I've got my family to think about. I'm plenty scared."

"Would you feel safer if your family were in our regimental barracks?" Falkenberg looked at Hamner critically. "It could be arranged."

"It's about time we had something out," George said. "Yes, I'd feel safer with my wife and children under your protection. But I want you to level with me. Those marines of yours—those aren't penal battalion men. I've watched them. And those battle banners they've got on the regimental standard . . . they didn't win those in any peanut actions in three months on this planet! Just who are those troops, Colonel?"

John smiled thinly. "Wondering when you'd ask. Why haven't you brought this up with Budreau?"

"I don't know. Trust you more than I do Bradford, maybe . . . if the president dismissed you, there'd be nobody able to oppose Ernie. Hadley's going downhill so fast another conspirator more or less can't make any difference. . . . You still haven't answered my question."

"The battle banners are from the 42nd CD Marine Regiment," Falkenberg answered slowly. "Decommissioned as part of the budget cuts."

"Forty-second." Hamner thought for a second, remembering the files he'd seen on Falkenberg. "Your regiment."

"A battalion of it," John agreed. "Their women are waiting to join them when we get settled. When the 42nd was decommissioned, the men decided to stay together if they could."

"So you brought not only the officers, but the men as well. . . . What's your game, Colonel? You want something more than just pay for your troops. What is it? I wonder if I shouldn't be more afraid of you than of Bradford."

Falkenberg shrugged. "Decision you have to make, Mr. Hamner. I could give you my word that we mean you no harm, but what would that be worth? I will pledge to take care of your family. If you want us to."

There was another shout from the stadium. Bradford and Lieutenant Colonel Cordova left their table, still talking in low tones. The conversation was animated, with violent gestures, as if Cordova were trying to talk Bradford into something. As they left, Bradford agreed.

George watched them leave the room, then nodded thoughtfully to Falkenberg. "I'll send Laura and the kids over to your headquarters this afternoon. There isn't much time, is there? Whatever you've got planned, it's going to have to be quick."

John shook his head slowly. "You seem to think I have some kind of master plan, Mister Vice-President. I'm only a soldier in a political situation."

"With Professor Whitlock to advise you," Hamner reminded him. "That cornball stuff of his doesn't fool me, I looked him up. He's another part of the puzzle I don't understand. Why doesn't he come to the president instead of moving around the city like a ghost? He must have fifty political agents out there." Hamner watched Falkenberg's face closely. "Surprised you with that one, didn't I? I'm not quite so stupid as I look . . . but I can't fit the pieces together. Maybe I ought to use whatever influence I have left to get you out of the picture entirely."

"Go ahead." Falkenberg's smile was cold. "Who watches your wife for you after that? The chief of police? Listen." The stadium roared again, an angry sound that swelled in volume.

"You win." Hamner left the table, walked slowly back toward the council room, his head swirling with doubts. One thing stood out clearly: John Christian Falkenberg controlled the only military force on Hadley that could oppose both Bradford's people and the Freedom Party gangsters. He kept that firmly in mind as he turned, went downstairs to the apartment he'd been assigned. The sooner Laura was in the marine barracks, the safer he'd feel . . . Was he sending her to another enemy? But what could Falkenberg use her for? Mercenary or not, the man was honorable. Boris Karantov had been emphatic about that. And he hadn't any reason to hate George Hamner. Keep remembering that, he told himself. Keep remembering that and try not to remember the rest of it. The crowd screamed again. "Power to the people!" George heard it, and walked faster.

Bradford's grin was back. It was the first thing Hamner noticed as he came into the council chamber. The little man stood at the table with an amused smile.

"Ah, here is our minister of technology," Bradford grinned. "Just in time. Mister President, that gang outside is threatening the city. I'm sure you'll all be pleased to know that I've taken steps to end the situation. At this moment, Colonel Cordova is arresting the leaders of the opposition. Including, Mister President, the Engineers' and Technicians' Association leaders who have joined them. This rebellion will be over within the hour."

Hamner stared at the man. "You fool! You'll have every technician in the city joining the FP! And they control the power plants, our last influence over the crowd! You bloody damn fool!"

Bradford's smirk widened, as he spoke with exaggerated surprise. "I thought you'd be pleased, George. And naturally I've sent men to the power plants as well. Ah, listen."

The crowd outside wasn't chanting any more. There was a confused babble, a welling of sound that turned ugly, but nothing coherent. Then a rapid fusillade of shots.

"My God!" Budreau stared wildly in confusion. "Who are they shooting at? You've started open civil war!"

"It takes stern measures, Mister President," Bradford said calmly. "Perhaps too stern for you?" He shook his head slightly. "The time is come for harsh measures, Mister President. Hadley cannot be governed by weak-willed men. Our future belongs to those who have the will to grasp it!"

Hamner stood, went to the door. Before he reached it, Bradford called to him. "Please, George," he said pleasantly. "I'm afraid you can't leave just yet. It wouldn't be safe for you. I took the liberty of ordering Colonel Cordova's men to, uh, guard this room while my troops restore order."

An uneasy quiet had settled on the stadium, and they waited for long minutes. Then there were screams, more shots, and the sounds were moving closer, as if they were outside the stadium. Bradford frowned slightly, but no one said anything. They waited for what seemed a lifetime as the firing continued, guns, shouts, screams, sirens and alarms.

The door burst open. Cordova, now wearing the insignia of a full colonel, came into the room, glanced about wildly. "Mister Bradford—could you come outside, please?"

"You will make your report to the cabinet," Budreau ordered. "Now, sir."

Cordova glanced at Bradford, who nodded. "Yes, sir," the young officer said. "As directed by Vice-President Bradford, elements of the fourth battalion proceeded to the stadium and arrested some forty leaders of the so-called constitutional convention. Our plan was to enter quickly and take the men out through the Presidential Box into the Palace. However, when we attempted to make the arrests we were opposed by armed men, many of them in the uniforms of household guards. There were not supposed to be any weapons in the stadium, but this was in error. The crowd overpowered my officers and released their prisoners. When we attempted to recover them, we were attacked by the mob and forced to fight our way out of the stadium."

"Good Lord," Budreau sighed.

"The power plants! Did you secure them?" Hamner demanded.

Cordova looked miserable. "No, sir. My men were not admitted. A council of technicians holds the power plants and threatens to destroy them if we attempt forcible entry. We will try to seal them off from outside support, but I don't think that will be possible with only my battalion. In my judgment, we will require the full complement of constabulary to restore order."

Hamner sat heavily, tried to think. Council of technicians. He'd know most of them, they'd be his friends . . . but did they trust him now? Was this good or bad? At least Bradford didn't control the plants.

"What is the current status outside?" Budreau demanded. They could still hear firing in the streets.

"Uh, there's a mob barricaded in the market, another in the theater across from the Palace, sir. My troops are trying to dislodge them."

"Trying. I take it they weren't able to succeed." Budreau struck his hands together, suddenly rose and went to the anteroom door. "Colonel Falkenberg?" he called.

"Yes, sir?" John entered the room as the president beckoned.

"Colonel, are you familiar with the situation outside?"

"Yes, sir."

"Damn it, man, can you do something?"

"What does the president suggest that I do?" Falkenberg looked at the Cabinet. "For three months we have attempted to restore order in this city. Even with the cooperation of the technicians we have been unable to do so for reasons which ought to be obvious. Now there is open rebellion and you have alienated one of the most powerful blocs within your party. We no longer control either the power plants or the food processing centers. I repeat, what does the president suggest I do now?"

Budreau nodded. "A fair enough criticism."

He was interrupted by Bradford. "Disperse that mob! Use those precious troops of yours to fight!"

"Will the president draw up a proclamation of martial law?" Falkenberg asked.

Budreau nodded. "I have to."

"Very well," John continued. "But I want something made clear. If I am to enforce martial law, I must have command of all government forces, including the fourth battalion. I will not attempt to restore order when some of the troops are not responsive to my policies."

"No!" Bradford stared wildly at Falkenberg. "I see what you're trying to do! You're against me too. You always have been. That's why it was never time to make me president, you're planning to take over this planet yourself! You want to be dictator. Well, you won't get away with it. Cordova, arrest that man!"

Cordova licked his lips, glanced at Falkenberg. "Lieutenant Hargreave!" he called. The door to the anteroom opened fully, but no one came in. "Hargreave!" Cordova shouted again. He put his hand to his pistol "You're under arrest, Colonel Falkenberg."

"This is absurd," Budreau shouted. "Colonel Cordova, take your hand off that weapon! I will not have my cabinet meeting turned into a farce."

Bradford stared intently at the president. "You too, huh? Arrest Budreau, Colonel Cordova. As for you, Mister Traitor George Hamner, you'll get what's coming to you. I've got men all through this Palace; I knew I might have to do this."

"What is this, Earnest?" Budreau asked. He seemed bewildered. "Are you serious?"

"Oh, shut up, old man," Bradford snarled. "I suppose you'll have to be shot as well."

"I think we've heard enough," Falkenberg said carefully. His voice rang through the room, although he hadn't shouted. "And I refuse to be arrested."

"Kill him!" Bradford shouted. He reached under his tunic.

Cordova put his hand back on his pistol. There were shots from the doorway, impossibly loud, filling the room. Hamner's ears rang from the muzzle blast. Bradford spun toward the door, a surprised look on his face, then his eyes glazed and he slid to the floor, the half-smile still on his lips. More shots, a crash of automatic weapons, and Cordova was flung against the wall of the council chamber, held there for an incredibly long moment. Bright red blotches spurted across his uniform. Sergeant-Major Calvin came into the room with three marines in battle dress, leather over bulging body armor, their helmets dull in the bright blue sunlight streaming from the chamber's windows.

Falkenberg nodded, holstered his pistol. "All secure, Sergeant-Major?"

"Sir!"

Falkenberg nodded again. "To quote Mister Bradford, I took the liberty of securing the corridors, Mister President. Now, if you'll issue that proclamation, I'll see to the situation in the streets outside. I believe Captain Fast has already drawn it up for your signature."

"But—" Budreau's tone was hopeless. "All right. Not that there's much chance." The president sat at the head of the table, still bewildered by the rapid events. Too much had happened, too much to do. The battle sounds outside were louder, and the room was filled with the sharp copper odor of blood.

"You'd better speak to the President's Guard," Falkenberg told Hamner. "They won't know what to do."

"Aren't you going to use them in the street fight?"

Falkenberg shook his head. "I doubt if they'd fight. They live here in the city, too many friends on both sides. They'll protect the Palace, but they won't be reliable for anything else."

"Have we got a chance?"

"Depends on how good the people we're fighting are. If they've got a commander half as good as I think, we won't win this battle."

Two hours proved him right. Fierce attacks drove the rioters away from the immediate area of the Palace, but Falkenberg's regiment paid for every yard they gained. Whenever they took a building, the enemy left it blazing. When the regiment trapped one large group of rebels, Falkenberg was forced to abandon the assault to aid in evacuating a hospital that the enemy torched. In three hours, fires were raging all around the Palace.

There was no one in the council chamber with Budreau and Hamner when Falkenberg came back to report.

"They've got good leaders," John told them. "When they left the stadium, im-

The Mercenary　　　　　　　　　　　　　　　　　　　　　　　　　　　　　　　　211

mediately after Cordova's assault, they stormed the police barracks. Took the weapons, distributed them to their allies, and butchered the police. And we're not fighting just the mob out there. We've repeatedly run up against well-armed men in household forces uniform. I'll try again in the morning, but for now, Mister President, we don't hold much more than half a kilometer around the Palace."

The fires burned all night, but there was little fighting. In the morning the regiment sallied out again, moved northward toward the concentration points of the rioters. Within an hour they were heavily engaged against rooftop snipers, barricaded streets, and everywhere burning buildings.

The fourth regiment, Bradford's former troops, were decimated in repeated assaults against the barricades. Hamner accompanied the soldiers to Falkenberg's field headquarters, watched the combat operations.

"You're using up those men pretty fast, aren't you?" he asked.

"Not by choice," Falkenberg told him. "The president has ordered me to break the enemy resistance. That squanders soldiers. I'd as soon use the fourth battalion as to blunt the fighting edge of the rest of the regiment."

"But we're not getting anywhere."

"No. The opposition's too good, and there are too many of them. We can't get them concentrated for an all-out battle, they simply set fire to part of the city and retreat under cover of the flames." He stopped, listened to reports from a runner, then spoke quietly into a communicator. "Fall back to the Palace."

"You're retreating?"

"I have to. I can't hold this thin a perimeter. I've only two battalions—and what's left of the fourth."

"Where's the third? The Progressive partisans? My people?"

"Out at the power plants and food centers," Falkenberg answered. "We can't get in without giving the techs time to wreck the place, but we can keep any of the rebels from getting in. The third isn't as well trained as the rest of the regiment—and besides, the techs may trust them."

They walked through burned-out streets, the sounds of fighting following them as the regiment retreated. Worried Presidential Guards let them into the Palace, swung heavy doors shut behind them.

President Budreau was in the ornate office with Lieutenant Banners. "I was going to send for you," Budreau said. "We can't win this, can we?"

"Not the way it's going."

"That's what I thought. Pull your men back to barracks, Colonel. I'm going to surrender."

"But you can't," George protested. "Everything we've dreamed of . . . You'll doom Hadley. The Freedom Party can't govern . . ."

"Precisely. You've seen it too, haven't you? How much governing are we doing?

Before it came to an open break, perhaps we had a chance. Not now. Bring your men back to the Palace, Colonel Falkenberg. Or are you going to resist my commands?"

"No, sir. The men are retreating already. They'll be here in a few minutes."

Budreau sighed loudly. "I told you the military answer wouldn't work here, Falkenberg."

"We might have accomplished something in the past months if we'd been given the chance."

"You might. You might not, also. It doesn't matter now. This isn't three months ago. It's not even yesterday. I might have bargained with them then. But it's today, and we've lost. You're not doing much besides burning down the city . . . at least I can spare Hadley that. Banners, go tell the Freedom Party people I can't take anymore." The Guard officer saluted and left, his face an unreadable mask.

"So you're resigning," Falkenberg said slowly.

Budreau nodded.

"Have you resigned, sir?" Falkenberg asked deliberately.

"Yes, blast it. Banners has promised to get me out of here. On a boat, I can sail up the coast, cut inland to the mines. There'll be a starship come in there sometime, I can get out on it. You'd better come with me, George." He put his face to his hands for a moment, then looked up. "What will you do, Colonel Falkenberg?"

"We'll manage. There are plenty of boats in the harbor. For that matter, the new government will need soldiers."

"The perfect mercenary," Budreau said with contempt. He sighed, looked around the office. "It's a relief. I don't have to decide things anymore." He stood suddenly, his shoulders no longer stooped. "I'll get the family. You'd better be moving too, George."

"I'll be along, sir. Don't wait for us—as the colonel says, there are plenty of boats." He waited until Budreau had left the office. "All right, what now?" he asked Falkenberg.

"Now we do what we came here for," Falkenberg snapped. "You haven't been sworn in as president yet, and you won't get the chance until I've finished. And there's nobody to accept your resignation, either."

Hamner looked at him carefully. "So you do have an idea. Let's hear it."

"You're not president yet," Falkenberg answered. "Under Budreau's proclamation of martial law, I am to take whatever action I deem necessary to restore order in Refuge. That order is valid until a new president rescinds it. And at the moment there's no president."

"But—Budreau's surrendered! The Freedom Party will elect one!"

"Under Hadley's constitution only the Senate and Assembly in joint session can make a change in the order of succession. They're scattered across the city, their meeting chambers have been burned . . . to play guardhouse lawyer, Mr. Hamner, Budreau doesn't have the authority to appoint a new president. With Bradford dead, you're in charge here—but not until you appear before a magistrate and take the oath of office."

"I see . . . and there aren't any magistrates around. How long do you think you can stay in control here?"

"As long as I have to." Falkenberg turned to his aides. "Corporal, I want Mr. Hamner to stay with me. You're to treat him with respect but he goes nowhere and sees no one without my permission. Understood?"

"Sir!"

"And now what?" Hamner asked.

"And now we wait," John said softly. "But not too long . . ."

Hamner and Falkenberg sat in the council chambers. When Captain Fast came in periodically to give reports on the combat situation, Falkenberg didn't seem interested; but when Dr. Whitlock's agents came in from time to time, the soldier was attentive. After a long wait the regiment was assembled in the Palace courtyard, while the Presidential Guard still held the Palace entrances, refused to admit the rioters. The rebels were obviously instructed to leave the Guardsmen alone so long as they took no action against them, giving an uneasy truce.

After Banners reported the president's surrender, the crowd began to flow into the stadium, shouting with triumph. Still they waited, Falkenberg with outward calm, Hamner with growing tension.

An hour later Dr. Whitlock came into the council room. He looked at Falkenberg and Hamner, then sat easily in the president's chair. "Don't reckon I'll get another chance to sit in the seat of the mighty," he grinned. "It's 'bout like you figured, Colonel. Mob's moved right into the stadium. Nobody wants to be left out now they think they've won. Got some senators out there on the field, fixin' to elect themselves a brand-new president."

"The election won't be valid," Hamner said.

"Naw, suh, but that don't seem to stop 'em none. They figure they've won the right, it seems. And the Guard has already said they're goin' to honor the people's choice." Whitlock smiled ironically.

"How many of my technicians are out there in that mob?" Hamner asked. "They'd listen to me, I know they would."

"Not so many as there used to be," Whitlock replied. "Most of 'em couldn't stomach the burnin' and lootin'. Still, there's a fair number."

"Can you get them out?" Falkenberg asked.

"Doin' that right now." Whitlock grinned. "Got some of my people goin' round tellin' them they already got Mister Hamner as president, why would they want somebody else? Seems to be working, too. Should have all that's goin' out of there in a half hour or so."

Falkenberg nodded. "Let's speed them on their way, shall we?" He strode to the control wall of the council chamber, opened a panel. "Mister Hamner, I can't give you orders, but I suggest you make a speech. Say you're going to be president and things are going to be different. Then order them to go home or face charges as rebels."

Hamner nodded. It wasn't much of a speech, and from the roar outside the crowd didn't hear much of it anyway. He promised amnesty for anyone who left the stadium, tried to appeal to the Progressives who were caught up in the rebellion. When he put the microphone down, Falkenberg nodded. "Half an hour, Dr. Whitlock?" he asked.

"About that," the historian agreed.

"Let's go, Mister President." Falkenberg was insistent.

"Where?" Hamner asked.

"To see the end of this. You want to watch, or would you like to join your family? You can go anywhere you like except to a magistrate or to someone who might accept your resignation."

"Colonel, this is ridiculous. You can't force me to be president! And I don't understand what's going on."

Falkenberg's smile was grim. "Nor do I want you to. Yet. You'll have enough trouble living with yourself anyway. Let's go."

The first and second battalions were assembled in the Palace courtyard. The men stood in ranks, synthileather battle dress stained with dirt from training and the recent street fighting. Their armor bulged under the uniforms of the impassive men. Hamner thought they might have been carved from stone.

Falkenberg led the way to the stadium entrance. Lieutenant Banners stood in the doorway. "Halt," he commanded.

"Really, Lieutenant? Would you fight my troops?" Falkenberg indicated the grim lines behind him.

"No, sir," Banners protested. "But we have barred the doors. The emergency meeting of the Senate is electing a new president out there. When he's sworn in, the Guard will be under his command—until then, we can't permit your mercenaries to interfere."

"I have orders from Vice-President Hamner to arrest the leaders of the rebellion, and a valid proclamation of martial law," Falkenberg insisted.

"I'm sorry, sir." Banners seemed to mean it. "Our council of officers has decided that President Budreau's surrender is valid. We intend to honor it."

"I see." Falkenberg withdrew. "Hadn't expected this. It would take a week to fight through those guardrooms . . ." he thought for a moment. "Give me your keys!" he snapped at Hamner.

Bewildered, George took them out. Falkenberg examined them, grinned. "There's another way into there, you know . . . Major Savage! Take G and H companies of second battalion to secure the stadium exits. Place anyone who comes out under arrest.

And you'd better dig the men in pretty good, they'll be coming out fighting. But I don't expect them to be well-organized."

"Yes, sir. Do we fire on armed men?"

"Without warning, Major. Without warning." Falkenberg turned to the assembled soldiers. "Follow me."

He led them to the tunnel entrance, unlocked the doors. Hamner trailed behind him as they wound down stairways, across under the field. He could hear the long column of armed men tramp behind them. They moved up the stairways on the other side, marching briskly until Hamner was panting, but the men didn't seem to notice. Gravity difference, Hamner thought. And training.

They reached the top, moved along the passageways. Falkenberg stationed men at each exit, came back to the center doors. "MOVE OUT!" he commanded.

The doors burst open. The armed troopers moved quickly across the top of the stadium. Most of the mob was below, and a few unarmed men were struck down when they tried to oppose the regiment. Rifle butts swung, then there was a moment of calm. Falkenberg took a portable speaker from a corporal attendant.

"ATTENTION. ATTENTION. YOU ARE UNDER ARREST BY THE AUTHORITY OF THE MARTIAL LAW PROCLAMATION OF PRESIDENT BUDREAU. LAY DOWN YOUR WEAPONS AND YOU WILL NOT BE HARMED. IF YOU RESIST, YOU WILL BE KILLED."

Someone below fired at them. Hamner heard the flat snap of the bullet as it rushed past, then the crack of the rifle.

One of the leaders on the field had a speaker, shouted orders. "ATTACK THEM! THERE AREN'T MORE THAN A THOUSAND OF THEM, WE'RE THIRTY THOUSAND STRONG. ATTACK, KILL THEM!" There were more shots. Several of Falkenberg's men fell.

"PREPARE FOR VOLLEY FIRE!" Falkenberg called. "MAKE READY! TAKE AIM. IN VOLLEY, FIRE!"

Seven hundred rifles crashed as one.

"FIRE!"

Someone screamed, a long drawn-out cry, a plea without words.

"FIRE!"

It was like one shot, very loud, lasting far longer than a rifle shot ought to, but impossible to hear individual weapons.

"THE FORTY-SECOND WILL ADVANCE. FIX BAYONETS. FORWARD, MOVE. FIRE! FIRE AT WILL."

Now there was a continuous crackle of weapons. The leather-clad lines moved forward, down the stadium seats, inexorably toward the press below.

"SERGEANT-MAJOR!"

"SIR!"

"MARKSMEN AND EXPERTS. FIRE ON ALL ARMED MEN."

"SIR!"

Calvin spoke into his communicator. Two sections fell out of the advancing line, took cover behind seats. They began to fire, carefully but rapidly. Anyone below who raised a weapon died.

Hamner was sick. The screams of wounded men could be heard everywhere.

"GRENADIERS, PREPARE TO THROW," Falkenberg ordered. "THROW!" A hundred grenades arched out, down into the milling crowds below. Their muffled explosions were masked by the screams of terror. "IN VOLLEY, FIRE!"

The regiment advanced, made contact with the mob below. There was a brief struggle. Rifles fired, bayonets flashed red, the line halted momentarily. Then it moved on, leaving behind a ghastly trail.

Men were jammed at the stadium exits, trampling each other in a scramble to escape. There was a rattle of gunfire from outside.

"You won't even let them out!" he screamed at Falkenberg.

"Not armed. And not to escape." The colonel's face was hard, cold, the eyes narrowed to slits as he peered down at the battle.

"Are you going to kill them all?"

"All who resist."

"But they don't deserve this!" Hamner insisted.

"No one does, George. Sergeant-Major!"

"Sir!"

"Half the marksmen may concentrate on the leaders now."

"Sir!" Calvin spoke quietly into his command set. As Hamner watched, the snipers began concentrating their fire on the Presidential Box across from them. Centurions ran up and down the line of hidden troops, pointing out targets. The marksmen kept up a steady fire.

The leather lines of armored men advanced inexorably, almost reached the lower tiers of seats. There was less firing now, but the scarlet painted bayonets could be seen everywhere. A section fell out of the line, moved to guard a tiny number of prisoners at one end of the stadium. The rest of the line moved on.

When the regiment reached ground level, their progress was slower. There was not much opposition, but the sheer mass of people in front of them held the troopers. In some places there were pockets of armed fighting, which held for long moments until flying squads rushed up to reinforce the line. Falkenberg watched the battle calmly, spoke into his communicator. Below, more men died.

A company of troopers formed, rushed up a stairway on the opposite side of the stadium, fanned out across the top. Their rifles leveled, crashed in another terrible volley.

Suddenly it was over. There was no opposition, only screaming crowds, men throwing away weapons to run with their hands in the air, falling to their knees to beg for quarter. A final volley crashed out, then a deathly quiet fell over the stadium.

But it wasn't quiet, Hamner discovered. The guns were silent, men no longer shouted, but there was sound. Screams of wounded men.

Falkenberg nodded grimly. "Now we can find a magistrate, Mister President. Now."

"I—oh my God!" Hamner stood at the top of the stadium, held a column to steady his weakened legs. The scene below was unreal. There was too much of it, too much blood, rivers of blood, blood cascading down the steps, pouring down stairwells, soaking the grassy field below.

"It's over," Falkenberg said gently. "For all of us. The regiment will be leaving as soon as you're properly in command. You shouldn't have any trouble with the power plants, your technicians will trust you now that Bradford's gone. And without their leaders, the city people won't resist. You can ship as many as you have to out to the interior, disperse them among the loyalists where they won't do you any harm. That amnesty of yours—it's only a suggestion, but I'd keep it."

Hamner turned dazed eyes toward Falkenberg. "Yes. There's been too much slaughter today. . . . Who are you, Falkenberg?"

"A mercenary soldier, Mister President. Nothing more."

"But—who are you working for?"

"That's the question nobody asked before. Grand Admiral Lermontov."

"Lermontov—but you've been dismissed from the CoDominium! You mean that—you were hired by the admiral? As a mercenary?"

Falkenberg nodded coldly. "More or less. The Fleet's a little sick of being used to mess up people's lives without having a chance to—to leave things in working order."

"And now you're leaving?"

"Yes. We couldn't stay here, George. Nobody is going to forget this. You couldn't keep us on and build a government that worked. I'll take first and second battalions, there's more work for us. The third will stay here to help you. We put all the married locals, the solid people in third and sent it off to the power plants where they wouldn't have to fight." He looked across the stadium, turned back to Hamner. "Blame it all on us, George. You weren't in command. You can say Bradford ordered the slaughter, killed himself in remorse . . . people will want to believe that. They'll want to think somebody was punished for—for this." He waved expressively. A child was sobbing out there somewhere.

"It had to be done," Falkenberg insisted. "Didn't it? There was no way out, nothing you could do to keep civilization . . . Dr. Whitlock estimated a third of the population would die when things collapsed. Fleet intelligence put it higher than that. Now you have a chance." Falkenberg was speaking rapidly, and George wondered who he was trying to convince. "Move them out while they're still dazed . . . you won't need much help for that. We've got the railroad running again, use it fast and ship them to the farms. It'll be rough with no preparation, but it's a long time until winter . . ."

Hamner nodded. "I know what to do." He leaned against the column, gathered new strength from the thought. "I've known all along what had to be done. Now we can do it. We won't thank you for it, but—you've saved a whole world, John."

Falkenberg looked at him grimly, then pointed to the bodies below. "Damn you, don't say that!" he shouted. "I haven't saved anything. All a soldier can do is buy time . . . I haven't saved Hadley. You have to do that. God help you if you don't."
∎

NO SHOULDER TO CRY ON
Hank Davis

Human beings tend to see things as black or white, overlooking the many shades of gray between. Some look at the destructive power of unprecedented weapons and see an awesome choice with a yawning chasm between them: now, it seems, we must surely either utterly destroy ourselves or learn to live happily ever after. But that argument overlooks a very important subtlety. . . .

THIS SHIP PURRED AS IT BORED A tunnel through space; purred like a pampered and petted kitten.

It is, I was thinking, a hell of a noise for a spaceship to make.

A spaceship should roar like all the enraged lions that have ever walked the earth roaring *fortissimo* and in unison. It should spew flame burning more brightly than any tiger in any jungle—even Blake's bright burner.

This spaceship, however, spurned the more flamboyant traits of feline heritage and purred like an enormous kitten.

If it weren't for the purring, I thought, I wouldn't know that we were moving—the purring and the violet shift.

My shirt had been white when I left Earth. It now appeared to be a delicate violet hue. The field which allowed the ship to cheat Einstein and cover light-years in a matter of days shifted all light within the ship slightly toward the violet end of the spectrum. During the first few days of flight the shift had been irritating, giving me an irrational feeling that something was wrong with my eyes. I had compulsively rubbed my eyes until they were red and throbbing.

Now I scarcely noticed the shift. But I couldn't get used to the purring.

Maybe I associated it with cats. But that shouldn't have bothered me. Cats to me were like spinach. Some people love the stuff and some people hate it. I'm apathetic.

I'm edgy because of what Arthon said yesterday, I decided. I'm just reading something sinister into what he said. It's silly to get cold feet just as mankind's salvation comes out of the skies at the eleventh hour, I told myself. There's no reason to be afraid. There should be an end to fear now that there will be no atomic doom.

There had been the usual bumper crop of brushfire wars, some smoldering, some flaming brightly; all to the background music of rattling sabers. Dangerous, merrily blazing little brushfire wars in a world of deadly thermonuclear inflammables. There had been the arms race, more crowded than before by the entry of Cuba with its A-bomb.

But there had also been visitors from interstellar space. Before the moon bases had been developed beyond the level of extraterrestrial summer camps, before man had gone to Mars in person, the stars had come to see him. And brought hope.

The old argument: we have scarcely begun to crawl in space, but look how far we have come in killability. Before we can send our own carcasses—and not some electronic gimmick, some glorified and hopped-up Brownie camera—in person to Mars, we are able to sterilize the globe. If we can keep from blowing our collective brains out for just a little longer, we might even reach Pluto, chilly outpost of the sun's domain.

But to go beyond Pluto and reach the stars would require time; much time. To survive long enough to graduate from the solar system surely would require that we find the magic formula for peace; the therapy to prevent Terracide.

No Shoulder to Cry On

And, similarly, wouldn't visitors from extrasolar systems have found the key to *pacem in terris*; or, rather, *extraterris*?

Scant surprise, then, that *everybody* was ecstatic over the arrival of live and kicking unbombed and unirradiated neighbors from Out There. Those who had advocated a hard line in foreign policy, consequently being villified as warmongers, were happiest of all, for it is a hard and lonely thing to advocate a necessary evil.

Immediately, all parties concerned got down to work on each other's languages. They learned ours before we learned theirs, naturally. They had more teachers than we did. When said language exchange had been reasonably well accomplished, and all the "hello there" rituals had been suffered through, the first question from our side was, in essence: "How can three point nine billion—and more on the way—highly belligerent people coexist on the same eight thousand-mile-diameter life raft without one or more groups of passengers capsizing the shaky thing and drowning one and all?"

The answer, again in essence, was: "We would have to study your history and culture in depth to determine what factors are responsible for any differences between our civilization and yours with respect to war or anything else, and the time required would be prohibitive; would put us so far behind schedule that our home planets would be concerned. Why not let us ferry experts of your planet to our planets and let them study our civilizations at their leisure? When they have determined the causes of differences in our civilizations, we will return them to Earth."

It made sense. If a group of people, all of the same IQ, were placed on an island as children and allowed to grow up, would they ever develop the concept of intelligence? Could a man who grew up on a plain conceive of either mountains, or valleys, without seeing them? If the aliens had never slaughtered each other *en masse,* would it ever occur to them that there was anything unusual about the peaceful state of affairs, any more than we think it unusual that man can't fly by wiggling his ears? If the man who had grown up on a plain ever wanted to learn all the various techniques involved in mountain climbing, he would have to go to where the mountains are.

Which was why I, Howard M. Nelson, Esq., Ph.D. in political science, and wearer of a white shirt, that happened to look violet at the moment, happened to be on a purring spaceship hurtling through space at several hundred times the speed of light.

My mother didn't raise her boy to be a spaceman, I thought. I didn't look the part. An astronaut is as near to physical perfection as flesh born of mere man and woman can be, has the reflexes of a cougar with hypertension, has stamina enough to get out and carry the ship back home, should the rockets fail. This was common knowledge—so common that it had passed into the exalted category of things that "everyone knows." Yet here I was, receding hairline, advancing waistline and all, flying farther and faster than any of the smiling young spacefarers of Projects Mercury, Gemini, Apollo, *et al.*

Aside from some mild panic at takeoff, which had been overwhelmed by the greater fear that I would show the panic and make a fool of myself, all had gone well until yesterday. I had been talking to Arthon, the pilot and entire crew of the ship, and he had hit me between the eyes with an umpteen hundred megaton firecracker—one of the ones that my little thirty-seven light-year jaunt would cover, hopefully, with cobwebs.

"There is so much that we can learn from you," I had said, "it's a shame that there is no way we can repay you."

"The reverse is that which is true," he had replied. "That which we can learn from you is greater than that which you can learn from us."

Feeling as if a gallon of ice water had been poured into my BVDS, I had said, "Oh, gee. Yeah, sure. Uh." We he-men always have a little trouble speaking our minds; especially when hit with brain-scrambling firecrackers like the aforementioned.

"Pardon? Perhaps I have not the mastery of your language which I thought was mine," Arthon had said, his features clouded with very human concern.

By now, I had re-erected the facade behind which we humans, masters of Earth, spend our lives hiding. "But you are so much more advanced than we, what can we possibly teach you?"

"You underestimate your people and in a way that is unjust, Howard," he replied, smiling a very human smile. "As for what that is known by you that can benefit us"—sorrow flowed across his face and spilled over into his voice—"I think that that will be left as a surprise for the time which will be that of arrival."

Judging from his new mood, the surprise would be as cheery as an unexpected visit by Jack the Ripper.

Now, some twenty-four hours later and about thirty minutes from arrival, I was in a very calm state of hysteria. Damnit, why had Arthon looked like Gloom & Doom, Inc. when he told me that there was much that we Earthside primitives could teach his side—which consisted of some fifty odd inhabited planets in a loose federation.

Arthon had been very chummy during the trip. He looked very human except for his light blue fur and prehensile tail. He was more human on the inside than the administrators back at my university. I had thought that we were becoming fast friends, as the Rover Boys would say. . . . Maybe he was going to have to throw me to the lions when we arrived and he was regretting it.

But what could *they* learn from *us?*

Maybe we had followed up pathways of discovery that they had neglected. The American Indians were around for a long time without inventing the wheel.

Suppose they developed their space drive without ever developing atomic power.

Arthon had said that the drive had no moving parts. I didn't have the mathematical background to understand how it worked, he said, but he could easily show me how to make one. If it was that simple, could the extrasolarites, as I called them, have hit upon the drive by accident and still be, with the exception of the drive, in a more primitive state of technological development than man? Then they wouldn't have the wherewithal to bump each other off and wouldn't need any magic formula for peace. Arthon's planet was out to get the know-how for nuclear power and lick the other planets in the federation. *That* was what his people could learn from me!

Nope—because Earth had been discovered by a *fleet* of extrasolarites; one ship from each planet in the Federation. And each ship had taken back one (1) Earthling to its home planet; so no planet would have an advantage over any other. Moreover, each Earthling taken was just like me—an ultra-departmentalized specialist in the social sciences whose total knowledge of atomic power consisted of: "Well, there're some bombs that have uranium in them and some that have hydrogen and the ones with hydrogen make bigger bangs and the bombs cause fallout; yup, yup, yup."

My son was a bug about science and electronics. They could have found out more about atomic power by snatching him than by carting me off.

What if, instead of the planets of the Federation fighting among themselves, they have ganged up and go around looking for other planets to clobber?

Nope—in that case, why did they contact us instead of just going back home with the news of fresh prey? And, if they wanted to size us up as to what kind of a fight we would give them, why were they taking social scientists back with them instead of military experts?

My train of thought was derailed by Arthon's entrance. "Howard, the time which will be that of the breaking out of pseudospace will be ten minutes from this time," he informed me. "Would that which you want be to see it?"

"Lead on, MacDuff," I said. The misquote fit my mood.

I went with him down the corridor, which was throbbing with the engine's pussy-noise galore, and followed him into the control room. We sat down in deep-cushioned seats, both with slots for a prehensile tail, and looked through the viewscreen at the rippling violet shell that surrounded the ship.

"You promised me a surprise," I reminded him.

"At this time the surprise would be that which I could only tell you. In five minutes, it will be that which can be seen with those eyes which are your own." He paused. "It is afraid that I am, Howard, that honest is not what we have been with you."

Little crawling bits of fear were in my spinal column, as numerous as ants in an anthill. "How is that?"

"You are hoping that the secret of peace is something which can be obtained from us, are you not?"

"Yes. We were expecting a rain of death from the skies any day. Then you came and we, well . . . had hope again."

"For how long had this rain of death from your skies been something that you had expected?"

"What?"

"Let me ask again the question in another shape. How long has atomic power been with you humans?"

My heart sank. "Well, uh, since 1945. Almost forty years, that is."

"And how many times has a war seen the use of atomic weapons?"

"Well, twice. Both times in the same year—1945."

"So, you have not used the weapons of which you have great fear for almost as long as you have had them—for forty of your years."

"Well . . . yes." I frowned.

"Atomic power was our discovery over three hundred of your years ago."

"And you haven't wiped yourselves out? Now I know that you must have the key to peace, Arthon!" (But, still, something was calling the short hairs on the back of my neck to military attention.)

"The terribleness of nuclear weapons has not the final greatness that you think it does, Howard. There are perfect defenses against them. There are fields which are such that a fission bomb will not explode within them. There are other fields for fusion bombs and antimatter bombs."

"Then you've survived because you have defenses against atomic weapons. You can give them to us and there will be no atomic war."

"Understanding is that which you do not yet have, Howard. There are weapons which have a deadliness far greater than the weapons that are those I have named. There are biological weapons. There are X-ray lasers. The knowledge is ours which can convert a sunspot into a laser and incinerate the sunlit half of a planet. And defenses are ours which nullify these weapons. And others that are more terrible."

"To have survived such dangers proves that you have the key to peace that I seek."

"As I have said, Howard, honest is not what we have been with you. We have misled your people. Happiness was ours when we saw that to study us was your wish and so we gladly took you and your fellows to the planets which were ours, because there is that which we must learn from you."

He paused. My tongue was looking for a hole to crawl into and hide.

"As you once told me, and exactly as you told me, 'A common characteristic equally shared by a group is not evident to the group as a characteristic until they encounter another group which has the characteristic to a different degree.' As you said, 'A colony of people, all having the same IQ, would have no awareness of intelligence as a variable.' True would be what this statement would be even if the colony were one of geniuses, would it not, Howard?"

He had amazed me by quoting me verbatim. He must have a photographic memory. "Yes, Arthon," I answered.

"Earth is a colony of geniuses, Howard. In the forty years which have been those of your development of atomic weapons you have used only two bombs, both small ones. In my planet's first forty years that were the same, we used hundreds, many of them more powerful than any that are yours now. Your population is expanding so fast as to be that which is a problem to you. Our population is now one tenth of that which it was when we discovered atomic energy. The time of our discovery was more than three of your centuries back. The number of planets which are those in our Federation, as you call it, is shrinking. Eighty-seven planets which once were among those which are members are lifeless balls rolling through space now."

The violet curtain parted and we began the approach to Arthon's planet on slow drive. My white shirt was no longer violet, but I ignored it. I was looking at the ugly craters on the planet's surface, which were plainly visible, even at this distance, like planetary smallpox scars. I could easily see the black areas where nothing green grew.

A tear, running ahead to act as scout for the main body, crept out of Arthon's left eye.

"The job of keeping the peace is that which you humans think you have done poorly," he said in a voice soft as a crumbling dream. "Teach us how to do a job that is as poor. Please!" ■

THE BULLY AND THE CRAZY BOY
Marc Stiegler

So it's up to us. We cannot rely on someone else to solve our problems of survival and tranquillity—and please note that survival is a prerequisite *for tranquillity. Some enemies may allow even the most dedicated seeker of peace no choice but to die or to fight back by means that seem, in the short run, irrational.*

WEIGHTLESS, FLEET ADMIRAL ENCRAI launched himself off the wall of the C-Cubed room, arched, snapped against the far wall on his front paws, twisted, and sprang back across the room. Ordinarily the lithe power of his body would have pleased him; but now he paced in fury, trying to regain his feline poise.

Damn! Damn! How could he have expected the stupid primates to be insane? Why hadn't the psychologists warned him? Granted, they'd told him the species hadn't completed its evolution to a communal hunting animal. Granted, they'd warned him to expect strange behavior. But this! How could he predict that, after crushing the puny defenses around Uranus, the primates' orbital city would accept his ships, then blow itself up? Unbelievable! Not rational! What kind of creatures *were* these?

Again Encrai questioned the wisdom of taking this solar system now; certainly it'd be more sensible to let this species ripen a bit, let them gain a measure of non-primitiveness (he hated to call it sophistication—certainly no *primate* could achieve *that*) so they'd be useful slaves.

His pacing slowed; at last he shrugged. The High Command's decision was made, their orders given. Encrai's full F class fleet would knock off the primates quickly, before the retrenchment wars began.

"Admiral—an enemy fleet just broke toward us from a planetoid fragment." Captain Taress spoke crisply from across the room.

Touching the controls on his magnetic harness, Encrai curved through the air to his command station. Floating between his webcradle and his console, he looked up at the holoscreen, which covered the whole front wall of the room. Part of that wall teemed with statistics and gauges, changing endlessly as the Flagship staff and the Command/Control/Communication staff requested new data.

But Encrai barely noticed these. His attention centered on the 3-D display of fleet dispositions. Part of that display now detached itself, to expand for detailed analysis in the tactical viewer. A dense handful of numbered ellipses, the primate fleet, approached the dispersed center of Encrai's fleet—approached Encrai's flagship itself! Unbelievable!

Chief Assistant Mrech, a bright young strategist, glanced back at him. "Looks to me like Jirbri's in position to pick them off fastest. Shall I punch it out?"

Encrai hissed. "No, it could be another pack of suicidal idiots. I'd better take care of them myself." Besides, he needed something fun to do; the disaster at the primate Outbase still rankled.

As he punched out commands on his console, a handful of ships on the tactical screen broke from the Kalixi formation to swirl around the opposing clay pigeons. But the swirling was careful—no Kalixi ship approached the pigeons closely enough to be destroyed by the explosion of a primate's main thrust chamber.

The battle was over at its beginning. A final blasting pass cooked the two biggest enemy ships; a handful of lifeboats scattered from them. Kalixi ships turned to mop up the lifeboats; but Encrai forbade it.

The chief assistant cocked his head. "You're going to pick them up?"

Encrai swished his tail in acknowledgment. "Only if they agree to leave the lifeboats and get picked up in spacesuits. I don't think a primate can be very dangerous with just the weapons he carries in his spacesuit, do you? And I need the information." In particular, he needed to know why the stupid creatures were so eager to blow themselves up.

The admiral yawned. "Have Jirbri question them. When he's done, buzz." The assistant mrowed understanding; Encrai stretched forward from his console, and floated out of the room.

A burrstinger buzzed close to him, spinning around him, waiting for him to stop trying to track it, so it could land. His nose, his nose was the stinger's target.

But his eyes were closed, and when he opened them he saw it was the intercom buzzing at him, and he himself was doing the spinning, tethered in the center of his room. Encrai touched his harness. "Yes?" he yawned.

"We found something interesting when we took the prisoners, Admiral." The assistant's voice almost purred.

"Something interesting with the *primates?*"

"One of the prisoners is special." Encrai could almost see Mrech sniffing the high air.

"Very funny, Colonel. A special primate, indeed."

"It's true—apparently one of our guests is the creature that developed the primate defense strategy. He's an admiral, of sorts. He seems quite eager to help us defeat him, since we pointed out how unpleasant his alternatives are."

Encrai opened his mouth, then closed it. With a furious swish of his tail he bounded into the hall.

Soaring gracefully back into the Command/Control/ Communications room, Encrai watched marine guards manacle a primate to the prison chair, next to the admiral's control station. Encrai frowned for a moment; the chair had been designed to immobilize all kinds of intelligent beings—but all kinds of intelligent beings generally meant felines, canines, and low-gravity arachnoids. The chair didn't fit on the primate very well.

But then, these primates were weak little creatures, according to the pre-campaign analyses. The chair wouldn't have to fit to hold him. Encrai smiled. Besides, what could a primate do, even if he got free, amidst full-grown, full-clawed Kalixi? The admiral turned to the psychmed accompanying the marines. "Is this the primate," he curled his lips, "who calls himself an admiral?"

The psychmed swished his tail. "Yes, sir. He seems to be the originator of the primate battle plans. The other prisoners support his statements under all forms of extraction." The psychmed ruffled his fur. "Naturally, when we found out that this," he tapped the primate with his tail, "was supposed to be an admiral, we examined his mind, such as it is, a bit more carefully. He has a number of implanted psycho-blocks, presumably protecting important information."

Encrai smiled. "No doubt he's protecting top secret technological details."

The psychmed laughed. "I wouldn't be surprised. Anyway, his blocks are sophisticated enough so that he might be damaged if I try to penetrate them hastily. Whatever is inside those blocks will stay there 'til after the campaign. Unless he tells us willingly."

Encrai raised an eyebow. "Willingly?"

"Yes, we gave him a drug that stimulates verbosity. He'll probably be telling you a lot more than you ask for. I'm not sure it was necessary—*all* these creatures like to talk, it seems—but if you don't ask a question just the right way, you'll probably get the information you want anyway. Remember, though, it still won't register on the lie-sniffer if he just answers the poorly worded question truthfully."

"As if he had any secrets that could hurt us."

"Indeed."

Encrai's lips pulled back in a ferocious grin, exposing a vast collection of murderous teeth. "This is great! I've never planned a battle with the enemy admiral giving me advice before. Such a shame it couldn't have happened in the battle with Valesh and his damned Crusairs."

The psychmed saluted. "Maybe next time, sir." He turned to leave, then turned back again. "Oh, one last thing. Two of the primate's teeth are filled with a chemical—a stimulant of some kind, leaking slowly into his mouth. The primate said the chemical keeps him alive, so we left it. It seems harmless enough."

"Fine. Let's hope he lives long enough to be useful."

The psychmed pushed toward the doorway.

Floating in his webcradle, Encrai examined the prisoner. He seemed small, even for a primate. Black hair and ashen skin seemed his dominant features. Frail was the best one-word descriptor. But the jaw was set in determination, even though the eyes stayed downcast. For a moment the primate reminded Encrai of a pouting kitten.

The Kalixi admiral tapped his webcradle and drifted toward the prisoner, into the gentle breeze from behind the prison chair that made it possible for the great cat to be downwind of the primate. He closed his eyes to focus on the primate's scents: the bitter organic staleness of its soft body wrapping, the sweet saltiness of its perspiration, the flavor of its most recent meal—an almost fruity flavor it was, mixed with acidic digestive juices. How strange that fruitiness was! Encrai had never met an intelligent omnivore before. Not even a semi-intelligent one.

He tapped the pad on the translator. "I understand you're the admiral of the primate fleet," Encrai said. The translator repeated the words in the local barbarism of a language.

The creature just nodded its head up and down.

Encrai swished his tail. "Well, are you or are you not the admiral of the primate fleet?"

The primate looked at him with big eyes, then broke into laughter. "When I nod my head that means 'yes' in our language. Yes, my name is Craig Thearsporn, and I'm the Campaign Admiral for the Fleet of Interplanetary Alliance." He looked Admiral Encrai over. "Are you the admiral for the Kalixi fleet?"

"Who do you think is doing the questioning here?"

The prisoner shrugged his shoulders. Gestures and expressions seemed to be important methods of communication with the creatures; Encrai decided to watch more closely. It wouldn't be difficult to infer the meanings; Encrai had a knack for such empathic intuitions.

The admiral touched the lock button on his harness, to prevent any drifting while he questioned the primate. "What were you doing out here?"

The prisoner shrugged again. "The Kalixi we captured from your exploratory fleet told us that an admiral always hangs far back, if possible. So we came to get you."

"Did you really expect to destroy me and my flagship?"

The primate turned his eyes down again, heaved a sob. "No, not really."

Encrai swished his tail. "And why'd you let us take you alive?"

The primate smiled. "For one thing, I wanted to live."

Encrai mrowed understanding.

The liesniffer's requirements were fulfilled, but the primate went on. "Besides, I wanted to meet you." He shook his head back and forth. "Ever since that first exploratory hunting party slaughtered every person on the first space city it found, I've known something's terribly wrong with the universe. So *wrong*. Why are you so vicious, so cruel, so determined to destroy and conquer? Why not come as traders, benefitting us both?"

Encrai snorted, then laughed. He shouldn't have bothered to answer, but he was vain about his species, and proud of his vanity. "Why don't we trade? Because, primate, the Kalixi are conquerors, not traders." His claws extended, retracted, extended. "For a thousand years we were slaves, as you'll be. We were declawed. We, the Kalixi!" The claws extended one last time. "But we were patient, learning in secret, as our masters weakened and waned and were replaced by other masters." His paw raked through the air, tearing the throat from an ephemeral opponent. "And under the terrible oppression, those of us who were weak died, and those of us who were strong gained strength. Now our enemies know us in our power and glory."

"You've defeated them?"

Encrai hissed. "We've destroyed them. The species who subjugated us are extinct, by our claws. Now we are the masters, and others are the slaves."

"So you're continuing the system you despised."

"It's a good system—the strong live and conquer, the weak serve and die." Encrai smiled. "You're lucky to be conquered by the Kalixi. We're the Destined Ones, fated to conquer the galaxy. Already we have over 600 solar systems and 150 slave species. No other single species has subjugated that many others for millions of years."

The primate seemed shaken. "Don't you have any allies? What about your enemies? Why don't *they* form an alliance? I can't believe the universe is so devoid of cooperation. Even among us, at least hate is powerful enough to mold friendships."

Encrai laughed. "Poor naive omnivore. I guess that with your background, it's understandable." Encrai looked the creature in the eye. "The universe is the domain of the carnivores, primate. Planetary evolution dictates it. With few, few exceptions, the carnivores develop intelligence first—and once a carnivore develops intelligence, no other species has a chance." He smiled; had he not become an admiral, Encrai might well have been a university professor. "But regardless of how much our intelligence expands, still we retain our ancient instincts. We know the love of the good hunt, and the joy of the final kill." He spoke the words with relish. "And as we hunt and are hunted, our intelligence and instincts develop apace."

The primate shook its head; water gathered in its eyes. "Dear God, no! Are all the other species really like yours?"

Encrai swished his tail. "Of course not; they are much less sophisticated. From your point of view, though, they're similar." He rolled his eyes. "Actually, I've heard rumors of a group of omnivorous species that've united to protect themselves from the carnivores. But I doubt the rumors. How could omnivores survive long enough to find each other?"

A funny expression spread over the primate's face; for some reason, it made the admiral uneasy. "Perhaps they survive by being just a little bit insane."

What did *that* mean? Encrai slitted his eye. Oh well—at least it brought them to the topic of insanity; and that was the thing that interested Encrai. "Perhaps they have. Though it certainly didn't help the primates at the Uranus Outbase. Tell me, primate—why did that Outbase destroy itself?"

The primate wrestled with the chair, trying to get more comfortable. "That's a long story. Have you ever heard the story of the Bully and the Crazy Boy?"

The verbosity drug had definitely taken effect. "No, nor do I want to hear it now. Just tell me why they blew themselves up."

The primate shrugged. "We struck at you through the only weakness we could find."

Encrai turned bright eyes to his captive. "Indeed!"

The primate nodded.

"Well, goodness! Don't keep me in suspense, primate, tell me. I'm always trying to correct my defects." He wondered if primates were able to recognize sarcasm.

"Your flaw is that you're altogether too rational."

What a stupid thing to say! Faagh! Yet the admiral's spine tingled.

"Yes, that was the only flaw we could find," the primate continued, "aside from a tendency to overconfidence. I fear you never let your overconfidence influence important decisions."

"Um. And, ah—just how did you figure out that we are, um, too rational?"

"Well, that's a good story too. I'm the one who realized you had this flaw—not because I'm the smartest admiral we have, but because I've fought this fight before." He looked down at himself, then continued, "I'm a sort of small man, as you may have noticed, and—"

Encrai saw a complete autobiography coming, which he wished to avoid. "From all this I gather that the rest of your ships will behave as suicidally and insanely as the Outbase did?"

The shadow of a snarl passed over the primate's face. "With a vengeance, Admiral, with a vengeance."

"I see." The admiral adjusted his harness, and returned to his control station. The central battlescreen brightened to full vigor as he touched the pads. Two disjoint sections appeared, the left one filled with the shape of the Kalixi fleet, the right one containing Saturn and its many moons. To the far left of the right section, two tiny dots represented the advanced scouts recording the Saturn scene; to the right of Saturn, on the sunward side, a small group of large objects approached the planet and its system.

"Tell me, primate, what are those clumsy objects moving toward Saturn?" A pointer appeared on the screen and drew the skeleton of a sphere around the spots of light.

"They're the battle stations from Earth, I imagine. Admiral Springrain deduced that you'd come from this direction. It's the obvious line of approach, if you plan to take the planets one at a time. When we realized that we'd have to meet you at Titan, the Terran Federate sent its battle stations to help defend Titan." The primate smiled. "Actually, I should thank you, after a manner. You're the first thing that's united mankind since the beginning of history."

"That's right, I'd forgotten. Your species wars against itself, doesn't it?" Amazing. At least they'd make a fascinating study for the xenologists. Evolution had been short-circuited here. Lessons could be learned.

Another thought struck Encrai. "So you anticipated our coming this way. I'm impressed."

"We assumed you'd take the simplest route. That destroys the element of surprise, but you can beat us without surprise. Your technology and tactics should beat us regardless."

Encrai appreciated that; it was exactly the conclusion *he'd* come to, of course. "You admit we'll win?"

Water collected in the primate's eyes. "How can you lose! You have more people, more resources, better technology. You're certainly more vicious, and . . . if the handful of prisoners we took from your exploratory group are any indication, you're even . . . you're even," the primate's voice choked on a sob. "You're even smarter than we are." The primate's face contorted with bright dogged anger. "And we intend to beat your damned tails down your throats, and stomp you into pulp and spit on you when we're done."

The admiral smiled broadly. "Good for you." So they were realistic—but spunky. "Tell me, where are your fleets, and where are they going to be, in order to carry out this commendable operation?"

The primate told him, expansively. He described the details of the designs of the ships in each fleet. He explained their tactical theory upon entering the conflict.

Returning to his console, Encrai set up a new scene on the display, a close-up of Titan and its neighbors, and started the games. Fleets entered the 3-D playing area and splintered into ships. The ships in turn branched into sets of potentialities, vectors for their possible actions. Then, one by one, inferior potentiality branches dissolved, and optimal ones solidified. The scene commanded all of Encrai's attention; this was one of the parts of war he enjoyed most.

The battle's dance slowed as primate ships winked out of existence in the midst of their optimal paths; none escaped the Kalixi guns. "You know, it's almost a shame your species hasn't learned to compensate for acceleration without locking everybody in a stasis box. This could be a pleasant battle, if your ships could maneuver."

The primate just floated in his chair.

Encrai took careful note of a flaw in the design of the primate strategy, and played out a second scenario. The new game ran quickly to completion, as Encrai had predicted. "Why commit your fleets in such a loosely coupled fashion? There're large gaps in the pattern."

The primate nodded. "Yeah, we left some openings for the research ships to watch through."

"Research ships?"

Again the primate nodded. "Assuming we survive this time, we'll have to know a lot more to survive again. The Martian Republic donated its research fleet. We hope to get detailed pictures of your ships in the instants before they explode, after our missiles strike. By putting enough of those fragments together, along with the remains of the destroyed ships, maybe the next time you come to the solar system, you'll be facing ships just like your own."

Encrai snorted. "Fools! You think you can understand *our* technology? Just by taking pictures and collecting debris?" He searched his memory for an analogy, something out of the alien's own history. "Could a medieval primate build an airplane just by looking at the construction diagrams? It's absurd."

The primate winced. "I don't know. Certainly no ordinary medieval man could have done it. But a medieval man who knew the scientific method might be able to, given time. The scientific method is our greatest strength. It's the best method for learning there is." A look of—horror? Yes, a look of horror passed over the primate's face. "Unless you've found something better than the scientific method. If you've learned a better way to learn, we're lost." His eyes held a plea. "You don't have anything better than science, do you?"

The great cat hissed; Captain Taress turned to look at him with puzzlement.

The alien was right. Science was the key, and the Kalixi had nothing better. For the first time, a chill of fear ran along his spine—a chill he very quickly suppressed.

Encrai punched in a new set of orders for his fleet, modifying their battle plan. "You shall pay dearly for the opportunity to learn from the Kalixi," he muttered grimly. The new orders detailed a massive incursion into the gaps between the alien fleets, breaking their flanks and splintering them in chaos.

Encrai yawned, and stretched. He turned to Chief Assistant Mrech. "Colonel, watch after things, will you?" With a look at the timetable, he turned to the alien. "I'll be back in about six hours. We'll watch the battle together." He smiled. "May the best minds win."

The burrstinger closed, closed, and—Encrai opened his eyes with a start; his whole body was bent with tension, ready to pounce.

It was wrong—something was wrong in this campaign, but he didn't know what it was. And his hunches seldom erred.

But until his hunch blossomed into understanding, he could do nothing. And soon it would be irrelevant, anyway. The battle was starting. It was time to go see the show.

Encrai hurtled through the air at terrifying velocity, snagging the edge of his web-cradle with outstretched claws as he passed. Back at his console, he created a new display upon the holoscreen; now the two scenes, one of Titan and the other of his fleet, coalesced. Saturn lay dead center, straddled by two opposing armadas. The humans far outnumbered the Kalixi. They looked quite imposing on the screen, but it was only an illusion. In the first conflict, between a Kalixi Class J fleet and the Martian Second Fleet, twenty-five Kalixi vessels knocked off 180 primate ships before the primates pegged their first Kalixi ship; even after that, the Kalixi lost only three more ships, while the humans lost another forty-six. Armor alloy and fusion missiles just couldn't contest the clean power of gammaxers and gravshields. For the upcoming battle, the High Command anticipated the destruction of eleven human ships for every Kalixi; considering the weakness Encrai had found in the alien strategy, newer figures suggested a ratio of seventeen to one. And the human's suicidal tendency made no difference—insanity worked once, but only once.

Then why did Encrai's intuition disagree?

Encrai turned to the prisoner. "I wish to compliment you on the accuracy of your reporting. The fleets are indeed arriving just as you said they would, in just the disposition you described. Thank you."

"Yeah." Shadows hung under the prisoner's eyes, and stubble darkened his chin. The Kalixi admiral chose not to notice.

Instead he turned back to the holoscreen. It was all so beautiful. Simple and elegant. There was, he told himself, nothing to fear.

Then the outer edge broke away from the battlescreen, forming a set of new displays far removed from the battle. These new sections held no fleets, just scattered ships—but the ships were moving at incredible speeds. The Kalixi advance scouts had just detected them. And though they were far away, they were unquestionably heading for the battle zone, and they were accelerating at the fastest pace that the best of the alien stasis boxes could handle and still keep the occupants alive. Encrai played with the controls, and potentialities expanded from those ships in narrow, senseless patterns.

To get to the battle in time, they'd have to continue to accelerate, and when they arrived they'd be going so fast they'd only be in the battle for a few seconds before they flashed past, hopelessly out of control, to speed beyond the limits of the solar system and die—for the aliens had no interstellar jumpdrive, nothing that could get those ships home again. It was truly suicidal, and in that sense at least it seemed typical of these primates.

"Where did those ships come from?" Encrai asked in tense bewilderment. "Where are they *going?*"

Somehow, the prisoner's silence seemed ominous. Encrai turned to the alien, and saw that he was no longer haggard and tired. His eyes were bright with a new emotion—was it pride? Could a primate feel pride? "Tell me, primate Admiral, what are those ships doing out there?"

The man smiled broadly, and Encrai's gnawing tension leaped in his throat. Instantly he swung over the human, claws extended, ready for the killing stroke. "Tell me," he spat.

The man leaned back, squirming away from the claws. "Where'd they come from? They came from the far side of the sun, beyond the bounds of the solar system. They've been accelerating since we figured out your timetable." He paused, and Encrai came closer with his claws. "They're on their way to the battle, obviously. They're on their way to *win.*"

"How? They'll only be *in* the battle for a few seconds before they leave again, as swiftly as they came. They'll hardly have time to fire, much less time to aim."

The prisoner raised an eyebrow. "Well, in one sense you're even more right than you realize—many won't get to fire at all. By the time they get to the battle, they'll be traveling at almost a third of the speed of light. Many of those ships'll be dead hulls even before they get *to* the battle."

Encrai cocked his head, questioning.

"Don't you see? At one-third the speed of light, every dust particle in the solar system is their enemy—because in *their* reference frame, those particles are traveling at a third of the speed of light. Those dust particles, then, are slow—but incredibly massive—cosmic rays."

Encrai's eyes widened in dawning horror as he leaped to the console. He trembled as he composed the fleet's evacuation orders.

And as he worked, the prisoner's words taunted him, telling him what he already knew. "Of course, that works both ways. Those ships, those ships, *Admiral,* are the biggest damn cosmic rays in the universe right now. They won't *have* to aim their missiles—they aren't even going to try. Their warheads are just hunks of lead, with enough deuterium to vaporize. They'll explode way in front of your ships, leaving clouds of lead nuclei cosmic rays to blast through your damn gravshields. How long can your gravshields take *that,* Admiral?"

The evacuation orders sped from the admiral's console. He finished, looked at an instrument display, and sagged in his cradle in agony. "Too late," he sobbed in a cracked voice. "I'm too far away. My beam'll take half an hour to get to Saturn from here. The suiciders will arrive before my message does."

The man broke into hysterical laughter. "We didn't have a chance, not a chance in the world. But we tried, goddammit, we *had* to try, and we *won!*"

Encrai was too numb to respond. He looked dully at the display, saw a small mystery resolved. "Those gaps between your fleets—they're for the suiciders, aren't they?" The gaps into which Encrai had sent so many Kalixi ships.

The human admiral nodded. "They're really for the research ships, but they're tunnels for the suiciders as well."

Burning, paralyzing terror fought with cold, penetrating thought in Encrai's mind; but he was Kalixi, and thought won over terror. He set his teeth in determination. "That still won't destroy my fleet, Admiral. You'll hurt us, terribly, but we'll win anyway. We're warriors, Admiral. Even this can't bring you victory."

The human admiral shook his head again. "You've missed the most important part of the attack. We aren't counting on a single pass to destroy you—because those ships won't ever get to pass. Look at the trajectories and the timings on those ships. Go ahead and look, Admiral."

Encrai turned to the holoscreen. Under his direction, the senseless patterns branched again—then, far faster than anything he'd ever seen before, the branches fell away and a handful of single solid certainties locked into place. The certainties emanated from a single point in the center of the Kalixi formation, radiating out in a cone to the suiciders' ships. Encrai gasped. "Spiders in web! They're going to collide with each other!"

The human—what was his name! Thearsporn? Thearsporn nodded again—an awful custom, this nodding was. "We hope to get ten to fifteen of them to ram together within five nanoseconds of each other. The explosion won't be as bright as a star, but it'll be pretty close."

New waves of shock washed through Encrai's brain, waning as his mind froze, waxing each time a coherent thought tried to form. "My fleet. The center of my fleet." He shuddered. "But your own ships! That star will destroy your own ships as well!"

Thearsporn turned sober. "Yes, it will. Only the farthest research vessels will survive."

Encrai ripped deep tears in his web, unbelieving, incapable of believing. "Why? How?"

The admiral's voice answered gently. "Let me tell you the story of the Bully and the Crazy Boy."

Encrai had no answer.

"Once there was a crazy boy who always walked home from school. One day a bully confronted him, and dared the boy to get around him. The boy tried to cajole the bully, but failed. So they fought. And the bully beat the boy unmercifully. But in the course of the fighting the boy got in one good blow, and bloodied the bully's nose."

The voice through the translator was soft, soothing; by concentrating on the voice, Encrai could think again.

"The next day, the bully and the crazy boy met and fought again, and the boy was brutally beaten, but again he got in one good blow, kicking the bully in the knee."

Encrai noticed Thearsporn's face; it became increasingly contorted as he spoke. The words were heated now, and Thearsporn's eyes, which were bright before, now burned.

"And they continued to meet and fight for a week. By then the crazy boy was a bruised mass of ruptured flesh. But despite all the bruises he wasn't defeated. In fact, he looked up at the bully and pleaded, 'Please, please don't make me hurt you again.' The bully laughed at him, knowing he was a crazy, stupid boy—but he stopped laughing because laughing hurt, because the boy'd split his lip the day before, and the bully put his hand to his lips, and felt the swelling from his eye that still hadn't subsided, and felt the pain in his knee as he shifted his weight. And the bully looked at the crazy boy with horror, and turned and hurried away."

Encrai felt bile rise in his throat. Insanity, insanity was what this man was about. Why couldn't Thearsporn and his kind just accept the idea of slavery, like rational beings, when the alternative was death?

Encrai's numbness was gone; rational thought replaced the emptiness.

And with new thoughts came a new wave of horror. He formed new orders on his console; orders for his flagship and personal guard.

Captain Taress gasped as he read the orders. "Twenty-five G's! The compensators won't be able to handle it all."

"I know that, Captain," Encrai growled. "Do it anyway!" Encrai turned back to the human admiral. "Are any of those suicidal ships headed for *us?*"

Thearsporn shook his head. "Nope, 'fraid not."

A stench from the liesniffer assailed Encrai's senses; his snarl was cut off as a hammer of acceleration nailed him in his webcradle. The human snapped sideways in his chair, awkwardly positioned to survive such force. "Where are they?" Encrai demanded of his prisoner. "How soon will the suiciders get here?"

Thearsporn twisted into the acceleration, trying to get away from the even more terrible agony assaulting him from the pain transmitters in the chair. "They're, they're off to one side, away from the scouts. Coming from an off angle. Should be here any minute."

Even as Thearsporn spoke, Encrai saw a dozen cosmic rays blossom into existence on his flagship's own scanners. With a strangled cry, Encrai screamed interception orders for his ships, orders they had only seconds to execute.

But Encrai's officers were the best in the universe, and they made it. The guardships lurched forward, spraying death even as the guards themselves died. The flagship's acceleration rotated ninety degrees and doubled. And the dead crews of the suicide ships couldn't retarget on the dodging flagship.

"We made it," Encrai muttered, then shouted in joy, "we made it!"

His thoughts turned to the future even as his happiness swept away his horrors. They would have to send another fleet to this system, he realized. His personal career was destroyed, of course, but there was something more important here. These crazy primates had to be subdued.

It would be difficult to convince the High Command to send another fleet now, with the retrenchment wars coming, but Encrai would convince them. And it wouldn't take much; even a Class H fleet, hardly bigger than the original exploratory group, could beat the remains of the human defenses. Yes, a Class H fleet . . . and a single Planetburster, just in case the fleet failed to conquer. Yes. Encrai turned cheerfully to his prisoner.

The prisoner was clamping his jaw, swallowing hard. Encrai remembered the psychmed talking about a stimulant in the primate's teeth.

"What . . ." Encrai started, then slapped his hand down on the alarm button. The man's complexion darkened, perspiration erupted from his face, and Encrai could smell the man's anger as he tore himself from the ill-fitting prison chair in the 5-G gravity.

With a powerful lunge Encrai was upon the beast—for beast Thearsporn was, with the light of insanity in his eyes. Closing swiftly, Encrai delivered a lethal stroke of his claws.

But Thearsporn snapped away, and the lethal stroke merely raked across his side, drawing a swath of skin and blood. Thearsporn extended his fist with impossible strength, and bones snapped in Encrai's side as he crashed through the air.

Disregarding his pain, Encrai followed as Thearsporn dodged down the corridors. A marine appeared and fired a lasgun through Thearsporn's abdomen, but it didn't diminish his speed. He disappeared around the corner.

The Bully and the Crazy Boy

Encrai realized that he was heading for the fusion pool at ship's center.

The creature was insane, no doubt about it. Worse, he was dying—he was already dead, if he would just realize it; no doubt about it. But he would not realize it, and he would get to the fusion pool; there was no doubt about that either. Encrai wondered briefly how the admiral knew where to go and how to get there.

Not that it mattered. Encrai started to take a deep breath, found it was a terrible mistake. The broken bones in his chest must have punctured a lung. And an artery. Moist warmth collected near his throat. He was dying.

Not that it mattered. In a few moments he would become part of another, even smaller, star. Admiral Thearsporn's star.

Encrai sighed. He felt a certain sense of guilt, failing his people like this, but the guilt seemed remote. Poor, poor Kalixi. He wished he could tell them; he wished he could tell them how much they still had to learn before they could conquer.

But for now the learning was too late; and soon the fury of atoms in bondage conquered all. ∎

THUNDER AND ROSES
Theodore Sturgeon

It has never really been possible to make wise decisions on the basis of short-term considerations alone, but the kinds of destructive power available to us and our descendants make it even less possible than ever before. Some of the most important and agonizing choices, in fact, may require an extremely long view.

WHEN PETE MAWSER LEARNED about the show, he turned away from the GHQ bulletin board, touched his long chin, and determined to shave, in spite of the fact that the show would be video, and he would see it in his barracks. He had an hour and a half. It felt good to have a purpose again—even the small matter of shaving before eight o'clock. Eight o'clock Tuesday, just the way it used to be. Everyone used to say, Wednesday morning, "How about the way Starr sang *The Breeze and I* last night?"

That was a while ago, before the attack, before all those people were dead, before the country was dead. Starr Anthim—an institution, like Crosby, like Duse, like Jenny Lind, like the Statue of Liberty. (Liberty had been one of the first to get it, her bronze beauty volatilized, radio-activated, and even now being carried about in vagrant winds, spreading over the earth. . . .)

Pete Mawser grunted and forced his thoughts away from the drifting, poisonous fragments of a blasted liberty. Hate was first. Hate was ubiquitous, like the increasing blue glow in the air at night, like the tension that hung over the base.

Gunfire crackled sporadically far to the right, swept nearer. Pete stepped out to the street and made for a parked truck. There was a WAC sitting on the short runningboard.

At the corner a stocky figure backed into the intersection. The man carried a tommygun in his arms, and he was swinging it to and fro with the gentle, wavering motion of a weather-vane. He staggered toward them, his gun-muzzle hunting. Someone fired from a building and the man swiveled and blasted wildly at the sound.

"He's—blind," said Pete Mawser, and added, "he ought to be," looking at the tattered face.

A siren keened. An armored jeep slewed into the street. The full-throated roar of a brace of .50-caliber machine-guns put a swift and shocking end to the incident.

"Poor crazy kid," Pete said softly. "That's the fourth I've seen today." He looked down at the WAC. She was smiling. "Hey!"

"Hello, Sarge." She must have identified him before, because now she did not raise her eyes nor her voice. "What happened?"

"You know what happened. Some kid got tired of having nothing to fight and nowhere to run to. What's the matter with you?"

"No," she said. "I don't mean that." At last she looked up at him. "I mean all of this. I can't seem to remember."

"You—well, it's not easy to forget. We got hit. We got hit everywhere at once. All the big cities are gone. We got it from both sides. We got too much. The air is becoming radioactive. We'll all—" He checked himself. She didn't know. She'd forgotten. There was nowhere to escape to, and she'd escaped inside herself, right here. Why tell her about it? Why tell her that everyone was going to die? Why tell her that other, shameful thing: that we hadn't struck back?

But she wasn't listening. She was still looking at him. Her eyes were not quite straight. One held his, but the other was slightly shifted and seemed to be looking at his temple. She was smiling again. When his voice trailed off she didn't prompt him. Slowly, he moved away. She did not turn her head, but kept looking up at where he had been, smiling a little. He turned away, wanting to run, walking fast.

How long could a guy hold out? When you were in the army they tried to make you be like everybody else. What did you do when everybody else was cracking up? He blanked out the mental picture of himself, as the last one left sane. He'd followed that one through before. It always led to the conclusion that it would be better to be one of the first. He wasn't ready for that yet. Then he blanked that out, too. Every time he said to himself that he wasn't ready for that yet, something within him asked "Why not?" and he never seemed to have an answer ready.

How long could a guy hold out?

He climbed the steps of the QM Central and went inside. There was nobody at the reception switchboard. It didn't matter. Messages were carried by jeep, or on motorcycles. The Base Command was not insisting that anybody stick to a sitting job these days. Ten desk-men could crack up for every one on a jeep, or on the soul-sweat squads. Pete made up his mind to put in a little stretch on a squad tomorrow. Do him good. He just hoped that this time the adjutant wouldn't burst into tears in the middle of the parade ground. You could keep your mind on the manual of arms just fine until something like that happened.

He bumped into Sonny Weisefreund in the barracks corridor. The tech's round young face was as cheerful as ever. He was naked and glowing, and had a towel thrown over his shoulder.

"Hi, Sonny. Is there plenty of hot water?"

"Why not?" grinned Sonny. Pete grinned back, wondering if anybody could say anything about anything at all without one of these reminders. Of course, there was hot water. The QM barracks had hot water for three hundred men. There were three dozen left. Men dead, men gone to the hills, men locked up so they wouldn't—

"Starr Anthim's doing a show tonight."

"Yeah, Tuesday night. Not funny, Pete. Don't you know there's a war—"

"No kidding," Pete said swiftly. "She's here—right on the base."

Sonny's face was joyful. "Gee." He pulled the towel off his shoulder and tied it around his waist. "Starr Anthim here! Where are they going to put on the show?"

"HQ, I imagine. Video only. You know about public gatherings."

"Yeah. And a good thing, too," said Sonny. "Somebody'd be sure to crack up. I wouldn't want her to see anything like that. How'd she happen to come here, Pete?"

"Drifted in on the last gasp of a busted-up Navy helicopter."

"Yeah, but why?"

"Search me. Get your head out of that gift-horse's mouth."

He went into the washroom, smiling and glad that he still could. He undressed and put his neatly folded clothes down on a bench. There were a soap-wrapper and an empty tooth-paste tube lying near the wall. He picked them up and put them in the catchall, took the mop that leaned against the partition and mopped the floor where Sonny had splashed after shaving. Someone had to keep things straight. He might have worried if it were anyone else but Sonny. But Sonny wasn't cracking up. Sonny always had been like that. Look there. Left his razor out again.

Pete started his shower, meticulously adjusting the valves until the pressure and temperature exactly suited him. He did nothing carelessly these days. There was so much to feel, and taste, and see now. The impact of water on his skin, the smell of soap, the consciousness of light and heat, the very pressure of standing on the soles of his feet . . . he wondered vaguely how the slow increase of radioactivity in the air, as the nitrogen transmuted to Carbon 14, would affect him if he kept carefully healthy in every way. What happens first? Blindness? Headaches? Perhaps a loss of appetite or slow fatigue?

Why not look it up?

On the other hand, why bother? Only a very small percentage of the men would die of radioactive poisoning. There were too many other things that killed more quickly, which was probably just as well. That razor, for example. It lay gleaming in a sunbeam, curved and clean in the yellow light. Sonny's father and grandfather had used it, or so he said, and it was his pride and joy.

Pete turned his back on it, and soaped under his arms, concentrating on the tiny kisses of bursting bubbles. In the midst of a recurrence of disgust at himself for thinking so often of death, a staggering truth struck him. He did not think of such things because he was morbid, after all! It was the very familiarity of things that brought death-thoughts. It was either "I shall never do this again" or "This is one of the last times I shall do this." You might devote yourself completely to doing things in different ways, he thought madly. You might crawl across the floor this time, and next time walk across on your hands. You might skip dinner tonight, and have a snack at two in the morning instead, and eat grass for breakfast.

But you had to breathe. Your heart had to beat. You'd sweat and you'd shiver, the same as always. You couldn't get away from that. When those things happened, they would remind you. Your heart wouldn't beat out its *wunklunk, wunklunk* any more. It would go *one-less, one-less,* until it yelled and yammered in your ears and you had to make it stop.

Terrific polish on that razor.

And your breath would go on, same as before. You could sidle through this door, back through the next one and the one after, and figure out a totally new way to go through the one after that, but your breath would keep on sliding in and out of your nostrils like a razor going through whiskers, making a sound like a razor being stropped.

Sonny came in. Pete soaped his hair. Sonny picked up the razor and stood looking at it. Pete watched him, soap ran into his eyes, he swore, and Sonny jumped.

"What are you looking at, Sonny? Didn't you ever see it before?"

"Oh, sure. Sure. I just was—" He shut the razor, opened it, flashed light from its blade, shut it again. "I'm tired of using this, Pete. I'm going to get rid of it. Want it?"

Want it? In his foot-locker, maybe. Under his pillow. "Thanks, no, Sonny. Couldn't use it."

"I like safety razors," Sonny mumbled. "Electrics, even better. What are we going to do with it?"

"Throw it in the—no." Pete pictured the razor turning end over end in the air, half open, gleaming in the maw of the catchall. "Throw it out the—" No. Curving out into the long grass. He might want it. He might crawl around in the moonlight looking for it. He might find it.

"I guess maybe I'll break it up."

"No," Pete said. "The pieces—" Sharp little pieces. Hollow-ground fragments. "I'll think of something. Wait'll I get dressed."

He washed briskly, toweled, while Sonny stood looking at the razor. It was a blade now, and if it were broken it would be shards and glittering splinters, still razor sharp. If it were ground dull with an emery wheel, somebody could find it and put another edge on it because it was so obviously a razor, a fine steel razor, one that would slice so—

"I know. The laboratory. We'll get rid of it," Pete said confidently.

He stepped into his clothes, and together they went to the laboratory wing. It was very quiet there. Their voices echoed.

"One of the ovens," said Pete, reaching for the razor.

"Bake-ovens? You're crazy!"

Pete chuckled. "You don't know this place, do you? Like everything else on the base, there was a lot more went on here than most people knew about. They kept calling it the bakeshop. Well, it *was* research headquarters for new high-nutrient flours. But there's lots else here. We tested utensils and designed vegetable-peelers and all sorts of things like that. There's an electric furnace in there that—" He pushed open a door.

They crossed a long, quiet, cluttered room to the thermal equipment. "We can do everything here from annealing glass, through glazing ceramics, to finding the melting point of frying pans." He clicked a switch tentatively. A pilot light glowed. He swung open a small, heavy door and set the razor inside. "Kiss it goodbye. In twenty minutes it'll be a puddle."

"I want to see that," said Sonny. "Can I look around until it's cooked?"

"Why not?"

They walked through the laboratories. Beautifully equipped they were, and too quiet. Once they passed a major who was bent over a complex electronic hook-up on one of the benches. He was watching a little amber light flicker, and he did not return their salute. They tip-toed past him, feeling awed at his absorption, envying it. They saw the models of the automatic kneaders, the vitaminizers, the remote signal thermostats and timers and controls.

"What's in there?"

"I dunno. I'm over the edge of my territory. I don't think there's anybody left for this section. They were mostly mechanical and electronic theoreticians. Hey!"

Sonny followed the pointing hand. "What?"

"That wall-section. It's loose, or—well, what do you know!"

He pushed at the section of wall which was very slightly out of line. There was a dark space beyond.

"What's in there?"

"Nothing, or some semi-private hush-hush job. These guys used to get away with murder."

Sonny said, with an uncharacteristic flash of irony, "Isn't that the Army theoretician's business?"

Cautiously they peered in, then entered.

"Why—*hey!* The door!"

It swung swiftly and quietly shut. The soft click of the latch was accompanied by a blaze of light.

The room was small and windowless. It contained machinery—a "trickle" charger, a bank of storage batteries, an electric-powered dynamo, two small self-starting gas-driven light plants and a diesel complete with sealed compressed-air starting cylinders. In the corner was a relay rack with its panel-bolts spot-welded. Protruding from it was a red-topped lever.

They looked at the equipment wordlessly for a time and then Sonny said, "Somebody wanted to make awful sure he had power for something."

"Now, I wonder what—" Pete walked over to the relay rack. He looked at the lever without touching it. It was wired up; behind the handle, on the wire, was a folded tag. He opened it cautiously. "To be used only on specific orders of the Commanding Officer."

"Give it a yank and see what happens."

Something clicked behind them. They whirled. "What was that?"

"Seemed to come from that rig beside the door."

They approached it cautiously. There was a spring-loaded solenoid attached to a bar which was hinged to drop across the inside of the secret door, where it would fit into steel gudgeons on the panel. It clicked again.

"A Geiger counter," said Pete disgustedly.

"Now why," mused Sonny, "would they design a door to stay locked unless the general radioactivity went beyond a certain point? That's what it is. See the relays? And the overload switch there? And this?"

"It has a manual lock, too," Pete pointed out. The counter clicked again. "Let's get out of here. I got one of those things built into my head these days."

The door opened easily. They went out, closing it behind them. The keyhole was cleverly concealed in the crack between two boards.

They were silent as they made their way back to the QM labs. The small thrill of violation was gone.

Back at the furnace, Pete glanced at the temperature dial, then kicked the latch control. The pilot winked out, and then the door swung open. They blinked and started back from the raging heat within. They bent and peered. The razor was gone. A pool of brilliance lay on the floor of the compartment.

"Ain't much left. Most of it oxidized away," Pete grunted.

They stood together for a time with their faces lit by the small shimmering ruin. Later, as they walked back to the barracks, Sonny broke his long silence with a sigh. "I'm glad we did that, Pete. I'm awful glad we did that."

At a quarter to eight they were waiting before the combination console in the barracks. All hands except Pete and Sonny and a wiry-haired, thick-set corporal named Bonze had elected to see the show on the big screen in the mess hall. The reception was better there, of course, but, as Bonze put it, "You don't get close enough in a big place like that."

"I hope she's the same," said Sonny, half to himself.

Why should she be? thought Pete morosely as he turned on the set and watched the screen begin to glow. There were many more of the golden speckles that had killed reception for the past two weeks. . . . Why should anything be the same, ever again?

He fought a sudden temptation to kick the set to pieces. It, and Starr Anthim, were part of something that was dead. The country was dead, a once real country—prosperous, sprawling, laughing, grabbing, growing, and changing, mostly healthy, leprous in spots with poverty and injustice, but systemically healthy enough to overcome any ill. He wondered how the murderers would like it. They were welcome to it, now. Nowhere to go. No one to fight. That was true for every soul on earth now.

"You hope she's the same," he muttered.

"The show, I mean," said Sonny mildly. "I'd like to just sit here and have it like—like—"

Oh, thought Pete mistily. Oh—that. Somewhere to go, that's what it is, for a few minutes. . . . "I know," he said, all the harshness gone from his voice.

Noise receded from the audio as the carrier swept in. The light on the screen swirled and steadied into a diamond pattern. Pete adjusted the focus, chromic balance and intensity. "Turn out the lights, Bonze. I don't want to see anything but Starr Anthim."

It *was* the same, at first. Starr Anthim had never used the usual fanfares, fade-ins, color and clamor of her contemporaries. A black screen, then *click!* a blaze of gold. It was all there, in focus; tremendously intense, it did not change. Rather, the eye changed to take it in. She never moved for seconds after she came on; she was there, a portrait, a still face and a white throat. Her eyes were open and sleeping. Her face was alive and still.

Thunder and Roses

Then, in the eyes which seemed green but were blue flecked with gold, an awareness seemed to gather, and they came awake. Only then was it noticeable that her lips were parted. Something in the eyes made the lips be seen, though nothing moved yet. Not until she bent her head slowly, so that some of the gold flecks seemed captured in the golden brows. The eyes were not, then, looking out at an audience. They were looking at me, and at *me*, and at ME.

"Hello—you," she said. She was a dream, with a kid sister's slightly irregular teeth.

Bonze shuddered. The cot on which he lay began to squeak rapidly. Sonny shifted in annoyance. Pete reached out in the dark and caught the leg of the cot. The squeaking subsided.

"May I sing a song?" Starr asked. There was music, very faint. "It's an old one, and one of the best. It's an easy song, a deep song, one that comes from the part of men and women that is mankind—the part that has in it no greed, no hate, no fear. This song is about joyousness and strength. It's—my favorite. Is it yours?"

The music swelled. Pete recognized the first two notes of the introduction and swore quietly. This was wrong. This song was not for—this song was part of—

Sonny sat raptly. Bonze lay still.

Starr Anthim began to sing. Her voice was deep and powerful, but soft, with the merest touch of vibrato at the ends of the phrases. The song flowed from her, without noticeable effort, seeming to come from her face, her long hair, her wide-set eyes. Her voice, like her face, was shadowed and clean, round, blue and green but mostly gold.

> *When you gave me your heart, you gave me the world,*
> *You gave me the night and the day,*
> *And thunder, and roses, and sweet green grass,*
> *The sea, and soft wet clay.*
> *I drank the dawn from a golden cup,*
> *From a silver one, the dark,*
> *The steed I rode was the wild west wind,*
> *My song was the brook and the lark.*

The music spiraled, caroled, slid into a somber cry of muted hungry sixths and ninths; rose, blared, and cut, leaving her voice full and alone:

> *With thunder I smote the evil of earth,*
> *With roses I won the right,*
> *With the sea I washed, and with clay I built,*
> *And the world was a place of light!*

The last note left a face perfectly composed again, and there was no movement in it; it was sleeping and vital while the music curved off and away to the places where music rests when it is not heard.

Starr smiled.

"It's so easy," she said. "So simple. All that is fresh and clean and strong about mankind is in that song, and I think that's all that need concern us about mankind." She leaned forward. "Don't you see?"

The smile faded and was replaced with a gentle wonder. A tiny furrow appeared between her brows; she drew back quickly. "I can't seem to talk to you tonight," she said, her voice small. "You hate something."

Hate was shaped like a monstrous mushroom. Hate was the random speckling of a video plate.

"What has happened to us," said Starr abruptly, impersonally, "is simple too. It doesn't matter who did it—do you understand that? *It* doesn't matter. We were attacked. We were struck from the east and from the west. Most of the bombs were atomic—there were blast-bombs and there were dust-bombs. We were hit by about five hundred and thirty bombs altogether, and it has killed us."

She waited.

Sonny's fist smacked into his palm. Bonze lay with his eyes open, open, quiet. Pete's jaws hurt.

"We have more bombs than both of them put together. We *have* them. We are not going to use them. *Wait!*" She raised her hands suddenly, as if she could see into each man's face. They sank back, tense.

"So saturated is the atmosphere with Carbon 14 that all of us in this hemisphere are going to die. Don't be afraid to say it. Don't be afraid to think it. Is is a truth, and it must be faced. As the transmutation effect spreads from the ruins of our cities, the air will become increasingly radioactive, and then we must die. In months, in a year or so, the effect will be strong overseas. Most of the people there will die too. None will escape completely. A worse thing will come to them than anything they have given us, because there will be a wave of horror and madness which is impossible to us. We are merely going to die. They will live and burn and sicken, and the children that will be born to them—" She shook her head, and her lower lip grew full. She visibly pulled herself together.

"Five hundred and thirty bombs . . . I don't think either of our attackers knew just how strong the other was. There has been so much secrecy." Her voice was sad. She shrugged slightly. "They have killed us, and they have ruined themselves. As for us—we are not blameless, either. Neither are we helpless to do anything—yet. But what we must do is hard. We must die—without striking back."

She gazed briefly at each man in turn, from the screen. "We must *not* strike back. Mankind is about to go through a hell of his own making. We can be vengeful—or merciful, if you like—and let go with the hundreds of bombs we have. That would sterilize the planet so that not a microbe, not a blade of grass could escape, and nothing new could grow. We would reduce the Earth to a bald thing, dead and deadly.

"No—it just won't do. We can't do it.

"Remember the song? *That* is humanity. That's in all humans. A disease made other humans our enemies for a time, but as the generations march past, enemies become friends and friends enemies. The enmity of those who have killed us is such a tiny, temporary thing in the long sweep of history!"

Her voice deepened. "Let us die with the knowledge that we have done the one noble thing left to us. The spark of humanity can still live and grow on this planet. It will be blown and drenched, shaken and all but extinguished, but it will live if that song is a true one. It will live if we are human enough to discount the fact that the spark is in the custody of our temporary enemy. Some—a few— of his children will live to merge with the new humanity that will gradually emerge from the jungles and the wilderness. Perhaps there will be ten thousand years of beastliness; perhaps man will be able to rebuild while he still has his ruins."

She raised her head, her voice tolling. "And even if this is the end of humankind, we dare not take away the chances some other life-form might have to succeed where we failed. If we retaliate, there will not be a dog, a deer, an ape, a bird or fish or lizard to carry the evolutionary torch. In the name of justice, if we must condemn and destroy ourselves, let us not condemn all other life along wth us! Mankind is heavy enough with sins. If we must destroy, let us stop with destroying ourselves!"

There was a shimmering flicker of music. It seemed to stir her hair like a breath of wind. She smiled.

"That's all," she whispered. And to each man listening she said, "Good night. . . ."

The screen went black. As the carrier cut off (there was no announcement) the ubiquitous speckles began to swarm across it.

Pete rose and switched on the lights. Bonze and Sonny were quite still. It must have been minutes later when Sonny sat up straight, shaking himself like a puppy. Something besides the silence seemed to tear with the movement.

He said, softly, "You're not allowed to fight anything, or to run away, or to live, and now you can't even hate any more, because Starr says no."

There was bitterness in the sound of it, and a bitter smell to the air.

Pete Mawser sniffed once, which had nothing to do with the smell. He sniffed again. "What's that smell, Son?"

Sonny tested it. "I don't— Something familiar. Vanilla—no . . . No."

"Almonds. Bitter— Bonze!"

Bonze lay still with his eyes open, grinning. His jaw muscles were knotted, and they could see almost all his teeth. He was soaking wet.

"Bonze!"

"It was just when she came on and said 'Hello—you,' remember?" whispered

Pete. "Oh, the poor kid. That's why he wanted to catch the show here instead of in the mess-hall."

"Went out looking at her," said Sonny through pale lips. "I—can't say I blame him much. Wonder where he got the stuff."

"Never mind that!" Pete's voice was harsh. "Let's get out of here."

They left to call the ambulance. Bonze lay watching the console with his dead eyes and his smell of bitter almonds.

Pete did not realize where he was going, or exactly why, until he found himself on the dark street near GHQ and the communications shack, reflecting that it might be nice to be able to hear Starr, and see her, whenever he felt like it. Maybe there weren't any recordings; yet her musical background was recorded, and the signal corps might have recorded the show.

He stood uncertainly outside the GHQ building. There was a cluster of men outside the main entrance. Pete smiled briefly. Rain, nor snow, nor sleet, nor gloom of night could stay the stage-door Johnnie.

He went down the side street and up the delivery ramp in the back. Two doors along the platform was the rear exit of the Communications section.

There was a light on in the communications shack. He had his hand out to the screen door when he noticed someone standing in the shadows beside it. The light played daintily on the golden margins of a head and face.

He stopped. "S—Starr Anthim!"

"Hello, soldier. Sergeant."

He blushed like an adolescent. "I—" His voice left him. He swallowed, reached up to whip off his hat. He had no hat. "I saw the show," he said. He felt clumsy. It was dark, and yet he was very conscious of the fact that his dress-shoes were indifferently shined.

She moved toward him into the light, and she was so beautiful that he had to close his eyes. "What's your name?"

"Mawser. Pete Mawser."

"Like the show?"

Not looking at her, he said stubbornly, "No."

"Oh?"

"I mean—I liked it some. The song."

"I—think I see."

"I wondered if I could maybe get a recording."

"I think so," she said. "What kind of reproducer have you got?"

"Audiovid."

"A disc. Yes; we dubbed off a few. Wait, I'll get you one."

She went inside, moving slowly. Pete watched her, spellbound. She was a silhouette, crowned and haloed; and then she was a framed picture, vivid and golden. He waited, watching the light hungrily. She returned with a large envelope, called good night to someone inside, and came out on the platform.

"Here you are, Pete Mawser."

"Thanks very—" he mumbled. He wet his lips. "It was very good of you."

"Not really. The more it circulates, the better." She laughed suddenly. "That isn't meant quite as it sounds. I'm not exactly looking for new publicity these days."

The stubbornness came back. "I don't know that you'd get it, if you put on that show in normal times."

Her eyebrows went up. "Well!" she smiled. "I seem to have made quite an impression."

"I'm sorry," he said warmly. "I shouldn't have taken that tack. Everything I think and say these days is exaggerated."

"I know what you mean." She looked around. "How is it here?"

"It's okay. I used to be bothered by the secrecy, and being buried miles away from civilization." He chuckled bitterly. "Turned out to be lucky after all."

"You sound like the first chapter of *One World or None*."

He looked up quickly. "What do you use for a reading list—the Government's own *Index Expurgatorius*!"

She laughed. "Come now, it isn't as bad as all that. The book was never banned. It was just—"

"Unfashionable," he filled in.

"Yes, more's the pity. If people had paid more attention to it in the forties, perhaps this wouldn't have happened."

He followed her gaze to the dimly pulsating sky 'How long are you going to be here?"

"Until—as long as—I'm not leaving."

"You're not?"

"I'm finished," she said simply. "I've covered all the ground I can. I've been everywhere that . . . anyone knows about."

"With this show?"

She nodded. "With this particular message."

He was quiet, thinking. She turned to the door, and he put out his hand, not touching her. "Please—"

"What is it?"

"I'd like to—I mean, if you don't mind, I don't often have a chance to talk to—maybe you'd like to walk around a little before you turn in."

"Thanks, no, Sergeant. I'm tired." She did sound tired. "I'll see you around."

He stared at her, a sudden fierce light in his brain. "I know where it is. It's got a red-topped lever and a tag referring to orders of the commanding officer. It's really camouflaged."

She was quiet so long that he thought she had not heard him. Then, "I'll take that walk."

They went down the ramp together and turned toward the dark parade ground.

"How did you know?" she asked quietly.

"Not too tough. This 'message' of yours; the fact that you've been all over the country with it; most of all, the fact that somebody finds it necessary to persuade us not to strike back. Who are you working for?" he asked bluntly.

Surprisingly, she laughed.

"What's that for?"

"A moment ago you were blushing and shuffling your feet."

His voice was rough. "I wasn't talking to a human being. I was talking to a thousand songs I've heard, and a hundred thousand blonde pictures I've seen pinned up. You'd better tell me what this is all about."

She stopped. "Let's go up and see the colonel."

He took her elbow. "No. I'm just a sergeant, and he's high brass, and that doesn't make any difference at all now. You're a human being, and so am I, and I'm supposed to respect your rights as such. I don't. You'd better tell me about it."

"All right," she said, with a tired acquiescence that frightened something inside him. "You seem to have guessed right, though. It's true. There are master firing keys for the launching sites. We have located and dismantled all but two. It's very likely that one of the two was vaporized. The other one is—lost."

"Lost?"

"I don't have to tell you about the secrecy," she said. "You know how it developed between nation and nation. You must know that it existed between State and Union, between department and department, office and office. There were only three or four men who knew where all the keys were. Three of them were in the Pentagon when it went up. That was the third blast-bomb, you know. If there was another, it could only have been Senator Vanercook, and he died three weeks ago without talking."

"An automatic radio key, hmm?"

"That's right. Sergeant, must we walk? I'm so tired."

"I'm sorry," he said impulsively. They crossed to the reviewing stand and sat on the lonely benches. "Launching racks all over, all hidden, and all armed?"

"Most of them are armed. There's a timing mechanism in them that will disarm them in a year or so. But in the meantime, they are armed—and aimed."

"Aimed where?"

"It doesn't matter."

"I think I see. What's the optimum number again?"

"About six hundred and forty; a few more or less. At least five hundred and thirty have been thrown so far. We don't know exactly."

"Who are *we?*" he asked furiously.

"Who? Who?" She laughed weakly. "I could say, 'The Government,' perhaps.

If the President dies, the Vice-President takes over, and then the Secretary of State, and so on and on. How far can you go? Pete Mawser, don't you realize yet what's happened?"

"I don't know what you mean."

"How many people do you think are left in this country?"

"I don't know. Just a few million, I guess."

"How many are here?"

"About nine hundred."

"Then, as far as I know, this is the largest city left."

He leaped to his feet. *"No!"* The syllable roared away from him, hurled itself against the dark, empty buildings, came back to him in a series of lower-case echoes: nonono*no . . . no*-no.

Starr began to speak rapidly, quietly. "They're scattered all over the fields and the roads. They sit in the sun and die. They run in packs, they tear at each other. They pray and starve and kill themselves and die in the fires. The fires—everywhere, if anything stands, it's burning. Summer, and the leaves all down in the Berkshires, and the blue grass burnt brown; you can see the grass dying from the air, the death going out wider and wider from the bald-spots. Thunder and roses. . . . I saw roses, new ones, creeping from the smashed pots of a greenhouse. Brown petals, alive and sick, and the thorns turned back on themselves, growing into the stems, killing. Feldman died tonight."

He let her be quiet for a time. Then:

"Who is Feldman?"

"My pilot." She was talking hollowly into her hands. "He's been dying for weeks. He's been on his nerve-ends. I don't think he had any blood left. He buzzed your GHQ and made for the landing strip. He came in with the motor dead, free rotors, giro. Smashed the landing gear. He was dead, too. He killed a man in Chicago so he could steal gas. The man didn't want the gas. There was a dead girl by the pump. He didn't want us to go near. I'm not going anywhere. I'm going to stay here. I'm tired."

At last she cried.

Pete left her alone, and walked out to the center of the parade ground, looking back at the faint huddled glimmer on the bleachers. His mind flickered over the show that evening, and the way she had sung before the merciless transmitter. "Hello, you."

"If we must destroy, let us stop with destroying ourselves!"

The dimming spark of humankind . . . what could it mean to her? How could it mean so much?

"Thunder and roses." Twisted, sick, non-survival roses, killing themselves with their own thorns.

"And the world was a place of light!" Blue light, flickering in the contaminated air.

The enemy. The red-topped lever. Bonze. "They pray and starve and kill themselves and die in the fires."

What creatures were these, these corrupted, violent, murdering humans? What right had they to another chance? What was in them that was good?

Starr was good. Starr was crying. Only a human being could cry like that. Starr was a human being.

Had humanity anything of Starr Anthim in it?

Starr was a human being.

He looked down through the darkness for his hands. No planet, no universe, is greater to a man than his own ego, his own observing self. These hands were the hands of all history, and like the hands of all men, they could by their small acts make human history or end it. Whether this power of hands was that of a billion hands, or whether it came to a focus in these two—this was suddenly unimportant to the eternities which now enfolded him.

He put humanity's hands deep in his pockets and walked slowly back to the bleachers.

"Starr."

She responded with a sleepy-child, interrogative whimper.

"They'll get their chance, Starr. I won't touch the key."

She sat straight. She rose, and came to him, smiling. He could see her smile, because, very faintly in this air, her teeth fluoresced. She put her hands on his shoulders. "Pete."

He held her very close for a moment. Her knees buckled then, and he had to carry her.

There was no one in the Officers' Club, which was the nearest building. He stumbled in, moved clawing along the wall until he found a switch. The light hurt him. He carried her to a settee and put her down gently. She did not move. One side of her face was as pale as milk.

He stood looking stupidly at it, wiped it on the sides of his trousers, looking dully at Starr. There was blood on her shirt.

A doctor . . . but there was no doctor. Not since Anders had hanged himself. "Get somebody," he muttered. *"Do* something."

He dropped to his knees and gently unbuttoned her shirt. Between the sturdy, unfeminine GI bra and the top of her slacks, there was blood on her side. He whipped out a clean handkerchief and began to wipe it away. There was no wound, no puncture. But abruptly there was blood again. He blotted it carefully. And again there was blood.

It was like trying to dry a piece of ice with a towel.

He ran to the water cooler, wrung out the bloody handkerchief and ran back to her. He bathed her face carefully, the pale right side, the flushed left side. The handkerchief reddened again, this time with cosmetics, and then her face was pale all over, with great blue shadows under the eyes. While he watched, blood appeared on her left cheek.

"There must be somebody—" He fled to the door.

"Pete!"

Running, turning at the sound of her voice, he hit the doorpost stunningly, caromed off, flailed for his balance, and then was back at her side. "Starr! Hang on, now! I'll get a doctor as quick as—"

Her hand strayed over her left cheek. "You found out. Nobody else knew, but Feldman. It got hard to cover properly." Her hand went up to her hair.

"Starr, I'll get a—"

"Pete, darling, promise me something?"

"Why, sure; certainly, Starr."

"Don't disturb my hair. It isn't—all mine, you see." She sounded like a seven-year-old, playing a game. "It all came out on this side. I don't want you to see me that way."

He was on his knees beside her again. "What is it? What happened to you?" he asked hoarsely.

"Philadelphia," she murmured. "Right at the beginning. The mushroom went up a half-mile away. The studio caved in. I came to the next day. I didn't know I was burned, then. It didn't show. My left side. It doesn't matter, Pete. It doesn't hurt at all, now."

He sprang to his feet again. "I'm going for a doctor."

"Don't go away. Please don't go away and leave me. Please don't." There were tears in her eyes. "Wait just a little while. Not very long, Pete."

He sank to his knees again. She gathered both his hands in hers and held them tightly. She smiled happily. "You're good, Pete. You're so good."

(She couldn't hear the blood in his ears, the roar of the whirlpool of hate and fear and anguish that spun inside of him.)

She talked to him in a low voice, and then in whispers. Sometimes he hated himself because he couldn't quite follow her. She talked about school, and her first audition. "I was so scared that I got a vibrato in my voice. I'd never had one before. I always let myself get a little scared when I sing now. It's easy." There was something about a window-box when she was four years old. "Two real live tulips and a pitcher-plant. I used to be sorry for the flies."

There was a long period of silence after that, during which his muscles throbbed with cramp and stiffness, and gradually became numb. He must have dozed; he awoke with a violent start, feeling her fingers on his face. She was propped up on one elbow. She said clearly, "I just wanted to tell you, darling. Let me go first, and get everything ready for you. It's going to be wonderful. I'll fix you a special tossed salad. I'll make you a steamed chocolate pudding and keep it hot for you."

Too muddled to understand what she was saying, he smiled and pressed her back on the settee. She took his hands again.

The next time he awoke it was broad daylight, and she was dead.

Sonny Weisefreund was sitting on his cot when he got back to the barracks. He handed over the recording he had picked up from the parade-ground on the way back. "Dew on it. Dry it off. Good boy," he croaked, and fell face downward on the cot Bonze had used.

Sonny stared at him. "Pete! Where you been? What happened? Are you all right?"

Pete shifted a little and grunted. Sonny shrugged and took the audiovid disc out of its wet envelope. Moisture would not harm it particularly, though it could not be played while wet. It was made of a fine spiral of plastic, insulated between laminations. Electrostatic pickups above and below the turntable would fluctuate with changes in the dielectric constant which had been impressed by the recording, and these changes were amplified for the scanners. The audio was a conventional hill-and-dale needle. Sonny began to wipe it down carefully.

Pete fought upward out of a vast, green-lit place full of flickering cold fires. Starr was calling him. Something was punching him, too. He fought it weakly, trying to hear what she was saying. But someone else was jabbering too loud for him to hear.

He opened his eyes. Sonny was shaking him, his round face pink with excitement. The audiovid was running. Starr was talking. Sonny got up impatiently and turned down the volume. "Pete! Pete! Wake up, will you? I got to tell you something. Listen to me! Wake up, will yuh?"

"Huh?"

"That's better. Now listen. I've just been listening to Starr Anthim—"

"She's dead," said Pete.

Sonny didn't hear. He went on, explosively, "I've figured it out. Starr was sent out there, and all over, to *beg* someone not to fire any more atom bombs. If the government was sure they wouldn't strike back, they wouldn't've taken the trouble. Somewhere, Pete, there's some way to launch bombs at those murdering cowards—and I've got a pret-ty shrewd idea of how to do it."

Pete strained groggily toward the faint sound of Starr's voice. Sonny talked on. "Now, s'posing there was a master radio key—an automatic code device something like the alarm signal they have on ships, that rings a bell on any ship within radio range when the operator sends four long dashes. Suppose there's an automatic code machine to launch bombs, with repeaters, maybe, buried all over the country. What would it be? Just a little lever to pull; that's all. How would the thing be hidden? In the middle of a lot of other equipment, that's where; in some place where you'd expect to find crazy-looking secret stuff. Like an experiment station. Like right here. You beginning to get the idea?"

"Shut up, I can't hear her."

Thunder and Roses 257

"The hell with her! You can listen to her some other time. You didn't hear a thing I said!"

"She's dead."

"Yeah. Well, I figure I'll pull that handle. What can I lose? It'll give those murderin'—*what?*"

"She's dead."

"Dead? Starr Anthim?" His young face twisted, Sonny sank down to the cot. "You're half asleep. You don't know what you're saying."

"She's dead," Pete said hoarsely. "She got burned by one of the first bombs. I was with her when she—she— Shut up now and get out of here and let me listen!" he bellowed hoarsely.

Sonny stood up slowly. "They killed her, too. They killed her! That does it. That just fixes it up." His face was white. He went out.

Pete got up. His legs weren't working right. He almost fell. He brought up against the console with a crash, his outflung arm sending the pickup skittering across the record. He put it on again and turned up the volume, then lay down to listen.

His head was all mixed up. Sonny talked too much. Bomb launchers, automatic code machines—

"You gave me your heart," sang Starr. *"You gave me your heart. You gave me your heart. You. . . ."*

Pete heaved himself up again and moved the pickup arm. Anger, not at himself, but at Sonny for causing him to cut the disc that way, welled up.

Starr was talking, stupidly, her face going through the same expression over and over again. *"Struck from the east and from the struck from the east and from the. . . ."*

He got up again wearily and moved the pickup.

"You gave me your heart you gave me . . ."

Pete made an agonized sound that was not a word at all, bent, lifted, and sent the console crashing over. In the bludgeoning silence he said, "I did, too."

Then, "Sonny." He waited.

"Sonny!"

His eyes went wide then, and he cursed and bolted for the corridor.

The panel was closed when he reached it. He kicked at it. It flew open, discovering darkness.

"Hey!" bellowed Sonny. "Shut it! You turned off the lights!"

Pete shut it behind them. The lights blazed.

"Pete! What's the matter?"

"Nothing's the matter, son," croaked Pete.

"What are you looking at?" said Sonny uneasily.

"I'm sorry," said Pete as gently as he could. "I just wanted to find something out, is all. Did you tell anyone else about this?" He pointed to the lever.

"Why, no. I only just figured it out while you were sleeping, just now."

Pete looked around carefully, while Sonny shifted his weight. Pete moved toward a tool-rack. "Something you haven't noticed yet, Sonny," he said softly, and pointed. "Up there, on the wall behind you. High up. See?"

Sonny turned. In one fluid movement Pete plucked off a fourteen-inch box wrench and hit Sonny with it as hard as he could.

Afterward he went to work systematically on the power supplies. He pulled the plugs on the gas-engines and cracked their cylinders with a maul. He knocked off the tubing of the diesel starters—the tanks let go explosively—and he cut all the cables with bolt-cutters. Then he broke up the relay rack and its lever. When he was quite finished, he put away his tools and bent and stroked Sonny's tousled hair.

He went out and closed the partition carefully. It certainly was a wonderful piece of camouflage. He sat down heavily on a workbench nearby.

"You'll have your chance," he said into the far future. "And, by Heaven, you'd better make good."

After that he just waited. ■

LATE NIGHT FINAL
Eric Frank Russell

How can our descendants "make good"? How can they build societies with the dual strengths of peace within themselves and the ability to withstand outside threats? If anybody had all the answers now, the world might already be a very different place. But the key to that hope just may lie in the realization—the very deep, widespread realization—of a startlingly simple truth.

COMMANDER CRUIN WENT DOWN THE extending metal ladder, paused a rung from the bottom, placed one important foot on the new territory, and then the other. That made him the first of his kind on an unknown world.

He posed there in the sunlight, a big bull of a man meticulously attired for the occasion. Not a spot marred his faultlessly cut uniform of gray-green on which jeweled orders of merit sparkled and flashed. His jack boots glistened as they had never done since the day of launching from the home planet. The golden bells of his rank tinkled on his heel-hooks as he shifted his feet slightly. In the deep shadow beneath the visor of his ornate helmet his hard eyes held a glow of self-satisfaction.

A microphone came swinging down to him from the air lock he'd just left. Taking it in a huge left hand, he looked straight ahead with the blank intentness of one who sees long visions of the past and longer visions of the future. Indeed, this was as visionary a moment as any there had been in his world's history.

"In the name of Huld and the people of Huld," he enunciated officiously, "I take this planet." Then he saluted swiftly, slickly, like an automaton.

Facing him, twenty-two long, black spaceships simultaneously thrust from their forward ports their glorypoles ringed with the red-black-gold colors of Huld. Inside the vessels twenty-two crews of seventy men apiece stood rigidly erect, saluted, broke into well-drilled song, "Oh, heavenly fatherland of Huld."

When they had finished, Commander Cruin saluted again. The crews repeated their salute. The glorypoles were drawn in. Cruin mounted the ladder, entered his flagship. All locks were closed. Along the valley the twenty-two invaders lay in military formation, spaced equidistantly, noses and tails dead in line.

On a low hill a mile to the east a fire sent up a column of thick smoke. It spat and blazed amid the remnants of what had been the twenty-third vessel—and the eighth successive loss since the fleet had set forth three years ago. Thirty then. Twenty-two now.

The price of empire.

Reaching his cabin, Commander Cruin lowered his bulk into the seat behind his desk, took off his heavy helmet, adjusted an order of merit which was hiding modestly behind its neighbor.

"Step four," he commented with satisfaction.

Second Commander Jusik nodded respectfully. He handed the other a book. Opening it, Cruin meditated aloud.

"Step one: Check planet's certain suitability for our form of life." He rubbed his big jowls. "We know it's suitable."

"Yes, sir. This is a great triumph for you."

"Thank you, Jusik." A craggy smile played momentarily on one side of Cruin's broad face. "Step two: Remain in planetary shadow at distance of not less than one diameter while scout boats survey world for evidence of superior life forms. Three:

Late Night Final 261

Select landing place far from largest sources of possible resistance but adjacent to a source small enough to be mastered. Four: Declare Huld's claim ceremoniously, as prescribed in manual on procedure and discipline." He worked his jowls again. "We've done all that."

The smile returned, and he glanced with satisfaction out of the small port near his chair. The port framed the smoke column on the hill. His expression changed to a scowl, and his jaw muscles lumped.

"Fully trained and completely qualified," he growled sardonically. "Yet he had to smash up. Another ship and crew lost in the very moment we reach our goal. The eighth such loss. There will be a purge in the astronautical training center when I return."

"Yes, sir," approved Jusik, dutifully. "There is no excuse for it."

"There are no excuses for anything," Cruin retorted.

"No, sir."

Snorting his contempt, Cruin looked at his book. "Step five: Make all protective preparations as detailed in defense manual." He glanced up into Jusik's lean, clearcut features. "Every captain has been issued with a defense manual. Are they carrying out its orders?"

"Yes, sir. They have started already."

"They better had! I shall arrange a demotion of the slowest." Wetting a large thumb, he flipped a page over. "Step six: If planet does hold life forms of suspected intelligence, obtain specimens." Lying back in his seat he mused a moment, then barked: "Well, for what are you waiting?"

"I beg your pardon, sir?"

"Get some examples," roared Cruin.

"Very well, sir." Without blinking, Jusik saluted, marched out.

The self-closer swung the door behind him. Cruin surveyed it with a jaundiced eye. "Curse the training center," he rumbled. "It has deteriorated since I was there."

Putting his feet on the desk, he waggled his heels to make the bells tinkle while he waited for the examples.

Three specimens turned up of their own accord. They were seen standing wide-eyed in a row near the prow of number twenty-two, the endmost ship of the line. Captain Somir brought them along personally.

"Step six calls for specimens, sir," he explained to Commander Cruin. "I know that you require ones better than these, but I found these under our nose."

"Under your nose? You land and within short time other life forms are sightseeing around your vessel? What about your protective precautions?"

"They are not completed yet, sir. They take some time."

"What were your lookouts doing—sleeping?"

"No, sir," assured Somir desperately. "They did not think it necessary to sound a general alarm for such as these."

Reluctantly, Cruin granted the point. His gaze ran contemptuously over the trio. Three kids. One was a boy, knee-high, snubnosed, chewing at a chubby fist. The next, a skinny-legged, pigtailed girl obviously older than the boy. The third was another girl almost as tall as Somir, somewhat skinny, but with a hint of coming shapeliness hiding in her thin attire. All three were freckled, all had violently red hair.

The tall girl said to Cruin: "I'm Marva—Marva Meredith." She indicated her companions. "This is Sue and this is Sam. We live over there, in Williamsville." She smiled at him and suddenly he noticed that her eyes were a rich and startling green. "We were looking for blueberries when we saw you come down."

Cruin grunted, rested his hands on his paunch. The fact that this planet's life manifestly was of his own shape and form impressed him not at all. It had never occurred to him that it could have proved otherwise. In Huldian thought, all superior life must be humanoid and no exploration had yet provided evidence to the contrary.

"I don't understand her alien gabble and she doesn't understand Huldian," he complained to Somir. "She must be dull-witted to waste her breath thus."

"Yes, sir," agreed Somir. "Do you wish me to hand them over to the tutors?"

"No. They're not worth it." He eyed the small boy's freckles with distaste, never having seen such a phenomenon before. "They are badly spotted and may be diseased. *Pfaugh!*" He grimaced with disgust. "Did they pass through the ray-sterilizing chamber as they came in?"

"Certainly, sir. I was most careful about that."

"Be equally careful about any more you may encounter." Slowly, his authoritative stare went from the boy to the pigtailed girl and finally to the tall one. He didn't want to look at her, yet knew that he was going to. Her cool green eyes held something that made him vaguely uncomfortable. Unwillingly he met those eyes. She smiled again, with little dimples. "Kick 'em out!" he rapped at Somir.

"As you order, sir."

Nudging them, Somir gestured toward the door. The three took hold of each other's hands, filed out.

"Bye!" chirped the boy, solemnly.

"Bye!" said pigtails, shyly.

The tall girl turned in the doorway. "Good-by!"

Gazing at her uncomprehendingly, Cruin fidgeted in his chair. She dimpled at him, then the door swung to.

"Good-by." He mouthed the strange word to himself. Considering the circumstances in which it had been uttered, evidently it meant farewell. Already he had picked up one word of their language.

"Step seven: Gain communication by tutoring specimens until they are proficient in Huldian."

Teach them. Do not let them teach you—teach *them*. The slaves must learn from the masters, not the masters from the slaves.

"Good-by." He repeated it with savage self-accusation. A minor matter, but still an infringement of the book of rules. There are no excuses for anything.

Teach them.

The slaves—

Rockets rumbled and blasted deafeningly as ships maneuvered themselves into the positions laid down in the manual of defense. Several hours of careful belly-edging were required for this. In the end, the line had reshaped itself into two groups of eleven-pointed stars, noses at the centers, tails outward. Ash of blast-destroyed grasses, shrubs and trees covered a wide area beyond the two menacing rings of main propulsion tubes which could incinerate anything within one mile.

This done, perspiring, dirt-coated crews lugged out their forward armaments, remounted them pointing outward in the spaces between the vessels' splayed tails. Rear armaments still aboard already were directed upward and outward. Armaments plus tubes now provided a formidable field of fire completely surrounding the double encampment. It was the Huldian master plan conceived by Huldian master planners. In other more alien estimation, it was the old covered wagon technique, so incredibly ancient that it had been forgotten by all but most earnest students of the past. But none of the invaders knew that.

Around the perimeter they stacked the small, fast, well-armed scouts of which there were two per ship. Noses outward, tails inward, in readiness for quick take-off, they were paired just beyond the parent vessels, below the propulsion tubes, and out of line of the remounted batteries. There was a lot of moving around to get the scouts positioned at precisely the same distances apart and making precisely the same angles. The whole arrangement had that geometrical exactness beloved of the military mind.

Pacing the narrow catwalk running along the top surface of his flagship, Commander Cruin observed his toiling crews with satisfaction. Organization, discipline, energy, unquestioning obedience—those were the prime essentials of efficiency. On such had Huld grown great. On such would Huld grow greater.

Reaching the tail-end, he leaned on the stop-rail, gazed down upon the concentric rings of wide, stubby venturis. His own crew were checking the angles of their two scouts already positioned. Four guards, heavily armed, came marching through the ash with Jusik in the lead. They had six prisoners.

Seeing him, Jusik howled: "Halt!" Guard and guarded stopped with a thud of boots and a rise of dust. Looking up, Jusik saluted.

"Six specimens, sir."

Cruin eyed them indifferently. Half a dozen middle-aged men in drab, sloppily fitting clothes. He would not have given a snap of the fingers for six thousand of them.

The biggest of the captives, the one second from the left, had red hair and was sucking something that gave off smoke. His shoulders were wider than Cruin's own though he didn't look half the weight. Idly, the commander wondered whether the fellow had green eyes; he couldn't tell that from where he was standing.

Calmly surveying Cruin, this prisoner took the smoke-thing from his mouth and said, tonelessly: "By hokey, a brasshat!" Then he shoved the thing back between his lips and dribbled blue vapor.

The others looked doubtful, as if either they did not comprehend or found it past belief.

"Jeepers, *no!*" said the one on the right, a gaunt individual with thin, saturnine features.

"I'm telling you," assured Redhead in the same flat voice.

"Shall I take them to the tutors, sir?" asked Jusik.

"Yes." Unleaning from the rail, Cruin carefully adjusted his white gloves. "Don't bother me with them again until they are certified as competent to talk." Answering the other's salute, he paraded back along the catwalk.

"See?" said Redhead, picking up his feet in time with the guard. He seemed to take an obscure pleasure in keeping in step with the guard. Winking at the nearest prisoner, he let a curl of aromatic smoke trickle from the side of his mouth.

Tutors Fane and Parth sought an interview the following evening. Jusik ushered them in, and Cruin looked up irritably from the report he was writing.

"Well?"

Fane said: "Sir, these prisoners suggest that we share their homes for a while and teach them to converse there."

"How did they suggest that?"

"Mostly by signs," explained Fane.

"And what made you think that so nonsensical a plan had sufficient merit to make it worthy of my attention?"

"There are aspects about which you should be consulted," Fane continued stubbornly. "The manual of procedure and discipline declares that such matters must be placed before the commanding officer whose decision is final."

"Quite right, quite right." He regarded Fane with a little more favor. "What are these matters?"

"Time is important to us, and the quicker these prisoners learn our language the better it will be. Here, their minds are occupied by their predicament. They think too much of their friends and families. In their own homes it would be different, and they could learn at great speed."

"A weak pretext," scoffed Cruin.

"That is not all. By nature they are naive and friendly. I feel that we have little to fear from them. Had they been hostile they would have attacked by now."

Late Night Final

"Not necessarily. It is wise to be cautious. The manual of defense emphasizes that fact repeatedly. These creatures may wish first to gain the measure of us before they try to deal with us."

Fane was prompt to snatch the opportunity. "Your point, sir, is also my final one. Here, they are six pairs of eyes and six pairs of ears in the middle of us, and their absence is likely to give cause for alarm in their home town. Were they there, complacency would replace that alarm—and we would be the eyes and ears!"

"Well put," commented Jusik, momentarily forgetting himself.

"Be silent!" Cruin glared at him. "I do not recall any ruling in the manual pertaining to such a suggestion as this. Let me check up." Grabbing his books, he sought through them. He took a long time about it, gave up, and said: "The only pertinent rule appears to be that in circumstances not specified in the manual the decision is wholly mine, to be made in light of said circumstances providing that they do not conflict with the rulings of any other manual which may be applicable to the situation, and providing that my decision does not effectively countermand that or those of any senior ranking officer whose authority extends to the same area." He took a deep breath.

"Yes, sir," said Fane.

"Quite, sir," said Parth.

Cruin frowned heavily. "How far away are these prisoners' homes?"

"One hour's walk." Fane made a persuasive gesture. "If anything did happen to us—which I consider extremely unlikely—one scout could wipe out their little town before they'd time to realize what had happened. One scout, one bomb, one minute!" Dexterously, he added, "At your order, sir."

Cruin preened himself visibly. "I see no reason why we should not take advantage of their stupidity." His eyes asked Jusik what he thought, but that person failed to notice. "Since you two tutors have brought this plan to me, I hereby approve it, and I appoint you to carry it through." He consulted a list which he extracted from a drawer. "Take two psychologists with you—Kalma and Hefni."

"Very well, sir." Impassively, Fane saluted and went out, Parth following.

Staring absently at his half-written report, Cruin fiddled with his pen for a while, glanced up at Jusik, and spat: "At what are you smiling?"

Jusik wiped it from his face, looked solemn.

"Come on. Out with it!"

"I was thinking, sir," replied Jusik, slowly, "that three years in a ship is a very long time."

Slamming his pen on the desk, Cruin stood up. "Has it been any longer for others than for me?"

"For you," said Jusik, daringly but respectfully, "I think it has been longest of all."

"Get out!" shouted Cruin.

He watched the other go, watched the selfcloser push the door, waited for its last click. He shifted his gaze to the port, stared hard-eyed into the gathering dusk. His heelbells were silent as he stood unmoving and saw the invisible sun sucking its last rays from the sky.

In short time, ten figures strolled through the twilight toward the distant, tree-topped hill. Four were uniformed; six in drab, shapeless clothes. They went by conversing with many gestures, and one of them laughed. He gnawed his bottom lip as his gaze followed them until they were gone.

The price of rank.

"Step eight: Repel initial attacks in accordance with techniques detailed in manual of defense." Cruin snorted, put up one hand, tidied his orders of merit.

"There have been no attacks," said Jusik.

"I am not unaware of the fact." The commander glowered at him. "I'd have preferred an onslaught. We are ready for them. The sooner they match their strength against ours the sooner they'll learn who's boss now!" He hooked big thumbs in his silver-braided belt. "And besides, it would give the men something to do. I cannot have them everlastingly repeating their drills of procedure. We've been here nine days and nothing has happened." His attention returned to the book. "Step nine: Follow defeat of initial attacks by taking aggressive action as detailed in manual of defense." He gave another snort. "How can one follow something that has not occurred?"

"It is impossible," Jusik ventured.

"Nothing is impossible," Cruin contradicted, harshly. "Step ten: In the unlikely event that intelligent life displays indifference or amity, remain in protective formation while specimens are being tutored, meanwhile employing scout vessels to survey surrounding area to the limit of their flight-duration, using no more than one-fifth of the numbers available at any time."

"That allows us eight or nine scouts on survey," observed Jusik, thoughtfully. "What is our authorized step if they fail to return?"

"Why d'you ask that?"

"Those eight scouts I sent out on your orders forty periods ago are overdue."

Viciously, Commander Cruin thrust away his book. His broad, heavy face was dark red.

"Second Commander Jusik, it was your duty to report this fact to me the moment those vessels became overdue."

"Which I have," said Jusik, imperturbably. "They have a flight-duration of forty periods, as you know. That, sir, made them due a short time ago. They are now late."

Cruin tramped twice across the room, medals clinking, heel-bells jangling. "The answer to nonappearance is immediately to obliterate the areas in which they are held. No half-measures. A salutary lesson."

"Which areas, sir?"

Stopping in mid-stride, Cruin bawled: "*You* ought to know that. Those scouts had properly formulated route orders, didn't they? It's a simple matter to—"

Late Night Final

He ceased as a shrill whine passed overhead, lowered to a dull moan in the distance, curved back on a rising note again.

"Number one." Jusik looked at the little timemeter on the wall. "Late, but here. Maybe the others will turn up now."

"Somebody's going to get a sharp lesson if they don't!"

"I'll see what he has to report." Saluting, Jusik hurried through the doorway.

Gazing out of his port, Cruin observed the delinquent scout belly-sliding up to the nearest formation. He chewed steadily at his bottom lip, a slow, persistent chew which showed his thoughts to be wandering around in labyrinths of their own.

Beyond the fringe of dank, dead ash were golden buttercups in the grasses, and a hum of bees, and the gentle rustle of leaves on trees. Four engine-room wranglers of ship number seventeen had found this sanctuary and sprawled flat on their backs in the shade of a big-leafed and blossom-ornamented growth. With eyes closed, their hands plucked idly at surrounding grasses while they maintained a lazy, desultory conversation through which they failed to hear the ring of Cruin's approaching bells.

Standing before them, his complexion florid, he roared: "Get up!"

Shooting to their feet, they stood stiffly shoulder to shoulder, faces expressionless, eyes level, hands at their sides.

"Your names?" He wrote them in his notebook while obediently they repeated them in precise, unemotional voices. "I'll deal with you later," he promised. "March!"

Together, they saluted, marched off with a rhythmic pounding of boots, one-two-three-hup! His angry stare followed them until they reached the shadow of their ship. Not until then did he turn and proceed. Mounting the hill, one cautious hand continually on the cold butt of his gun, he reached the crest, gazed down into the valley he'd just left. In neat, exact positioning, the two star-formations of the ships of Huld were silent and ominous.

His hard, authoritative eyes turned to the other side of the hill. There, the landscape was pastoral. A wooded slope ran down to a little river which meandered into the hazy distance, and on its farther side was a broad patchwork of cultivated fields in which three houses were visible.

Seating himself on a large rock, Cruin loosened his gun in its holster, took a wary look around, extracted a small wad of reports from his pocket and glanced over them for the twentieth time. A faint smell of herbs and resin came to his nostrils as he read.

"I circled this landing place at low altitude and recorded it photographically, taking care to include all the machines standing thereon. Two other machines which were in the air went on their way without attempting to interfere. It then occurred to me that the signals they were making from the ground might be an invitation to land, and I decided to utilize opportunism as recommended in the manual of procedure. Therefore

I landed. They conducted my scout vessel to a dispersal point off the runway and made me welcome."

Something fluted liquidly in a nearby tree. Cruin looked up, his hand automatically seeking his holster. It was only a bird. Skipping parts of the report, he frowned over the concluding words.

". . . lack of common speech made it difficult for me to refuse, and after the sixth drink during my tour of the town I was suddenly afflicted with a strange paralysis in the legs and collapsed into the arms of my companions. Believing that they had poisoned me by guile, I prepared for death . . . tickled my throat while making jocular remarks . . . I was a little sick." Cruin rubbed his chin in puzzlement. "Not until they were satisfied about my recovery did they take me back to my vessel. They waved their hands at me as I took off. I apologize to my captain for overdue return and plead that it was because of factors beyond my control."

The flutter came down to Cruin's feet, piped at him plaintively. It cocked its head sidewise as it examined him with bright, beady eyes.

Shifting the sheet he'd been reading, he scanned the next one. It was neatly typewritten, and signed jointly by Parth, Fane, Kalma and Hefni.

"Do not appear fully to appreciate what has occurred . . . seem to view the arrival of a Huldian fleet as just another incident. They have a remarkable self-assurance which is incomprehensible inasmuch as we can find nothing to justify such an attitude. Mastery of them should be so easy that if our homing vessel does not leave too soon it should be possible for it to bear tidings of conquest as well as of mere discovery."

"Conquest," he murmured. It had a mighty imposing sound. A word like that would send a tremendous thrill of excitement throughout the entire world of Huld.

Five before him had sent back ships telling of discovery, but none had gone so far as he, none had traveled so long and wearily, none had been rewarded with a planet so big, lush, desirable—and none had reported the subjection of their finds. One cannot conquer a rocky waste. But this—

In peculiarly accented Huldian, a voice behind him said, brightly: "Good morning!"

He came up fast, his hand sliding to his side, his face hard with authority.

She was laughing at him with her clear green eyes. "Remember me—Marva Meredith?" Her flaming hair was windblown. "You see," she went on, in slow, awkward tones, "I know a little Huldian already. Just a few words."

"Who taught you?" he asked, bluntly.

"Fane and Parth."

"It is your house to which they have gone?"

"Oh, yes. Kalma and Hefni are guesting with Bill Gleeson; Fane and Parth with us. Father brought them to us. They share the welcome room."

"Welcome room?"

"Of course." Perching herself on his rock, she drew up her slender legs, rested her chin on her knees. He noticed that the legs, like her face, were freckled. "Of course. Everyone has a welcome room, haven't they?"

Cruin said nothing.

"Haven't you a welcome room in your home?"

"Home?" His eyes strayed away from hers, sought the fluting bird. It wasn't there. Somehow, his hand had left his holster without realizing it. He was holding his hands together, each nursing the other, clinging, finding company, soothing each other.

Her gaze was on his hands as she said, softly and hesitantly, "You have got a home . . . somewhere . . . haven't you?"

"No."

Lowering her legs, she stood up. "I'm so sorry."

"*You* are sorry for *me?*" His gaze switched back to her. It held incredulity, amazement, a mite of anger. His voice was harsh. "You must be singularly stupid."

"Am I?" she asked, humbly.

"No member of my expedition has a home," he went on. "Every man was carefully selected. Every man passed through a screen, suffered the most exacting tests. Intelligence and technical competence were not enough; each had also to be young, healthy, without ties of any sort. They were chosen for ability to concentrate on the task in hand without indulging morale-lowering sentimentalities about people left behind."

"I don't understand some of your long words," she complained. "And you are speaking far too fast."

He repeated it more slowly and with added emphasis, finishing, "Spaceships undertaking long absence from base cannot be handicapped by homesick crews. We picked men without homes because they can leave Huld and not care a hoot. They are pioneers!"

" 'Young, healthy, without ties,' " she quoted. "That makes them strong?"

"Definitely," he asserted.

"Men especially selected for space. Strong men." Her lashes hid her eyes as she looked down at her narrow feet. "But now they are not in space. They are here, on firm ground."

"What of it," he demanded.

"Nothing." Stretching her arms wide, she took a deep breath, then dimpled at him. "Nothing at all."

"You're only a child," he reminded, scornfully. "When you grow older—"

"You'll have more sense," she finished for him, chanting it in a high, sweet voice. "You'll have more sense, you'll have more sense. When you grow older you'll have more sense, tra-la-la-lala!"

Gnawing irritatedly at his lip, he walked past her, started down the hill toward the ships.

"Where are you going?"

"Back!" he snapped.

"Do you like it down there?" Her eyebrows arched in surprise.

Stopping ten paces away, he scowled at her. "Is it any of your business?"

"I didn't mean to be inquisitive," she apologized. "I asked because . . . because—"

"Because what?"

"I was wondering whether you would care to visit my house."

"Nonsense! Impossible!" He turned to continue downhill.

"Father suggested it. He thought you might like to share a meal. A fresh one. A change of diet. Something to break the monotony of your supplies." The wind lifted her crimson hair and played with it as she regarded him speculatively. "He consulted Fane and Parth. They said it was an excellent idea."

"They did, did they?" His features seemed molded in iron. "Tell Fane and Parth they are to report to me at sunset." He paused, added, "Without fail!"

Resuming her seat on the rock, she watched him stride heavily down the slope toward the double star-formation. Her hands were together in her lap, much as he had held his. But hers sought nothing of each other. In complete repose, they merely rested with the ineffable patience of hands as old as time.

Seeing at a glance that he was liverish, Jusik promptly postponed certain suggestions that he had in mind.

"Summon captains Drek and Belthan," Cruin ordered. When the other had gone, he flung his helmet onto the desk, surveyed himself in a mirror. He was still smoothing the tired lines on his face when approaching footsteps sent him officiously behind his desk.

Entering, the two captains saluted, remained rigidly at attention. Cruin studied them irefully while they preserved wooden expressions.

Eventually, he said: "I found four men lounging like undisciplined hoboes outside the safety zone." He stared at Drek. "They were from your vessel." The stare shifted to Belthan. "You are today's commander of the guard. Have either of you anything to say?"

"They were off-duty and free to leave the ship," exclaimed Drek. "They had been warned not to go beyond the perimeter of ash."

"I don't know how they slipped through," said Belthan, in official monotone. "Obviously the guards were lax. The fault is mine."

"It will count against you in your promotion records," Cruin promised. "Punish these four, and the responsible guards, as laid down in the manual of procedure and discipline." He leaned across the desk to survey them more closely. "A repetition will bring ceremonial demotion!"

"Yes, sir," they chorused.

Dismissing them, he glanced at Jusik. "When tutors Fane and Parth report here, send them in to me without delay."

"As you order, sir."

Late Night Final

Cruin dropped the glance momentarily, brought it back. "What's the matter with you?"

"Me?" Jusik became self-conscious. "Nothing, sir."

"You lie! One has to live with a person to know him. I've lived on your neck for three years. I know you too well to be deceived. You have something on your mind."

"It's the men," admitted Jusik, resignedly.

"What of them?"

"They are restless."

"Are they? Well, I can devise a cure for that! What's making them restless?"

"Several things, sir."

Cruin waited while Jusik stayed dumb, then roared: "Do I have to prompt you?"

"No, sir," Jusik protested, unwillingly. "It's many things. Inactivity. The substitution of tedious routine. The constant waiting, waiting, waiting right on top of three years' close incarceration. They wait—and nothing happens."

"What else?"

"The sight and knowledge of familiar life just beyond the ash. The realization that Fane and Parth and the others are enjoying it with your consent. The stories told by the scouts about their experiences on landing." His gaze was steady as he went on. "We've now sent out five squadrons of scouts, a total of forty vessels. Only six came back on time. All the rest were late on one plausible pretext or another. The pilots have talked, and shown the men various souvenir photographs and a few gifts. One of them is undergoing punishment for bringing back some bottles of paralysis-mixture. But the damage has been done. Their stories have unsettled the men."

"Anything more?"

"Begging your pardon, sir, there was also the sight of you taking a stroll to the top of the hill. They envied you even that!" He looked squarely at Cruin. "I envied you myself."

"I am the commander," said Cruin.

"Yes, sir." Jusik kept his gaze on him but added nothing more.

If the second commander expected a delayed outburst, he was disappointed. A complicated series of emotions chased each other across his superior's broad, beefy features. Laying back in his chair, Cruin's eyes looked absently through the port while his mind juggled with Jusik's words.

Suddenly, he rasped: "I have observed more, anticipated more, and given matters more thought than perhaps you realize. I can see something which you may have failed to perceive. It has caused me some anxiety. Briefly, if we don't keep pace with the march of time we're going to find ourselves in a fix."

"Indeed, sir?"

"I don't wish you to mention this to anyone else: I suspect that we are trapped in a situation bearing no resemblance to any dealt with in the manuals."

"Really, sir?" Jusik licked his lips, felt that his own outspokenness was leading into unexpected paths.

"Consider our present circumstances," Cruin went on. "We are established here and in possession of power sufficient to enslave this planet. Any one of our supply of bombs could blast a portion of this earth stretching from horizon to horizon. But they're of no use unless we apply them effectively. We can't drop them anywhere, haphazardly. If parting with them in so improvident a manner proved unconvincing to our opponents, and failed to smash the hard core of their resistance, we would find ourselves unarmed in a hostile world. No more bombs. None nearer than six long years away, three there and three back. Therefore we must apply our power where it will do the most good." He began to massage his heavy chin. "We don't know where to apply it."

"No, sir," agreed Jusik, pointlessly.

"We've got to determine which cities are the key points of their civilization, which persons are this planet's acknowledged leaders, and where they're located. When we strike, it must be at the nerve-centers. That means we're impotent until we get the necessary information. In turn, that means we've got to establish communication with the aid of tutors." He started plucking at his jaw muscles. "And that takes time!"

"Quite, sir, but—"

"But while time crawls past the men's morale evaporates. This is our twelfth day and already the crews are restless. Tomorrow they'll be more so."

"I have a solution to that, sir, if you will forgive me for offering it," said Jusik, eagerly. "On Huld everyone gets one day's rest in five. They are free to do as they like, go where they like. Now if you promulgated an order permitting the men say one day's liberty in ten, it would mean that no more than ten percent of our strength would be lost on any one day. We could stand that reduction considering our power, especially if more of the others are on protective duty."

"So at last I get what was occupying your mind. It comes out in a swift flow of words." He smiled grimly as the other flushed. "I have thought of it. I am not quite so unimaginative as you may consider me."

"I don't look upon you that way, sir," Jusik protested.

"Never mind. We'll let that pass. To return to this subject of liberty—there lies the trap! There is the very quandary with which no manual deals, the situation for which I can find no officially prescribed formula." Putting a hand on his desk, he tapped the polished surface impatiently. "If I refuse these men a little freedom, they will become increasingly restless—naturally. If I permit them the liberty they desire, they will experience contact with life more normal even though alien, and again become more restless—naturally!"

"Permit me to doubt the latter, sir. Our crews are loyal to Huld. Blackest space forbid that it should be otherwise!"

"They were loyal. Probably they are still loyal." Cruin's face quirked as his memory brought forward the words that followed. "They are young, healthy, without ties. In space, that means one thing. Here, another." He came slowly to his feet, big, bulky and imposing. "I *know!*"

Looking at him, Jusik felt that indeed he did know. "Yes, sir," he parroted, obediently.

"Therefore the onus of what to do for the best falls squarely upon me. I must use my initiative. As second commander it is for you to see that my orders are carried out to the letter."

"I know my duty, sir." Jusik's thinly drawn features registered growing uneasiness.

"And it is my final decision that the men must be restrained from contact with our opponents, with no exceptions other than the four technicians operating under my orders. The crews are to be permitted no liberty, no freedom to go beyond the ash. Any form of resentment on their part must be countered immediately and ruthlessly. You will instruct the captains to watch for murmurers in their respective crews and take appropriate action to silence them as soon as found." His jowls lumped, and his eyes were cold as he regarded the other. "All scout-flights are canceled as from now, and all scout-vessels remain grounded. None moves without my personal instructions."

"That is going to deprive us of a lot of information," Jusik observed. "The last flight to the south reported discovery of ten cities completely deserted, and that's got some significance which we ought to—"

"I said the flights are canceled!" Cruin shouted. "If I say the scout-vessels are to be painted pale pink, they will be painted pale pink, thoroughly, completely, from end to end. I am the commander!"

"As you order, sir."

"Finally, you may instruct the captains that their vessels are to be prepared for my inspection at midday tomorrow. That will give the crews something to do."

"Very well, sir."

With a worried salute, Jusik opened the door, glanced out and said: "Here are Fane, Kalma, Parth and Hefni, sir."

"Show them in."

After Cruin had given forcible expression to his views, Fane said: "We appreciate the urgency, sir, and we are doing our best, but it is doubtful whether they will be fluent before another four weeks have passed. They are slow to learn."

"I don't want fluency," Cruin growled. "All they need are enough words to tell us the things we want to know, the things we *must* know before we can get anywhere."

"I said sufficient fluency," Fane reminded. "They communicate mostly by signs even now."

"That flame-headed girl didn't."

"She has been quick," admitted Fane. "Possibly she has an above-normal aptitude for languages. Unfortunately she knows the least in any military sense and therefore is of little use to us."

Cruin's gaze ran over him balefully. His voice became low and menacing. "You have lived with these people many days. I look upon your features and find them different. Why is that?"

"Different?" The four exchanged wondering looks.

"Your faces have lost their lines, their space-gauntness. Your cheeks have become plump, well-colored. Your eyes are no longer tired. They are bright. They hold the self-satisfied expression of a fat *skodar* wallowing in its trough. It is obvious that you have done well for yourselves." He bent forward, his mouth ugly. "Can it be that you are in no great hurry to complete your task?"

They were suitably shocked.

"We have eaten well and slept regularly," Fane said. "We feel better for it. Our physical improvement has enabled us to work so much the harder. In our view, the foe is supporting us unwittingly with his own hospitality, and since the manual of—"

"Hospitality?" Cruin cut in, sharply.

Fane went mentally off-balance as vainly he sought for a less complimentary synonym.

"I give you another week," the commander harshed. "No more. Not one day more. At this time, one week from today, you will report here with the six prisoners adequately tutored to understand my questions and answer them."

"It will be difficult, sir."

"Nothing is difficult. Nothing is impossible. There are no excuses for anything." He studied Fane from beneath forbidding brows. "You have my orders—obey them!"

"Yes, sir."

His hard stare shifted to Kalma and Hefni. "So much for the tutors; now *you*. What have you to tell me? How much have you discovered?"

Blinking nervously, Hefni said: "It is not a lot. The language trouble is—"

"May the Giant Sun burn up and perish the language trouble! How much have you learned while enjoyably larding your bellies?"

Glancing down at his uniform-belt as if suddenly and painfully conscious of its tightness, Hefni recited: "They are exceedingly strange in so far as they appear to be highly civilized in a purely domestic sense but quite primitive in all others. This Meredith family lives in a substantial, well-equipped house. They have every comfort, including a color-television receiver."

"You're dreaming! We are still seeking the secrets of plain television even on Huld. Color is unthinkable."

Kalma chipped in with: "Nevertheless, sir, they have it. We have seen it for ourselves."

"That is so," confirmed Fane.

"Shut up!" Cruin burned him with a glare. "I have finished with you. I am now dealing with these two." His attention returned to the quaking Hefni: "Carry on."

"There is something decidedly queer about them which we've not yet been able to understand. They have no medium of exchange. They barter goods for goods without any regard for the relative values of either. They work when they feel like it. If they don't feel like it, they don't work. Yet, in spite of this, they work most of the time."

"Why?" demanded Cruin, incredulously.

"We asked them. They said that one works to avoid boredom. We cannot comprehend that viewpoint." Hefni made a defeated gesture. "In many places they have small factories which, with their strange, perverted logic, they use as amusement centers. These plants operate only when people turn up to work."

"Eh?" Cruin looked baffled.

"For example, in Williamsville, a small town an hour's walk beyond the Meredith home, there is a shoe factory. It operates every day. Some days there may be only ten workers there, other days fifty or a hundred, but nobody can remember a time when the place stood idle for lack of one voluntary worker. Meredith's elder daughter, Marva, has worked there three days during our stay with them. We asked her the reason."

"What did she say?"

"For fun."

"Fun . . . fun . . . fun?" Cruin struggled with the concept. "What does that mean?"

"We don't know," Hefni confessed. "The barrier of speech—"

"Red flames lick up the barrier of speech!" Cruin bawled. "Was her attendance compulsory?"

"No, sir."

"You are certain of that?"

"We are positive. One works in a factory for no other reason than because one feels like it."

"For what reward?" topped Cruin, shrewdly.

"Anything or nothing." Hefni uttered it like one in a dream. "One day she brought back a pair of shoes for her mother. We asked if they were her reward for the work she had done. She said they were not, and that someone named George had made them and given them to her. Apparently the rest of the factory's output for that week was shipped to another town where shoes were required. This other town is going to send back a supply of leather, nobody knows how much—and nobody seems to care."

"Senseless," defined Cruin. "It is downright imbecility." He examined Hefni as if suspecting him of inventing confusing data. "It is impossible for even the most primitive of organizations to operate so haphazardly. Obviously you have seen only part of the picture; the rest has been concealed from you, or you have been too dull-witted to perceive it."

"I assure you, sir," began Hefni.

"Let it pass," Cruin cut in. "Why should I care how they function economically? In the end, they'll work the way *we* want them to!" He rested his heavy jaw in one hand. "There are other matters which interest me more. For instance, our scouts have brought in reports of many cities. Some are organized but grossly under-populated; others are completely deserted. The former have well-constructed landing places with air-machines making use of them. How is it that people so primitive have air-machines?"

"Some make shoes, some make air-machines, some play with television. They work according to their aptitudes as well as their inclinations."

"Has this Meredith got an air-machine?"

"No." The look of defeat was etched more deeply on Hefni's face. "If he wanted one he would have his desire inserted in the television supply-and-demand program."

"Then what?"

"Sooner or later, he'd get one, new or secondhand, either in exchange for something or as a gift."

"Just by asking for it?"

"Yes."

Getting up, Cruin strode to and fro across his office. The steel heel-plates on his boots clanked on the metal floor in rhythm with the bells. He was ireful, impatient, dissatisfied.

"In all this madness is nothing which tells us anything of their true character on their organization." Stopping his stride, he faced Hefni. "You boasted that *you* were to be the eyes and ears." He released a loud snort. "Blind eyes and deaf ears! Not one word about their numerical strength, not one—"

"Pardon me, sir," said Hefni, quickly, "there are twenty-seven millions of them."

"Ah!" Cruin registered sharp interest. "Only twenty-seven millions? Why, there's a hundred times that number on Huld, which has no greater area of land surface." He mused a moment. "Greatly underpopulated. Many cities devoid of a living soul. They have air-machines and other items suggestive of a civilization greater than the one they now enjoy. They operate the remnants of an economic system. You realize what all this means?"

Hefni blinked, made no reply. Kalma looked thoughtful. Fane and Parth remained blank-faced and tight-lipped.

"It means two things," Cruin pursued. "War or disease. One or the other, or perhaps both—and on a large scale. I want information on that. I've got to learn what sort of weapons they employed in their war, how many of them remain available, and where. Or, alternatively, what disease ravished their numbers, its source, and its cure." He tapped Hefni's chest to emphasize his words. "I want to know what they've got hidden away, what they're trying to keep from your knowledge against the time when they can bring it out and use it against us. Above all, I want to know which people will issue orders for their general offensive and where they are located."

"I understand, sir," said Hefni, doubtfully.

"That's the sort of information I need from your six specimens. I want information, not invitations to meals!" His grin was ugly as he noted Hefni's wince. "If you can get it out of them before they're due here, I shall enter the fact on the credit side of your records. But if I, your commander, have to do your job by extracting it from them myself—" Ominously, he left the sentence unfinished.

Hefni opened his mouth, closed it, glanced nervously at Kalma who stood stiff and dumb at his side.

"You may go," Cruin snapped at the four of them. "You have one week. If you fail me, I shall deem it a front-line offense and deal with it in accordance with the active-service section of the manual of procedure and discipline."

They were pale as they saluted. He watched them file out, his lips curling contemptuously. Going to the port, he gazed into the gathering darkness, saw a pale star winking in the east. Low and far it was—but not so far as Huld.

In the mid-period of the sixteenth day, Commander Cruin strode forth polished and bemedaled, directed his bell-jangling feet toward the hill. A sour-faced guard saluted him at the edge of the ash and made a slovenly job of it.

"Is that the best you can do?" He glared into the other's surly eyes. "Repeat it!"

The guard saluted a fraction more swiftly.

"You're out of practice," Cruin informed. "Probably all the crews are out of practice. We'll find a remedy for that. We'll have a period of saluting drill every day." His glare went slowly up and down the guard's face. "Are you dumb?"

"No, sir."

"Shut up!" roared Cruin. He expanded his chest. "Continue with your patrol."

The guard's optics burned with resentment as he saluted for the third time, turned with the regulation heel-click and marched along the perimeter.

Mounting the hill, Cruin sat on the stone at the top. Alternately he viewed the ships lying in the valley and the opposite scene with its trees, fields and distant houses. The metal helmet with its ornamental wings was heavy upon his head but he did not remove it. In the shadow beneath the projecting visor, his cold eyes brooded over the landscape to one side and the other.

She came eventually. He had been sitting there for one and a half periods when she came as he had known she would—without knowing what weird instinct had made him certain of this. Certainly, he had no desire to see her—no desire at all.

Through the trees she tripped light-footed, with Sue and Sam and three other girls of her own age. The newcomers had large, dark, humorous eyes, their hair was dark, and they were leggy.

"Oh, hello!" She paused as she saw him.

"Hello!" echoed Sue, swinging her pigtails.

" 'Lo!" piped Sam, determined not to be left out.

Cruin frowned at them. There was a high gloss on his jack boots, and his helmet glittered in the sun.

"These are my friends," said Marva, in her alien-accented Huldian. "Becky, Rita, and Joyce."

The three smiled at him.

"I brought them to see the ships."

Cruin said nothing.

"You don't mind them looking at the ships, do you?"

"No," he growled with reluctance.

Lankily but gracefully she seated herself on the grass. The others followed suit with the exception of Sam, who stood with fat legs braced apart sucking his thumb and solemnly studying Cruin's decorated jacket.

"Father was disappointed because you could not visit us."

Cruin made no reply.

"Mother was sorry, too. She's a wonderful cook. She loves a guest."

No reply.

"Would you care to come this evening?"

"No."

"Some other evening?"

"Young lady," he harshed, severely, "I do not pay visits. Nobody pays visits."

She translated this to the others. They laughed so heartily that Cruin reddened and stood up.

"What's funny about that?" he demanded.

"Nothing, nothing." Marva was embarrassed. "If I told you, I fear that you would not understand."

"I would not understand." His grim eyes became alert, calculating as they went over her three friends. "I do not think, somehow, that they were laughing at me. Therefore they were laughing at what I do not know. They were laughing at something I ought to know but which you do not wish to tell me." He bent over her, huge and muscular, while she looked up at him with her great green eyes. "And what remark of mine revealed my amusing ignorance?"

Her steady gaze remained on him while she made no answer. A faint but sweet scent exuded from her hair.

"I said that nobody pays visits," he repeated. "That was the amusing remark—nobody pays visits. And I am not a fool!" Straightening, he turned away. "So I am going to call the rolls!"

He could feel their eyes upon him as he started down the valley. They were silent except for Sam's high-pitched, childish, "Bye!" which he ignored.

* * *

Without once looking back, he gained his flagship, mounted its metal ladder, made his way to the office and summoned Jusik.

"Order the captains to call their rolls at once."

"Is something wrong, sir?" inquired Jusik, anxiously.

"Call the rolls!" Cruin bellowed, whipping off his helmet. "Then we'll know whether anything is wrong." Savagely, he flung the helmet onto a wall hook, sat down, mopped his forehead.

Jusik was gone for most of a period. In the end he returned, set-faced, grave.

"I regret to report that eighteen men are absent, sir."

"They laughed," said Cruin, bitterly. "They laughed—because they *knew!*" His knuckles were white as his hands gripped the arms of his chair.

"I beg your pardon, sir?" Jusik's eyebrows lifted.

"How long have they been absent?"

"Eleven of them were on duty this morning."

"That means the other seven have been missing since yesterday?"

"I'm afraid so, sir."

"But no one saw fit to inform me of this fact?"

Jusik fidgeted. "No, sir."

"Have you discovered anything else of which I have not been informed?"

The other fidgeted again, looked pained.

"Out with it, man!"

"It is not the absentees' first offense," Jusik said with difficulty. "Nor their second. Perhaps not their sixth."

"How long has this been going on?" Cruin waited a while, then bawled: "Come on! You are capable of speech!"

"About ten days, sir."

"How many captains were aware of this and failed to report it?"

"Nine, sir. Four of them await your bidding outside."

"And what of the other five?"

"They . . . they—" Jusik licked his lips.

Cruin arose, his expression dangerous. "You cannot conceal the truth by delaying it."

"They are among the absentees, sir."

"I see!" Cruin stamped to the door, stood by it. "We can take it for granted that others have absented themselves without permission, but were fortunate enough to be here when the rolls were called. That is their good luck. The real total of the disobedient cannot be discovered. They have sneaked away like nocturnal animals, and in the same manner they sneak back. All are guilty of desertion in the face of the enemy. There is one penalty for that."

"Surely, sir, considering the circ—"

"Considering nothing!" Cruin's voice shot up to an enraged shout. "Death! The penalty is death!" Striding to the table, he hammered the books lying upon it. "Summary execution as laid down in the manual of procedure and discipline. Desertion, mutinous conduct, defiance of a superior officer, conspiracy to thwart regulations and defy my orders—all punishable by death!" His voice lowered as swiftly as it had gone up. "Besides, my dear Jusik, if we fail through disintegration attributable to our own deliberate disregard of the manuals, what will be the penalty payable by *us?* What will it be, eh?"

"Death," admitted Jusik. He looked at Cruin. "On Huld, anyway."

"We are on Huld! *This* is Huld! I have claimed this planet in the name of Huld and therefore it is part of it."

"A mere claim, sir, if I may say—"

"Jusik, are *you* with these conspirators in opposing my authority?" Cruin's eyes glinted. His hand lay over his gun.

"Oh, no, sir!" The second commander's features mirrored the emotions conflicting within him. "But permit me to point out, sir, that we are a brotherly band who've been cooped together a long, long time and already have suffered losses getting here as we shall do getting back. One can hardly expect the men to—"

"I expect obedience!" Cruin's hand remained on the gun. "I expect iron discipline and immediate, willing, unquestionable obedience. With those, we conquer. Without them, we fail." He gestured to the door. "Are those captains properly prepared for examination as directed in the manuals?"

"Yes, sir. They are disarmed and under guard."

"Parade them in." Leaning on the edge of his desk, Cruin prepared to pass judgment on his fellows. The minute he waited for them was long, long as any minute he had ever known.

There had been scent in her hair.
And her eyes were cool and green.
Iron discipline must be maintained.
The price of power.

The manual provided an escape. Facing the four captains, he found himself taking advantage of the legal loophole to substitute demotion for the more drastic and final penalty.

Tramping the room before them while they stood in a row, pale-faced and rigid, their tunics unbuttoned, their ceremonial belts missing, the guards impassive on either side of them, he rampaged and swore and sprinkled them with verbal vitriol while his right fist hammered steadily into the palm of his left hand.

"But since you were present at the roll call, and therefore are not technically guilty of desertion, and since you surrendered yourself to my judgment immediately you were called upon to do so, I hereby sentence you to be demoted to the basic rank, the circumstances attending this sentence to be entered in your records." He dismissed them with a curt flourish of his white-gloved hand. "That is all."

They filed out silently.

He looked at Jusik. "Inform the respective lieutenant captains that they are promoted to full captains and now must enter recommendations for their vacated positions. These must be received by me before nightfall."

"As you order, sir."

"Also warn them to prepare to attend a commanding officer's court which will deal with the lower-ranking absentees as and when they reappear. Inform Captain Somir that he is appointed commander of the firing squad which will carry out the decisions of the court immediately they are pronounced."

"Yes, sir." Gaunt and hollow-eyed, Jusik turned with a click of heels and departed.

When the closer had shut the door, Cruin sat at his desk, placed his elbows on its surface, held his face in his hands. If the deserters did not return, they could not be punished. No power, no authority could vent its wrath upon an absent body. The law was impotent if its subjects lacked the essential feature of being present. All the laws of Huld could not put memories of lost men before a firing squad.

It was imperative that he make an example of the offenders. Their sly, furtive trips into the enemy's camp, he suspected, had been repeated often enough to have become a habit. Doubtless by now they were settled wherever they were visiting, sharing homes—welcome rooms—sharing food, company, laughter. Doubtless they had started to regain weight, to lose the space lines on their cheeks and foreheads, and the light in their eyes had begun to burn anew; and they had talked with signs and pictures, played games, tried to suck smoke things, and strolled with girls through the fields and the glades.

A pulse was beating steadily in the thickness of his neck as he stared through the port and waited for some sign that the tripled ring of guards had caught the first on his way in. Down, down, deep down inside him at a depth too great for him to admit that it was there, lay the disloyal hope that none would return.

One deserter would mean the slow, shuffling tread of the squad, the hoarse calls of "Aim!" and "Fire!" and the stepping forward of Somir, gun in hand, to administer the mercy shot.

Damn the manuals.

At the end of the first period after nightfall Jusik burst into the office, saluted, breathed heavily. The glare of the ceiling illumination deepened the lines of his thin features, magnified the bristles on his unshaven chin.

"Sir, I have to report that the men are getting out of control."

"What d'you mean?" Cruin's heavy brows came down as he stared fiercely at the other.

"They know of the recent demotions, of course. They know also that a court will assemble to deal with the absentees." He took another long-drawn breath. "And they also know the penalty these absentees must face."

"So?"

"So more of them have deserted—they've gone to warn the others not to return."

"Ah!" Cruin smiled lopsidedly. "The guards let them walk out, eh? Just like that?"

"Ten of the guards went with them," said Jusik.

"Ten?" Coming up fast, Cruin moved near to the other, studied him searchingly. "How many went altogether?"

"Ninety-seven."

Grabbing his helmet, Cruin slammed it on, pulled the metal chin strap over his jaw muscles. "More than one complete crew." He examined his gun, shoved it back, strapped on a second one. "At that rate they'll all be gone by morning." He eyed Jusik. "Don't you think so?"

"That's what I'm afraid of, sir."

Cruin patted his shoulder. "The answer, Jusik, is an easy one—we take off immediately."

"Take off?"

"Most certainly. The whole fleet. We'll strike a balanced orbit where it will be impossible for any man to leave. I will then give the situation more thought. Probably we'll make a new landing in some locality where none will be tempted to sneak away because there'll be nowhere to go. A scout can pick up Fane and his party in due course."

"I doubt whether they'll obey orders for departure, sir."

"We'll see, we'll see." He smiled again, hard and craggy. "As you would know if you'd studied the manuals properly, it is not difficult to smash incipient mutiny. All one has to do is remove the ringleaders. No mob is composed of men, as such. It is made up of a few ringleaders and a horde of stupid followers." He patted his guns. "You can always tell a ringleader—invariably he is the first to open his mouth!"

"Yes, sir," mouthed Jusik, with misgivings.

"Sound the call for general assembly."

The flagship's siren wailed dismally in the night. Lights flashed from ship to ship, and startled birds woke up and squawked in the trees beyond the ash.

Slowly, deliberately, impressively, Cruin came down the ladder, faced the audience whose features were a mass of white blobs in the glare of the ships' beams. The captains and lieutenant captains ranged themselves behind him and to either side. Each carried an extra gun.

"After three years of devoted service to Huld," he enunciated pompously, "some men have failed me. It seems that we have weaklings among us, weaklings unable to stand the strain of a few extra days before our triumph. Careless of their duty they disobey orders, fraternize with the enemy, consort with our opponents' females, and try to snatch a few creature comforts at the expense of the many." His hard, accusing eyes went over them. "In due time they will be punished with the utmost severity."

They stared back at him expressionlessly. He could shoot the ears off a running man at twenty-five yards, and he was waiting for his target to name itself. So were those at his side.

None spoke.

"Among you may be others equally guilty but not discovered. They need not congratulate themselves, for they are about to be deprived of further opportunities to exercise their disloyalty." His stare kept flickering over them while his hand remained ready at his side. "We are going to trim the ships and take off, seeking a balanced orbit. That means lost sleep and plenty of hard work for which you have your treacherous comrades to thank." He paused a moment, finished with: "Has anyone anything to say?"

One man holding a thousand.

Silence.

"Prepare for departure," he snapped, and turned his back upon them.

Captain Somir, now facing him, yelped: "Look out, commander!" and whipped up his gun to fire over Cruin's shoulder.

Cruin made to turn, conscious of a roar behind him, his guns coming out as he twisted around. He heard no crack from Somir's weapon, saw no more of his men as their roar cut off abruptly. There seemed to be an intolerable weight upon his skull, the grass came up to meet him, he let go his guns and put out his hands to save himself. Then the hazily dancing lights faded from his eyesight and all was black.

Deep in his sleep he heard vaguely and uneasily a prolonged stamping of feet, many dull, elusive sounds as of people shouting far, far away. This went on for a considerable time, and ended with a series of violent reports that shook the ground beneath his body.

Someone splashed water over his face.

Sitting up, he held his throbbing head, saw pale fingers of dawn feeling through the sky to one side. Blinking his aching eyes to clear them, he perceived Jusik, Somir, and eight others. All were smothered in dirt, their faces bruised, their uniforms torn and bedraggled.

"They rushed us the moment you turned away from them," explained Jusik, morbidly. "A hundred of them in the front. They rushed us in one united frenzy, and the rest followed. There were too many for us." He regarded his superior with red-rimmed optics. "You have been flat all night."

Unsteadily, Cruin got to his feet, teetered to and fro. "How many were killed?"

"None. We fired over their heads. After that—it was too late."

"Over their heads?" Squaring his massive shoulders, Cruin felt a sharp pain in the middle of his back, ignored it. "What are guns for if not to kill?"

"It isn't easy," said Jusik, with the faintest touch of defiance. "Not when they're one's own comrades."

"Do you agree?" The commander's glare challenged the others.

They nodded miserably, and Somir said: "There was little time, sir, and if one hesitates, as we did, it becomes—"

"There are no excuses for anything. You had your orders; it was for you to obey them." His hot gaze burned one, then the other. "You are incompetent for your rank. You are both demoted!" His jaw came forward, ugly, aggressive, as he roared: "Get out of my sight!"

They mooched away. Savagely, he climbed the ladder, entered his ship, explored it from end to end. There was not a soul on board. His lips were tight as he reached the tail, found the cause of the earth-rocking detonations. The fuel tanks had been exploded, wrecking the engines and reducing the whole vessel to a useless mass of metal.

Leaving, he inspected the rest of his fleet. Every ship was the same, empty and wrecked beyond possibility of repair. At least the mutineers had been thorough and logical in their sabotage. Until a report-vessel arrived, the home world of Huld had no means of knowing where the expedition had landed. Despite even a systematic and wide-scale search it might well be a thousand years before Huldians found this particular planet again. Effectively the rebels had marooned themselves for the rest of their natural lives and placed themselves beyond reach of Huldian retribution.

Tasting to the full the bitterness of defeat, he squatted on the bottom rung of the twenty-second vessel's ladder, surveyed the double star-formations that represented his ruined armada. Futilely, their guns pointed over surrounding terrain. Twelve of the scouts, he noted, had gone. The others had been rendered as useless as their parent vessels.

Raising his gaze to the hill, he perceived silhouettes against the dawn where Jusik, Somir, and the others were walking over the crest, walking away from him, making for the farther valley he had viewed so often. Four children joined them at the top, romped beside them as they proceeded. Slowly the whole group sank from sight under the rising sun.

Returning the flagship, Cruin packed a patrol sack with personal possessions, strapped it on his shoulders. Without a final glance at the remains of his once-mighty command he set forth away from the sun, in the direction opposite to that taken by the last of his men.

His jack boots were dull, dirty. His orders of merit hung lopsidedly and had a gap where one had been torn off in the fracas. The bell was missing from his right boot;

he endured the pad-*ding*, pad-*ding* of its fellow for twenty steps before he unscrewed it and slung it away.

The sack on his back was heavy, but not so heavy as the immense burden upon his mind. Grimly, stubbornly he plodded on, away from the ships, far, far into the morning mists—facing the new world alone.

Three and a half years had bitten deep into the ships of Huld. Still they lay in the valley, arranged with mathematical precision, noses in, tails out, as only authority could place them. But the rust had eaten a quarter of the way through the thickness of their tough shells, and their metal ladders were rotten and treacherous. The field mice and the voles had found refuge beneath them; the birds and spiders had sought sanctuary within them. A lush growth had sprung from encompassing ash, hiding the perimeter for all time.

The man who came by them in the midafternoon rested his pack and studied them silently, from a distance. He was big, burly, with a skin the color of old leather. His deep gray eyes were calm, thoughtful as they observed the thick ivy climbing over the flagship's tail.

Having looked at them for a musing half hour he hoisted his pack and went on, up the hill, over the crest and into the farther valley. Moving easily in his plain, loose-fitting clothes, his pace was deliberate, methodical.

Presently he struck a road, followed it to a stone-built cottage in the garden of which a lithe, dark-haired woman was cutting flowers. Leaning on the gate, he spoke to her. His speech was fluent but strangely accented. His tones were gruff but pleasant.

"Good afternoon."

She stood up, her arms full of gaudy blooms, looked at him with rich, black eyes. "Good afternoon." Her full lips parted with pleasure. "Are you touring? Would you care to guest with us? I am sure that Jusik—my husband—would be delighted to have you. Our welcome room has not been occupied for—"

"I am sorry," he chipped in. "I am seeking the Merediths. Could you direct me?"

"The next house up the lane." Deftly, she caught a falling bloom, held it to her breast. "If their welcome room has a guest, please remember us."

"I will remember," he promised. Eying her approvingly, his broad, muscular face lit up with a smile. "Thank you so much."

Shouldering his pack he marked on, conscious of her eyes following him. He reached the gate of the next place, a long, rambling, picturesque house fronted by a flowering garden. A boy was playing by the gate.

Glancing up as the other stopped near him, the boy said: "Are you touring, sir?"

"Sir?" echoed the man. *"Sir?"* His face quirked. "Yes, sonny, I am touring. I'm looking for the Merediths."

"Why, I'm Sam Meredith!" The boy's face flushed with sudden excitement. "You wish to guest with us?"

"If I may."

"Yow-ee!" He fled frantically along the garden path, shrieking at the top of his voice, "Mom, Pop, Marva, Sue—we've got a guest!"

A tall, red-headed man came to the door, pipe in mouth. Coolly, calmly, he surveyed the visitor.

After a little while, the man removed the pipe and said: "I'm Jake Meredith. Please come in." Standing aside, he let the other enter, then called, "Mary, Mary, can you get a meal for a guest?"

"Right away," assured a cheerful voice from the back.

"Come with me." Meredith led the other to the veranda, found him an easy-chair. "Might as well rest while you're waiting. Mary takes time. She isn't satisfied until the legs of the table are near to collapse—and woe betide you if you leave anything."

"It is good of you." Seating himself, the visitor drew a long breath, gazed over the pastoral scene before him.

Taking another chair, Meredith applied a light to his pipe. "Have you seen the mail ship?"

"Yes, it arrived early yesterday. I was lucky enough to view it as it passed overhead."

"You certainly were lucky considering that it comes only once in four years. I've seen it only twice, myself. It came right over this house. An imposing sight."

"Very!" endorsed the visitor, with unusual emphasis. "It looked to me about five miles long, a tremendous creation. Its mass must be many times greater than that of all those alien ships in the valley."

"Many times," agreed Meredith.

The other leaned forward, watching his host. "I often wonder whether those aliens attributed smallness of numbers to war or disease, not thinking of large-scale emigration, nor realizing what it means."

"I doubt whether they cared very much, seeing that they burned their boats and settled among us." He pointed with the stem of his pipe. "One of them lives in that cottage down there. Jusik's his name. Nice fellow. He married a local girl eventually. They are very happy."

"I'm sure they are."

They were quiet a long time, then Meredith spoke absently, as if thinking aloud. "They brought with them weapons of considerable might, not knowing that we have a weapon truly invincible." Waving one hand, he indicated the world at large. "It took us thousands of years to learn about the sheer invincibility of an idea. That's what we've got—a way of life, an idea. Nothing can blast that to shreds. Nothing can defeat an idea—except a better one." He put the pipe back in his mouth. "So far, we have failed to find a better one.

"They came at the wrong time," Meredith went on. "Ten thousand years too late."

He glanced sidewise at his listener. "Our history covers a long, long day. It was so lurid that it came out in a new edition every minute. But this one's the late night final."

"You philosophize, eh?"

Meredith smiled. "I often sit here to enjoy my silences. I sit here and think. Invariably I end up with the same conclusion."

"What may that be?"

"That if I, personally, were in complete possession of all the visible stars and their multitude of planets I would still be subject to one fundamental limitation"—bending, he tapped his pipe on his heel—"in this respect—that no man can eat more than his belly can hold." He stood up, tall, wide-chested. "Here comes my daughter, Marva. Would you like her to show you your room?"

Standing inside the welcome room, the visitor surveyed it appreciatively. The comfortable bed, the bright furnishings.

"Like it?" Marva asked.

"Yes, indeed." Facing her, his gray eyes examined her. She was tall, red-haired, green-eyed, and her figure was ripe with the beauty of young womanhood. Pulling slowly at his jaw muscles, he asked: "Do you think that I resemble Cruin?"

"Cruin?" Her finely curved brows crinkled in puzzlement.

"The commander of that alien expedition."

"Oh, him!" Her eyes laughed, and the dimples came into her cheeks. "How absurd! You don't look the least bit like him. He was old and severe. You are *young*—and far more handsome."

"It is kind of you to say so," he murmured. His hands moved aimlessly around in obvious embarrassment. He fidgeted a little under her frank, self-possessed gaze. Finally, he went to his pack, opened it. "It is conventional for the guest to bring his hosts a present." A tinge of pride crept into his voice. "So I have brought one. I made it myself. It took me a long time to learn . . . a long time . . . with these clumsy hands. About three years."

Marva looked at it, raced through the doorway, leaned over the balustrade and called excitedly down the stairs. "Pop, Mom, our guest has a wonderful present for us. A clock. A clock with a little metal bird that calls the time."

Beneath her, feet bustled along the passage and Mary's voice came up saying: "May I see it? Please let me see it." Eagerly, she mounted the stairs.

As he waited for them within the welcome room, his shoulders squared, body erect as if on parade, the clock whirred in Cruin's hands and its little bird solemnly fluted twice.

The hour of triumph. ∎